This remarkable collection very nicely combines conceptual, political and critical perspectives on the Anthropocene. All articles show that political science can contribute to a better understanding of the Anthropocene, but also that political science has to evolve in order to take up the challenges we face in this new era.

— **Markus Lederer**, *Chair of International Relations, Technical University of Darmstadt, Germany*

Can a geological epoch have politics? *The Anthropocene Debate and Political Science* invites us to take this question seriously and to bring political analysis into the center of contemporary environmental debates. A timely and innovative investigation into the political life of the Anthropocene.

— **Eva Lövbrand**, *Department of Thematic Studies: Environmental Change, Linköping University, Sweden*

The Anthropocene has conquered most public and scholarly debates on the human-nature nexus – and has often been greeted without deeper reflection about the term's social and political implications. This superb and innovative volume addresses this gap and brings political science into a timely and much-needed dialogue with the Anthropocene concept.

— **Fariborz Zelli**, *Associate Professor, Department of Political Science, Lund University, Sweden*

The Anthropocene Debate and Political Science

Anthropocene has become an environmental buzzword. It denotes a new geological epoch that is human-dominated. As mounting scientific evidence reveals, humankind has fundamentally altered atmospheric, geological, hydrological, biospheric and other Earth system processes to an extent that the risk of an irreversible system change emerges. Human societies must therefore change direction and navigate away from critical tipping points in the various ecosystems of our planet. This hypothesis has kicked off a debate not only on the geoscientific definition of the Anthropocene era, but increasingly also in the social sciences. However, the specific contribution of the social sciences disciplines and in particular that of political science still needs to be fully established.

This edited volume analyses, from a political science perspective, the wider social dynamics underlying the ecological and geological changes, as well as their implications for governance and politics in the Anthropocene. The focus is on two questions: (1) What is the contribution of political science to the Anthropocene debate, e.g., in terms of identified problems, answers and solutions? (2) What are the conceptual and practical implications of the Anthropocene debate for the discipline of political science?

Overall, this book contributes to the Anthropocene debate by providing novel theoretical and conceptual accounts of the Anthropocene, engaging with contemporary politics and policy-making in the Anthropocene, and offering a critical reflection on the Anthropocene debate as such. The volume will be of great interest to students and scholars of political science, global environmental politics and governance, and sustainable development.

Thomas Hickmann is a Postdoctoral Researcher and Lecturer at the Faculty of Economics and Social Sciences of the University of Potsdam in Germany.

Lena Partzsch is a Professor of Environmental and Development Policy at the University of Freiburg in Germany.

Philipp Pattberg is a Professor of Transnational Environmental Governance and Policy at Vrije Universiteit Amsterdam in The Netherlands.

Sabine Weiland is an Associate Professor of Political Science at Lille Catholic University, affiliated with the European School of Political and Social Sciences (ESPOL) in France.

Routledge Research in Global Environmental Governance
Series Editors: Philipp Pattberg
VU University Amsterdam and the Amsterdam Global
Change Institute (AGCI), the Netherlands
Agni Kalfagianni
Utrecht University, the Netherlands

Global environmental governance has been a prime concern of policymakers since the United Nations Conference on the Human Environment in 1972. Yet, despite more than nine hundred multi-lateral environmental treaties coming into force over the past forty years and numerous public-private and private initiatives to mitigate global change, human-induced environmental degradation is reaching alarming levels. Scientists see compelling evidence that the entire Earth system now operates well outside safe boundaries and at rates that accelerate. The urgent challenge from a social science perspective is how to organise the co-evolution of societies and their surrounding environment; in other words, how to develop effective and equitable governance solutions for today's global problems.

Against this background, the *Routledge Research in Global Environmental Governance* series delivers cutting-edge research on the most vibrant and relevant themes within the academic field of global environmental governance.

Grassroots Environmental Governance
Community Engagements with Industry
Edited by Leah S. Horowitz and Michael J. Watts

Traditions and Trends in Global Environmental Politics
International Relations and the Earth
Edited by Olaf Corry and Hayley Stevenson

Regime Interaction and Climate Change
The Case of International Aviation and Maritime Transport
Beatriz Martinez Romera

The Anthropocene Debate and Political Science
Edited by Thomas Hickmann, Lena Partzsch, Philipp Pattberg
and Sabine Weiland

For more information about this series, please visit: www.routledge.com/
Routledge-Research-in-Global-Environmental-Governance/book-series/RRGEG

The Anthropocene Debate and Political Science

Edited by
**Thomas Hickmann, Lena
Partzsch, Philipp Pattberg and
Sabine Weiland**

LONDON AND NEW YORK

First published 2019 by Routledge

2 Park Square, Milton Park, Abingdon, Oxfordshire OX14 4RN
52 Vanderbilt Avenue, New York, NY 10017

Routledge is an imprint of the Taylor & Francis Group, an informa business

First issued in paperback 2020

British Library Cataloguing-in-Publication Data
A catalogue record for this book is available from the British Library

Library of Congress Cataloging-in-Publication Data
A catalog record for this book has been requested

ISBN: 978-0-8153-8614-8 (hbk)
ISBN: 978-0-367-53495-0 (pbk)

Typeset in Times New Roman
by Apex CoVantage, LLC

Contents

Figures

Tables

Contributors

Basil Bornemann has an interdisciplinary background in environmental sciences and holds a doctoral degree in political science from Leuphana University of Lüneburg, Germany. In line with his overall interest in understanding the governance of societal transformations toward sustainability, he has extensively studied policy integration in the context of sustainable development strategies in his PhD thesis. Basil is a Postdoctoral Researcher at the Sustainability Research Group, University of Basel, Switzerland, and was a fellow at the Institute for Advanced Sustainability Studies (IASS), Potsdam, Germany. In his current work, he focuses on the relationship between governance, sustainable development and democracy within various fields, such as energy and food policy. He is also interested in the principles, practices and political implications of transdisciplinary and transformative sustainability science.

Achim Brunnengräber is an Associate Professor at the Department of Political and Social Sciences at Freie Universität Berlin, Germany. He is the coordinator of the research project "Methods and measures to deal with socio-technical challenges in storage and disposal of radioactive waste management" (SOTEC-radio) and works in the research project "The political economy of e-mobility. An analysis on the potentials and obstacles in the transformation to a sustainable transport policy in Germany and the European Union" at the Environmental Policy Research Centre (FFU). From 2009 to 2012, Achim was Visiting Professor at the Department of International Politics at the Technical University of Dresden, and from 2007 to 2008 Visiting Professor of International Political Economy at Freie Universität Berlin. There, he led the interdisciplinary research project 'Global governance and climate change' from 2002 to 2007.

Judith Nora Hardt works as an Associated Postdoctoral Researcher with the Research Group 'Climate Change and Security' (CLISEC), as part of the Cluster of Excellence 'Integrated Climate System Analysis and Prediction' (CliSAP) at the University of Hamburg, Germany, and is affiliated with the Fondation Maison des Sciences de l'Homme (FMSH) in Paris, France, and with the Wissenschaftszentrum Berlin für Sozialforschung (WZB). Her research is based on a critical-normative approach and aims to develop the conceptualisations of security, conflict, human well-being, and justice via the new readings of human-nature relations in the Anthropocene. Further constitutive elements of her research are the forms and roles of agency, expertise, power and normative foundations within global governance.

Till Hermanns is an independent researcher and holds a PhD in geography from the Georg-August University Göttingen, Germany. He has worked in the interdisciplinary research project "Developing Integrated Land Management through Sustainable Utilization of Water and Substances in North-East Germany" at the Leibniz-Centre for Agricultural Landscape Research (ZALF). The goal of this project was to explore options for sustainable land management in northeast Germany. His subproject and thesis have dealt with a framework to sustainability impact assessment of land use scenarios. Before his work at ZALF, he studied geography at the Georg-August University Göttingen. His research and publications deal with sustainable land management, land use functions, urban-rural interactions, and sustainability impact assessment of land use changes.

Lukas Hermwille is a Senior Research Fellow at the Wuppertal Institute for Climate, Environment and Energy in Germany. He has been working in the field of international climate policy since 2008. At the Wuppertal Institute, he has particularly focused on market-based mitigation instruments as well as questions of the overall governance architecture of the climate regime. Furthermore, he has worked on the transformation of energy sectors from a global perspective. Lukas is an external PhD candidate at the Institute for Environmental Studies (IVM) at Vrije Universiteit Amsterdam. In his dissertation project, he aims at integrating theoretical perspectives from transition studies and international governance theory. He graduated with a diploma in Regional Sciences of Latin America with a special focus on energy and environmental economics.

Thomas Hickmann is a Postdoctoral Researcher and Lecturer at the Faculty of Economics and Social Sciences, University of Potsdam in Germany. In 2014, he finished his doctoral dissertation which was published with Routledge under the title "Rethinking Authority in Global Climate Governance: How Transnational Climate Initiatives Relate to the International Climate Regime". Together with Harald Fuhr and Markus Lederer, he co-leads the research project *Carbon Governance Arrangements and the Nation-State: The Reconfiguration of Public Authority in Developing Countries* funded by the German Research Foundation (DFG). His research deals with global sustainability governance, the role and function of transnational actors in world politics, the impact of new modes of governance on public-administrative systems in developing countries, and the growing interaction of international bureaucracies with sub- and non-state actors.

Chris Höhne is a research associate and PhD candidate at the Technical University of Darmstadt, Germany, working in the DFG-funded research project 'Carbon Governance Arrangements and the Nation-State'. Until September

2016, he worked in the same research project at the University of Münster. He was a Visiting Researcher at the Centre for Policy Research (CPR) in New Delhi, India (2018), the Indian Institute of Technology (IIT) in Mandi, India (2018), the Centre for International Forestry Research (CIFOR) in Bogor, Indonesia (2017), and the Bogor Agricultural University (IPB) in Bogor, Indonesia (2017). He conducted several research trips to India and Indonesia where he studied climate governance on the national and subnational level, and their impacts on policy-making in the forest, energy and transport sector. He studied political science and economics at the University of Trier, Germany, the IEP Sciences Po Bordeaux, France, and the University of Colorado at Boulder.

Qirui Li is a Research Associate at the Leibniz Institute of Ecological Urban and Regional Development (IOER) in Dresden, Germany. He is working in the EU Horizon 2020 project "Transition towards urban sustainability through socially integrative cities in the EU and in China". He holds a PhD from Humboldt-Universität Berlin in agricultural economics. His thesis explored the livelihood security and adaptive strategies of farm households under payments for ecosystem services programmes, and how to promote rural livelihoods in response to the land use policy shock in China. His research interests lie in the area of social-ecological systems, concerning urban-rural interactions, smallholder agriculture development, sustainable livelihoods, and resilience and adaptation.

Johannes Lundershausen is a Junior Researcher at the International Centre for Science Ethics at Eberhard Karls University Tübingen, Germany. He has been investigating ways of thinking and acting upon global environmental change the concept of the Anthropocene enables. He is particularly interested in the multiple and ambiguous meanings of the Anthropocene and their impact on the broader sustainability discourse. This interest is reflected in his postgraduate degree in environmental politics and sociology from University College London, UK, as well as in his past working experience. In particular, he worked at the "International Human Dimensions Programme on Global Environmental Change" at the United Nations University in Bonn and in the research group "Science Policy" at the Social Science Research Centre Berlin. In addition, Johannes is versed in the topic of climate change adaptation in the Global South – particularly in India and Tanzania. Currently, Johannes works as a Science Officer at the Secretariat of the German Committee Future Earth.

Jens Marquardt is working on environmental governance, climate politics and development. His current research deals with the politics of sustainability transitions and the contested nature of climate governance in times of political disruption. He is particularly interested in the links between social sciences and environmental technologies, the role of power and coordination in multi-level governance systems, and the challenging process of policy implementation. Having investigated the complex relations between power and environmental governance in Southeast Asia, Jens received his PhD in political science at Freie Universität Berlin, Germany, in 2015. His book *How Power Shapes*

Energy Transitions in Southeast Asia was published with Routledge. Jens is currently a Visiting Research Fellow at the Program on Science, Technology & Society at Harvard, USA, a Lecturer at the University of Halle, Germany, and associated with the Environmental Policy Research Centre in Berlin.

Franziska Müller is research group leader based at the University of Kassel, Germany. She holds a PhD in political science and an MA in political science and cultural anthropology. Her PhD focused on European Union-Africa relations and analysed the change of this postcolonial relationship as a change of governance and normative power, culminating in the advent of characteristic liberal and postliberal governmentalities. Previously, she was based at the Technical University of Darmstadt and at the Cluster of Excellence 'Normative Orders' at the University of Frankfurt. Coming from the fields of international relations theory and global environmental governance, her current work focuses on the intersections of International Relations and political ecology in postcolonial contexts and under circumstances of liberal governance. Her research group "GLOCALPOWER – funds, tools and networks for an African energy transition" analyses glocal energy transitions in South Africa, Zambia and Ghana from the perspectives of global/local environmental governance and international political economy.

Lena Partzsch is a Professor of Environmental and Development Policy at the University of Freiburg, Germany. Her research interests lie in the fields of international relations and sustainability governance. Her work has been published in leading scientific journals. She received the GAIA Best Paper Award in 2016, and *Global Governance: A Review of Multilateralism and International Organizations* chose her forthcoming article "Take action now: The legitimacy of celebrity power in international relations" as the best paper of the year in 2018 for translation into Spanish and additional publication in *Foro Internacional*, the journal of El Colegio de Mexico.

Philipp Pattberg is a Professor of Transnational Environmental Governance and Policy and head of the Department of Environmental Policy Analysis, Institute for Environmental Studies (IVM), Vrije Universiteit Amsterdam in The Netherlands. He teaches master's courses in environmental governance at the Faculty of Sciences and the Faculty of Social Sciences, VU Amsterdam. Philipp specialises in the study of global environmental politics, with a focus on private transnational governance, multi-stakeholder partnerships, network theory and institutional analysis. His work has been published in leading scientific journals including *Annual Review of Environment and Resources, European Journal of International Relations, Global Environmental Politics, Governance* and *Science*.

Sandra Schwindenhammer is an Assistant Professor at the Department of Political Science at Justus Liebig University Giessen, Germany. She is co-principal investigator for the project TANNRE (*The Transformation Potential of Interinstitutional Arrangements and the Norm of Sustainability in the Global*

Regime Complex for Food, 2017–2020) funded by the German Federal Ministry of Education and Research. She received her PhD in political science from Technical University of Darmstadt (2011) and held an interim professorship of International Politics at Humboldt University of Berlin (2015–2016). She is a founding member of the Research Network *Food Policy and Governance* at the European Consortium for Political Research. Her areas of expertise include international norms, norm contestation, norm entrepreneurship, food and agricultural politics, and the legitimacy and effectiveness of public and private organisations.

Dörte Themann holds a bachelor of science in environmental sciences from the Leuphana University Lüneburg, Germany, and is currently about to finish the master's programme Environmental Policy and Planning at Freie Universität Berlin and Technical University of Berlin. From 2016 to 2017, she was working as a student assistant at the Environmental Policy Research Centre (FFU) at Freie Universität Berlin in the research project on "Multi level governance – perspective on management of nuclear waste disposal". Since 2018, she has been working as a research fellow at FFU in the project "Methods and measures to deal with socio-technical challenges in storage and disposal of radioactive waste management".

Jörg Tremmel is a Permanent Lecturer (Privatdozent) at Eberhard Karls University of Tübingen, Germany. He holds two PhDs, one in philosophy and one in social sciences. From 2009 to 2010, he was a Research Fellow at the London School of Economics and Political Science, both at the Centre for Philosophy of Natural and Social Science and the Grantham Institute for Climate Change Research. From 2010 to 2016, Jörg was a Junior Professor in Intergenerationally Just Policies at the Institute for Political Science of Tübingen University. His master's thesis in political science, "Sustainability as an analytical and political category", won the Procter & Gamble Award for exceptional final thesis in environmental science. Jörg is one of the editors of the peer-review journal *Intergenerational Justice Review*.

Maike Weißpflug is a political theorist and currently a Postdoctoral Researcher at the Natural History Museum Berlin, Germany. She studied social sciences, philosophy and German literature at RWTH Aachen University, Germany. In her research, she works on concepts of nature, citizen science and the effects of digitalisation on scientific research. She has published on Hannah Arendt, critical theory and methods in the history of ideas.

Sabine Weiland is an Associate Professor of Political Science at Lille Catholic University, affiliated with the European School of Political and Social Sciences (ESPOL) in France, and the director of the MA food policy programme. Sabine holds a PhD in social sciences from the University of Göttingen, Germany. She participated in various German, European and international research projects in the fields of environmental governance, policy assessment, and science-policy interface. Before her appointment at Lille Catholic University she was working at the Helmholtz Centre for Environmental Research – UFZ, Leipzig, and Freie Universität Berlin, both in Germany, Catholic University Louvain, Belgium and IDDRI/Sciences Po Paris, France. Her researches focusses on issues of environmental and sustainability governance, food governance, reflexivity and policy learning, and the role of knowledge in political processes.

Acknowledgements

We are thankful to a couple of people that supported the publication of this book. First and foremost, we want to thank all participants of the conference "Global Environmental Politics in the Anthropocene" organised by the working group *Environmental Politics and Global Change* of the *German Political Science Association* at the University of Potsdam in April 2017. The keynote speeches, presentations and discussions at this conference laid the foundation for the ideas we developed in this edited volume. Moreover, we are grateful to Per-Olof Busch, Jobst Conrad, Alejandro Esguerra, Sylvia Kruse and Markus Lederer who provided constructive comments and suggestions on individual chapters as well as the whole book project. In this context, we would also like to thank two anonymous reviewers that commented on the initial book proposal. Their reviews helped us clarify and refine the overall goal of the edited volume and provided us with confidence that we have identified a key research topic for coming decades. Last but not least, we are indebted to Christiane Barna for her patience and great work in copyediting the different chapters of this book.

Thomas Hickmann, Lena Partzsch,
Philipp Pattberg and Sabine Weiland

1 Introduction

A political science perspective on the Anthropocene

Thomas Hickmann, Lena Partzsch,
Philipp Pattberg and Sabine Weiland

Overview

Over the past decades, it has become more and more obvious that ongoing global-isation processes have substantial impacts on the natural environment. Studies reveal that intensified global economic relations have caused or accelerated dra-matic changes in the Earth system, defined as the sum of our planet's interacting physical, chemical, biological and human processes (Schellnhuber et al. 2004). Climate change, biodiversity loss, disrupted biogeochemical cycles, and land degradation are often cited as emblematic problems of global environmental change (Rockström et al. 2009; Steffen et al. 2015). In this context, the term Anthropocene has lately received widespread attention and gained some promi-nence in the academic literature.

Although still controversial among different scholar groups, the term *Anthro-pocene* denotes a new geological epoch in the Earth's history in which humans have become the main drivers of change (Crutzen 2002). Human-induced climate change, species extinction, ocean acidification, plastic seas, desertifica-tion, overexploitation of natural resources, and other problems prompted by economic globalisation restrain and endanger the habitability of the planet. Governments at all levels and other political actors are now at a critical junc-ture to set sustainable development paths for the 21st century and beyond (Bier-mann et al. 2012). The key challenge is to alter the way we work, trade and do business on a global scale in order to reconcile our economies and ways of living with the natural basis of life on Earth. Thus, human societies must change direction and navigate away from critical tipping points in the Earth system.

The new geological epoch of the Anthropocene would follow the epoch of the Holocene after only ten thousand years. Several studies underscore that humans are driving or dramatically accelerating global environmental change which, in turn, is linked to the danger of an irreversible system transformation (Lewis and Maslin 2015). This hypothesis has kicked off a debate not only on the geos-cientific definition of the Anthropocene era, but increasingly also in the social sciences. However, the specific contribution of the social sciences disciplines and in particular that of political science still needs to be fully established. Against this backdrop, we address two fundamental questions in this edited volume:

- What is the contribution of political science to the Anthropocene debate, e.g., in terms of identified problems, answers and solutions?
- What are the conceptual and practical implications of the Anthropocene debate for the discipline of political science?

This introduction proceeds as follows: Next, we briefly refer to the origins and background of the Anthropocene concept and explain why it is a research object of political science. After that, we review the evolving political science literature on the Anthropocene and state what we think could be the key contribution of our discipline to the current debate on the human age. Then, inversely, we highlight the implications of the Anthropocene debate for political science. As such, the Anthropocene can be a linchpin in the debate that offers far-reaching opportunities to reflect upon the political and social dimensions of global environmental change. Finally, we outline the general structure of the edited volume and summarise the main arguments put forward by the authors of the individual chapters of this volume.

The Anthropocene as a research object of political science

The central idea of the Anthropocene is that humans are a new and influential natural force in the Earth system and hence became a 'geological factor'. This is considered a unique event in planetary history: "For the first time a single species dominates the entire surface, sits at the top of all terrestrial and oceanic food chains, and has taken much of the biosphere for its own purposes" (Langmuir and Broecker 2012, 597). At the same time, this characterises a fundamental change in the human-environment-relation, which now centres on human dominance over biological, chemical and geological processes on Earth. Paul Crutzen and Christian Schwägerl describe this relation as follows: "It's no longer us against 'Nature'. It's we who decide what nature is and what it will be" (Crutzen and Schwägerl 2011).

The hypothesis of the 'production' of nature draws attention to the political and social implications of the Anthropocene concept. The concept underlines the urgency to act in order to fight climate change, species extinction and other global problems. On the one hand, as impressively demonstrated in climate politics, political actors have struggled to agree on measures against anthropogenic climate change. Despite some progress in addressing the problem of climate change in the past few years, it is still very unclear whether global warming can be limited to 2° Celsius or even below compared to pre-industrial levels (Rockström et al. 2016). Indeed, the Paris Agreement stands for a far-reaching intergovernmental agreement, in which almost all countries on Earth committed themselves to individual steps to reduce or limit their national greenhouse gas emissions (Keohane and Oppenheimer 2016; Peters et al. 2017). However, the

United States lately announced their withdrawal from the Paris Agreement and, in other countries, the required ambition levels as well as concrete implementation programmes are lacking. In this context, we have to understand the Anthropocene as a threatening scenario and as a call for action.

On the other hand, the Anthropocene concept also changes the perspective regarding the 'controllability' of global environmental change. In this context, several authors highlight human stewardship to preserve the natural resources of Earth (Steffen et al. 2011). It is thus up to us how we design this human-dominated epoch and whether it will end in a catastrophe, or not. We can observe tendencies to simply accept conditions and causes of the Anthropocene as given, followed by suggestions how to deal with them. A further line of discussion deals with the options to transfer threatening systemic change into a stage of 'good Anthropocene'. Central to this perception is the idea that there already exist approaches how to positively influence the Anthropocene (Bennett et al. 2016). Others, by contrast, have criticised the Anthropocene outlook that humanity stands out from or above other species, and hence feeds further transformation of the Earth by humans (Manemann 2014). In both cases, the amenability of natural cycles by humans is taken as an opportunity or a justification to selectively interfere with ecological processes, with the claim to repair them (Vaughan and Lenton 2011). Visions of 'geo-engineering' and models of a planetary management of the Earth system, often based on hierarchical and authoritative visions of steering, have been put forward (Eckersley 2015). They are rooted in a firm belief in technological progress and the desirability of dominating nature – topics that have long been identified by political science scholarship.

Phantasies of dominating global environmental change stand in clear contrast to key findings of the Earth System Governance Project (e.g., Biermann 2014a). This line of research emphasises the complex and inherently political dimension of governance at all levels of the system and is hence opposed to simplified ideas of management and control. Central to this research are also local and transnational actors, such as various social movements on degrowth and alternative ways of living (for example, food sharing, car sharing, and other forms of a shared economy). The idea of controlling and managing global environmental change, quite the reverse, is top-down and primarily based on technocratic and expertocratic solutions. As a result, while the debate on the Anthropocene addresses questions that are inherently political, it apparently tends to depoliticise these societal aspects. From our perspective, the tension between politics and non- or post-politics characterises the new quality of the Anthropocene debate within the political science and more general within the social sciences.

The contribution of political science to the Anthropocene debate

According to some critical thinkers, we live in a 'post-political' age (Žižek 2004). From this perspective, the Anthropocene is not a neutral term describing an epochal transformation, as the natural sciences suggest, but the manifestation of an epoch in which political debates are replaced by economic management and expert views. The debate on the Anthropocene gets firmly 'a-political' if Earth politics merely becomes a consensual question of 'good governance' instead of something for which it is worth arguing (Swyngedouw 2013, 2014). Bülent Diken and Carsten Laustsen contend that, under post-political conditions, "everything is politicized, can be discussed, but only in a non-committal way and as a non-conflict. Absolute and irreversible choices are kept away; politics becomes something one can do without making decisions that divide and separate" (Diken and Laustsen 2004, 15). While focusing on consensus, post-politics neglects differences among ideas and ideologies. It reduces the political terrain to a purely technical and administrative management of global climate and environmental problems. Critical voices hence see the Anthropocene as a justification of a new global technocracy, in which post-politics replaces conflictual disputes (Stirling 2014).

Moreover, universalism is a main characteristic to the debate. The concept of the Anthropocene refers to the whole of humanity. It is humanity that causes global environmental change, and thus should collectively carry the respective burdens. This perception neglects the fact that only a small percentage of humanity is responsible for the various ongoing adverse global environmental changes (Luke 2015). Human impact on the environment has always been unequal and variable over the course of time. Simon Lewis and Mark Maslin elaborate different options in their discussion on the Anthropocene (Lewis and Maslin 2015). The so-called 'Orbis hypothesis' denotes the beginning to the clash of the Anthropocene, colonialism and mercantilism. In contrast, the 'Great Acceleration' hypothesis depicts the beginning to the clash between the Anthropocene, post-war capitalism and the geopolitics of the Cold War. Others suggest the term Capitalocene (Bonneuil 2015; Moore 2016) to highlight the causal role of capitalism for irreversible environmental impacts and the emergence of the new epoch.

No matter which hypothesis one follows, it is crucial for the Anthropocene debate to reflect the societal circumstances and their meaning for the course of history. It is imperative to study the relations between the Anthropocene and capitalism, their parallels and common problems. The Anthropocene appears as a grand narrative of global systemic development, even though postcolonial and postfeminist approaches, for example, demonstrate such a claim to be untenable (Gibson-Graham 1996; Chakrabarty 2015; Caputi 2016; Grusin 2017). Despite differences in detail, all of these approaches emphasise the plurality of humanity, which clusters into classes, genders and generations. The definition and history of the Anthropocene would look different – representatives of these theories argue – if not only considered from a Eurocentric or techno-masculine perspective, on which the dominant narrative of the Anthropocene is based.

While humanity is not equally responsible for the causes, humanity does also not suffer equally from the consequences of environmental change. Global environmental changes affect in particular poor and marginalised people that are highly vulnerable and generally less resilient to rising sea levels, floods and draughts, crop losses, ongoing land degradation, and other adverse effects of ongoing global environmental change, especially in the so-called Global South (Malm and Horn-borg 2014). The idea of a general history of the Anthropocene stands on shaky ground, and it should be replaced by a plurality of – partial – narratives. This plu-rality would inevitably bring the political dimension back into the analysis and underline the great repertoire and enormous potential of a more pronounced polit-ical science perspective on the current Anthropocene debate.

The implications of the Anthropocene debate for political science

We do not understand the Anthropocene as a one-way street through which natural scientists diffuse their perception of the world in order to establish them in society, as it has sometimes been the case so far (for a critical note on this, see Castree et al. 2014; Lövbrand et al. 2015). The participation and the commitment of diverse dis-ciplines are necessary for an informed discussion. From our perspective, simplified assumptions of Earth system *management* need to be replaced by more profound studies of governance and politics (including power-, interest- and knowledge-based approaches) in the Anthropocene (Biermann 2014b). Perceived as a political concept, the Anthropocene can be a linchpin that offers far-reaching opportunities to reflect upon the efficacy and the creative power of humanity. Despite an evolv-ing political science literature, representatives of this discipline have only recently begun to attract wider attention in the Anthropocene debate (e.g., Hamilton et al. 2015; Lövbrand et al. 2015; Pattberg and Zelli 2016).

The core of the debate on the Anthropocene – we argue – is not about the new geological epoch, but rather about the political and social dimensions of global environmental change. We can approach these dimensions through using *theories and concepts*. In this regard, our understanding of human-nature relations is central. It is imperative to the Anthropocene debate to reconsider and redefine this relation, without falling back into old patterns of nature domination. Anthro-pogenic, hence not naturally given changes are not without alternatives; they are the consequence of political action. At the same time, humanity is a central part of the history of nature. In this vein, the Anthropocene points out the inescapability of politics. This inescapability includes the urgency which the 'non-political pol-itics' (Swyngedouw 2013) of the Anthropocene concept discloses. In other words, the current debate is very much focused on the question of how humanity can adapt to the various environmental changes, whereas the actual political and societal causes of the changes are largely neglected.

Political scientists should more actively follow-up on this reflection and respective studies than they have done so far. It is not enough to only superficially point to the relevance of the discipline of political science, while the debate con-tinues to be based on perceptions of the relation between technology or humans and nature back from the 1970s or earlier. Eva Lövbrand et al. come to a similar conclusion: "We believe that a deeper involvement of critical social science in global environmental change research represents an important step out of this post-political situation" (Lövbrand et al. 2015, 214). The repoliticisation of the

Anthropocene gives us the opportunity to discuss *governance and practices* from new ontological angles, and this discussion should fundamentally go beyond the pragmatic defence of the status quo (keyword: post-politics).

The main objective of political science research should be to identify a diversity of understandings, problem descriptions and future ideas about the design of environmental and sustainability politics in the Anthropocene. Thereby, spaces for *critical perspectives and implications* can be created. Such spaces would allow the Anthropocene to be not the 'end of politics' but the contrary: An epoch in which humans become genuinely environmentally aware and actively engage with the Earth system and the ecosystems they live in. These three areas of political science scholarship, (i) theories and concepts, (ii) governance and practices, and (iii) critical perspectives and implications, constitute the broad sections of this edited volume. In each of these parts, the authors seek to clarify the genuine contribution of political science to the Anthropocene debate as well as the implications of *Anthropocene thinking* for political science as a discipline and intellectual endeavour.

The implications of human-induced global system changes for political science research are diverse. As natural scientists dominate the debate on the Anthropocene, scholars have not sufficiently reflected upon these changes yet. In the following section, we take up major lines of discussion in the debate on the Anthropocene, around which the volume is organised. We aim to shed light on the political and social dimensions of the concept. As the social sciences have so far been involved rather superficially into the debate, these dimensions have not seriously been taken into consideration. In particular, we seek to understand the reasons of this blind spot. Therefore, we strive for more political science engagement to foster a broader and deeper debate on the Anthropocene between scholars from the natural sciences and the social sciences.

Structure of this volume

This edited volume offers a series of original analyses from the discipline of political science and contributes to the current Anthropocene debate in three respects: First, the book provides novel theoretical and conceptual accounts of the Anthropocene (*Part I: Theories and concepts*). These chapters address the question: What is the political dimension of the Anthropocene debate and how does the proclaimed human age change the foundations of existing theoretical and conceptual approaches? Second, the book examines contemporary politics as well as policy-making in the Anthropocene and lays out a political science research agenda for the field (*Part II: Governance and practices*). These chapters deal with the question: What are the political repercussions of the human age for individual policy domains, such as climate change, agriculture and security? Third, the book takes one step back and reflects upon the Anthropocene debate as such (*Part III: Critical perspectives and implications*). These chapters raise the question: What are the societal responsibilities in the human age and what do they imply for our democratic political-administrative systems and for future generations?

Part I of the volume on 'theories and concepts' is opened with a contribution from Maike Weißpflug (chapter 2), who demonstrates that the Anthropocene debate can draw from a rich body of theories and concepts of political science. She proposes to rethink the Anthropocene with two key political science scholars, Hannah Arendt and Theodor W. Adorno. Both offer a critique of abstract 'grand' narratives and call for acknowledging the more complex, decentralised human-nature relations. The Anthropocene has been framed as a normative narrative from the very beginning, and Weißpflug analyses the 'grand' storytelling of the Anthropocene. As this is detached from everyday actions and real-world experiences, it becomes difficult to rethink our relation to and responsibility for the natural world. Acknowledging the complexity, diversity and local dimensions of how societies relate to nature opens up ways to redefine and reshape these relations and a shared responsibility towards humanity and the natural world we live in.

In chapter 3, Johannes Lundershausen evaluates the Anthropocene as a scientific description of the Earth system that is inherently linked to normative statements about past, present and future states of that system. In particular, the argument elaborates on the distinction between the Anthropocene depicted as a 'crisis' and 'opportunity' as two ways of understanding the history of humans on Earth. Lundershausen argues that opening up the different normative logics underpinning scientific representations helps scientists and others to understand the entanglement of scientific research on global change in ethical and political decision-making. Furthermore, the author clarifies the implications for responses to global change by elucidating how they invigorate existing proposals of Earth System Governance and geo-engineering, respectively.

In chapter 4, Basil Bornemann studies the consequences of the Anthropocene debate for concepts of governance, starting from the assumption that *Anthropocene thinking* has already entered politics and political science in recent years. The proclamation of the geological epoch challenges not only perceptions and practices of environmental and sustainability politics, but also the conceptual foundations of politics more generally. Bornemann argues that, from a political science perspective, understandings of governance in the Anthropocene debate are simplistic and under-complex. In particular, he criticises the linear and centralist perception of authority as well as the lack of a contextual view. However, Bornemann also sees potential in the Anthropocene debate to challenge, reflect upon and further innovate existing governance thinking in political science. The Anthropocene debate points to gaps and biases that call for a reconsideration of concepts and practices of governance. He highlights especially the need for a re-materialisation of politics and political theory, in form of an internalisation of nature in its conception construction.

In chapter 5, Franziska Müller analyses how the Anthropocene enters the field of International Relations (IR) as a rupture. This has significant repercussions for classical IR theory, in declaring a crisis of the liberal world order, acknowledging other species besides human agency and requesting new problem-solving strategies. The call for a different understanding of 'the political' provides ontological and epistemological challenges for the discipline. Müller discusses strategies for transforming IR theories to conceptualise the Anthropocene challenge. An ongoing debate that evolved around the 'Manifesto for the end of IR' (Burke et al. 2016) serves as a reference point for identifying Holocene features within IR theories. This builds the ground for a more in-depth discussion regarding the Anthropocene's systemic, normative and governance implications for theory development and IR's research agenda. It refers especially to Holocene and Anthropocene conceptualisations of the international system, actors and agency beyond man and state, as well as modes of governance and problem-solving strategies.

Part II of the volume on 'governance and practices' starts off with the contribution of Judith Nora Hardt (chapter 6) on how the Anthropocene has entered one of the central sub-disciplines of International Relations and political science: security studies. Hardt critically contrasts the security conceptions of different worldviews of *Anthropocene thinking* (a dynamic interrelated human-nature world) and *Holocene thinking* (natural processes acting as a background for human action). She then scrutinises the contributions that the critical approaches to security studies have on the Anthropocene debate. As Hardt argues, there exist opportunities along the threat-response logic and the focus on central values and fears in relation to the Anthropocene discourse. Consequently, developing an *Anthropocene thinking* of security could advance a research agenda that focuses more explicitly on these fundamental questions for humankind.

In chapter 7, Lukas Hermwille emphasises that the very notion of the Anthropocene implies that we are already transforming the world, and we do so at the grandest imaginable scale. Building on theoretical perspectives of transition research, he argues that such transformations can be actively governed, although not in the sense of a universalist, control-type of style. He conceptualises global climate governance as a 'boundary object' to enable researchers from different disciplines to work together on this issue. In particular, Hermwille brings together concepts of landscape, regime and niche from socio-technical system analysis with multilevel governance approaches from the political science. He discusses their compatibility and implications for Anthropocene governance. While socio-technical system analysis finds transformations to start in niches, political science research still tends to assume that it is possible to govern the Anthropocene at a supranational or regime level.

In chapter 8, Chris Höhne further elaborates the issue of global climate governance with a focus on Indonesia. As an emerging economy, Indonesia is among the highest greenhouse gas emitters in the world. While Höhne highlights the crucial role of emerging economies in shaping the geological epoch of the Anthropocene, he finds that Indonesia has increasingly become aware of its responsibility in this field. For instance, Indonesia committed itself to Nationally Appropriate Mitigation Actions (NAMAs) as a result of the 2007 Conference of the Parties (COP) 13 in Bali. The contribution sheds light on how and why developments in the UNFCCC have triggered institutional and policy changes for mitigating climate change in Indonesia. It builds upon an analysis of the Anthropocene debate in the International Relations literature, and applies a multi-level global governance framework to account for the dynamics between the global and the domestic governance of the Anthropocene. Höhne finds that, despite only 'talking the talk' without 'walking the walk', i.e., incorporation of climate rhetoric without practical consequences on the ground, the Indonesian government meanwhile shares the norms of climate mitigation.

In chapter 9, Sandra Schwindenhammer connects findings from (critical) constructivist International Relations research with recent theoretical works on environmental governance and politics in the Anthropocene. It conceives the Anthropocene as a social construction. This in turn requires more nuanced conceptions of agency, norms and technological innovations. The empirical focus of the chapter is on global agricultural production and governance. Schwindenhammer outlines a constructivist research agenda including three main dimensions for future research: The dimension of agency deals with the material and normative embeddedness of norm entrepreneurship in the Anthropocene and sheds light on who is conceived as an agent in charge of governing agricultural systems and why. The dimension of norms highlights the (conflictive) normative foundations and interpretations of societal problems in the agri-food system in the Anthropocene. The dimension of technological innovations discusses the rise of transformative technologies in light of normative debates about agricultural governance in the Anthropocene. Overall, the chapter highlights the important contributions of constructivist IR research to the Anthropocene debate.

Part III on 'critical perspectives and implications' begins with the contribution by Till Hermanns and Qirui Li (chapter 10) on sustainable land use in the Anthropocene. The authors present a framework for sustainability impact assessment (SIA), which is a tool to support political decision-making concerning sustainable human space usage. The debate on the Anthropocene calls for social science approaches for an integrative and spatially explicit SIA of land use changes. It influences scientific approaches to the SIA of land use changes due to increasing evidence that planetary boundaries are being exceeded by humankind and that societal value systems are changing. To correctly identify land use claims, Hermanns and Li argue, SIA approaches are required that include a representation of humankind as a major geological driver of land use changes. In future SIA research, anthropogenic land use claims and patterns should be linked with the boundaries of bio-geophysical thresholds of the Earth system. This will help to integrate the knowledge base on sustainability gains and deficits of land use changes when addressing issues of global governance.

In chapter 11, Dörte Themann and Achim Brunnengräber interpret the Anthropocene as expression of the interdependencies between a radically transformed nature, the man-made technosphere with its path dependencies and internal dynamics, and societies. Humans are both driving forces of the Anthropocene as well as they are affected by it. The authors use the handling of nuclear remnants and the final disposal of high-level radioactive waste as an example to demonstrate the changed relationship between nature, technology and society, which they interpret as a characteristic of the Anthropocene. They argue that the technosphere challenges present and future generations with an increasing phenomenon called 'unknown unknowns', i.e., societies have to deal with incalculable timescales, path dependencies and increasing uncontrollability of the technosphere. This calls for novel governance concepts that comply better with the interrelations between nature, technology and society, capable of taking uncertainties and uncontrollable dynamics into account.

In chapter 12, Jens Marquardt critically addresses the universalism of the Anthropocene concept. In times of massive global environmental threats, proponents of the Anthropocene often call for a global transformation towards sustainability in all societies around the world. Marquardt challenges this universalism and asks how voices and ideas from the Global South contribute to the Anthropocene discourse. In a review of more than 1,200 journal articles from 2002 to 2016, the contributions from scholars from the Global South to the Anthropocene debate were analysed. Marquardt finds that the ideas, worldviews and concepts from the Global South are rarely recognised in the Anthropocene discourse despite the concept's global aspirations. To include these voices would allow for additional perspectives and critical reflections on the Anthropocene related to human-nature relations, power struggles and widespread technocentrism.

In chapter 13, Jörg Tremmel engages with the important question of implications that the proclamation of the Anthropocene should have for the pivotal concept of democracy. More particularly, Tremmel argues that the transition into a new geological phase also necessitates a further advancement of our form of government. Democracy, as it has been conceived of and been practiced until now, has to a large extent ignored the problem of 'presentism'. The contribution suggests an extension of the 300-year-old separation of powers between the legislative, executive and judicial branches. In order to make our political system more future-oriented, there is an urgent need for a new fourth branch that ensures that the interests of future generations are taken into account within today's decision-making processes. A newly established 'future council' could introduce respective legislation, integrating the competences of this new institution with those of the parliament.

In sum, the debate on the Anthropocene, which so far has largely been dominated by scholars from the natural sciences, needs to be opened up. Contributions from the discipline of political science have only recently started to attract the attention of authors concerned with the so-called human age. This edited volume joins the new wave of studies within the field of global environmental politics that explore the underlying social dynamics of the various ecological and geological changes in the Earth system, as well as their implications for governance and politics in the Anthropocene. The overarching goal of this book is to complement the Anthropocene debate with a well-grounded reflection on how the planetary scale crisis alters the ways in which humans respond to the most pressing environmental challenges in the 21st century. Our ambition is to establish political science as a central voice in the Anthropocene debate, without neglecting the important impulses and challenges that emerge from the Anthropocene debate for the discipline of political science. In fact, the concept of the Anthropocene raises numerous questions with regard to environmental and development policy-making and provides a unique opportunity for re-thinking core concepts of the scholarship on global sustainability politics. The following chapters explore these intriguing questions in-depth.

References

Bennett, E.M., Solan, M., Biggs, R., McPhearson, T., Norström, A.V., Olsson, P., Pereira, L., Peterson, G.D., Raudsepp-Hearne, C. and Biermann, F. (2016) "Bright spots: Seeds of a good Anthropocene" *Frontiers in Ecology and the Environment*, 14(8), 441–448.

Biermann, F. (2014a) "The Anthropocene: A governance perspective" *The Anthropocene Review*, 1(1), 57–61.

Biermann, F. (2014b) *Earth System Governance: World Politics in the Anthropocene* MIT Press, Cambridge, MA.

Biermann, F., Abbott, K., Andresen, S., Backstrand, K., Bernstein, S., Betsill, M.M., Bulkeley, H., Cashore, B., Clapp, J., Folke, C., Gupta, A., Gupta, J., Haas, P.M., Jordan, A., Kanie, N., Kluvankova-Oravska, T., Lebel, L., Liverman, D., Meadowcroft, J., Mitchell, R.B., Newell, P., Oberthur, S., Olsson, L., Pattberg, P., Sanchez-Rodriguez, R., Schroeder, H., Underdal, A., Vieira, S.C., Vogel, C., Young, O.R., Brock, A. and Zondervan, R. (2012) "Navigating the Anthropocene: Improving Earth system governance" *Science*, 335(6074), 1306–1307.

Bonneuil, C. (2015) "The geological turn: Narratives of the Anthropocene" in Hamilton, C., Bonneuil, C. and Gemenne, F. eds., *The Anthropocene and the Global Environmental Crisis* Routledge, London, 17–31.

Burke, A., Fishel, S., Mitchell, A., Dalby, S. and Levine, D.J. (2016) "Planet politics: A manifesto from the end of IR" *Millennium: Journal of International Studies*, 44(3), 499–523.

Caputi, J. (2016) "Mother earth meets the Anthropocene" in Godfrey, P. and Torres, D. eds., *Systemic Crisis of Global Climate Change: Intersections of Race, Class and Gender* Routledge, New York, 20–33.

Castree, N., Adams, W.M., Barry, J., Brockington, D., Büscher, B., Corbera, E., Demeritt, D., Duffy, R., Felt, U. and Neves, K. (2014) "Changing the intellectual climate" *Nature Climate Change*, 4(9), 763–768.

Chakrabarty, D. (2015) "The Anthropocene and the convergence of histories" in Hamilton, C., Christophe, B. and Gemenne, F. eds., *The Anthropocene and the Global Environmental Crisis* Routledge, London, 44–56.

Crutzen, P.J. (2002) "Geology of mankind" *Nature*, 415(6867), 23.

Crutzen, P.J. and Schwägerl, C. (2011) *Living in the Anthropocene: Toward a New Global Ethos: Yale Environment 360* (http://e360.yale.edu/feature/living_in_the_anthropocene_toward_a_new_global_ethos/2363) Accessed 3 April 2017.

Diken, B. and Laustsen, C.B. (2004) *7/11, 9/11, and Post-Politics* (www.comp.lancs.ac.uk/sociology/papers/diken-laustsen-7-11-9-11-post-politics.pdf) Accessed 31 October 2017.

Eckersley, R. (2015) *Anthropocene Raises Risks of Earth without Democracy and without Us* (https://theconversation.com/anthropocene-raises-risks-of-earth-without-democracy-and-without-us-38911U) Accessed 31 March, 2017.

Gibson-Graham, J.K. (1996) *The End of Capitalism (As We Knew It): A Feminist Critique of Political Economy* Blackwell, Oxford.

Grusin, R. (2017) *Anthropocene Feminism* University of Minnesota Press, Minneapolis.

Hamilton, C., Gemenne, F. and Bonneuil, C. eds. (2015) *The Anthropocene and the Global Environmental Crisis: Rethinking Modernity in a New Epoch* Routledge, London.

Keohane, R.O. and Oppenheimer, M. (2016) "Paris: Beyond the climate dead end through pledge and review?" *Politics and Governance*, 4(3), 142–151.

Langmuir, C.H. and Broecker, W. (2012) *How to Build a Habitable Planet: The Story of Earth from the Big Bang to Humankind* Princeton University Press, Princeton, NJ.

Lewis, S.L. and Maslin, M.A. (2015) "Defining the Anthropocene" *Nature*, 519, 171–180.

Lövbrand, E., Beck, S., Chilvers, J., Forsyth, T., Hedrén, J., Hulme, M., Lidskog, R. and Vasileiadou, E. (2015) "Who speaks for the future of earth? How critical social science can extend the conversation on the Anthropocene" *Global Environmental Change*, 32, 211–218.

Luke, T. (2015) "Introduction: Political critiques of the Anthropocene" *Telos*, 172, 3–14.

Malm, A. and Hornborg, A. (2014) "The geology of mankind? A critique of the Anthropocene narrative" *The Anthropocene Review*, 1(1), 62–69.

Manemann, J. (2014) *Kritik des Anthropozäns: Plädoyer für eine neue Humanökologie* Transcript Verlag, Bielefeld.

Moore, J.W. (2016) *Anthropocene or Capitalocene? Nature, History, and the Crisis of Capitalism* Verso, Oakland.

Pattberg, P. and Zelli, F. (2016) *Environmental Politics and Governance in the Anthropocene: Institutions and Legitimacy in a Complex World* Routledge, London.

Peters, G.P., Andrew, R.M., Canadell, J.G., Fuss, S., Jackson, R.B., Korsbakken, J.I. and Nakicenovic, N. (2017) "Key indicators to track current progress and future ambition of the Paris agreement" *Nature Climate Change*, 7(2), 118–122.

Rockström, J., Schellnhuber, H.J., Hoskins, B., Ramanathan, V., Schlosser, P., Brasseur, G.P., Gaffney, O., Nobre, C., Meinshausen, M. and Rogelj, J. (2016) "The world's biggest gamble" *Earth's Future*, 4(10), 465–470.

Rockström, J., Steffen, W., Noone, K., Persson, Å., Chapin, F.S., Lambin, E.F., Lenton, T.M., Scheffer, M., Folke, C. and Schellnhuber, H.J. (2009) "A safe operating space for humanity" *Nature*, 461(7263), 472–475.

Schellnhuber, H.J., Crutzen, P.J., Clark, W.C., Claussen, M. and Held, H. eds. (2004) *Earth System Analysis for Sustainability* MIT Press, Cambridge, MA.

Steffen, W., Persson, Å., Deutsch, L., Zalasiewicz, J., Williams, M., Richardson, K., Crumley, C., Crutzen, P., Folke, C. and Gordon, L. (2011) "The Anthropocene: From global change to planetary stewardship" *AMBIO: A Journal of the Human Environment*, 40(7), 739–761.

Steffen, W., Richardson, K., Rockström, J., Cornell, S.E., Fetzer, I., Bennett, E.M., Biggs, R., Carpenter, S.R., de Vries, W. and de Wit, C.A. (2015) "Planetary boundaries: Guiding human development on a changing planet" *Science*, 347(6223), 1259855.

Stirling, A. (2014) *Emancipating Transformations: From Controlling 'the Transition' to Culturing Plural Radical Progress* University of Sussex, Sussex.

Swyngedouw, E. (2013) "The non-political politics of climate change" *ACME: An International E-Journal for Critical Geographies*, 12(1), 1–8.

Swyngedouw, E. (2014) "Anthropocenic politicization: From the politics of the environment to politicizing environments" in Bradley, K. and Hedrén, J. eds., *Green Utopianism: Perspectives, Politics, and Micro-Practices* Routledge, London, 24–37.

Vaughan, N.E. and Lenton, T.M. (2011) "A review of climate geoengineering proposals" *Climatic Change*, 109(3–4), 745–790.

Žižek, S. (2004) "Afterword: The lesson of Rancière" in Rancière, J. ed., *The Politics of Aesthetics: The Distribution of the Sensible* Continuum, London, 69–79.

Part I
Theories and concepts

2 A natural history for the 21st century

Rethinking the Anthropocene narrative with Arendt and Adorno

Maike Weißpflug

Introduction

In a heavily disputed article for *The New Yorker*, the American novelist Jonathan Franzen addressed an ethical dilemma in the Anthropocene: Do we have to choose between global climate protection and local nature conservation? The text also points to the important question of how we tell the narrative of the Anthropocene. As temperatures continue to rise due to human activities, the approaches to climate change mitigation often tend to be as abstract or 'grand' as the problem itself, particularly the visions of climate engineering. Accordingly, the scale at which these changes are taking place seems simply too large to feel connected to or even responsible for, as an individual or as a society. Classical nature conservation policies, by contrast, correspond to a Franciscan ethic: "you're helping something you love, something right in front of you, and you can see the results" (Franzen 2015). Franzen was strongly criticised for prioritising local nature conservation above climate action, and he revoked his statement in the light of Trump's presidency, saying it was a mistake to turn both against each other (Franzen 2017).

Yet, how do we tell the story of the Anthropocene, and how does it come to life as a narrative, reframing the way humans relate to the Earth? Why is how we tell the Anthropocene's story important? These questions frame my inquiry and proposal to dig deeper into the history, meaning and normative dimensions of the Anthropocene.

First, I argue that the term Anthropocene – although it also has been discussed as a purely scientific geological concept – has been framed as a *normative narrative* from the very beginning, starting with the original article by Paul Crutzen and Eugene Stoermer (2000). However, in these texts, the Anthropocene narrative has been told from the abstract point of view Jonathan Franzen calls 'eschatological' – from an 'end of the world' or god-like perspective. Detached from everyday actions and real-world experiences, this kind of 'grand' storytelling, however, seems to be utterly unhelpful to rethink our relation to and responsibility for the natural world.

In a second step, I propose to rethink the Anthropocene narrative by reading two 20th century philosophers, Hannah Arendt and Theodor W. Adorno. Both offer a critique of abstract 'grand' narratives and call for more complex, decentralised human-nature relations. These two example inquiries are used to explore the ways the Anthropocene is deeply embedded in ideas about the relationship between man and nature, which has developed within the discourse of modernity. Arendt's critique of the 'Archimedean point', her understanding of politics as care for the world, Adorno's idea of a natural history, his critical reflections on nature domination and the question of technology are vantage points to rethink the philosophical framework for a more resonating Anthropocene narrative that reconnects our actions with the consequences for the world we live in.

Finally, I follow an argument recently made by Ellis et al. (2016) who demanded an involvement of social sciences and humanities in defining the Anthropocene, by including them into the Anthropocene Working Group of the International Commission on Stratigraphy. To gain a 'deeper and thicker' (Ellis et al. 2016) understanding of the Anthropocene, I advocate for practical inter- and transdisciplinary, participatory studies of natural history with strong social and historical perspectives, that acknowledge the complexity, diversity and local dimensions of how societies relate to nature, and open up ways to redefine and reshape these relations.

Contested narratives of the Anthropocene

In a very broad sense, narratives can be understood as a fundamental form of world disclosure. One of the most cited definitions, by the French structuralist Roland Barthes, reflects this universalistic quality of narratives:

> There are countless forms of narratives in the world. . . . Narrative is present in myths, legends, fables, tales, short stories, epics, history, . . . movies, local news, conversation. Moreover, in this infinite variety of forms, it is present at all times, in all places, in all societies; indeed narrative starts with the history of mankind; there is not, there has never been anywhere, a people without narrative. . . . Like life itself, it is there, international, transhistorical, transcultural.
>
> (Barthes 1975, 237)

This strong social dimension of narratives has been acknowledged since what we now call the narrative turn in the social sciences. Since the 1970s, authors like Clifford Geertz (1973) or Alasdair MacIntyre (2007) and others have successfully claimed that narratives (1) can be understood as a form of social and cultural knowledge, (2) that they shape human interactions and their relations to the non-human world and (3) that they are inherently normative: this means they inform and define who we are (our identities) and what we do (our actions). In other words: Human beings "think, perceive, imagine, interact and make moral choices according to narrative structures" (Crossley 2000, 46). These narrative structures can be described as "having a setting, characters, plot and moral" (Jones and Crow 2017, 2).

A narrative of power and superiority

The term 'anthropocene' was first coined by Crutzen and Stoermer in 2000, in the Global Change Newsletter. The short definition they give in the opening sentences of the text already reveals the narrative, almost mythological character of the text: "Mankind's activities gradually grew into a significant geological, morphological force" (Crutzen and Stoermer 2000, 17). This impression is emphasised by the fact that Crutzen and Stoermer continue to develop the idea of the Anthropocene by referring to a broad range of historical approaches by authurs such as Antonio Stoppani, G.P. Marsh, Vladimir Vernadsky, Pierre Teilhard de Chardin and E. Le Roy who describe, or narrate, humankind as a planetary force a quite uncommon approach to introduce concepts into the natural sciences. Taking a closer look, these authors' ideas are bred not only from quite different backgrounds, but are also shared with varying characters, plots and morales. For Stoppani, the 'Anthropozoic era' is not an historical event or a new quality of human-nature relations but indeed the 'Age of Man' – he conflates anthropological and historical arguments:

> It is in this sense, precisely, that I do not hesitate in proclaiming the Anthropozoic era. The creation of man constitutes the introduction into nature of a new element with a strength by no means known to ancient worlds. And, mind this, that I am talking about physical worlds, since geology is the history of the planet and not, indeed, of intellect and morality. But the new being installed on the old planet, the new being that not only, like the ancient inhabitants of the globe, unites the inorganic and the organic world, but with a new and quite mysterious marriage unites physical nature to intellectual principle; this creature, absolutely new in itself, is, to the physical world, a new element, a new telluric force that for its strength and universality does not pale in the face of the greatest forces of the globe.
>
> (A. Stoppani, *Corso di Geologica*, trans.
> in: Turpin and Federighi 2012, 36)

The second author, George Perkins Marsh, is known as one of the founding fathers of the American environmental movement. He knew the ideas of Stoppani and was strongly influenced by Alexander von Humboldt's ecological thought (Wulf 2016, 366–367). However, Marsh set a different tone in the debate. He criticised the man-made destruction of the natural environment, which in his eyes had already reached a planetary scale. While describing the same setting, his story has a different morale: he did not hope that man as a 'telluric force' would shape the Earth in a positive sense: "man has brought the face of the earth to a desolation almost as complete as that of the moon" (Marsh, *The Earth as Modified by Human Action* (1864), cited from Lowenthal 2016, 7). But Marsh, in this aspect, seems to be the exemption.

The third group of authors Crutzen and Stoermer refer to take a strong progress narrative, fostering the idea that human reason will be able to successfully govern nature and planet Earth. Vernadsky, Teilhard de Chardin and Le Roy shaped the term 'noosphere', the development of a conscious biosphere dominated by human reason. Crutzen and Stoermer refer again to the noosphere in the last section of their text, sketching out solutions for the Anthropocene situation. They assume that "mankind will remain a major geological force for many millennia, maybe millions of years, to come", but only if a 'real functioning noosphere' prevents "major catastrophes like an enormous volcanic eruption, an unexpected epidemic, a large-scale nuclear war, an asteroid impact, a new ice age, or continued plundering of Earth's resources by partially still primitive technology" (Crutzen and Stoermer 2000, 18).

Yet, this imagination of technological progress and sovereign global control of nature, underpinned by the notion of the noosphere, is the flipside of the doomsday narrative: The aim of the narrative is to prevent the end of the world and lead the planet into a better future. From this description the authors derive a call to action for humankind, adding the strong normative connotation of 'planetary stewardship' to the concept of the Anthropocene: "To develop a worldwide accepted strategy leading to sustainability of ecosystems against human induced stresses . . . , requiring intensive research efforts and innovative application of the knowledge thus acquired in the noosphere, better known as knowledge or information society". For the authors, like Bonneuil (2015, 23) has pointed out, science is the *deus ex machina* in this narrative, which will lead humankind into a new and better world: It is not the task of societies or the people, but of the "global research and engineering community to guide mankind towards global, sustainable, environmental management" (Crutzen and Stoermer 2000, 18). In a follow-up article in 2002, Crutzen added the vision of geo-engineering as a planetary scale solution: "This will require appropriate human behavior at all scales, and may well involve internationally accepted, large-scale geo-engineering projects, for instance to 'optimize' climate" (Crutzen 2002, 23).

This "mainstream narrative of the Anthropocene" is in a nutshell the story of humanity evolving "from hunter-gatherers to global geologic force" (Steffen et al. 2011, 741). It encompasses the idea of a *new quality in the relationship between human societies and the natural environment*. The line between nature and culture is blurred – as a planetary force, humanity has become an undeniable part of nature; and nature, on the other side, is deeply shaped by human activities. This touches upon the way nature is understood: it is not the everlasting, unchangeable ground on which human culture evolves. Still, this does not automatically imply a new harmony between nature and culture, or that human activities suddenly have become a part of nature. It indeed turns out to be significant how this story is told. In the original version by Crutzen and Stoermer, it is also a narrative of power and domination, of the superiority of human intellect and the idea that a small elite – scientist and engineers – could manage and control human-nature relations. This narrative has its roots in older stories of progress (or destruction) and the need for humanity to rule the Earth (which is, of course, an even older, biblical element).

Narratives, disruptured

In the Anthropocene literature, this 'mainstream history' of the Anthropocene idea is quite well-established and often quoted. Yet, this history of the idea has been contested. Hamilton and Grinevald (2015) argue that the ideas of Stoppani, Marsh et al. do not capture the central aspect of the Anthropocene concept – the novelty of *scientific understanding* of the Earth as a complex system: "The giants of natural history, when thinking about civilized man as a geological force, lived in a world unaware of a disturbed global nitrogen cycle, a mass extinction event, and global climatic change due to the atmosphere's changing chemical composition" (Hamilton and Grinevald 2015, 61). Hamilton and Grinevald propose an alternative version of the Anthropocene narrative: a strictly rational one.

This narrative includes the interdisciplinary knowledge of the Earth system, of the changes in the global material (carbon, nitrogen, phosphorus) cycles through human interventions which have a stronger effect than natural factors. Secondly, it is this change that sets a new relationship between man and nature into motion: the dichotomy of culture (or history) and nature is dissolved into a more interconnected framework. Hamilton and Grinewald criticise the fact that Crutzen and Stoermer's history of the Anthropocene is based on the idea that humanity's history is one of salvation and progress. To avoid this, they speak of the Anthropocene as a 'rupture', to emphasise the suddenness, extent and irreversibility of human influence on the planetary environment:

> We are not arguing that the discovery of 'precursors' is deflationary because the credit is given to previous thinkers, but that the reference to authors in the 19th and early 20th century locates the origin and nature of the Anthropocene in a pre-Earth system world, thereby drawing the understanding of the Anthropocene into the processes of human alteration of the landscape and changes in the functioning of ecosystems. In so doing it 'gradualizes' the new epoch so that it is no longer a rupture due principally to the burning of fossil fuels but a creeping phenomenon due to the incremental spread of human influence over the landscape. This misconstrues the suddenness, severity, duration and irreversibility of the Anthropocene leading to a serious underestimation and mischaracterization of the kind of human response necessary to slow its onset and ameliorate its impacts.
>
> (Hamilton and Grinevald 2015, 8)

This rational version of the Anthropocene has a narrative structure, a setting (Earth system), characters (humanity), a plot (rupture) and a morale (need to act). One can even say that by rejecting the intellectual history of the Anthropocene, Hamilton and Grinevald introduce their own eschatological trait, believing that only a disruptive Anthropocene, the feeling of 'living in the end times' would lead to an adequate human reaction to the self-induced threats of the Anthropocene. Yet, this has much in common with the kind of narrative the authors criticised and intended to avoid. The strictly rational version of the Anthropocene seems to inherit the traits of the original version by Crutzen and Stoermer: It is in a similar way an abstract, 'grand' narrative, calling for grand and abstract solutions seems 'the kind of human response necessary'. Both versions fail, by over-emphasising the global perspective and the urgent need to find large-scale solutions, to address all complex dimensions of the Anthropocene situation, e.g., the biodiversity crisis with its many local implications. Yet, they evade the maybe more complex and difficult task, namely to provide an adequate response to the Anthropocene situation: How to change the way we, as a global civilisation or as community of global societies, relate to the Earth, to our natural environments, and how we define and value nature locally. This would be no less than a deep cultural chance, as these ideas and relations seems to be hard-wired into the normative texture of Western lifestyles, becoming more and more global.

Digging deeper: Arendt, Adorno and the idea of a natural history

However, the question of responsibility for the Earth points to the normative ambivalence of the concept of Anthropocene, which I have pointed out with Franzen in the beginning: As we have seen, the way in which we tell the story of the Anthropocene seems to influence and shape the calls for action. From a grand narrative, a stronger, even more controlling intervention in natural contexts (e.g., geo-engineering), can be derived. As Raffnsøe points out, a new responsibility for nature will not stem from such superior or sovereign position, but from a new sense of human dependence and precariousness: "A critical turn affecting the human condition is thus still in the process of arriving. Within this landscape, issues concerning the human – its finitude, responsiveness, responsibility, maturity and relationship to itself – appear rephrased and re-accentuated as decisive probing questions, not only for humans but also for the Earth at large" (Raffnsøe 2016, xii). This calls for decentralised, 'thick' Anthropocene narratives, taking into account the various places, landscapes, relationships, technologies and activities relating the human and the non-human world. The idea of thick description was introduced by Gilbert Ryle and Clifford Geertz, together with the idea that we can only understand human actions by describing the small, meaning-generating details (Geertz 1973). Later, the philosopher Bernard Williams adopted this idea and transferred it to evaluative terms, speaking of thick and thin ethical concepts, the latter referring to abstract evaluative terms like 'good' or 'bad' (Williams 2011).

Even though the idea of 'thick' and 'thin' is of later origin, the two philosophers I bring into the dialogue here can both be characterised by a shared advocacy for thick narratives, for their love of details and individual experiences. Their theories are based on a wide-ranging critique of the abstract, thin concepts of Western philosophy and its social conditions and impacts. However, Hannah Arendt and Theodor W. Adorno come from quite different, even oppositional, philosophical backgrounds. Yet, both offer powerful critiques of centralised viewpoints on human life and human relationships to the non-human world. And both claim the power of narratives to grasp the plurality of perspectives, moments and experiences. Their critique of single perspective narratives and the philosophical answers both give can help us to rethink the Anthropocene. As we will see, the Anthropocene debate can benefit from a reexamination of these traits. In the following, I will explore these traits in the philosophies of Arendt and Adorno.

Hannah Arendt: critique of the Archimedean point

According to Arendt, western scientific culture is based on a 'return to Archimedes' (Arendt 2012a, 391), the idea of a mechanical and manipulable nature. According to legend, Archimedes said that if he only had one fixed point and sufficient leverage, he could move the whole Earth. The metaphor of the lever, however, contains more than just a specific conception of the physical universe, it also determines the way in which scientists – and a science-dominated civilisation as a whole – relate to the world and the perspective from which knowledge is gained: "We must always distance ourselves from the objects we want to study, we must withdraw, so to speak" (Arendt 2012a, 394). The Archimedean paradigm is however not a purely physical one. What distinguishes modern science from everything that existed before is, according to Arendt, not the calculated and distanced gaze of the observer, but the notion that knowledge of a natural object can only be gained by exercising power over it. This view of science – we have not only decoded the DNA, but we can also *manipulate* it; the Higgs boson was discovered by *producing it* in a particle accelerator – has taken a long time to fully develop into modern scientific methods.

> For whatever we do today in physics – whether we release energy processes that ordinarily go on only in the sun, or attempt to initiate in a test tube the processes of cosmic evolution, or penetrate with the help of telescopes the cosmic space to a limit of two and even six billion light years, or build machines for the production and control of engines unknown in the household of earthly nature, or attain speeds in atomic accelerators which approach the speed of light, or produce elements not to be found in nature, or disperse radioactive particles, created by us through the use of cosmic radiation, on the Earth – we always handle nature from a point in the universe outside of Earth.
>
> (Arendt 1998, 262)

Arendt's critique of the Archimedean point has a certain closeness to the analysis of the Anthropocene narrative in the first part of this essay. Arendt asks herself if we, "who are Earth-bound creatures" may "have begun to act as though we were dwellers of the universe" (Arendt 1998, 3). For her, the problem is that humans are suddenly able to do thinks that are of such scale that it transcends the human ability to grasp and understand, to 'speak and think' about these actions – like the start of a satellite, the atom bomb or the splitting of the atom. Yet, Arendt is not only concerned about the human inability to understand and judge, but the fact that human activities alter nature itself. Arendt states that the laws of nature "lost their validity when *man entered into nature*" (Arendt 2002, 565). Arendt developed her critique of progress and technology in the context of the global debate on technical civilisation and the possibility of the nuclear destruction of the Cold War world in the 1950s and 1960s. In these passages, Arendt almost sounds like the pioneers of the ecology movement when she states that "the progress of science ... could mean the end of nature and the human race" (Arendt 1995, 34). Arendt also expands her proto-ecological criticism to the production paradigm and a destructive consumerism that misuses the things and may lead to a 'really major collapse':

> This 'progress', accompanied by the incessant noise of the advertising agencies, took place at the expense of the world in which we live and at the expense of the things themselves, in which wear and tear was now built in and which we no longer use, but which we misuse and throw away. The fact that we are now suddenly interested in the dangers threatening the environment is the first ray of hope in this development, although, as far as I can see, no one has yet found a remedy for this out-of-control economy, which would not cause a really major collapse.
>
> (Arendt 2012b, 358–359)

In Arendt's analysis, it is not only the ability to completely destroy the Earth (by means of the atomic bomb) that completely changes the relationship between man and nature. The power to destroy the Earth corresponds to a new, and not at all metaphorical, view of the Earth: through space travel, the first satellites and finally man's journey to the moon, a view of the Earth from the outside becomes possible, which for the first time appears as a whole in the human field of vision.

As Margaret Canovan in her insightful introduction to Arendt's *The Human Condition* has emphasised, there are two quite paradoxical convictions linked with this abstract view: "on the one hand the belief that 'everything is possible'; and on the other that human beings are merely an animal species governed by laws of nature or history, in the service of which individuals are entirely dispensable" (Canovan 1998, 13). Arendt's concern is not primarily the concern that man might destroy nature. Quite contrary: She emphasises that the technical civilisation destroys the way people relate to the world and generate meaning for their lives – their self-respect. From the sky-high perspective of the Archimedean point, the single individual looks like an ant. For Arendt it is therefore not enough to limit – or even solve technically – the negative consequences of a technical civilisation that has gone out of control.

In Arendt's eyes, the 'paradox' of modernity is the 'reduction of self-esteem' (Arendt 2012a, 395) resulting from the tremendous increase in power and pull in the technology field: Man can only be lost in the vastness of the universe. This means that modern natural and engineering sciences do not ask human questions – in the sense of questions that can be opened up to the human senses and everyday mind – but ask what lies "behind the natural phenomena when they reveal themselves to the senses and the mind of man" (Arendt

2012b, 375). This analysis also applies to the Anthropocene situation. Climate science alone – like the reports of the IPCC – does not speak a human language. It is hard to connect to it, to create meaning or base local decisions on it. Arendt points out that this is not a phenomenon of a moral lagging behind scientific understanding, but a more general problem. Arendt contradicts the frequently voiced assertion that the humanities and social sciences lag behind developments of the natural sciences and technology. To her, the assumption that mankind fell politically – one could also say, morally – short of technical developments is nothing more than a 'red herring' in the debate.

The real problem for Arendt is not that morality has to adapt to technical progress, but "that man can do (and can do with success) what he cannot comprehend and express in daily human language" (Arendt 2002, 378). Arendt adds a second diagnosis to this gap between action and understanding: When we no longer understand what we are doing, we experience a radical loss of meaning. Trust in the world of 'mere phenomena' would be lost if the consequences of human action could no longer be sensitively grasped. Arendt attributes this to the attitude of modern scientists: "Rather, it was their search for 'true reality' that led them to lose faith in the phenomena, in the phenomena that she let herself reveal from the human mind and sense" (Arendt 2002, 378). Arendt helps to specify the question of the Anthropocene narrative: According to her analysis of the modern situation, it is not only important how we tell the story of our civilisation, but also how our actions relate to this story. Not understanding what we are doing leads to the inability to tell a meaningful, 'thick' narrative.

While Arendt's critique of the Archimedean point has an obvious parallel to the Anthropocene debate and the question from which perspective we tell the Anthropocene narrative, a second aspect in Arendt's writings is linked to the question discussed here. Arendt proposes a paradigm shift – from an expert culture to a participatory political culture. She states that the real experts of politics are the people: "As laymen, as ordinary people, we have the expertise – and not science, neither engineering nor the humanities – to recognize the dangers and pitfalls of technical civilization" (Arendt 2002, 378). Political judgement is something to be exercised not by specialists, but by ordinary people, from the perspective of the many.

This shifts perspective from the Archimedean point to the perspective of the citizens of the world, from one unified narrative to a plurality of stories. It is therefore too short-sighted to limit, or even solve technically, the negative consequences of a technical civilisation gone out of control. Arendt says quite clearly: As laymen, as citizens, as ordinary people, we – and neither science, nor engineering nor the humanities – have the expertise to recognise, understand, judge and express the dangers of technical civilisation. The question is: How can a policy of 'care for the Earth' be conceived as a policy of human self-respect? Can we think of the "possibility of non-destructive contact with nature", which "lie in the specific, non-sovereign conservation and care of nature and the world" (Jalušič 2011, 292)? Not mastery of nature, but rather a reciprocal relationship with the environment, in which we can find ourselves as individuals, because it remains 'romantically' complex and which is still determined by the metabolism with nature would then be the basis of such a policy. This is also one of the main concerns of Theodor W. Adorno's philosophy.

Theodor W. Adorno's 'idea of natural history'

In 1932, Theodor W. Adorno held a lecture with the title 'The Idea of a Natural History'. Right in the beginning, Adorno states that his own term 'natural history' has nothing to do with the term used by the natural sciences (Adorno 1990, 345) – yet, many of the ideas expressed in this text seem to anticipate quite exactly what is happening in the Anthropocene debate and in the interdisciplinary field of life sciences today. Most interestingly, Adorno's idea of a natural history may come even closer to how we today understand this particular field of study than he might have anticipated. However, his ideas enable us to rethink the Anthropocene situation. The fact that human impact on nature has surpassed natural forces does not mean that humanity is – or will ever be – in full sovereign control over nature. For Adorno, the idea of sovereignty is a fantasy and only the flipside of the cruel natural law of 'eat and being eaten'. Adorno's intellectual work can be understood as an effort to overcome this binary opposition of dominance and heteronomy in human-nature relations and find a third alternative.

From this, he intends to "abandon the usual antithesis of nature and history" (Adorno 1990, 345), to develop a new understanding of nature and history. He opposes the idea that nature is historically unstable, the invariable backdrop against that history unfolds. First, he notes that contemporary philosophy – namely ontology and phenomenology – is based on the "duality of nature and history" (Adorno 1990, 349) in a way that it is always presupposed. Adorno criticises the idea of seeing nature as the eternal, the imperishable, and the kingdom of laws: 'Nature itself is transient' (Adorno 1990, 359). His own idea of a natural history is aimed at a fundamental 'change of perspective', which is more than "a synthesis of natural and historical methods" (Adorno 1990, 356). On the other hand, however, not only the concept of nature is subject to change; the concept of history also has been redefined in the light of the new understanding of nature as dynamic and changing: history is then no longer the realm of freedom and meaning. The historical and social process confronts the individual as 'second nature' just as naturally unchangeably. In *Negative Dialectics*, Adorno formulates this in a pointed way: "Human history, the progressive domination of nature, continues unconscious nature, eating and being eaten" (Adorno 2003a, 348). The "conventional antithesis of nature and history" is 'true and false' at the same time. It is true in that it pronounces "what happened to the moment of nature" to have become the object of human domination.

Programmatically, Horkheimer and Adorno have elucidated the motif of nature control in the *Dialectics of Enlightenment*: "Enlightenment, understood in the widest sense as the advance of thought, has always aimed at liberating human beings from fear and installing them as masters" (Horkheimer and Adorno 1988, 13). However, it is false, "in so far as it apologetically repeats the concealment of the natural growth of history by means of its conceptual reconstruction"

(Adorno 2003a, 351). As Deborah Cook has pointed out, "our understanding of ourselves is seriously flawed" (Cook 2011, 9) because we are not able to see our own – or our history's – entwinement with nature. The same problem of interpretation seems to be at the centre of the Anthropocene debate. How can we, as humans, understand our growing or even disruptive impact on the natural world? Have we, as humans, ourselves become a force of nature? And who is that 'we'? Are human societies able to take responsibility and change the way we relate to the natural environment? I discussed the eschatological trait of the Anthropocene concept in the first section. Adorno seems to discuss a similar idea: the fatality of human history.

So, is human history doomed? Are we dominated by a self-driven technosphere? Adorno gives a twofold answer that can be explored further by turning to the question of technology and the dual nature of technological progress. Yet, humanity is not completely dominated by the forces of technological progress. There are different qualities of new technologies: some are more or less destructive, while others may have the potential "to depart from domination, centralism, violence against nature" (Adorno 2003b, 363). Yet, the choice of technologies is, in Adorno's analysis, always a question of power; the use of technologies is never neutral, it is embedded in social conditions. "Not technology is the fatality, but rather its entanglement with the social conditions in which it is embedded" (Adorno 2003b, 363).

Many of the motifs in Adorno's texts reappear in the narrative of the Anthropocene: Nature is no longer imperishable and boundless, but limited, a planet with finite resources and sensitive ecosystems. Human actions interfere with nature and change it, thus making it a part of history. On the other hand, human activities and the use of technologies become at the same time natural forces with heavy and irreversible impact on the planet. The most important insight of the Anthropocene lies in the fact that nature is transient and therefore, historical, leads to a new discussion about how human societies relate to the natural environment and the question of human responsibility. Adorno can thus be read as a critical correction of the Anthropocene narrative, as a reflection and objection to the progressive control of nature. However, Adorno's criticism of the control of nature is not to be understood as a brief call to preserve nature but aims at a different relationship between history and nature.

Changing narratives: a natural history for the 21st century

Although we have seen that many of the motifs in the Anthropocene narrative already present and reflected upon in the 20th century, it is first and foremost one aspect that sets the world of Hannah Arendt and Theodor W. Adorno apart from our current situation: Climate change, the dramatic loss of biodiversity, soil degradation and ocean acidification and pollution are not mere philosophical, but real-world problems that need real-world solutions. It does not only call for a mere reflection of human-nature relations, but actions. So, what follows from these philosophical re-readings from the history of political thought for our situation today? Two interventions with Arendt and Adorno, and two further conclusions, will be detailed in the following section.

Decentralising the Anthropocene narrative: from one to many stories

The first idea follows Arendt's critique of the 'Archimedean point' and aims at decentralising the Anthropocene narrative – from a single perspective story about 'man' or 'humankind' to the manifold stories of people connected to their environment, to animals, plants, landscapes and cities. The Anthropocene situation itself is complex and does not fit into one grand narrative: climate change has multitudes of impacts and biodiversity loss occurs across many scales, these changes take various forms and extents and exist within diverse cultural and historical contexts. The same is true for soil degradation, pollution, air and water quality. We can name and lament these things, but in this abstract form they will remain 'thin' narratives, if narratives at all. The way nature and nature destruction affect people is as diverse and complex as nature and people themselves. Instead of one grand but 'thin' narrative, thick descriptions and narratives have to be told, recent and old narratives about human-environment relations. The texts and cultural resources we can rely on for this adventure are numberless and spread through space and time, like these verses from Sophocles' *Antigone* (Murray 1941):

> *Chorus.*
> Wonders are many, but none there be
> So strange, so fell, as the Child of Man.
> He rangeth over the whitening sea,
> Through wintry winds he pursues his plan:
> About his going the deeps unfold,
> The crests o'erhang, but he passeth clear.
> Oh, Earth is patient, and Earth is old,
> And a mother of Gods, but he breaketh her,
> To-ing, froing, With the plough-teams going,
> Tearing the body of her year by year.

Against nature domination

The second intervention is inspired by Adorno's critique of nature domination. Does the idea of an 'age of man' suggest a new stage of humanity's sovereignty over nature, like in the original narrative by Crutzen and Stoermer? Or can the Anthropocene be retold as a critical narrative helping us to rethink human-environment relations and our modern life form? For examining the possibility of redefining human-environmental relations, which is not based on the principle of natural control, we have to understand the deep cultural roots of today's technological civilisation and its human-nature relationship. But we should not only understand the genealogy and history of human-nature relations in western societies, but also explore non-Western models of nature-culture webs, like in the groundbreaking study of Philippe Descola (Descola 2011). With reference to Adorno, Peter Sloterdijk has outlined this new relationship with the concept of 'cohabitation': "The concept of the Anthropocene contains the spontaneous minima moralia of the present age: it implies the concern for the cohabitation of the citizens of the Earth in both human and non-human form" (Sloterdijk 2015, 271).

Yet the limits of the Anthropocene idea also seem to lie in its misleading and ambiguous terminology – we should not only consider merely *human* activity, but more specifically the systematic challenges of a *technological* culture.

> More seriously, we are witnessing a contemporary recovery of the idea of a second creation in the reframing of the Anthropocene as an event to be celebrated rather than lamented and feared. Instead of the final proof of the damage done by human arrogance, a new breed of 'eco-modernists' welcomes the new epoch as a sign of our ability to transform and control.
>
> (Hamilton et al. 2015, 41)

Another problem of the Anthropocene narrative is that about it focuses too heavily on humans. As important this reflective dimension is – as I explained before – it tends to render invisible what is actually at the centre of it: nature.

New ways of creating knowledge

One may regard the Anthropocene narrative critically. But what it achieves is to enable us to discuss and understand groundbreaking changes in human-environment relations. The Anthropocene narrative opens up a critical evaluation of what human agency, modern life forms and the use of technologies inflict on planet Earth. The insight into this new quality of human impact is new, but the reflection of modernity's relation to the natural world – without doubt the basis and precondition of today's situation – can be found all along within modernity. I have picked two 'high crest' authors, but of course these conflicts and debates can be found elsewhere – in the history of ideas, in literature and the arts, and in all products of culture. The Anthropocene as a new world might also require a new science (Tocqueville), a paradigm change based on a redefinition of the basic understandings of nature and human activities. This change is already on the way and should be observed and described carefully. This entails a set of shifts in the structure and organisation of the scientific system.

The first is the blurring of the nature-history divide, bringing the humanities and the sciences closer together. The separation of nature and culture-history is no longer the meaningful framework for understanding the state of the world and human action in it. The second is the 'participatory turn', blurring the line between experts and the public: exploring and understanding how nature evolves into a societal endeavour. These shifts are already underway in several disciplines and fields, e.g., the science and technology studies, the inter- and transdisciplinary field of environmental and sustainability studies, environmental humanities, in natural history museums and in participatory research and citizen science approaches. Yet, it is still to be determined what this blurring of lines between sciences and humanities, nature and culture, experts and citizens means and what the implications for the way we conduct science and discuss societal issues are. For example, scientists could define their interventions into nature, e.g., genetic manipulations, as 'natural' and therefore legitimate. This is, again, a question of how we tell the story of the Anthropocene.

Conclusion

The Anthropocene should not be told from a single perspective, but from many. The 'sovereign' version of the Anthropocene narrative we find in the original texts by Crutzen, is already contested in the scientific debate. Still, these debates seem to need some further decentralising and contextualising by adding historical, philosophical and transdisciplinary perspectives, and through connecting science, humanities and public engagement. Understanding the Anthropocene as a narrative of nature and human-nature relations helps to connect the scientific and inter disciplinary work on the Anthropocene concept with a genealogy of human-environment relations and reflections on the interconnectedness of culture, technology and human agency. In my inquiry of Adorno and Arendt, I have undertaken some first steps to show that precisely the normative discussion of the Anthropocene narrative can sustain fruitful stimuli from the philosophical discourse of modernity. The Anthropocene – or however we might call this narrative about current human-nature relations – is first and foremost a diagnosis of the current global situation and an attempt to tell the story of the civilisation that created this situation. For a better understanding of humanity's complex, diverse and 'novelistic' relations to the natural world, it will be fruitful to investigate the ideas, practices and norms that brought us here – by digging deeper into the histories and narratives of the human-nature fabric (see also Höhne and Schwindenhammer, in this volume). This may also help to engage in a broader public, critical and participatory debate about the modern lifestyle, the possibility and conditions of cultural change and the experimental search for new life forms. In the end, the way we live and the technologies we choose, abandon or reject, will shape the way we, as a global culture, walk into the future. At the same time, this will be a question of our shared responsibility towards humanity and the natural world we live in.

Finally, it all depends on the most crucial question of the Anthropocene narrative – who this 'we' is, and who the 'anthropos' may refer to. This not a normative question of what we should do, but a political question depending on and decided by real-world actions. At the moment, the Anthropocene narrative already has gained some power in guiding public reason and decision-making, but remains contested, with many societies experiencing a cleavage between those who identify themselves with this kind of narrative and those who do not. As I have tried to argue, we need to enable new and manifold ways to reinvent how our lives and societies relate to nature. The 'grand' but 'thin' original version of the

Anthropocene narrative may, as I have tried to show with my narrative analysis and the philosophical critique of Arendt and Adorno, not be the right vessel for this – another, decentralised version is yet to be told. Decentralised narratives of the Anthropocene would connect us with the nature around us, while still taking into account the dire and radical global consequences of our lifestyles and actions for the Earth system.

References

Adorno, T.W. (1990) "Die Idee der Naturgeschichte" in Adorno, T.W., *Philosophische Frühschriften* Suhrkamp, Frankfurt am Main, 345–336.

Adorno, T.W. (2003a) *Negative Dialektik, Jargon der Eigentlichkeit* Suhrkamp, Frankfurt am Main.

Adorno, T.W. (2003b) "Spätkapitalismus oder Industriegesellschaft?" in Adorno, T.W., *Soziologische Schriften I* Suhrkamp, Frankfurt am Main, 354–370.

Arendt, H. (1995) *Macht und Gewalt* 10th ed. Piper, München.

Arendt, H. (1998) *The Human Condition* 2nd ed. University of Chicago Press, Chicago.

Arendt, H. (2002) *Vita activa oder Vom tätigen Leben* Piper, München.

Arendt, H. (2012a) "Der archimedische Punkt" in Arendt, H., *In der Gegenwart. Übungen im politischen Denken II* Piper, München, 389–402.

Arendt, H. (2012b) "Zweihundert Jahre Amerikanische Revolution" in Arendt, H., *In der Gegenwart. Übungen im politischen Denken II* Piper, München, 354–369.

Barthes, R. (1975) "An introduction to the structural analysis of narrative" *New Literary History*, 6(2), 237–272.

Bonneuil, C. (2015) "The geological turn: Narratives of the Anthropocene" in Hamilton, C., Bonneuil, C. and Gemenne, F. eds., *The Anthropocene and the Global Environmental Crisis* Routledge, London, New York, 17–31.

Canovan, M. (1998) "Introduction" in Arendt, H., *The Human Condition* University of Chicago Press, Chicago, vii–xx.

Cook, D. (2011) *Adorno on Nature* Acumen, Durham.

Crossley, M. (2000) *Introducing Narrative Psychology: Self, Trauma and the Construction of Meaning* Open University Press, Buckingham, Philadelphia.

Crutzen, P.J. (2002) "Geology of mankind" *Nature*, 415(6867), 23

Crutzen, P.J. and Stoermer, E.F. (2000) "The 'Anthropocene'" *Global Change Newsletter*, 41, 17–18.

Descola, P. (2011) *Jenseits von Natur und Kultur* Suhrkamp, Berlin.

Ellis, E., Maslin, M., Boivin, N. and Bauer, A. (2016) "Involve social scientists in defining the Anthropocene" *Nature News*, 540(7632), 192.

Franzen, J. (2015) "Carbon capture: Has climate change made it harder for people to care about conservation?" *The New Yorker*, 91(7), 56–65.

Franzen, J. (2017) "Is it too late to save the world? Jonathan Franzen on one year of Trump's America" *The Guardian*, 4 November.

Geertz, C. (1973) "Thick description: Toward an interpretive theory of culture" in Geertz, C., *The Interpretation of Cultures: Selected Essays* Basic Books, New York, 3–30.

Hamilton, C., Bonneuil, C. and Gemenne, F. eds. (2015) *The Anthropocene and the Global Environmental Crisis* Routledge, London, New York.

Hamilton, C. and Grinevald, J. (2015) "Was the Anthropocene anticipated?" *The Anthropocene Review*, 2(1), 59–72.

30 *Maike Weißpflug*

Horkheimer, M. and Adorno, T.W. (1988) *Dialektik der Aufklärung. Philosophische Fragmente* Fischer, Frankfurt am Main.

Jalušič, V. (2011) "Leben/Natur" in Heuer, W., Heiter, B. and Rosenmüller, S. eds., *Arendt-Handbuch. Leben, Werk, Wirkung* Metzler, Stuttgart, 289–292.

Jones, M. and Crow, D. (2017) "How can we use the 'science of stories' to produce persuasive scientific stories?" *Palgrave Communications*, 3(1), 53.

Lowenthal, D. (2016) "Origins of Anthropocene awareness" *The Anthropocene Review*, 3(1), 52–63.

MacIntyre, A. (2007) *After Virtue: A Study in Moral Theory* 3rd ed. University of Notre Dame Press, Notre Dame, IN.

Murray, G. (1941) *Sophocles, the Antigone* Allen & Unwin, London.

Raffnsøe, S. (2016) *Philosophy of the Anthropocene: The Human Turn* Palgrave Macmillan, Hampshire.

Sloterdijk, P. (2015) "The Anthropocene: A process-state on the edge of geohistory?" in Klingan, K. ed., *Textures of the Anthropocene: Ray* MIT Press, Cambridge, MA, London, 257–271.

Steffen, W., et al. (2011) "The Anthropocene: From global change to planetary stewardship" *AMBIo*, 40, 739–761.

Turpin, E. and Federighi, V. (2012) "A new element, a new force, a new input: Antonio Stoppani's Anthropozoic" in Ellsworth, E. and Kruse, J. eds., *Making the Geologic Now* Punctum Books, Brooklyn, 34–41.

Williams, B. (2011) *Ethics and the Limits of Philosophy* Taylor & Francis, London.

Wulf, A. (2016) *Alexander von Humboldt und die Erfindung der Natur* 2nd ed. Bertelsmann, München.

3 Disentangling descriptions of and responses to the Anthropocene

Norms and implications of scientific representations of the Earth system

Johannes Lundershausen

Introduction

In 2000, Nobel laureate in chemistry Paul Crutzen and biologist Eugene Stoermer termed the 'Anthropocene' – the most recent epoch in Earth history in which the cumulative actions of (some) humans are driving the Earth system out of its Holocene state (Crutzen and Stoermer 2000). In spite of the ongoing debate about the official geological status of the Anthropocene (Zalasiewicz et al. 2017a), it has become a popular term within and outside of academia highlighting the vast extent and novel quality of anthropogenic Earth system change.

On the side of policy, decision makers increasingly refer to the Anthropocene for an explanation of global change and sustainable responses to it (Steiner 2016; Ban 2014; Hendricks 2015). From a political science perspective, researchers connect the empirical insights about the Anthropocene analysis to recommendations of how to act on global changes (Future Earth 2014; Whitmee et al. 2015). As Steffen et al. (2011b, 741) have argued: "One of the key developments in moving from problem definition to solution formulation is the concept of the Anthropocene" (Steffen et al. 2011b, 741). These efforts are idiosyncratic because the original description of the Anthropocene reveals relatively little about the social driving forces and consequences of global change (Bonneuil and Fressoz 2016; Palsson et al. 2013). But the interest in the Anthropocene as a framework for solutions indicates that "the Anthropocene is implicated in the deepening ethical-political entanglements of scientific research" (Clark 2014, 26). Commentators have argued that scientists are responsible to "guid[e] society towards environmentally sustainable management during the era of the Anthropocene" (Crutzen 2002, 23; Barnosky et al. 2014; Brasseur and van der Pluijm, B. 2013), and Anthropocene-specific research agendas have been advanced to achieve this aim (Kotchen and Young 2007; Bai et al. 2015).

In this chapter, I highlight the normative logics incorporated in scientific descriptions of the Anthropocene and demonstrate which ways of acting on the Anthropocene they can produce. In order to do so, I proceed in three steps. Firstly, I identify two relevant scientific representations of the Anthropocene that are based on very different interpretations of past and contemporary Earth system changes and the concomitant development of human civilisations. Whereas one depicts the Anthropocene as 'a crisis for sustainability', the other regards it 'as an opportunity' to increase human well-being. Secondly, the chapter shows that these scientific interpretations also contain certain normative logics. I refer to the 'end of nature' debate in order to demonstrate that the lack or adherence to an *a priori* environmental baseline defines the different normative outlooks of the two interpretations. Thirdly, I sketch out the connection between these normative logics and existing policy responses to global change. Namely, I explain how the normative logics identified respectively invigorate proposals for Earth System Governance and for geo-engineering. The chapter concludes by providing an outlook of the kind of approaches needed to generate different responses to the Anthropocene.

The co-production of scientific knowledge and social practices

This chapter starts from the socio-political embeddedness of the scientific analyses of the Anthropocene. Scholars in the field of science and technology studies (STS) have highlighted that knowledge about the world (including the Earth) is inseparable from the ways in which we govern our lives. This idea of 'co-production' between social and natural order, prominently advanced by Sheila Jasanoff (2004, 2–3), draws attention to the social performativity and contingency of scientific knowledge: "Scientific knowledge ... both embeds and is embedded in social practices, identities, norms, conventions, discourses, instruments and institutions – in short, in all the building blocks of what we term the social".

Incorporating this insight into an understanding of the Anthropocene is consequential. Brian Cook and Angeliki Balayannis (2015, 277) emphasised that recognising "the co-production of knowledge and governance means that proposals such as the Anthropocene ... must take into account the normative commitments entailed" in the Earth system sciences in which the term originates. The concept of co-production thus challenges both producers and users of scientific knowledge about the Anthropocene to consider if their normative commitments align with those of the scientific analyses of the Anthropocene. In this vein, Lauren Rickards (2015, 338) highlights that "the Anthropocene is a call (back) to science": we are asked to examine the prescriptive claims underpinning the representations of the Anthropocene require closer examination. This chapter follows this call by highlighting the logics for acting on the Anthropocene that inhere in scientific descriptions of the latter.

Two representations of the Anthropocene Earth system

Before evaluating the 'Anthropocene as crisis' and 'Anthropocene as opportunity', it needs to be emphasised that the two representations comprehensively describe neither the science of the Anthropocene nor its popular discourse (Dalby 2016). The debate about the Anthropocene is constantly evolving and this evolution is periodically assessed by commentators (Castree 2014). In this chapter, I focus on a limited number of seminal contributions to the debate. I am concerned predominantly with norms and implications of the science of the Anthropocene and thus attend to publications that are most revealing in this regard. I focus on articles that employ the concept of the Anthropocene to discuss the human impact on the Earth system. As a result, I do not review publications that debate the status of the Anthropocene as an official stratigraphic unit.

Given the diversity of the debates, categorising the scientific descriptions of the Anthropocene as two opposed paradigms is inevitably a simplification. But this dichotomy is a defendable heuristic that advances our understanding about the actions that scientific descriptions of the Anthropocene invoke, in spite of our limited knowledge about their actual socio-political consequences. Several academics writing on the Anthropocene justify this approach by cautiously contrasting positions at the ends of a wider spectrum (Cook et al. 2015; Cook and Balayannis 2015; Davison 2015; Karlsson 2015; Steffen et al. 2016). They emphasise the multiple ways in which the grand narrative of the Anthropocene can be interpreted, rather than to suggest that there are only two such interpretations. In this vein, the dichotomy between descriptions of the Anthropocene 'as crisis' and 'as opportunity' highlights the contradictory qualities that the Anthropocene combines.

The Anthropocene as a crisis of sustainability

Many scientists originally working on the Anthropocene define it as an anthropogenic state of the Earth system that is both unprecedented and unsustainable (Crutzen and Steffen 2003). This judgement is made because the Anthropocene would end "the Holocene-like state ... of the Earth system [which] is the only one that *we can be sure* provides an accommodating environment for the development of humanity" (Steffen et al. 2011b, 753 – emphasis added). This negative representation of the Anthropocene draws on the observation that humanity required the 'safe operating space' of the Holocene Earth system to develop complex civilisations with historically exceptional levels of human welfare. Although it is possible from this perspective to imagine human development in alternative Earth systems, this is generally disregarded as a counterfactual vision of the past that is not supported by empirical observation. To leave the safe space of the Holocene risks permanently overwhelming current strategies to maintain and increase present levels of human development. the Anthropocene marks a transition towards a new state of the Earth system that is exceedingly more variable and inherently more dynamic than known modes of Earth system functioning (Steffen et al. 2004; Steffen et al. 2016). This is unlike climate change, which may be regarded as a temporary (if long on human timescales) perturbation within regular patterns of Earth system variability between glacial and inter-glacial phases (Steffen et al. 2011b, 755).

The instability of the Anthropocene and the associated notion of unsustainability is further quantified by the concept of Planetary Boundaries, which articulates the negative representation of the Anthropocene in a more openly normative fashion (Castree 2014, 441). Even though the concept of Planetary Boundaries and that of the Anthropocene have different origins, many prominent scientists regard the former as a normative operationalisation of the latter (Brown 2015).

The concept of Planetary Boundaries starts from the notion that biophysical processes underpin the functioning of the subsystems of the Earth and that an alteration of these processes beyond certain thresholds risks non-linear changes in those subsystems and, for some 'core boundaries', the Earth system itself (Rockström et al. 2009b; Steffen et al. 2015). On the basis of these considerations, Planetary Boundaries define the safe distance from these thresholds. In case of climate change, for example, the control variables of atmospheric CO_2 concentrations and radiative forcing should stay below the limits of 350–450 ppm and +1.0–1.5 W m^{-2} compared to pre-industrial levels, respectively (Steffen et al. 2015).

Regardless of the recognition that the idea of Planetary Boundaries is "surrounded by large uncertainties and knowledge gaps" (Rockström et al. 2009b, 1) concerning both scientific understanding of thresholds (e.g., their globality and interactions) and normative judgements on acceptable environmental change (Steffen et al. 2015), this quantitative operationalisation of the idea of a 'safe operating space' is an explicitly normative one that aims to "meet the challenge of maintaining the Holocene state" of the Earth system (Rockström et al. 2009a, 472). Planetary Boundaries add a sense of urgency to that aim by showing that four of the specified boundaries (climate change, loss in biodiversity, land-system change, altered biogeochemical cycles) have already been crossed (Steffen et al. 2015).

In doing so, the concept of Planetary Boundaries contributes to a vision of the Anthropocene as an 'emerging limit experience' (Alberts 2011, 7). In terms of the current trajectory to confront those limits, Planetary Boundaries indicate a crisis of human development on a finite planet. In any case, the idea of the 'safe operating space' of the Holocene implies that entering the Anthropocene would risk not only the demise of humanity's potential to shape the Earth system but also the end of contemporary societies (Steffen et al. 2015).

While the concept of Planetary Boundaries consequently constitutes a normative framework to weigh the uncertainties and risks associated with leaving the Holocene Earth system, its advocates ground it in Earth system science. Although proponents of the concept acknowledge that what it means 'to be safe' is a normative question and that their answer to it is informed by a risk-averse and conservative approach to human development (Rockström et al. 2009b, 3), they are adamant that planetary thresholds "exist independent of human actions or desires" (Steffen et al. 2011a, 860) and that Planetary Boundaries are a first attempt to define the '*non-negotiable* planetary preconditions' of human development (Rockström et al. 2009b, 2 – emphasis added). To be sure, this approach does not deny that humans are increasingly able to influence Earth system changes intentionally. But this ability is circumscribed by the geophysical thresholds of the Holocene Earth system that cannot be surpassed by human ingenuity.

The Anthropocene as an opportunity for sustainability

The negative description of the Anthropocene can be contrasted with a positive one that emphasises the benefits of the ability of humans to alter their environment and overcome environmental limits. In this positive description of the Anthropocene, contemporary Earth system change does not primarily depict a crisis of human development on a finite planet but evidences the unprecedented capacity of humans to transform their environment on a planetary scale and thus to change the conditions of their very existence. The human activities that have led to extensive global change were not undertaken with the intention of causing the latter. Yet, the human potential to do so has led to the idea that they should embrace Earth system change as a solution to some of the predicaments of contemporary socio-environmental relations, rather than as an invigoration of their problematique. Highlighting the human ability to navigate environmental changes in advantageous ways thus enables a description of the Anthropocene Earth system change as a positive development that affords opportunities to achieve long-term sustainability.

The same rationale appears in the wider debate about 'novel ecosystems', i.e., ecosystems that differ from pristine ones in that they are created by and embedded in human systems (Hobbs et al. 2006). Although many existing novel ecosystems, like brownfields or agricultural land, were not intentionally created as sanctuaries of ecological diversity, the prospects of using these artificial habitats as sites of socio-ecological experiments entice restoration ecologists. These ecosystems are seen to provide new opportunities for focusing on what humans want to create rather than on the risks they seek to reduce (Marris 2009; Lehman and Nelson 2014). The contentious extension of these arguments to the global scale is a central feature of positive descriptions of the Anthropocene.

A prominent positive description has been advanced by Erle Ellis who first described a 'good Anthropocene' in a 2011 publication of the Breakthrough Institute (Ellis 2011a) that has been at the forefront of a 'new environmentalism' movement (for a critique see Szerszynski 2015). Ellis outlined a historical perspective on Earth system change and argued that modern humans have always extensively altered ecological systems across most of the terrestrial biosphere. This argument aligns with the suggested 'early Anthropocene' hypothesis that dates anthropogenic environmental change back to the Neolithic Revolution thousands of years ago (Ruddiman et al. 2011). Stratigraphers officially tasked with defining the inception of the Anthropocene have challenged this hypothesis (Zalasiewicz et al. 2017b) and Ellis (Ellis et al. 2016) has reacted by developing his arguments. As a result of setting an early baseline for extensive anthropogenic impact on the environment, changes to the Earth system in the Anthropocene appear not as fundamentally new but as a recent advancement of the human potential.

This view of historical socio-environmental relations implies a 'logic of human ingenuity': humans have always been able to shape their environment, so it becomes conducive to their development. Following this arguments, 'human system boundaries' (Ellis 2011a, 37–38) will define human activities in the

Anthropocene more than Planetary Boundaries. For, transgressing natural boundaries and adapting to new environmental conditions have been central means of human development

At the same time, the 'logic of human ingenuity' is contingent on the idea that the Earth system is already locked into an Anthropocene future that cannot completely be reversed to a Holocene trajectory even if 'human system boundaries' such as social values, systems of governance and technologies were to change (Ellis 2011b). Since the Earth system cannot be returned to the Holocene, pragmatism ostensibly relegates concerns with environmental limits. From this perspective, focusing on the possibilities provided by novel ecosystems or 'anthropogenic biomes' (Ellis and Ramankutty 2008) allows for adapting to and mending the conditions of an Anthropocene Earth system. Although Ellis does not contend that a human-driven Earth system is 'particularly good' (Ellis 2011a, 42), attending to these 'planetary opportunities' (DeFries et al. 2012) will arguably help to create a beneficial version of the Anthropocene.

Normative logics for Earth system change in the Anthropocene

The discussion above shows that scientific descriptions of the Anthropocene differ regarding their interpretation of past and contemporary Earth system change. From the perspective of philosophy of science, it is not unusual that interpretations are incommensurable with each other, even if they are consistent with the evidence (Evans and Collins 2008). This section takes this argument further by showing that these different scientific interpretations contain certain normative logics. They are 'epistemic-moral hybrids', i.e., scientific analyses of reality that are closely linked to evaluative and normative statements (Potthast 2010).

The competing normative logics that underpin the Anthropocene 'as crisis' and 'as opportunity' are elucidated a wider discussion about whether or not nature has ended. This debate gained prominence particularly after the publication of Bill McKibben's *The End of Nature* in 1989 (2006) in which he maintained that the traditional empirical understanding of nature as apart from humans is no longer viable. The acknowledgement of close interactions between humans and natural systems is central to both descriptions of the Anthropocene 'as crisis' and 'as opportunity'. They differ, however, on whether or not geophysical processes inevitably provide the basis of human conduct. While, in the negative description of the Anthropocene, Earth system processes constrict and enable intentional human action (Clark 2014), they cease to be the residual context of such action in the positive description (Dalby 2014).

In this sense, the description of the 'Anthropocene as opportunity' implies a 'culturalist logic' in which natural processes are determined by human actions. Ellis's comment that 'nature is gone' is suggestive here (Ellis 2009, unpaginated). It is because of this culturalism of some scientific representations that the Anthropocene analysis has been criticised for underestimating the nature-constructedness of humans (Clark 2012) and for unifying nature and culture under the mastery of the latter (Baskin 2014). In contrast, the description of the 'Anthropocene as crisis' highlights that human flourishing is inherently circumscribed by thresholds of the Earth system. It thus stresses that there is an essential quality to the Earth system that requires protection. As such it carries a 'naturalist logic' which is diametrically opposed to culturalism and seeks to understand social phenomena through natural processes.

This difference is consequential for the normative outlooks that the two perspectives enable. In the 'naturalist logic', contemporary civilisation will – by design or by disaster – have to adhere to the limits of the Earth system. In the 'culturalist logic', environmental conditions can be surpassed in order to advance human development. The former logic insists on the primacy of nature. Consequently, it lends itself to proposals to strictly prevent further change of the Holocene Earth system state which is regarded as the only operational mode of the Earth system. In doing so, the 'naturalist logic' already outlines a specific normative understanding of what humans should value most in nature. Such an understanding is missing in the 'culturalist logic', which rejects the notion of an 'optimal' past state of the Earth system. This logic thus lacks an explicit *a priori* environmental baseline upon which normative judgements and decision-making can be based. This is not to say that the 'culturalist logic' refrains from normalising a certain view of the Earth system. But its normalisation is not based on geophysical parameters of that system.

Conservation biology provides a good reference point when characterising these normative logics because conservation biologists have recently surrendered a strict distinction between fact and value when talking about the normative content of scientific representations. The 'naturalist logic' is in line with concerns to preserve or restore the integrity of natural ecosystems, reflecting in terms of norms the breath of traditional environmental ethics (Elliot 1995). In contrast, the 'culturalist logic' better reflects the recently popular idea of 'intervention biology' (Hobbs et al. 2006) as well as the norms of ecomodernism (Fisher and Freudenburg 2001).

To summarise the above argument, scientific descriptions of the Anthropocene Earth system are not neutral. They embody normative logics about whether humans should advance their influence on the Earth system or give ground to geophysical processes of the latter and respect their limits. At the basis of these statements lie different answers to the question if there is an essence to nature that provides the inevitable background for sustainable development and can thus function as a normative guide.

From representations of the Anthropocene towards responses to it

In this section, I show that the normative logics identified above engender different ways of acting on the Anthropocene. Whereas the focus in the 'naturalist logic' is on limiting the magnitude of global change, managing the direction of that change is of foremost importance in the 'culturalist logic'. I make this case by drawing parallels between the two scientific representations analysed above and proposed responses to the Anthropocene. On the one hand, Earth System Governance, which promotes political institutions that produce more sustainable socio-environmentalrelations, builds on an understanding of the 'Anthropocene as crisis' and the embodied 'naturalist logic'. On the other hand, the vision of 'Anthropocene as opportunity' and the connected 'culturalist logic' enables geo-engineering, which advocates deliberate large-scale intervention in the Earth system as a sustainable response to global change.

It needs to be emphasised, however, that neither the desirability nor the likelihood of different political measures can be deduced from the scientific representations of the Anthropocene. There is no linear relationship that would lead "politics and ethics [to] simply flow from science" of the Anthropocene (Randalls 2015, 334; Schmidt et al. 2016). Scientific descriptions of global change do not automatically result in corresponding action because the former cannot fully dissolve political disagreement about the latter (Oreskes 2004). Yet, while scientific representations of the Anthropocene cannot tell us what we ought to do, their scientific logics do engender different political logics. The ways in which we know a phenomenon affect the ways in which we act upon that phenomenon (Lövbrand et al. 2009). This is particularly the case for responses to global phenomena of environmental change, which are contingent upon the scientific discourse. These phenomena would not exist as recognisable matters of concern without that discourse (Urry 2011).

Governing the crisis of the Anthropocene

Global environmental governance is a long-standing concern of political science. Recently, it has been aligned more closely with scientific approaches that focus on the Earth as an integrated system. Accordingly, proposals have been developed for Earth System Governance (hereafter ESG), which purportedly responds both to scientific insights and the needs of policymakers (Biermann et al. 2010). The integrative approach of ESG promises to go beyond "traditional notions of environmental policy, ... [which] do not capture current global developments that transform the bio-geophysical ... processes of our planet" (Biermann et al. 2010, 203). This section shows that ESG has lately fulfilled this raison d'être by referring to Planetary Boundaries as a justification for political action as well as its own approach.

From an ESG perspective, the sustainability problems of the Anthropocene largely result from political processes and institutions that inadequately govern the human impact on the environment (Schroeder 2014). ESG does not, as the name might suggest, advocate direct management of the Earth system but it aims to steer the political processes that have adversely changed the latter (Biermann 2014b). ESG seeks to invest in *political ingenuity* to induce social changes that reduce human interference with the Earth system. Accordingly, it differs from the 'Anthropocene as opportunity', which puts hope in the *technological ingenuity* of human systems to advance the means of controlling nature.

Furthermore, the maintenance of the Holocene Earth system is a specific motivation of ESG (Biermann 2014b 59) and functions as an *a priori* environmental baseline for decision-making. ESG is underpinned by the 'naturalist logic'. This is the more evident because ESG adopts Planetary Boundaries as conceptual framework (Galaz et al. 2011). Frank Biermann, who has notably advanced the idea of ESG, most clearly outlines the relevance of Planetary Boundaries for governance by arguing that the concept "specifies an overall environmental target corridor" (Biermann 2012, 4) and thus helps to concretely define and balance the three pillars of sustainable development.

To be sure, the relationship of ESG to Planetary Boundaries and the primacy of nature argument is ambiguous. Although Biermann values a further quantification of Planetary Boundaries, he also cautions that they cannot generally guide governance because they are in 'principle neutral to human values' and simply highlight widely agreed relationships in the Earth system (Biermann 2012, 5). The normative questions that inhere in a quantitative definition of Planetary Boundaries (such as the assessment of scientific uncertainty, cost-benefit analyses and risk indicators), according to Biermann, acquire relevance only when the concept is 'operationalised' by political actors. But critics have argued that the science behind the Planetary Boundaries concept, rather than being absolute and independent, implies normative judgements regarding e.g., trade-offs between the multiple costs and benefits of environmental change (Nordhaus et al. 2012).

A plausible explanation why ESG nevertheless adopts Planetary Boundaries can be provided by referring to Simon Lewis (Lewis 2012, 417) who argues that Planetary Boundaries are

> Conceptually brilliant and politically seductive: clear, quantitative measurements with no obvious judgements on what is 'right' or 'wrong' to include. It is also liberating. Here is humanity's safe space: within it, do what you want.

In this vein, the primary function of Planetary Boundaries for ESG is to highlight the urgency of political action. The effect of this is twofold. On the one hand, the reference to ostensibly value-neutral and politically uninstructive Planetary Boundaries leaves considerable freedom as to the concrete measures of how to achieve sustainability. The proposed institutional reforms (Biermann 2014a, 2012), for example, are articulated quite independent of the individual Planetary Boundaries and instead encompass issue-specific solutions which largely follow social activities. On the other hand, the Planetary Boundaries concept helps to support the raison d'être of ESG. Whatever political solutions and institutional reforms are suggested by proponents of ESG, they can be legitimised as responses to the urgent "challenge of maintaining the Holocene state" (Rockström et al. 2009a, 472).

However, this double function incorporates a paradox: how can Planetary Boundaries simultaneously be indifferent to political choices and yet function to support concrete policy options? The paradox can be explained by Erik Swyngedouw's concept of 'de-politicisation of the environment' (2011), which demonstrates the normative importance of an *a priori* environmental baseline and of the 'naturalist logic' for ESG. The continuous commitment of the "normative theory of Earth System Governance ... [to the] needs and necessities of Earth system stability" (Biermann 2014a, 27) prescribes what humans should value most in nature. This is the case even where Planetary Boundaries are not explicitly highlighted as the basis for Earth System Governance (Biermann 2014a, 2014b). Consequently, the foremost criteria for evaluating suggested policies becomes whether or not the Earth system stays within the quantitatively defined limits delineated by the Planetary Boundaries concept.

An alternative framing of environmental governance that is more closely aligned with the description of the 'Anthropocene as opportunity' highlights the consequences of employing this normative logic. In contradistinction to the 'naturalist logic', John Dryzek (2014) has argued that global change requires current 'Holocene institutions' to overcome their path dependency on ideas of a stable nonhuman world including that of static boundaries. This difference to ESG is relevant for the concrete governance responses to global change. Because ESG focuses on governance options within a defined natural operating space with finite boundaries, it is much more concerned with allocation of and access to resources (Schroeder 2014). To the contrary, Dryzek (2014) suggests that adaptive governance (only one amongst five analytical problems of ESG (Biermann 2007)) is paramount because the subsystems of the Earth are not characterised by fixed thresholds but by instability and dynamism.

Geo-engineering as an opportunity of the Anthropocene

Another measure suggested to respond to the Anthropocene is geo-engineering. In spite of their long history (Fleming 2006), proposals for geo-engineering continue to be surrounded by considerable ambiguity relating e.g., to their demarcation from other technologies (Galaz 2012) as well as to their heterogeneous ethical and political implications (Hulme 2012). Notwithstanding this ambiguity, geo-engineering is increasingly seen as requiring strategic consideration (Dibley 2012). That this trend is strengthened by the arrival of the Anthropocene has been described as 'hardly surprising' (Clark 2012, 259) and 'inevitable' (Hamilton 2012, unpaginated). In this vein, geo-engineering has been called the 'posterchild of the Anthropocene' because it depicts the increasing power of humans to influence the environment on a global scale (Scott 2013, 316).

Conceptually, both 'Anthropocene as opportunity' and geo-engineering support the direct management of nature as a solution to Anthropogenic challenges. Particularly, geo-engineering's "'artificing of nature' [by] intentionally tweaking some of the Earth's basic processes" to create sustainable conditions (Preston 2012, 191) is evocative of the 'culturalist logic' of the 'Anthropocene as opportunity'. Proponents of geo-engineering like Schäfer et al. (2014) and Crutzen (2006), who also refer to the Anthropocene, are convinced that the development of geo-engineering technology and its deployment in the natural world can largely be determined by human intentions. This outlook aligns with the 'culturalist logic' that nature, even if it cannot be controlled fully, does not frustrate the realisation of human intentions (Yusoff 2013). In this logic, the historically grown capacity of humans to transform their environment on a large-scale is an opportunity to deal with current sustainability challenges. Whereas many of the phenomena that characterise the Anthropocene have been side-effects of the pursuit of various managerial and political goals, in conjuncture with the 'culturalist logic', they point towards the feasibility of managing the Earth system intentionally. As such, the 'culturalist logic' enables an endorsement of geo-engineering, which assumes that research and development can amplify the human capacity to direct Earth system processes to chosen ends (Hamilton 2012). The empirical analysis of the 'Anthropocene as opportunity' thus provides a 'geohistoric moment' (Yusoff 2013, 2800) that renders the deployment of geo-engineering imaginable.

Like in the scientific description of the 'Anthropocene as opportunity', natural limits rarely feature in geo-engineering debates. Instead, 'human system boundaries' such as governance and research are emphasised. Where governance is highlighted, it is distinct from Earth System Governance in that it seeks to advance institutional and procedural arrangements in order to enhance the management of nature itself and govern the competing interests involved in this. Conversely, Planetary Boundaries highlight the difficulty of realising intentional management of the Earth system by drawing attention to the possibility that respecting the boundaries of one subsystem of the Earth may lead to the crossing of another (Steffen et al. 2004). Geo-engineering has hence been described as 'antithetical' to the idea of Planetary Boundaries (Steffen et al. 2011a, 860) and is incompatible with the 'naturalist logic'.

It goes to show that some commentators have contributed both to Anthropocene and geo-engineering debates. Although only a few geo-engineering advocates directly refer to the Anthropocene, several Anthropocene scientists propose geo-engineering as a response option (Crutzen 2006; Steffen et al. 2011a, 2011b). They consider geo-engineering as a future possibility and advocate 'low-tech' mitigation measures such as afforestation as proximate solutions. In doing so, they follow the geo-engineering advocacy discourse, which seeks to break the taboo on the scientific exploration of associated technologies while remaining aware of geo-engineering's "dual prospect of large benefits and harms" (Parson and Keith 2013, 1278; Allenby 2007).

Fundamentally, the description of the 'Anthropocene as opportunity' provides a historical reference for large-scale human interference in the environment and thus extends the spatial and temporal scale of acceptable human disturbance. Even though authors like Simon Dalby (2016) have highlighted that a belief in technological solutions will not inevitably lead to geo-engineering, the description of the 'Anthropocene as opportunity' means that geo-engineering could be seen as a mere difference in degree rather than in kind to previous forms of environmental management. Spatially, authors like Ellis and Ramankutty (2008) imply that it is a small step from evident 'ecosystem engineering' to Earth system engineering. This thin line between faith in technological and ecological progress is a clear indicator for ecomodernist conception of the Earth (Davison 2015, 4).

Temporally, the description of the 'Anthropocene as opportunity' provides a historical analogy for global change and thus extends the futurism that underpins geo-engineering into the past. This bodes particularly well for a refutation of the common criticism that the deployment of geo-engineering would require considerable temporal commitment because it does not address the causes of anthropogenic environmental change (like rising carbon dioxide emissions) but merely treats its symptoms (Steffen et al. 2011b). According to critics (Preston 2012), the ensuing permanent and active management of the Earth system would assign humans an unbearable responsibility. But the description of the 'Anthropocene as opportunity', in conjuncture with the 'early Anthropocene' hypothesis, legitimises such a commitment by arguing that humans have influenced the Earth system for millennia.

Conclusion

This chapter has dichotomised the scientific descriptions of the Anthropocene 'as crisis' and 'as opportunity' in order to highlight the co-constitution of scientific and normative statements. It has explicated the normative logics about desirable states of the Earth system that these descriptions incorporate, and illustrated their implications for responses to Earth system change.

The analysis of scientific representations of the Anthropocene as 'epistemic-moral hybrids' (Potthast 2010) will trouble scientists who fear that their objectivity is being challenged. But the analysis conducted in this chapter should not be read as a judgement on the validity or the credibility of these representations. The latter are important not because they are right or wrong, objective or subjective, but because they can invoke action (Thrift 2004). This effect exists irrespective of the desirability of these actions. While the moral value of responses to environmental change can be judged by ethical analysis (Jamieson 2008), this has not been the aim of this chapter. Opening up normative logics of scientific representations and their political implications for debate, as done in this chapter, helps scientists and political actors alike to understand the entanglement of scientific research on global change in ethical and political decision-making.

Doubts may arise that the descriptions of the Anthropocene reviewed in this chapter can meaningfully contribute to distinctive responses to global change of unprecedented magnitude. Indeed, critics have questioned that Anthropocene representations can ground anything else than existing approaches to environmental management. They hold that its very analysis perpetuates, in case of the 'Anthropocene as opportunity', an anthropocentric worldview and destruction of nature (Crist 2013; Davison 2015), and, in case of the 'Anthropocene as crisis', "foregrounds a political imaginary of threat", precluding a focus on the particular processes that have led to the environmental crisis in the first place (Evans and Reid 2014, 4; Houston 2013).

We cannot expect different outcomes if we maintain the same normative assumptions. Although empirical descriptions of the Anthropocene advance our understanding of contemporary Earth system change, they need to be based on non-dualistic approaches to the 'end of nature' if they are to foster distinctive responses to the latter. A variety of such non-dualistic approaches have been developed within the social sciences and humanities (Lorimer 2012; Bingham and Hinchliffe 2008). They highlight that the Earth system is established both by different social ascriptions of objects as distinctive parts of it and by various practices that enact the materiality of these objects. Although the scientific representations of the Anthropocene analysed in this chapter highlight interrelations between the human and material world, future research needs to pay more attention to the actual practices of these processes. In addition, more reflection is required on the changed social, including scientific, ascriptions of objects and processes as constitutive of the Earth system.

Acknowledgements

This work has been supported by the Junior Research Group "Ethics in the Sciences for Sustainable Development" ("Wissenschaftsethik der Forschung für Nachhaltige Entwicklung") at the University of Tübingen, Germany, which is funded through the German Excellence Initiative (Zukunftskonzept 63).

References

Alberts, P. (2011) "Responsibility towards life in the early Anthropocene" *Angelaki*, 4, 5–17.
Allenby, B. (2007) "Earth systems engineering and management: A manifesto" *Environmental Science & Technology*, 41(23), 7960–7965.
Bai, X., van der Leeuw, S., O'Brien, K., Berkhout, F., Biermann, F., Brondizio, E.S., et al. (2015) "Plausible and desirable futures in the Anthropocene: A new research agenda" *Global Environmental Change*, 39, 351–362 [Epub ahead of print 23 September 2015].
Ban, K.-M. (2014) *Secretary-General's Remarks to Inaugural Meeting of His Scientific Advisory Board* (as prepared for delivery), Berlin. (http://www.un.org/sg/statements/index.asp?nid=7439) Accessed 21 October 2015.
Barnosky, A.D., Hadly, E.A., Dirzo, R., Fortelius, M. and Stenseth, N.C. (2014) "Translating science for decision makers to help navigate the Anthropocene" *The Anthropocene Review*, 1(2), 160–170.
Baskin, J. (2014) *The Ideology of the Anthropocene?* MSSI Research Paper No. 3, Melbourne Sustainable Society Institute, Melbourne.
Biermann, F. (2007) "'Earth system governance' as a crosscutting theme of global change research" *Global Environmental Change*, 17(3–4), 326–337.
Biermann, F. (2012) "Planetary boundaries and Earth system governance: Exploring the links" *Ecological Economics*, 81, 4–9.
Biermann, F. (2014a) *Earth System Governance: World Politics in the Anthropocene* MIT Press, Cambridge, MA.
Biermann, F. (2014b) "The Anthropocene: A governance perspective" *The Anthropocene Review*, 1(1), 57–61.
Biermann, F., Betsill, M.M., Vieira, S.C., Gupta, J., Kanie, N., Lebel, L., et al. (2010) "Navigating the Anthropocene: The Earth System Governance Project strategy paper" *Current Opinion in Environmental Sustainability*, 2(3), 202–208.
Bingham, N. and Hinchliffe, S. (2008) "Reconstituting natures: Articulating other modes of living together" *Geoforum*, 39(1), 83–87.
Bonneuil, C. and Fressoz, J.-B. (2016) *Shock of the Anthropocene: The Earth, History and Us* Verso, London.

Brasseur, G.P. and van der Pluijm, B. (2013) "Earth's future: Navigating the science of the Anthropocene" *Earth's Future*, 1(1), 1–2.

Brown, K. (2015) "Global environmental change II: Planetary boundaries: A safe operating space for human geographers?" *Progress in Human Geography*, 4(1), 118–130 [Epub ahead of print 30 September 2015].

Castree, N. (2014) "The Anthropocene and geography I: The back story" *Geography Compass*, 8(7), 436–449.

Clark, N. (2012) "Rock, life, fire: Speculative geophysics and the Anthropocene" *Oxford Literary Review*, 34(2), 259–276.

Clark, N. (2014) "Geo-politics and the disaster of the Anthropocene" *The Sociological Review*, 62, 19–37.

Cook, B.R. and Balayannis, A. (2015) "Co-producing (a fearful) Anthropocene" *Geographical Research*, 53(3), 270–279.

Cook, B.R., Rickards, L.A. and Rutherford, I. (2015) "Geographies of the Anthropocene" *Geographical Research*, 53(3), 231–243.

Crist, E. (2013) "On the poverty of our nomenclature" *Environmental Humanities*, 3, 129–147.

Crutzen, P.J. (2002) "Geology of mankind" *Nature*, 145, 23.

Crutzen, P.J. (2006) "Albedo enhancement by stratospheric sulphur injections: A contribution to resolve a policy dilemma?" *Climatic Change*, 77(3–4), 211–220.

Crutzen, P.J. and Steffen, W. (2003) "How long have we been living in the Anthropocene era: Editorial comment" *Climate Change*, 61, 251–257.

Crutzen, P.J. and Stoermer, E. (2000) "The Anthropocene" *IGBP Newsletter*, 41, 17.

Dalby, S. (2014) "Geographic pedagogy in the Anthropocene" in Johnson, E. and Morehouse, H. eds., "After the Anthropocene: Politics and geographic inquiry for a new epoch" *Progress in Human Geography*, 38(3), 442–444.

Dalby, S. (2016) "Framing the Anthropocene: The good, the bad and the ugly" *The Anthropocene Review*, 3(1), 33–51.

Davison, A. (2015) "Beyond the mirrored horizon: Modern ontology and amodern possibilities in the Anthropocene" *Geographical Research*, 53(3), 298–305.

DeFries, R., Ellis, E.C., Chapin, S.F., III, Matson, P., Turner, B.L., II, Agrawal, A., et al. (2012) "Planetary opportunities: A social contract for global change science to contribute to a sustainable future" *BioScience*, 62(6), 603–606.

Dibley, B. (2012) "'Nature is us': The Anthropocene and species-being" *Transformations*, 21, unpaginated.

Dryzek, J.S. (2014) "Institutions for the Anthropocene: Governance in a changing Earth system" *British Journal of Political Science*, 1–20 [Epub ahead of print 28 November 2014].

Elliot, R. (1995) *Environmental Ethics* Oxford University Press, Oxford, New York.

Ellis, E.C. (2009) *Stop Trying to Save the Planet* (www.wired.com/2009/05/ftf-ellis-1/) Accessed 19 February 2015.

Ellis, E.C. (2011a) "The Planet of no return: Human resilience on an artificial Earth" in Shellenberg, M. and Nordhaus, T. eds., *Love Your Monsters: Post Environmentalism and the Anthropocene*, Breakthrough Institute, Oakland, 37–46.

Ellis, E.C. (2011b) *Forget Mother Nature: This Is a World of Our Making* (www.newscientist.com/article/mg21028165-700-forget-mother-nature-this-is-a-world-of-our-making/) Accessed 20 October 2015.

Ellis, E.C., Maslin, M., Boivin, N. and Bauer, A. (2016) "Involve social scientists in defining the Anthropocene" *Nature*, 540(7632), 192–193.

Ellis, E.C. and Ramankutty, N. (2008) "Putting people in the map: Anthropogenic biomes of the world" *Frontiers in Ecology and the Environment*, 6(8), 439–447.

Evans, B. and Reid, J. (2014) *Resilient Life: The Art of Living Dangerously* Polity Press, Cambridge.

Evans, R. and Collins, H. (2008) "Expertise: From attribute to attribution and back again?" in Hackett, E.J., Amsterdamska, O., Lynch, M. and Wajcman, J. eds., *The Handbook of Science and Technology Studies* MIT Press, Cambridge, MA, 609–629.

Fisher, D.R. and Freudenburg, W.R. (2001) "Ecological modernization and its critics: Assessing the past and looking toward the future" *Society and Natural Resources*, 14, 701–709.

Fleming, J.R. (2006) "The pathological history of weather and climate modification: Three cycles of promise and hype" *Historical Studies in the Physical and Biological Sciences*, 37(1), 3–25.

Future Earth (2014) *Future Earth Launches Eight Initiatives to Accelerate Global Sustainable Development* (www.futureearth.info/news/future-earth-launches-eight-initiatives-accelerate-global-sustainable-development) Accessed 14 August 2014.

Galaz, V. (2012) "Geo-engineering, governance, and social-ecological systems: Critical issues and joint research needs" *Ecology and Society*, 17(1), unpaginated.

Galaz, V., Biermann, F., Crona, B., Loorbach, D., Folke, C., Olsson, P., et al. (2011) "Planetary boundaries-exploring the challenges for global environmental governance" *Current Opinion in Environmental Sustainability*, 4(1), 80–87.

Hamilton, C. (2012) *The Philosophy of Geoengineering* Mainz (www.clivehamilton.com/philosophy-of-geoengineering/) Accessed 9 August 2014.

Hendricks, B. (2015) *Rede der Bundesministerin Dr. Barbara Hendricks an der Humboldt-Universität zu Berlin* Berlin (www.bmub.bund.de/N50838/) Accessed 13 May 2015.

Hobbs, R.J., Arico, S., Aronson, J., Baron, J.S., Bridgewater, P., Cramer, V.A., et al. (2006) "Novel ecosystems: Theoretical and management aspects of the new ecological world order" *Global Ecology and Biogeography*, 15, 1–7.

Houston, D. (2013) "Crisis is where we live: Environmental justice for the Anthropocene" *Globalizations*, 10(3), 439–450.

Hulme, M. (2012) "Climate change: Climate engineering through stratospheric aerosol injection" *Progress in Physical Geography*, 36(5), 694–705.

Jamieson, D. (2008) *Ethics and the Environment: An Introduction* Cambridge University Press, Cambridge.

Jasanoff, S. (2004) "The idiom of co-production" in Jasanoff, S. ed., *States of Knowledge: The Co-Production of Science and Social Order* Routledge, London, 1–12.

Karlsson, R. (2015) "Three metaphors for sustainability in the Anthropocene" *The Anthropocene Review*, 3(1), 23–32 [Epub ahead of print 5 August 2015].

Kotchen, M.J. and Young, O.R. (2007) "Meeting the challenges of the anthropocene: Towards a science of coupled human-biophysical systems: Editorial" *Global Environmental Change*, 17(2), 149–151.

Lehman, J. and Nelson, S. (2014) "Experimental politics in the Anthropocene" in Johnson, E. and Morehouse, H. eds., "After the Anthropocene: Politics and geographic inquiry for a new epoch" *Progress in Human Geography*, 38(3), 444–447.

Lewis, S.L. (2012) "We must set planetary boundaries wisely" *Nature*, 485(7399), 417.

Lorimer, J. (2012) "Multinatural geographies for the Anthropocene" *Progress in Human Geography*, 36(5), 593–612.

Lövbrand, E., Stripple, J. and Wiman, B. (2009) "Earth system governmentality" *Global Environmental Change*, 19(1), 7–13.

Marris, E. (2009) "Ragamuffin Earth" *Nature Climate Change*, 460, 450–453.

McKibben, B. (2006) *The End of Nature* Random House Trade Paperbacks, New York.

Nordhaus, T., Shellenberg, M. and Blomqvist, L. (2012) *The Planetary Boundaries Hypothesis: A Review of the Evidence*, Breakthrough Institute, Oakland.

Oreskes, N. (2004) "Science and public policy: What's proof got to do with it?" *Environmental Science & Policy*, 7(5), 369–383.

Palsson, G., Szerszynski, B., Sörlin, S., Marks, J., Avril, B., Crumley, C., et al. (2013) "Reconceptualizing the 'Anthropos' in the Anthropocene: Integrating the social sciences and humanities in global environmental change research" *Environmental Science & Policy*, 28, 1–13.

Parson, E.A. and Keith, D.W. (2013) "Science and regulation: End the deadlock on governance of geoengineering research" *Science*, 339(6125), 1278–1279.

Potthast, T. (2010) "Epistemisch-moralische Hybride und das Problem interdisziplinärer Urteilsbildung" in Jungert, M., Romfeld, E., Sukopp, T. and Voigt, U. eds., *Interdisziplinarität: Theorie, Praxis, Probleme* Wissenschaftliche Buchgesellschaft, Darmstadt, 174–191.

Preston, C.J. (2012) "Beyond the end of nature: SRM and two tales of artificity for the Anthropocene" *Ethics, Policy & Environment*, 15(2), 188–201.

Randalls, S. (2015) "Creating positive friction in the Anthropo(s)cenes" *Dialogues in Human Geography*, 5(3), 333–336.

Rickards, L.A. (2015) "Metaphor and the Anthropocene: Presenting humans as a geological force" *Geographical Research*, 53(3), 280–287.

Rockström, J., Steffen, W., Noone, K., Persson, Å., Chapin, F.S., III, Stuart, F., Lambin, E., et al. (2009a) "A safe operating space for humanity" *Nature*, 461, 472–475.

Rockström, J., Steffen, W., Noone, K., Persson, Å., Chapin, F.S., III, Lambin, E., et al. (2009b) "Planetary boundaries: Exploring the safe operating space for humanity" *Economy and Society*, 14(2), unpaginated.

Ruddiman, W.F., Crucifix, M.C. and Oldfield, F.A. (2011) "Introduction to the early-Anthropocene special issue" *The Holocene*, 21(5), 713.

Schäfer, S., Stelzer, H., Maas, A. and Lawrence, M.G. (2014) "Earth's future in the Anthropocene: Technological interventions between piecemeal and utopian social engineering" *Earth's Future*, 2(4), 239–243.

Schmidt, J.J., Brown, P.G. and Orr, C.J. (2016) "Ethics in the Anthropocene: A research agenda" *The Anthropocene Review*, 3(3), 188–200.

Schroeder, H. (2014) "Governing access and allocation in the Anthropocene" *Global Environmental Change*, 26, A1–A3.

Scott, K.N. (2013) "International law in the Anthropocene: Responding to the geoengineering challenge" *Michigan Journal of International Law*, 34(309), 309–358.

Steffen, W., Grinevald, J., Crutzen, P.J. and McNeill, J. (2011a) "The Anthropocene: Conceptual and historical perspectives" in Zalasiewicz, J., Williams, M., Haywood, A. and Ellis, M.A. eds., "The Anthropocene: A new epoch of geological time?" *Philosophical Transactions of the Royal Society*, 369, 842–867.

Steffen, W., Leinfelder, R., Zalasiewicz, J., Waters, C.N., Williams, M., Summerhayes, C., et al. (2016) "Stratigraphic and Earth system approaches to defining the Anthropocene" *Earth's Future*, 4(8), 324–345.

Steffen, W., Persson, Å., Deutsch, L., Zalasiewicz, J., Williams, M., Richardson, K., et al. (2011b) "The Anthropocene: From global change to planetary stewardship" *AMBIO*, 40(7), 739–761.

Steffen, W., Richardson, K., Rockström, J., Cornell, S.E., Fetzer, I., Bennett, E.M., et al. (2015) "Planetary boundaries: Guiding human development on a changing planet" *Science*, 347(6223), 1–12.

Steffen, W., Sanderson, A., Tyson, P., Jäger, J., Matson, P., Moore, B., III, et al. (2004) *Global Change and the Earth System: A Planet under Pressure*, Springer, New York.

Steiner, A. (2016) *Stories from the Anthropocene: Lecture by UNEP Executive Director Achim Steiner at the Tongji University in Shanghai* (http://www.unep.org/NewsCentre/ default.aspx?DocumentID=27059&;ArticleID=36079) Accessed 6 March 2016.

Swyngedouw, E. (2011) "Depoliticized environments: The end of nature, climate change and the post-political condition" *Royal Institute of Philosophy Supplement*, 69, 253–274.

Szerszynski, B. (2015) "Getting hitched and unhitched with ecomodernists" *Environmental Humanities*, 7, 239–244.

Thrift, N.J. (2004) "Summoning life" in Cloke, P.J., Crang, P. and Goodwin, M. eds., *Envisioning Human Geographies*, Arnold, London, New York, 65–77, Distributed in the United States of America by Oxford University Press.

Urry, J. (2011) *Climate Change and Society*, Polity Press, Cambridge, Malden, MA.

Whitmee, S., Haines, A., Beyrer, C., Boltz, F., Capon, A.G., de Souza Dias, B.F., et al. (2015) "Safeguarding human health in the Anthropocene epoch: Report of The Rockefeller Foundation-Lancet Commission on planetary health" *The Lancet*, 386(10007), 1973–2028.

Yusoff, K. (2013) "The geoengine: Geoengineering and the geopolitics of planetary modification" *Environment and Planning A*, 45(12), 2799–2808.

Zalasiewicz, J., Waters, C.N., Summerhayes, C.P., Wolfe, A.P., Barnosky, A.D., Cearreta, A., et al. (2017b) "The working group on the Anthropocene: Summary of evidence and interim recommendations" *Anthropocene*, 19, 55–60.

Zalasiewicz, J., Waters, C.N., Wolfe, A., Barnosky, A., Cearreta, A., Edgeworth, M., et al. (2017a) "Making the case for a formal Anthropocene epoch: An analysis of ongoing critiques" *Newsletters on Stratigraphy*, 50(2), 205–226.

4 The Anthropocene and governance

Critical reflections on conceptual relations

Basil Bornemann

Introduction

After the 'sustainability turn' in the 1990s, environmental theory and practice currently face a new idea, which, in the eyes of some observers, heralds another, even more fundamental turn: the Anthropocene. In contrast to earlier ideas of human-nature relationships, the Anthropocene suggests that humans are no longer simply one factor among others influencing the Earth's system. Rather, human activities have reached levels of breadth and intensity that simply outperform the 'natural' dynamics of ecological systems and make humans *the* defining element of a post-geological epoch (Bonneuil 2015).

According to leading voices in the discourse, these deep transformations call for fundamental changes in virtually all spheres of society, including politics. In the Anthropocene, so goes the argument, we cannot simply proceed with established 'holocenic' politics. Rather, we are forced to adapt our ways of doing and knowing politics to the realities and challenges of the new epoch. In fact, the Anthropocene has already entered the discourse of politics and political science in recent years. From here, it seems to be ready to challenge not only the perceptions and practices of environmental/sustainability politics, but also the conceptual foundations of politics more generally (Hamilton et al. 2015; Biermann 2014b; Dryzek 2016; Wissenburg 2016).

In accordance with the overall goals of this book, my aim is to add to the emerging discussion about the implications of the Anthropocene for politics and political science. My focus lies in the relationship between the Anthropocene and governance, a core concept of political science that has also very much framed the theory and practice of environmental and sustainability politics in the last 20 years (Lemos and Agrawal 2006; Meadowcroft 2007). Governance, in a broad sense, covers a rich terrain of concepts, approaches and phenomena related to the organisation of collective action in contemporary societies. It is all about understanding the diversity of governing practices with which ever more differentiated and complex political systems address ever more complex problems (Haus 2010).

My focus on the relationship between the Anthropocene and governance is motivated by the observation that the Anthropocene discourse itself increasingly extends to governance terminology. In fact, there are more and more contributions dealing with the implications of the Anthropocene for conceptualising and practising collective action (see Pattberg and Zelli 2016b; Dryzek 2016). These contributions are also beginning to challenge established environmental and sustainability governance discourse by promoting 'anthropocenic governance' as the new way of knowing and doing future-oriented governance (Lövbrand et al. 2009; Biermann 2014a; Davies 2016). In light of this already ongoing and sometimes unquestioned process of conceptual and practical contestation and transformation, I see both the need and the opportunity to step back for a moment and enter into a critical reflection on the relationship between governance and the Anthropocene. However, since the discussion is still very much in flux, I frame this reflection in terms of an exploration of learning potentials in two directions.

On the one hand, I argue that concepts of anthropocenic governance can learn from established governance thinking. The latter can enlighten and improve the former by, for example, helping to uncover and overcome under-complex, simplistic or naive notions of governance that do not work in practice, have unexpected consequences, or are even repelled. On the other hand, I also see potential in the Anthropocene debate to challenge, reflect and further innovate existing governance thinking. The Anthropocene might point to gaps and biases in governance thinking that call for a reconsideration of the concepts and practices of governance.

In my effort to exploit these mutual learning potentials, I will look at the relationship between governance and the Anthropocene by asking the following questions: What does governance mean in the Anthropocene? How does anthropocenic governance appear in light of contemporary governance thinking? What are the implications of the Anthropocene for governance thinking more generally? In answering these questions, I will neither make new claims about whether the Anthropocene is a reality or 'a fact', nor will I judge the normative quality or practical utility of the term. Rather, I focus on how the Anthropocene and related conceptions of anthropocenic governance challenge, and are challenged by, governance thinking on a conceptual level.

My argument proceeds as follows: After a brief recapitulation of the Anthropocene discourse, I look at existing framings and conceptions of anthropocenic governance. Afterwards, I engage in critical reflections on the relationship between governance and the Anthropocene. To this end, I introduce a more systematic notion of governance thinking, based on which I reflect on the existing conceptions of anthropocenic governance and draw out implications of the Anthropocene for governance thinking more generally. In the final section, I discuss the consequences of my critique and argue for a normatively based conception of sustainability-oriented anthropocenic governance.

Understandings of the Anthropocene

The term 'Anthropocene' has been used for several years to refer to a new section on the official geological timescale. It denotes the era following the Holocene, suggesting that "the planetary system as a whole is undergoing an epoch-level transition" (Davies 2016, 2). An essential feature of this new epoch is the reference to

'Anthropos', which advances human activity as a new powerful force in the play of planetary and geophysical forces. Although the official recognition of the Anthropocene as a new geological epoch is still pending, the term is very often treated as referring to a fact, and has taken hold in varied scientific, social and political discourse in recent years (Görg 2016, 9). Here, the concept has been ascribed different, more specific meanings. From the point of view of decreasing reference to formal scientific criteria and increasing enrichment with cultural meaning, these meanings can be classified as stratigraphic, crisis-diagnostic, and culturalistic variants (for a similar suggestion, cf. Jahn et al. 2015; for alternative ways of sorting the discourse, see Semal 2015; Bonneuil 2015; Wissenburg 2016).

Firstly, the *stratigraphic interpretation* of the Anthropocene is based on a certain methodology – a set of objective scientific criteria and corresponding methods – for the delineation of geological epochs (Davies 2016). The crucial reference point for determining the Anthropocene is the objective manifestation of significant effects of human-influenced geobiological processes in certain rock strata (Davies 2016, 66). Given its focus on *characteristic* features of an epoch, the stratigraphic diagnosis of the Anthropocene does not imply that humans exclusively dominate the world; rather, human societies are regarded as the most vigorous and distinctive among an irreducibly various array of altered forces (Davies 2016, 76).

A second interpretation puts the Anthropocene as a *scientifically informed diagnosis of crisis* (Jahn et al. 2015, 93; see also Lundershausen, in this volume). As compared to the stratigraphic interpretation, the Anthropocene is not about the manifestation of human activity in certain rock strata, but about the destructive effects of human activities on critical 'planetary boundaries', which together constitute a 'safe operating space' of the Earth system (Rockstrom et al. 2009). The current or foreseeable crossing of these planetary boundaries, and the resulting catastrophic consequences, render the Anthropocene an epoch of Earth history, which is characterised by a fundamental crisis for humankind (Görg 2016, 10).

Finally, *culturalist interpretations* take the scientific diagnoses of the stratigraphers or Earth scientists as occasion for fundamental reconsiderations of the basic conditions of modernity, human civilisation and the human condition as such (Chakrabarty 2009; LeCain 2016; see also Weißpflug, in this volume). The Anthropocene signifies, in this reading, the transformation of humankind from a merely biological to a geological force (Chakrabarty 2009, 206). This insight, which deeply shakes previously undisputed achievements of human development, such as justice and freedom, and thus the foundations of humanity as such, not only makes the Anthropocene a 'geological turn', but also a 'post-humanist' turn (Arias-Maldonado 2016; Lövbrand et al. 2015), heralding the emergence of a 'transhuman Humanism' (LeCain 2016). The implications of this deep change vary between a narrative of 'humiliation' – the recognition of humankind's embeddedness in 'deep time' (Davies 2016, 11–12) – and a narrative of 'omnipotence', which, in the sense of a counter-Copernican turn, puts humankind back into the centre of attention (Davies 2016, 70; Arias-Maldonado 2016).

Overall, the Anthropocene is exposed to a fate similar to other concepts that transgress the ordering boundaries of scientific disciplines: Around the concept, a varied and partially controversial discourse about its diverse meanings and implications has emerged. Yet, despite these differences, there seems to be also some common ground in the discourse. First, all the interpretations agree that the Anthropocene signifies a virtually unprecedented change – a change that is so fundamental that it extends beyond the usual categories of historiography and justifies a switch to the time categories of geology. Secondly, and related to the first point, the different interpretations rely on natural, scientific knowledge as a basis for diagnosing the (actual or foreseeable) state of the Earth as Anthropocene. More specifically, they feature geological knowledge or knowledge produced by interdisciplinary Earth sciences, as an adequate basis for diagnosing the state of the Earth. Third, this knowledge basis endows the Anthropocene with universalist claims in at least two respects. From a spatial point of view, the Anthropocene connects all places on Earth in a single Earth system. In fact, there is no meaningful place on Earth 'outside' the Anthropocene. In terms of time, the Anthropocene combines hitherto separate and locally conceived human and natural histories into a common history of man and nature, integrated into the universal history of the Earth and the universe by means of geological nomenclature. Fourth, the Anthropocene in its different variants builds on a notion of the deep interconnectedness of human societies with geobiophysical dynamics. Interconnectedness implies both that humankind is fundamentally dependent on these dynamics and – as highlighted by the reference to Anthropos – the advancement of human activity as a unprecedented force in the play of planetary and geophysical forces: "Human societies are now among the most powerful ecological forces that operate on, and below the surface of the Earth" (Davies 2016, 10).

Anthropocenic governance

With the rise of Anthropocene discourse, questions about governance implications soon came up. In view of the fundamental change indicated by the Anthropocene, a common starting point for this discussion is the assumption that anthropocenic governance is fundamentally different from holocenic governance (Dryzek 2016). However, scholars are investigating these differences in various ways, implying different relationships between governance and the Anthropocene. Some scholars look for differences with an empirical twist, suggesting that not only the Anthropocene itself is a reality, but that it has already transformed governance. Following this interpretation, existing forms of governance are actually already expressions of *governance in the Anthropocene* (Biermann et al. 2016; Widerberg 2016). Other scholars discuss the Anthropocene (discourse) as a resource or framework for knowing and doing collective action (Lövbrand et al. 2009). This understanding of *governance with/by the Anthropocene* is present in the central texts of the Anthropocene discourse, for example, when Steffen et al. (2011, 741) stress the mobilising potential of the Anthropocene narrative as a "key development[s] in moving from problem definition to solution formulation" regarding the ongoing ecological crisis. Most prominently, however, questions of anthropocenic governance are discussed on a conceptual-prescriptive level – as if the Anthropocene was imminent and calling for a deliberate reconsideration of governance: How can and how should we govern in view of the Anthropocene? Several conceptions of *governance of the Anthropocene* have emerged around this question, which I discuss in more detail below.

Based on a continuum ranging from very concrete suggestions to rather abstract governance ideas, I distinguish five groups of conceptions. A first group defines very concrete *technological options for the governance of the Anthropocene.* Their understanding is based on the Earth scientists' notion of the Anthropocene, according to which the Earth system can be described by a number of global scale parameters that provide promising levers for a technology-oriented 'planetary management' (Stirling 2015b, 2015a). The geo-engineering technologies brought up by (parts of) the founding generation of Anthropocene thinkers are paradigmatic cases of this governance-by-technology approach (Wissenburg 2016). Underlying is a Promethean interpretation of the new epoch "based on the conviction that our technical ingenuity will not only save us from potential global chaos, but even enable us to extend our history of growth and progress for ages" (Semal 2015, 93). In fact, this much-criticised technological imagery seems to have become formative for the broader societal discussion about the Anthropocene and its governance.

A second group contains approaches that are less technologically oriented but still promote fairly *clear and concrete programmatic ideas of what governance in the Anthropocene is all about.* One paradigmatic example is a contribution by Tickell (2011), in which he discusses "societal responses to the Anthropocene". Arguing that "we cannot afford to be stupid", (927) and leaving no doubts that his suggestions are without alternatives, he promotes a set of policies with which the Anthropocene is to be governed. These policies include measures for, among others, population control, overcoming the predominant consumerist economy, the development of new ways of energy generation, the management of climate change as well as adaptation to climate destabilisation, nature conservation, and, finally, the development of the necessary institutional conditions for dealing with global problems in an increasingly interdependent world.

In contrast to the first and second group, which envision anthropocenic governance in terms of rather concrete technological or policy solutions to given problems, a third group of conceptions seeks to specify the *basic features of governance designs capable of coping with the Anthropocene.* The most prominent example is the Earth System Governance (ESG) concept (Biermann 2014b; Biermann et al. 2012; Biermann 2014a). According to its promoters, ESG is an explicit 'response to the Anthropocene' that reflects the fundamental changes this new epoch in planetary history implies with regard to "how we understand our political systems" (Biermann 2014b, 57). Understanding the "Earth as an integrated, interdependent system transformed by the interplay of human and non-human agency" (Biermann 2014b, 59), ESG seeks to make sense, both analytically and prescriptively, of this 'core tenet of the Anthropocene' in terms of governance. As opposed to technologically oriented conceptions, ESG does not explicitly envision the management of the Earth or the parameters of planetary evolution per se; rather, ESG focuses on "the societal steering of *human activities* with regard to long-term stability of geobiophysical systems" (Biermann 2014b, 59 – emphasis added). More specifically, ESG refers to the clarification of the prerequisites and conditions of governance that are adequate in view of the complexity of both the geobiophysical Earth system and the social governance system.

ESG promotes some overall and rather general conceptual hallmarks of governance in the Anthropocene. A key theme is, for example, the dysfunctional fragmentation of global governance systems calling for an improved architecture for the coordination of transformation processes at different levels and in different sectors with regard to the 'planetary boundaries'. Yet, ESG clearly refrains from one-fits-all solutions to the challenges of the Anthropocene. The ambition is rather to improve existing governance arrangements based on scientifically based empirical evidence (here the hybrid character of ESG as both a research programme and a prescriptive governance concept becomes evident). In fact, governance research under the ESG framework has come up with a rich variety of suggestions for the improvement of existing governance arrangements. These range from institutional changes at the global level to incremental policy change at the regional and local levels, from an improvement in private governance mechanisms to the increased involvement of civil society actors, from technological solutions to the fundamental transformations of lifestyles and behaviour (Biermann et al. 2012).

A fourth group of approaches to anthropocenic governance does not specify policy goals and means, nor does it make generalised statements about governance designs. The focus is rather on the *governance challenges that come with the Anthropocene*, and which have to be taken into account in the theoretical conceptualisation and the practical design of governance. For example, Pattberg and Zelli (2016a; Zelli and Pattberg 2016) identify a unique combination of three challenges for anthropocenic governance: *Urgency* points to the widespread call for immediate action in view of the speed, the dramatic effects and the potential irreversibility of global change towards the Anthropocene. Responsibility refers to the difficulty of a differentiated (empirical and normative) allocation of responsibilities in a world dominated on the one hand by the idea of a unified Anthropos and on the other hand by new and dynamic social fault lines and actor constellations. *Complexity* describes the growing interdependencies of material and social structures and processes in the Anthropocene.

A fifth group abstracts the understanding of appropriate forms of anthropocenic governance even further and draws out more *fundamental implications for thinking about 'politics' and 'collective action' in the Anthropocene*. Based on his stratigraphic reading of the Anthropocene, Davies (2016), for example, warns about all too fast programmatic answers, and outlines the contours of a new 'way of seeing' ecological politics in the Anthropocene. The basic political challenge of the transition from the dying Holocene to the birth of the Anthropocene is "to negotiate a way through the transition between these epochs" (148). The thrust of governance appropriate to this crippling situation cannot be the escape into a 'sustainable world', which is liberated from its historical dimension, but should be more sophisticated: "to live within the crisis, and to struggle to influence its course by working for the survival of complex, pluralistic ecosystems" (194). Based on this understanding, he suggests a new ecological politics for the environmental movement that revolves around a notion of global-local interconnectedness, acknowledgement of the interplay among human and non-human forces in shaping the Earth, the end of old-fashioned organic technologies, and a focus on divestment strategies. Starting from a similar scepticism of all too hasty institutional prescriptions, Dryzek argues for an approach of contextual empirical learning that builds on a concept of 'ecosystemic reflexivity' as the first virtue for political institutions in the Anthropocene (Dryzek 2016).

Overall, the Anthropocene discourse opens up a range of diverse governance ideas. Aside from different levels of concretion, there are also significant substantial differences cutting across the five groups. One difference refers to the explicit or implicit *goal orientation*. Some conceptions consider anthropocenic governance as an attempt towards 'restoring the Holocene' and seek to impose a kind of a 'U-turn' on the co-evolution of socio-ecological systems (groups 1 & 2). Other conceptions, in contrast, take the very conditions of the Anthropocene for granted and propose strategies for coping with it, and potentially transforming it towards some envisioned state of a better or good Anthropocene (3 & 5). Another difference relates to the envisioned *venue* of governance, that is, the place(s) where the Anthropocene is supposed to be governed. Some approaches clearly highlight the relevance of a correspondence between the planetary scale of the Anthropocene and the global reach of a fitting governance system (1 & 3). Other approaches argue more towards local or place-based governance arrangements (5). Still others highlight the multi-level character of adequate governance responses to the Anthropocene (3 & 5). Another distinction refers to the *objects* of anthropocenic governance. While some conceptions seem to be geared towards shaping the Earth system as a whole by putting hands on its geobiophysical parameters (1 & 2), other conceptions seem to put an emphasis on governing the social world and human activities (3). Still other conceptions refer to more complex co-evolutionary, socio-ecological systems as objects of governance (5).

Whether these substantial differences can be justified in view of the Anthropocene's diversity, or are merely a consequence of the fact that not all conceptions refer to the Anthropocene in a sophisticated and explicit manner, must remain open at this point. Instead, I focus on the plausibility of the conceptions of anthropocenic governance in view of a generic governance perspective.

Critical reflections

There is a growing critical discussion about the Anthropocene. Existing criticism, for example, focuses on the theoretical and empirical plausibility of the Anthropocene, on its obscured normativity or its problematic social implications (Davies 2016, 53–54; Lövbrand et al. 2015; Meyer 2016; Wissenburg 2016). My own critical take adds to this debate, but is more confined and prosaic in its ambition: It only focuses on the relationship between governance and the Anthropocene, and it builds on a merely descriptive notion of governance rather than employing strong normative concepts such as sustainability or democracy. Given the ongoing dynamic of the debate, my criticism should be understood as a stimulus for further reflection, rather than as a conclusive judgement. After briefly specifying the understanding of governance that serves as a yardstick for my reflections, I look at both the lessons governance can teach to anthropocenic governance and, vice versa, the implications of the Anthropocene for governance thinking.

Governance thinking

'Governance' is clearly a key concept in both scholarly and political debates in general (Pierre and Peters 2000; Kooiman 2007) as well as in environmental and sustainability politics in particular (Meadowcroft 2007; Adger and Jordan 2009). Although there is no consensus on its precise meaning and its analytical implications (Robichau 2011), there is agreement that governance refers to the problematic of how increasingly differentiated political systems organise collective action for dealing with an increasingly complex social reality. Like many social science concepts, governance denotes the rise of a new class of phenomena and a new analytical perspective on (new and old) empirical phenomena. These different uses are tensely interrelated in a hybrid governance discourse (Haus 2010, 2012).

The rise of governance discourse signifies a fundamental historical change in thinking about and doing political steering. Steering was for a long time considered a matter of the (rational) choice and design of adequate policy instruments and their hierarchical implementation by governments. When it became clear that practical steering efforts regularly failed, the very paradigm of political steering slowly eroded. It turned out that, besides policy instruments, power relations, institutional settings, political processes, and actor constellations were important factors for the success and failure of steering. Moreover, it became clear that the notion of political steering itself insufficiently captures the reality of political problem-solving. Rather than through goal-oriented steering by a hierarchical state, problems have been tackled in complex and multiple venues engaging diverse actors with different means and resources (Mayntz 2006).

These changes point to a post-modern pragmatic logic of governing: instead of a unifying, centralising and rationalist view of steering, the governance semantics unfold a diversifying, decentring and contextual-pragmatic view of collective action (Haus 2012, 137). First, governance comes with "a more diverse view of authority and its exercise" (Bevir 2013b, 29), which means that both functions and forms of collective action are ever more pluralised. The promotion of the common good is no longer linked to the realisation of a certain pre-defined model of society, but emerges from the interaction between multiple political and social actors. Second, decentring refers to a dispersion and spread of venues and resources of collective action throughout state and society. Problem-solving is no longer an exclusive function of the state, but is engendered in many different ways, by different actors at various levels and venues (Bevir 2013b). Governance signifies post-hierarchical political steering – with 'post' indicating that hierarchies have not been completely abandoned, but still prevail either as direct mode of steering or as a 'shadow' (Haus 2012). Third, a contextual view reflects the insight that governance is shaped by social, political and cultural contexts and unfolds therein. Practices of governance are always embedded in context-specific path dependencies, which shape the relations between the state, the market and (civil) society.

Drawing on these overall ontological features of governance thinking, governance as an analytical perspective seeks to capture conceptual understandings or empirical forms of governance in differentiated ways. It draws our attention to the multiple ways collective action takes form and plays out on the ground in diverse, complex cross-level and cross-sectoral governance arrangements. While there are many different frameworks for analysing empirical governance arrangements, I rely on an encompassing meta-framework that specifies basic dimensions and levels based on which specific governance arrangements can be described (Voss and Bornemann 2011; Lange et al. 2013; Treib et al. 2007). The dimensions include different constitutive elements of collective action, ranging from institutions and procedures ('polity'), actors and interactions ('politics'), to goals, strategies and practices ('policy'). These dimensions span the conceptual universe of governance thinking, which help to detect focal points as well as blind spots in empirical governance arrangements or conceptual proposals of governance, such as the conceptions described in the 'Anthropocenic governance' section above.

Implications of governance thinking for anthropocenic governance

What can we say about anthropocenic governance in the light of governance thinking as outlined in the previous section? According to my interpretation, the governance perspective reveals three critical issues, which are, however, of varying importance for different conceptions of anthropocenic governance.

The first issue refers to a *unifying tendency* in anthropocenic governance. In its different interpretations – as a geological epoch, as a planetary crisis, or as an era of post-humanist history – the Anthropocene refers to a universal scientific diagnosis regarding the state of the Earth (see above). One can discuss the plausibility of the universalist claims of the Anthropocene, and there are indeed convincing doubts in this regard (Malm and Hornborg 2014). In taking a governance perspective, however, I am concerned rather with how the universalistic claims of the Anthropocene all too easily translate into unified understandings of anthropocenic governance. Most obviously, this concern relates to technology- and policy-oriented conceptions (1 & 2), both of which obviously promote one-fits-all solutions to tackle the universal challenges of the Anthropocene in literally universal ways. However, a unifying logic seems also to shape other, more differentiated and more complex conceptions of anthropocenic governance (3–5). Deducing governance implications from natural scientific evidence regarding the state of the Earth, all conceptions embark on a basic scientific universalism: the claim that the Anthropocene is everywhere and literally inescapable. For example, this universalism shimmers through in ESG which, albeit acknowledging the need for contextual design and implementation, seeks to integrate multiple governance attempts under an overarching and unified framework of global governance. Universalist-unifying tendencies are also present when certain basic challenges – insecurity, complexity and urgency – or generic core features, such as 'ecosystem reflexivity', are identified as being constitutive for anthropocenic governance *per se*.

This universalist and unifying inclination of anthropocenic governance is at odds with governance thinking as introduced above. Despite its similar universal scope of aspiration and application, governance reminds us of the diversity and context-boundedness of all attempts to organise collective action. In fact, the very concept of governance itself has broadened our view towards the contextual particularities and varieties of existing forms of governance vis-à-vis older, unified models of collective action being bound to but one form of hierarchical government by the state (Levi-Faur 2012). Moreover, the governance concept carries with it a pragmatic legacy. Rather than deriving functions and forms of collective action from theoretical considerations, governance opens the view for the diversity of practices of collective action that emerge 'on the ground' (see Bevir 2013a).

A second challenge refers to a *control bias* in large parts of anthropocenic governance. The general understanding of governance underlying technology- and policy-oriented conceptions exhibit strong or even hyper-rational notions of 'governance as control'. This is most significantly expressed in metaphors such as the 'planetary machinery' (Steffen et al. 2005, 9), or "the engine room of the Earth System" (Schellnhuber 1999, C21), which imply that the Earth system as such can and should be steered based on scientifically monitored planetary processes. In a sense, it is the Promethean interpretation of the Anthropocene that has triggered new visions of and beliefs in a powerful humankind capable of steering human-natural systems (Hamilton et al. 2015). The related techno-scientific imaginaries of anthropocenic governance are possibly overstated visions that also serve the attraction of political attention and economic resources. However, there seems to be a link between the Anthropocene and the reactivation of control ideas of governance that also plays out in other less Promethean conceptions, such as ESG. Even though there is an awareness in ESG that steering capacities are limited – partly due to the complexities and uncertainties of co-evolutionary processes and partly because of the limited capacities of processing complexity – it still is geared towards realising a better coordination of transformation processes at different levels and in different areas, such that the overall transformation remains within planetary boundaries. Furthermore, the belief in control is reflected in the idea that forms of governance can be systematically designed and improved through scientific knowledge. While the idea of control accordingly still is present in ESG, it seems to vanish as the conceptions become more abstract. In particular, Davies' and Dryzek's conceptions imply a more complex, diverse and reflexive understanding of 'steering beyond control' that resonates with governance thinking.

In fact, the governance discourse recalls an entire history of disappointments with 'steering as control', which has finally resulted in a 'decontrolization' of political steering practice and theory. Apart from stressing an increasing diversity of governance venues (e.g., the rise of networks and multi-level-systems, the proliferation of participation venues), governance also opens the view towards alternative forms and interpretations of collective action (Haus 2010): governance as societal integration in view of ever-growing complexity (Lange and Schimank 2004); governance as regulation via re- and de-commodification (Jessop 1998), and governance as politicisation and democratisation (Sørensen and Torfing 2005). This is not to say that the governance discourse has completely abandoned ideas and practices of control (Mayntz and Scharpf 2005; Mayntz 2006; Haus 2010). Yet, the shift towards governance indicates that control is neither the only, nor only the most promising, option when it comes to organising collective action. Governance refers to constellations of more or less dispersed control and shared power – between multiple actors, levels and sectors.

In view of a governance perspective that emphasises the diversity of ways of organising collective action, control-oriented conceptions of anthropocenic governance seem to be too narrow, if not outdated. Neglecting the universe of governing practices and merely relying on approaches of 'governance as control', does not seem to be an adequate analytical and practical understanding. Anthropocenic governance conceptions would have to at least consider and reflect the limitations of control modes of governance and the potentials of alternative forms in view of the demands of the Anthropocene.

A third, closely related challenge of existing discourse can be termed the *order bias* of anthropocenic governance. This comes into view as soon as one looks at conceptions of anthropocenic governance from the perspective of encompassing multi-dimensional governance concepts, which emphasise the interplay between structures and norms (polity), actors and interactions (politics), and goals and means (policy). In the light of such a three-dimensional governance perspective, anthropocenic governance seems to focus on governance dimensions that can be associated with a notion of 'political order'. This is expressed by the fact that conceptions of anthropocenic governance revolve around, and are rather specific, regarding policy-related terminology, such as problems, goals and means. Moreover, they usually also refer to polity aspects, such as institutional conditions and norms (Dryzek 2016). Yet they remain relatively quiet about aspects of politics, which embody the 'disordered' or 'nasty' side of governance, such as concrete actor strategies, conflicts and power relations.

The deeper reasons for neglecting politics might lie in the overall scientific framework of *Anthropocene thinking*. In fact, the Anthropocene and the conceptions of anthropocenic governance seem to presuppose a world that is actually ordered by processes of co-evolution that are indeed insecure and complex, but in principle knowable, and that can therefore be ordered on the basis of rational insight and controlling interventions. In addition, the tendency to put a blind eye on politics might rest in the unifying tendencies of *Anthropocene thinking*. As underscored by many critical voices, the Anthropocene tends to obscure social and economic differences within humankind (Malm and Hornborg 2014). By eschewing these differences, the Anthropocene and related governance conceptions, by implication, downplay questions of distribution and redistribution, which give rise to conflicts and mobilisation, hence issues of politics.

What seems to be critical about neglecting politics is not only a lack of analytical and empirical clarity regarding the relevant agents and power relations. Neglecting politics means also disregarding an important functional ingredient of governance: collective action that seeks to tackle problems necessarily involves interactions and sometimes power struggles between actors as transformative momentum between different states of order. From this, it follows that understandings of anthropocenic governance need to include references to politics. They need to be specific about the politics that are involved in designing and performing collective action. Rather than conceiving of anthropocenic governance as ordered control, conceptions of anthropocenic governance would have to take account of the political struggle for transformations as an important analytical and practical dimension of contemporary governance. Indications in this direction can be found again in those parts of the anthropocenic governance discourse that feature a clearly politically oriented understanding of governance (Davies 2016; Wissenburg 2016).

Overall, the governance perspective points to three critical themes in the existing discourse around anthropocenic governance. Yet, given the conceptual differences within the discourse, these problems apply differently to different conceptions. In general, the more concrete the conceptions are (e.g., conceptions of the groups 1 and 2), the less adequate they appear from a nuanced governance perspective. Conceptions that commence from rather general problem features and design ideas (i.e., those belonging to the groups 3–5) tend to be more flexible and open to governance-fitted interpretations. Even though open approaches are also based on the universalism of the Anthropocene, they are less inclined towards notions of control and order, and tend to provide the leeway for the kind of contextual design and analysis of collective action arrangements in the Anthropocene that corresponds with critical governance thinking.

Implications of the Anthropocene for governance thinking

In the previous section, I adopted a governance perspective to reveal governance-related problems in the discourse about anthropocenic governance. In this section, I change my perspective and ask about the implications of the Anthropocene for governance theory and practice. What lessons can governance thinking learn from the Anthropocene? According to my reading, the Anthropocene challenges governance theory and practice, as we know it, in three important ways.

First, it challenges the *social bias* of governance. Governance is undoubtedly a concept that is rooted in the social world. It is all about social interactions and the institutions, procedures and instruments that result from and, at the same time, shape these interactions towards collective action. In contrast, the Anthropocene, in its different variants, is based on a notion of co-evolution between the social and natural spheres. It points to the inescapable interconnectedness and interplay between natural ('Earth') and social ('world') systems. This comes into play not only in a historical dimension – "in the Anthropocene era 'men' make . . . geological history" (Lövbrand et al. 2009, 11), while at the same time, the Earth system figures as "central player in human history" (Dryzek 2016, 953) – but challenges our understanding of contemporary governance and politics. In particular, the Anthropocene calls for a re-materialisation of politics and political theory, that is, the internalisation of nature in its conceptual construction (Hamilton et al. 2015, 10).

In view of the Anthropocene, governance thinking has to become aware of and take into consideration the interconnectedness of social and natural systems. In the Anthropocene, it is not only the social world shaping governance, but also the natural world: a natural-cum-social Earth-world. "Nature and Society are inextricably intertwined all around us" not only "in our bodies, our landscapes, our technologies" (Hornborg 2015, 58), but also in our governance. However, as Hornborg argues against some proponents of the Anthropocene, and contrary to earlier ideas of ecological politics (Meyer 2016), "the physical mixing of nature and society does not warrant the abandonment of their analytical distinction" (Hornborg 2015, 58). Rather, precisely their distinction can shed light on the ongoing co-evolutionary dynamics between social relations and the ecological conditions of human existence.

For governance analysis and practice, such co-evolutionary dynamics imply both a restriction and expansion of the governance space, that is, the range of options available for organising collective action. On the one hand, governance emerges from, and is limited by, socio-ecological dynamics. On the other hand, governance can actively address, shape and make use of these dynamics, which open new perspectives for (reflexive) governance design. The proposition that governance must be viewed as deeply entwined with co-evolutionary socio-ecological dynamics is obviously not new, but has been much reflected in the various strands of sustainability governance theory (Folke 2007; Voss and Kemp 2006). Yet, the Anthropocene suggests that this notion becomes part of governance thinking more generally.

The second challenge refers to the *problem bias* of governance. The overall, and sometimes only, implicit reference point and object of governance thinking are societal problems, broadly understood as discrepancies between actually existing and collectively desired target states in a given society (Mayntz 2006). Governance is all about organising collective action in such a way that problems are solved, meaning that actual states become desired target states. In modern and differentiated political systems, problems are frequently defined and dealt with in specialised policy areas, such as environmental, economic, or social policy.

The Anthropocene problematises the problem orientation underlying governance thinking in two respects. On the one hand, the Anthropocene seems to question the rather pragmatic focus on confined and sectoral problems in a favour of a more systematic and comprehensive view of interdependencies, externalities and dynamics, i.e., 'the big picture' (Lövbrand et al. 2009, 7) that is stressed by concepts such as 'planetary boundaries', 'development trajectories', or 'nexus problems'. The Anthropocene therefore highlights the problematic consequences of a sectoralised governance system that has been suspected for a while to be a source of sustainability problems (Bornemann 2014).

On the other hand, the Anthropocene seems to challenge the problem frame of governance thinking altogether. In the Anthropocene, one could argue, collective action is no longer geared towards (only) solving problems as defined by a certain confined political collective; it is rather concerned with shaping already ongoing co-evolutionary, socio-ecological dynamics and development trajectories such that they remain within a 'safe operating space'. This idea, which is most clearly expressed in notions of 'navigation', 'adaptation', 'transformation', suggests that actual states have become ever more fluid, insecure, dynamic and ambiguous, while the definition of target states is no longer a matter of collective negotiation and choice, but increasingly naturalised and objectivised.

Even though there are good reasons for a normative extension of anthropocenic governance (implying a partial de-naturalisation of target states, see below), the Anthropocene at least calls for a conceptual expansion of the notion of 'governance of problems' towards a 'governance of transformation' – with potentially far-reaching implications for the practice and analysis of governance. Practically, this expansion comes with the quest of shaping interconnected societal change in view of existing (and still problem-related!) governance arrangements. This requires new approaches and strategies of meta-governance that are geared towards coupling, integrating and redirecting multiple existing governance arrangements within an ever-diversified, dispersed and contextual governance world (Dryzek 2016). Analytically, this expansion comes with the quest of developing conceptual and empirical understandings of the meta-governance of transformations.

The third challenge refers to the *temporal frame* of contemporary governance thinking. Taking a pragmatic view on problems and the ways they are dealt with, governance thinking very much focuses on the near past and present. It seeks to clarify how actor constellations form around certain problems and bring about collective action to tackle the problems at stake. This is sometimes extended by historical analysis of the emergence and development of governance to explain why governance arrangements look like and function as they do (Blatter 2007). Yet, the Anthropocene problematises the temporal frame of governance thinking in multiple respects.

Most obvious is the expansion of time horizons in the Anthropocene. In the Anthropocene, the present, which existing governance arrangements are part of, becomes embedded in 'deep time', i.e., the long past and the far future (Davies 2016; Görg 2016; see also Tremmel, in this volume). This stresses, on the one hand, notions of co-evolution and path dependency. On the other hand, the expansion of the time horizon into the far future highlights that present governance will have long-term consequences and effects, which are deeply uncertain or unknown. Thus, the Anthropocene implies an understanding of governance developing on pathways of co-evolving social and ecological systems loaded with uncertainty.

Another temporal issue refers to the role of both irreversibilities and reversibilities in governance thinking. Given its pragmatic focus on present problems, much governance thinking rests on the assumption that the future is a horizon of limitless progress that can be principally shaped according to actually prevailing interests. Governance has been conceptualised as an attempt of problem-solving in an infinite world, in which, despite path dependencies, social change is considered reversible. Yet, the Anthropocene forces us to think about the governance of the irreversible: "With the Anthropocene ... undoing is no longer possible in the sense that the Earth system ... is now on a different trajectory with tremendous momentum" (Hamilton et al. 2015, 11).

At the same time, the Anthropocene comes with the rise of unprecedented reversibility posing new challenges to governance practice and analysis. This new reversibility refers to the assumption of collective, perpetual progress and emancipation underlying modern democratic societies and which may find its limits with the end of cheap energy and the achievement of 'peak-all' in a globally deteriorating environment (Semal 2015). In the long run, this might even lead to the end of humanity's geological power, that is, the exhaustion of precisely the conditions that constitute the Anthropocene. Governance will then have to deal with an ongoing anthropocenic trajectory under conditions of exhausted anthropocenic power.

Irreversibilities point to an understanding of governance as a 'permanent state of adaptation' (Hamilton et al. 2015, 11) and call for a consideration of themes such as collective precaution and collective self-limitation. The governance of reversibility, however, faces the challenge of instability and state shifts implying a revival of crisis and catastrophic thinking in governance analysis and practice (Dryzek 2016; Semal 2015).

Conclusion: towards future-oriented anthropocenic governance

In view of an emerging Anthropocene debate that challenges prevailing practices and understandings of governance and politics, this chapter engaged more systematically with the relationship between the Anthropocene and governance. I reconstructed existing conceptual understandings of the 'governance of the Anthropocene', critically reflected on their limitations in view of a broader governance perspective, and pondered the implications of the Anthropocene for governance thinking.

This analysis suggests that, on the one hand, the existing conceptions of anthropocenic governance come with certain limitations from a governance perspective. Some conceptions promote a flickering of yesterday's ideas of centralised steering and control. As a supposed conceptual innovation in future-oriented governance, anthropocenic governance actually builds on governance ideas of the past. The discourse, at least partially, sticks to those holocenic ideas of governance and control that are complicit in generating the unstable Earth system that now characterises the Anthropocene (see Dryzek 2016, 941). This seems to be neither a conceptual innovation nor a good fit for a governance world that harbours a post-modern logic of diversification, dispersion and contextualisation. On the other hand, the Anthropocene discourse also challenges existing governance theory in several respects, which implies that the latter in its current form is not a sufficient basis for conceptualising anthropocenic governance. In particular, the Anthropocene invokes a co-evolutionary, transformation-oriented and temporally extended understanding of governance.

In addition to gaps and weaknesses, the two-sided critical reflection also points to an enlightened understanding of anthropocenic governance. Such an understanding of anthropocenic governance that combines the gist of governance thinking with the fundamental claims of the Anthropocene revolves around the following basic features. First, it mediates between universalistic claims of the Anthropocene and particularistic governance interpretations thereof. Secondly, it conceives of collective action as being embedded in, i.e., being shaped by and, at the same time, shaping co-evolutionary socio-ecological dynamics. Third, it makes use of diverse ways and forms of thinking and doing collective action beyond control. And finally, it is located on a second order or metalevel to allow for both taking account of the diversity of contexts and forms of governance and referring to the big picture. Such a concept of governance might be an adequate basis for meeting the theoretical challenges of contemporary anthropocenic governance: a concept that does take account of both contemporary post-hierarchical governance and a potentially anthropocenic world.

Yet, is such an understanding also a sufficient basis for thinking about future-oriented governance? My answer is: no, not entirely. An enlightened conception of anthropocenic governance would provide a sound descriptive understanding of conceivable and functional forms of collective action in the face of a world that is both characterised by the Anthropocene and governance. However, it does not provide answers to the question *where do we want to go?* This is an essentially normative question, which has to be answered based on normative reasoning about goals based on explicit normative ideas and theories. Since neither the Anthropocene nor governance provide such goals, ideas and theories, anthropocenic governance is not a sufficient basis for future-oriented governance (see Tremmel, in this volume).

To provide meaningful prescriptions for future-oriented governance, anthropocenic governance would need to be endowed with normative orientation; it would need to be connected to some normative ground from which orientation and guidance for governance action can be derived. Until now, such a normative ground has not been established by the Anthropocene discourse. However, there is a different – 'old' – idea that still seems to be a good candidate: sustainable development. Sustainability can provide the missing normative essence of a meaningful future-oriented governance of the Anthropocene. Introducing sustainability into anthropocenic governance, however, induces new normative complexity and ambivalence (Stirling 2015b). More precisely, it leads to that kind of political debate about interpretations of desirable futures that appears suppressed in the existing discourse about anthropocenic governance, but which is crucial for governing social transformations in the Anthropocene in a democratic way.

Acknowledgements

Significant parts of this chapter were written during a fellowship at the Institute for Advanced Sustainability Studies (IASS), Potsdam, Germany. I am very grateful for the intellectual space IASS has given me. I particularly thank Henrike

Knappe, David Löw Beer, Frederic Hanusch, and Patrizia Nanz for the stimulating discussions during my stay at IASS. I thank Paul Burger from my home institution for giving me the time off.

References

Adger, N.W. and Jordan, A. eds. (2009) *Governing Sustainability* Cambridge University Press, Cambridge.
Arias-Maldonado, M. (2016) "Nature and the Anthropocene: The sense of an ending?" in Pattberg, P.H. and Zelli, F. eds., *Environmental Politics and Governance in the Anthropocene* Routledge, London, 31–46.
Bevir, M. (2013a) "Governance as theory, practice and dilemma" in Bevir, M. ed., *The Sage Handbook of Governance* Sage Publications, Los Angeles, 1–16.
Bevir, M. (2013b) *Key Concepts in Governance* Sage Publications, London.
Biermann, F. (2014a) *Earth System Governance: World Politics in the Anthropocene* MIT Press, Cambridge, MA.
Biermann, F. (2014b) "The Anthropocene: A governance perspective" *The Anthropocene Review*, 1, 57–61.
Biermann, F., et al. (2012) "Navigating the Anthropocene: Improving Earth system governance" *Science*, 335, 1306–1307.
Biermann, F., et al. (2016) "Down to Earth" *Global Environmental Change*, 39, 341–350.
Blatter, J.K. (2007) *Governance: Theoretische Formen und historische Transformationen* Nomos, Baden-Baden.
Bonneuil, C. (2015) "The geological turn" in Hamilton, C. Bonneuil, C. and Gemenne, F. eds., *The Anthropocene and the Global Environmental Crisis* Routledge, London, 17–31.
Bornemann, B. (2014) *Policy-Integration und Nachhaltigkeit* Springer VS, Wiesbaden.
Chakrabarty, D. (2009) "The climate of history" *Critical Inquiry*, 35, 197–222.
Davies, J. (2016) *The Birth of the Anthropocene* University of California Press, Oakland, CA.
Dryzek, J.S. (2016) "Institutions for the Anthropocene" *British Journal of Political Science*, 46, 937–956.
Folke, C. (2007) "Social-ecological systems and adaptive governance of the commons" *Ecological Research*, 22, 14–15.
Görg, C. (2016) "Zwischen Tagesgeschäft und Erdgeschichte. Die unterschiedlichen Zeitskalen in der Debatte um das Anthropozän" *GAIA: Ecological Perspectives for Science and Society*, 25, 9–13.
Hamilton, C., Bonneuil, C. and Gemenne, F. (2015) "Thinking the Anthropocene" in Hamilton, C., Bonneuil, C. and Gemenne, F. eds., *The Anthropocene and the Global Environmental Crisis* Routledge, London, 1–13.
Haus, M. (2010) "Governance-Theorien und Governance-Probleme: Diesseits und jenseits des Steuerungsparadigmas" *Politische Vierteljahresschrift*, 51, 457–479.
Haus, M. (2012) "Regieren als Schatten der Demokratie? Zum Verhältnis von Postdemokratie- und Governance-Diskurs" in Egner, B., Haus, M. and Terizakis, G. eds., *Regieren* VS Verlag für Sozialwissenschaften, Wiesbaden, 135–155.
Hornborg, A. (2015) "The political ecology of technocene" in Hamilton, C., Bonneuil, C. and Gemenne, F. eds., *The Anthropocene and the Global Environmental Crisis* Routledge, London, 57–67.
Jahn, T., Hummel, D. and Schramm, E. (2015) "Nachhaltige Wissenschaft im Anthropozän" *GAIA: Ecological Perspectives for Science and Society*, 24, 92–95.

Jessop, B. (1998) "The rise of governance and the risks of failure: The case of economic development" *International Social Science Journal*, 50, 29–45.

Kooiman, J. (2007) *Governing as Governance* Sage Publications, London.

Lange, P., et al. (2013) "Governing towards sustainability: Conceptualizing modes of governance" *Journal of Environmental Policy and Planning*, 15, 403–425.

Lange, S. and Schimank, U. (2004) "Governance und gesellschaftliche Integration" in Lange, S. and Schimank, U. eds., *Governance und gesellschaftliche Integration* VS Verlag für Sozialwissenschaften, Wiesbaden, 9–44.

LeCain, T.J. (2016) "Heralding a new humanism: The radical implications of Chakrabarty's 'four theses'" in Emmet, R. and Lekan, T. eds., Whose Anthropocene? *RCC Perspectives: Transformations in Environment and Society*, 2, 15–20.

Lemos, M.C. and Agrawal, A. (2006) "Environmental governance" *Annual Review of Environment and Resources*, 31, 297–325.

Levi-Faur, D. (2012) "From 'big government' to 'big governance'?" in Levi-Faur, D. ed., *Oxford Handbook of Governance* Oxford University Press, Oxford, 3–18.

Lövbrand, E., et al. (2015) "Who speaks for the future of Earth?" *Global Environmental Change*, 32, 211–218.

Lövbrand, E., Stripple, J. and Wiman, B. (2009) "Earth system governmentality" *Global Environmental Change*, 19, 7–13.

Malm, A. and Hornborg, A. (2014) "The geology of mankind?" *The Anthropocene Review*, 1, 62–69.

Mayntz, R. (2006) "Governance theory als fortentwickelte Steuerungstheorie?" in Schuppert, G.F. ed., *Governance-Forschung* Nomos, Baden-Baden, 11–20.

Mayntz, R. and Scharpf, F.W. (2005) "Politische Steuerung – Heute?" *Zeitschrift für Soziologie*, 34, 236–243.

Meadowcroft, J. (2007) "Who is in charge here? Governance for sustainable development in a complex world" *Journal of Environmental Policy and Planning*, 9, 299–314.

Meyer, J.M. (2016) "Politics in-but not of-the Anthropocene" in Emmet, R. and Lekan, T. eds., Whose Anthropocene? *RCC Perspectives: Transformations in Environment and Society* 2, 47–51.

Pattberg, P.H. and Zelli, F. (2016a) "Global environmental governance in the Anthropocene" in Pattberg, P.H. and Zelli, F. eds., *Environmental Politics and Governance in the Anthropocene* Routledge, London, 1–12.

Pattberg, P.H. and Zelli, F. eds. (2016b) *Environmental Politics and Governance in the Anthropocene* Routledge, London.

Pierre, J. and Peters, B.G. (2000) *Governance, Politics, and the State* St. Martin's Press, New York.

Robichau, R.W. (2011) "The mosaic of governance: Creating a picture with definitions, theories, and debates" *Policy Studies Journal*, 39, 113–131.

Rockstrom, J., et al. (2009) "A safe operating space for humanity" *Nature*, 461, 472–475.

Schellnhuber, H.J. (1999) "'Earth system' analysis and the second Copernican revolution" *Nature*, 402, C19–C23.

Semal, L. (2015) "Anthropocene, catastrophism and green political theory" in Hamilton, C., Bonneuil, C. and Gemenne, F. eds., *The Anthropocene and the Global Environmental Crisis* Routledge, London, 87–99.

Sørensen, E. and Torfing, J. (2005) "Network governance and post-liberal democracy" *Administrative Theory & Praxis*, 27, 197–237.

Steffen, W.L., et al. (2011) "The Anthropocene: From global change to planetary stewardship" *AMBIO*, 40, 739–761.

Steffen, W.L., et al. (2005) *Global Change and the Earth System* Springer, Berlin, New York.

Stirling, A. (2015a) "Reigning back the Anthropocene is hard-but Earth's worth it" (http://steps-centre.org/blog/reigning-back-the-anthropocene-is-hard-but-earths-worth-it/) Accessed 26 March 2016.

Stirling, A. (2015b) "Time to rei(g)n back the Anthropocene?" (http://steps-centre.org/blog/time-to-reign-back-the-anthropocene/) Accessed 26 March 2016.

Tickell, C. (2011) "Societal responses to the Anthropocene" *Philosophical Transactions of the Royal Society A: Mathematical, Physical, and Engineering Sciences*, 369, 926–932.

Treib, O., Bähr, H. and Falkner, G. (2007) "Modes of governance: Towards a conceptual clarification" *Journal of European Public Policy*, 14, 1–20.

Voss, J.-P. and Bornemann, B. (2011) "The politics of reflexive governance: Challenges for designing adaptive management and transition management" *Ecology and Society*, 16 (2), Art 9.

Voss, J.-P. and Kemp, R. (2006) "Sustainability and reflexive governance: Introduction" in Voss, J.-P., Bauknecht, D. and Kemp, R. eds., *Reflexive Governance for Sustainable Development* Edward Elgar, Cheltenham, 3–28.

Widerberg, O. (2016) "Mapping institutional complexity in the Anthropocene" in Pattberg, P.H. and Zelli, F. eds., *Environmental Politics and Governance in the Anthropocene* Routledge, London, 81–102.

Wissenburg, M. (2016) "The Anthropocene and the body ecologic" in Pattberg, P.H. and Zelli, F. eds., *Environmental Politics and Governance in the Anthropocene* Routledge, London, 15–30.

Zelli, F. and Pattberg, P. (2016) "Conclusions" in Pattberg, P.H. and Zelli, F. eds., *Environmental Politics and Governance in the Anthropocene* Routledge, London, 231–242.

5 International theory in the Anthropocene

Moving beyond species, state and governance

Franziska Müller

Introduction

The Anthropocene enters our world as a rupture. It invites us to reflect over the role of humankind as both a shaper and destroyer of the planetary ecosystem. Emphasising both human power and human powerlessness it points out how humankind has evolved as an extraordinarily successful species that has however accelerated the destruction of ecosystems. At the same time the concept refers to the powers of human creativity by accentuating how rationale agency may rebalance the planetary ecosystem. Based on 'planetary boundaries' (Rockström et al. 2009; Rockström 2010), this would allow regaining agency for regulating existential ecological threats such as climate change or loss of biodiversity. Thus, the Anthropocene is characterised by a conglomerate of failure and hope. On the one hand, an optimistic understanding acknowledges the loss of political control, yet counters this with deep trust in the possibility of a socio-ecological transformation and system preservation. On the other hand, a sceptical understanding regards the Anthropocene as proof for the failure of environmental governance and hence creates imaginaries of ecological apocalypse (Scranton 2015; Vince 2014). This understanding poses ethical questions that affirm human responsibility for ecological disasters and seek reasons for policy failure. This also gives way for more metaphysical thoughts concerning the further existence of humankind on the aftermath of ecocide, that is, the destruction of planetary ecosystems. Ultimately this understanding points to the impossibility of any environmental policy, and instead emphasises existentialist and spiritual aspects (Scranton 2015; Mitchell 2015).

As a gloomy narrative of human apocalypse, the advent of the Anthropocene calls for survival strategies and for a different understanding of 'the political'. Beyond usual subjects such as Earth sciences and environmental sciences, also International Relations (IR) are a discipline that has acquired quite a reputation in dealing with system change and system preservation, for instance, regarding the Cold War and the dangers of a 'nuclear winter' (Masco 2010; Sagan 1983). However, IR has so far focused on such questions primarily from the perspective of security policy. Thus, IR's typical categories might not be apt for analysing the Anthropocene *problematique*, that is, the danger of an ecocide (Mitchell 2017;

Burke et al. 2016). While the Anthropocene concept has mainly been debated in the context of global environmental governance, IR theory has stayed relatively silent so far, and seems to be locked in a Holocene cage, that aggravates the integration of Anthropocene worldviews, epistemologies and governance strategies.[1]

Based on the assumption that the Anthropocene is a powerful ontological concept that bears the ability to reorganise Holocene IR, the aim of this chapter is to identify the implications of the Anthropocene concept for IR theory, by investigating

- *Why and how* the Anthropocene challenges the conceptualisation of the international system as a whole;
- *Which* contours for Anthropocene IR can be found in the existing, 'Holocene' approaches of international theory; and
- *To what* extent epistemologies of IR theory need transformation.

The following sections will first give an introduction into the social science debate on the Anthropocene and the ways in which IR theory is currently approaching the Anthropocene. An ongoing debate that evolved around the 'Manifesto for the end of IR' (Burke et al. 2016) serves as a basis for reflecting IR perspectives on the Anthropocene and for identifying particularly Holocene features within IR strands of thought. This builds the ground for a more in-depth discussion of IR theories, which focuses on their capacities to integrate the Anthropocene concept and its systemic, normative and governance implications into their worldviews. This is followed by suggestions for research strategies that may pave the way towards a theory of Anthropocene IR.

Making sense of the Anthropocene: challenges for International Relations theories

International Relations have only recently started to engage with the Anthropocene as a conceptual framework. The Anthropocene concept was introduced into Earth science debates by climate scientist Paul Crutzen. In discussing the hypothesis that humankind itself has become a geological force, Crutzen depicts man-made geophysical alterations to the global ecosystem that are irreversible and will result in far-reaching ecological consequences. Some examples are the alteration of the Earth's atmosphere, as well as the creation of techno fossils out of nuclear fallout, aluminium or plastic (Crutzen 2002; Steffen et al. 2007).

However, to speak of the Anthropocene as a new geological era, it needs to be verified by the International Union of Geological Sciences that the 'geological signal' induced by such changes is significant enough to justify such a classification (Subcommission on Quarternary Stratigraphy 2016; Waters et al. 2016).[1] Nevertheless, it remains a political controversy to find an accurate cut-off date for the Anthropocene. According to Crutzen, the beginning of the industrial era can be taken as a significant marker, as the industrial expansion resulted in a far-reaching change of nature-society relations that led to massive ecological interventions, as the continuous rise of greenhouse gas emissions from fossil fuels clearly shows. At the same time, the 'Orbis Spike' – that is, the all-time low of CO_2 emissions in 1610 – highlights how the ever-closer relationship between colonial power and power over nature has developed (Hamilton 2016, 10). The Orbis Spike marks a slow decline of CO_2, which was caused by the conquistal genocide against indigenous peoples in the Americas. Estimations state that 50 million people lost their lives between 1492 and 1610, which meant that farming activities and CO_2 emissions reached an all-time low (Lewis and Maslin 2015, also see Mitchell 2015 from the perspective of postcolonial IR). Nevertheless, the Anthropocene working group has decided to take the 1950s era as the cut-off date, as in those days the 'Great Acceleration' of productive forces in the United States and Europe (McNeill and Engelke 2016) led to a highly intensified expansion of industrial activities, resulting in an exponential rise in CO_2 emissions (Zalasiewicz et al. 2015).

Beyond these debates the Anthropocene concept has mainly been reflected within the field of environmental studies. The concept of 'planetary boundaries' (Rockström et al. 2009; Rockström 2010; Steffen et al. 2011) bundles such research ambitions by offering a set of indicators,[2] that should guarantee a 'safe operating space' for humanity, with environmental/Earth sciences acting in a guardian-like manner. Within political science, especially authors from the field of global environmental governance have engaged with the Anthropocene concept. The idea of planetary boundaries closely corresponds with Frank Biermann's works on 'Earth System Governance' (Biermann 2007, 2014; Biermann et al. 2012), as this concept is in a similar fashion based on system preservation and system transformation. Anthropocene governance thus reaffirms the idea of a common responsibility for the global ecosystem, but also feeds the assumption that harmful ecological effects are governable and manageable.

While being quite characteristic for large parts of the Anthropocene discourse, this trust in governability and expert knowledge has come under critique from a socio-ecological perspective, as this can also be interpreted as a turn towards post-political 'Earth management', feeding the illusion that any ecological catastrophe can be brought under control without ever abolishing the economic growth imperative (Swyngedouw 2014, 23, also Dalby 2007). Also, socio-ecological theorists criticise interpretations of the Anthropocene narrative as universalist and therefore ahistorical, as the concept may replace historical responsibility for ecological harm by a community of responsibility on a global level. This may depoliticise global environmental governance and thwart historical legacies, especial colonial or northern responsibility for species extinction, climate change or soil degradation (Lövbrand et al. 2016; Chakrabarty 2012; Whyte 2016, 2017). At the same time, an understanding of nature as a space that needs to be meticulously measured (yet not cared for) may limit space for perceiving nature as a social, wild or even spiritual space. This would contribute to a functionalist and objectified perception of nature.

In their rejoinder, Biermann and his co-authors have integrated this critique by suggesting a less monolithic and more diverse conceptualisation of the Anthropocene, which is based on a "view of the planet as an interconnected, interdependent social-ecological system while considering both local variation and social inequalities" (Biermann et al. 2015, 2). This is achieved through a localisation of Anthropocene governance, which implies a connection between the 'planetary boundaries' and local counter-indicators, based on local/traditional knowledge. In a similar fashion, a repoliticisation of the Anthropocene would focus much more on civil society voices and intersectional perspectives, for instance, by including concepts such as 'environmental justice' or 'environmental racism' (Bullard 1994, 2000; Lövbrand et al. 2009, 2016). This would allow a deeper reflection also of the power relations that pervade the Anthropocene, not only in terms of nature-society relations, but also in identifying parallels between the colonisation of societies and the exploitation of nature.

Within the field of IR a similarly lively debate on the Anthropocene and its political implications is currently emerging (Young 2016; Hamilton 2016; Harrington 2016; Dalby 2007, 2013; Mitchell 2017; Burke et al. 2016; Chandler et al. 2018). While more 'mainstream' voices are still missing, at the fringe of the discipline the contours of controversies become visible. So far, we can state that IR's Anthropocene debate is driven by a critical reflection of the discipline in terms of epistemology and methodology, with a focus on failures of political theory facing ecological disasters. Thus, the debate has so far been shaped by a quite fundamental critique of both traditional and progressive approaches, yet misses out on already existing contours that would in fact foster Anthropocene theory development. A widely discussed example is the 'Manifesto for the end of IR' (Burke et al. 2016), which will be used here as a reference text for making sense of the Anthropocene from an IR perspective.

The manifesto states, that IR as a discipline and as a diplomatic practice had failed and would lack adequate theoretical instruments for developing global political solutions to the looming ecological catastrophe; thus IR "both a system of knowledge and institutional practice is undone by the reality of the planet" (Burke et al. 2016, 3). Indeed, theory development in IR has not so much been shaped by real-world problems and political change, but rather by its immanent debates, thereby establishing its distinguishing intellectual traditions and research paradigms. Furthermore, those historical events that shaped IR's theory development – the World Wars, the Holocaust and the end of the Warsaw Pact – were framed by classical foreign policy thought and created a demand for supposedly non-normative and objective theorising, which may now be IR's nemesis when facing the Anthropocene (Burke et al. 2016, 15). This results in IR being trapped in a set of categories such as power games or maximisation of interests that privilege epistemological and methodological nationalism (Wimmer and Schiller 2002). Also, political instruments such as international diplomacy have been largely northern-dominated and therefore do not seem adequate to counter Anthropocene challenges with a sound governance strategy. Overall Anthony Burke and his co-authors paint a bleak vision of the discipline, in claiming that the status of the planet remains unseen, when observed through IR's epistemological lenses (Burke et al. 2016, 3).

According to Burke and his co-authors, the Anthropocene thwarts thought patterns of IR, as "our existence is neither international nor global, but planetary.

Our anthropocentric, state-centric and capital-centric image of international relations and world politics is fundamentally wrong" (Burke et al. 2016, 5). Thus, the
main task for IR theory development would then be to learn from Earth system
science's systemic view (especially from the planetary boundaries framework)
and back the Anthropocene debate in environmental sciences by an international
political theory framework that offers an adequate discourse on the necessities of
social/political change in line with the planetary boundaries. This can be understood as 'planet politics' in a cooperative and cosmopolitan sense. Such a project
would build on existing approaches, namely 'Earth System Governance', while
being aware of the dangers any universalised and state-centric approach entails.
The authors eventually call for "a practice of governance and of subversion, of
regulation and resistance, at multiple scales and locales. Indeed as resistance it
is already underway, but as governance it is struggling to be born" (Burke
et al. 2016, 9). The ethical foundation for such an enterprise would require
going beyond mere 'Earth management' and would replace an anthropocentric
worldview by a more pluralistic one. This would have to be linked to a reform
of global environmental law, for instance by including environmental justice as
a norm and by countering environmental racism. Also new juridical standards
such as the right to an intact environment or crimes against biodiversity would
need to be introduced. In the end this would lead to an IR theory of ecosystem
survival (Burke et al. 2016, 19). This, however, would not call for a theory of
ever closer regulation and management, but rather for a theoretical design,
which would vigorously reject the total appropriation of the Earth and reflect
the mutual vulnerability of both Earth and humankind:

> Being Earth-worldly means embracing the collective threat that is the condi-
> tion of being. It means engaging in this complex and ultimately finite project
> with gratitude, attention, resolution, and, above all, with an amor mundi that
> embraces the Earth – not only human worlds.
>
> (Burke et al. 2016, 21)

The manifesto has provoked a critical reception by the IR community – ironically
though for not being radical enough. David Chandler and his co-authors (Chandler
et al. 2018) highlight contradictions by claiming that the authors problematise
global environmental governance's obsession with regulatory standards but keep
calling for a similar agenda that falls prey to liberal cosmopolitanism. The focus
on top-down global governance was in essence a reformist and anti-political strategy that reaffirms human power over the planet, instead of limiting it, as a post-
humanist perspective would do (Chandler et al. 2018, 7–8). The authors express
their discontent by a rally cry for a 'Non-Manifesto for the Capitalocene',
which denounces top-down global regulation, as well as the forces of the 'Capitalocene' that is, the global political economy that made the Anthropocene come
true. Instead they see an urge for re-enacting the relationship between economy
and ecology, inspired by post-humanist thought. The Manifesto crew counters
this by clarifying their understanding of the Anthropocene as a fundamental

rupture, with IR being reborn as a theory of global survival. In underlining their passion for a pluralist theoretical framework that brings together both postcolonial/indigenous, critical theory and cosmopolitan strands of thought, they point out their interest in carving out a kind of planetary politics that strives towards deep-reaching eco-social change on all scales (Fishel et al. 2018).

What do these engagements tell us about the dynamics within IR? Obviously, the Anthropocene concept poses several theoretical challenges that are thought-provoking for IR theory, as they deeply affect IR's epistemological paradigms and analytical categories. Anthropocene repercussions can be felt in various policy fields far from the 'usual suspects' such as climate, energy or biodiversity policies. Taking actor/agency, structure and governance into consideration, the Anthropocene seems not just relevant for certain policy fields, but questions central categories of Holocene IR, only to redefine them by carving out the con-tours of Anthropocene IR.

Moving beyond Holocene IR: steps and stages of theory development

The Anthropocene poses a challenge to IR theory on several levels. This refers to (1) worldviews and research paradigms, (2) analytical categories, especially the understanding of actor and agency, as this category is central for understand-ing the relation between human agency and man-made ecological crisis, and (3) problem-solving strategies, such as problematisations/problem definitions and modes of governance. On each of these levels the Anthropocene questions Holocene concepts of IR, while at the same time providing ideas for a different mindset that may eventually contribute to a theory of International Relations in the Anthropocene and corresponding research strategies.

(1) A Holocene understanding of the international system is shaped by an *anthro-pocentric worldview* that translates into specific assumptions on the shape and structure of the world system. So far, Holocene IR has conceptualised the interna-tional system in several ways, with state anarchy[3] being a common denominator: as an anarchical system driven by mutual security dilemmas and threat scenarios like in neorealist thought, as anarchy tamed by institutions, or as a norms-driven, mutu-ally constitutive actor/structure network as in constructivist IR theory. Neorealist threat scenarios and power games have been fundamentally reformulated in con-structivist thought through the seminal redefinition "anarchy is what the states make of it" (Wendt 1992: 391), which highlights the merits of de- and reconstruct-ing security policy norms and the potentials of mutual trust and learning between normative actors (see also Hardt, in this volume).

Still, facing Anthropocene conditions, the Westphalian Order[4] seems to be no longer apt as a fundamental structure for interstate relations, as it has acquired the shape of a golden cage that severely limits ecological agency. However, a recon-struction of the world system based on less competitive, but rather solidary forms of agency is still mostly a desideratum (cf. Ling 2013 for an alternative model of a world order beyond anarchy that focuses on dialogue, powers of listening and mutual understanding). The Holocene quality of IR world building lies mainly in the central assumption that humankind possesses unlimited powers, without ever questioning or problematising this ability as such. In the different IR schools of thought this is reflected by specific motivations for political agency: be it absolute or relative power gains, as in neorealist IR, be it objectifiable interests as in liberal intergouvernmentalism (Moravcsik 1997), or else be it normative orientations as a central motivation, as in large parts of constructivist thought (Onuf 2001).

While these schools share a long-standing history of ontological and epistemological 'great debates' (Mayer 2003), the *problematique* of unlimited human agency has remained a blind spot. Even though system preservation is an important concept especially for neorealism (for instance when identifying stabilising conditions in bipolar or multipolar state systems) literature on system preservation does not yet sufficiently cover ecological risks. A framing of Anthropocene dangers merely from the angle of security policy – as for example a process of 'securitisation' would imply – is unable to take other complex Anthropocene problems into account, such as the social or cultural dimension of any ecological catastrophe. Indeed, system preservation as it has been understood so far mainly focuses on the survival of humankind and on the prevention of genocide, with genocide being defined as the extermination of human populations, but not regarding a looming ecocide (Eckersley 2007).

From an Anthropocene perspective the structure of the international system looks considerably different than its Holocene counterpart, as it is not based on an anarchical, rule-less structure, but on a network of interdependent, self-organised relations. This change in perception means that the Earth's ecosystem becomes re-centered, so that the separation between man and nature, which was characteristic for Holocene system thinking can be overcome. This implies that the ecosystem's vulnerability as well as global change and environmental risks become a focal point for system preservation strategies. Re-centering the ecosystem also limits the power spheres of states as sovereign actors and plays out in an understanding of anarchy as organised interdependence, rather than the mere absence of rules.

The structure of the international system in an Anthropocene understanding of IR resembles an alternative conceptualisation designed by L.H.M. Ling (2013). Ling develops a world model that is based on mutual dialogue rather than on competition. This shift helps overcoming the mutual mistrust of the Hobbesian world model by means of political dialogue and mutual interest in each other. Her dialogic model is based on relationality (who communicates with whom?), resonance (which alternative discourses are possible, what are their ends and meanings?) and intersubjectivity (how can emphatic compassionate agency be encouraged?). Ling's model is helpful in creating a sense of mutual ecological responsibility and glocal interdependence but would also need some 'greening' to escape Holocene views and to integrate an ecosystemary perspective into the dialogic concept. In this sense, classical IR norms that have derived from the dogma of system preservation would need to be redefined in a way that embeds socio-ecological perspectives and leaves space for system transformation.

This points, for example, to an ecological understanding of mutual solidarity, a redefinition of the responsibility to protect as a directive for 'ecological intervention', or to an inter-species right to clean air. Also, a broadening of the security norm in terms of 'ecological security' would help to overcome the separation between international anarchy and the ecosystem by emphasising the relationship between humanity and the conditions of our own survival (Hardt, in this volume; McDonald 2017, 67–69).

(2) Holocene qualities are also visible within *analytical categories* that have shaped the realm of IR theorising: Holocene IR theories are based on a worldview which takes humankind and human agency as the initial analytical category. There is consent that the definition of actor and agency is based on the activities of human beings (read: man, according to Tickner 1988, or else: western researcher, according to Appadurai 2006), human interests and a cartesian worldview that sets a clear separation between society and nature (Freyberg-Inan 2004). Also, the focus on states as actors is characteristic for Holocene IR insofar as it effectively limits agency of actors other than states. This is only slightly altered in institutionalist or constructivist schools of thought, which highlight the formative power of international organisations respectively the power of norms and learning (Finnemore and Sikkink 1998). Even though IR theories have diversified in terms of world building, an anthropocentric worldview has remained a common denominator. While the limitations of this perspective have been acknowledged in practical philosophy (i.e., with regards to a biocentric or pathocentric perspective), IR has so far dealt with the ecological *problematique* mostly by regarding environmental problems as another 'issue' to be resolved by each specific theory. However, IR has only scarcely engaged with the ways in which green political thought questions anthropocentrism (Steans et al. 2005, 205, for a disambiguation between 'thinking green' and 'Green Thought', and between environmentalism and political ecology).

Furthermore, Anthropocene IR expands Holocene understandings of actor and agency. Theory development in the Anthropocene will have to deal with post-humanist worldviews as "a new reality, where humans, non-humans, things and materials co-exist in complex relations of life and non-life" (Harrington 2016, 5) that puts limitations to human agency, while being aware of anti-democratic and post-political tendencies some post-humanist readings bear. An anthropocentric understanding of actor and agency is replaced by a collective, post-human understanding, which highlights that "'we are in this all together' – humans, animals, ecologies, biosphere" (Burke et al. 2016, 2). This redefinition may however be formulated in different ways, either following post-positivist or positivist lines.

A post-positivist understanding of actor and agency questions actor definitions (neutral/male, individualist, utilitarist, interest-based) that remain widely unchallenged in large parts of IR theory and seeks to enrich them in a more pluralist way, with a focus on positionalities and 'strong objectivity' (Ziai 2010). An Anthropocene critique of Holocene actorness and agency starts from similar grounds but comes to different conclusions, as the limitations and dangers of

Holocene actorness and agency are brought to the fore. Anthropocene definitions of actor and agency can make way for including non-human actors – for instance, non-human animals or ecosystems – and their ways of expressing agency and allow emphasising their right to exist (Coward 2009; Cudworth and Hobden 2011). An ecological and post-human understanding of actor and agency involves a careful de- and re-centering: human agency is to be de-centered, while the survival of ecosystems – with humankind being a (special) part of it – is to be re-centered. Agency would in this sense be driven by inter-species/trans-species solidarity and empathy for each other's vulnerabilities, as those are everyone's 'Earth others' (Braidotti 2013, 49–50, also Braidotti (2010) or Haraway (2016) on 'making kin' as a way of granting personhood to other species). This also goes in line with a shift of environmental/carbon responsibility towards local or indigenous actors, which may bear both disciplinary, governmentalist and empowering qualities (Whyte 2016, 2017; Müller 2016, 2017).

To further develop these concepts, it seems necessary that IR engages more intensively with the extinction and extermination of species (Mitchell 2017). This would also have consequences for the concept of genocide, which would need to include also ecocides as crimes against nature. A blind spot of IR's problematisations, the man-made extinction of animal or plant species, would then no longer be negligible. Such an engagement would imply formulating a theory of ecosystemic survival in IR terms, combined with a reconceptualisation of the Westphalian Order (Young 2016). This however bears several caveats. As Chandler et al. (2018) point out, post-human thought can go so far as to question the legitimacy of normative orders such as human rights, and their emancipatory content, thus falling prey to post-political, organic ways of reasoning about Earth and life. Post-human discourse thus needs to engage with crypto-fascist tendencies to clearly carve out an emancipatory core. A fourth generation of (post) human rights might be a programmatic step in that sense.

In contrast, a positivist understanding of Anthropocene actorness and agency goes less far in its redefinitions, as it rather follows reformist intentions and recalls rationality as a shaping principle for agency (Young 2016). Agency is in this regard mainly motivated by the interest to work on the 'wicked problems'[5] (Levin et al. 2012; Churchman 1967), that are characteristic for the Anthropocene age and which cannot be reduced to simple environmental issues to be solved by effective environmental policies due to their transnational and complex nature. It is driven by a more optimist reading of the Anthropocene that comes along with a rally cry for using humankind's innovative strengths and unified political powers as a force for good to save the Earth's ecosystem. From this perspective actor and agency may also need reframing, yet not necessarily in a post-human way. Rather a different set of motivations for human agency would seem adequate, i.e., an understanding of agency as advocacy for the ecosystem. The concept of 'Earth stewardship' (Ogden et al. 2013) may serve as an example.

This refers for example to norm development in an Anthropocene sense. Normative orientations and principles for agency in an Anthropocene age find their foundation no longer in the preservation or expansion of power, but rather in an ecological-driven limitation of power, and a focus on ecosystem preservation or socio-ecological transformation. Extensions to existing norms could entail an ecological understanding of mutual solidarity, a redefinition of the responsibility to protect as a directive for 'ecological intervention' following suggestions by Robin Eckersley[6] (2007) or a human right to a clean climate. This is closely affiliated with the mindsets that underpin the concepts of 'planetary boundaries' and 'Earth System Governance' (Biermann 2007, 2014), especially with recent debates calling for a localisation of such boundaries, and a pluralisation of actors (Lövbrand et al. 2016; Lövbrand et al. 2009; Hamilton 2016). Also, a theory of norm development in and for the Anthropocene would however highly benefit from post/decolonial approaches (Tickner and Blaney 2013; Whyte 2017) that would bring in non-western thought on political ecology. This would mean to enrich theories of norm development and norm transfer with pluralist understandings of norms and with norms deriving from a non-western cosmovision. Regarding research agendas, 'Seeds of Good Anthropocenes',[7] a research group devoted to identifying positive examples of socially and ecologically desirable futures, represents such ambitions.

(3) Furthermore, Holocene qualities can be found in certain *modes of governance* proposed in IR thought. This refers specifically to 'wicked problems'. These kinds of problems pose considerable challenges for the established concepts of global governance. Due to their structure (transnational, long-term effects, widespread but historically and geographically differentiated vulnerabilities, large number of diverse actors) they remain difficult to handle within the classical multi-level governance frameworks and clearly mark the need for more flexible and diverse forms that can deal with glocality (Levin et al. 2012).

Anthropocene problem constellations furthermore imply that the glocality of problem constellations cannot yet be sufficiently conceptualised within the existing analytical frames and modes of governance. The mindset offered by the Westphalian Order – state sovereignty, territorial principle, principle of legality – unfolds as an anachronistic risk if the current global governance constellations fail to act in a quick and efficient way. Although being a supporter of global environmental regimes, Oran R. Young sees the limited progress of such regimes with deep scepticism, as it seems "hard to argue that the reformist strategy is producing real progress in the quest for a 'safe operating space for humanity'" (Young 2016, 245).

Widely debated concepts such as regime complexes or orchestration (Keohane and Victor 2010; Andonova and Chelminski 2016; Abbot et al. 2016) seem more able to offer such frameworks, as they allow working on beyond-border solutions, aiming to include a broad variety of stakeholders. This may make them more apt to tackle Anthropocene problems than conventional approaches. Concrete examples are the Intended National Determined Contributions developed within the UNFCCC (United Nations Framework Convention on Climate Change) system, the development of a clean energy regime complex (Andonova and Chelminski 2016) or glocal transnational networks that practice carbon budgeting or share good climate policy practice (C40 network of mutually carbon budgeting communities, World Bank Dedicated Grant Mechanism for Indigenous Peoples and Local Communities). However, even these promising examples of glocal governance need to be carefully assessed in terms of their appropriateness and aptitude for problem constellations in the Anthropocene, as they may still contain anthropocentric limitations, for instance regarding questions of political representation or actor proliferation.

As governance in the Anthropocene needs to act in a glocal and ubiquitous way, increased attention would have to be dedicated to the inclusion of plural – and often subaltern – actors, to avoid democratic and legitimatory dangers of a top-down bias. This refers especially to a top-down understanding of 'planetary boundaries' that perceives local actors only as docile implementers of global ecological norms. The field of glocal carbon budgeting – especially the governance of REDD+ programmes (Reducing Emissions from Deforestation and Forest Degradation) – provides vivid examples for empowerment and inclusion of local actors as carbon stewards, but also for disciplining and disenfranchising them (Müller 2017).

On a more abstract level, this also holds true for a hegemonial reading of the Anthropocene as a universalising concept that portrays humankind as a community of fate, that is, a community of equals (see Chakrabarty 2012, 13 for a postcolonial critique). While the quantification of ecological governance that is fostered through planetary boundaries may create important system and transition knowledge, ecological 'big data' approaches (Chandler 2015), such as carbon budgeting or smart-metering may also carry potentials for new forms of power abuse or technical/depoliticised regulation. Facing a historical link between the Anthropocene and colonialism, as Lewis and Maslin (2015) have pointed out, Anthropocene governance would therefore need to limit the role of eurocentric voices and encourage a greater plurality (see Whyte 2016, 2017, on the roles of indigenous voices in Anthropocene dialogues). Governance in the Anthropocene should therefore value local ecological practices and knowledge and should act in a bottom-up way.

Against this backdrop it becomes clear that a differentiation between Holocene and Anthropocene IR thwarts typical ways of categorising IR theories. Holocene thought can be found in neorealist and constructivist theories alike, as far as both find themselves caught in mindsets that may hinder the self-reflection of researchers, transgression of disciplinary borders or the transformation of the Westphalian Order. At the same time, various IR schools of thought can offer strategies for redefining emblematic IR categories such as 'actor and agency', 'the international system' or 'modes of governance'. The advent of the Anthropocene can thus be understood as a provocation (Harrington 2016, 6) for reformulating IR thought. Thus, a continuum for transitions towards an Anthropocene theory of IR gives an impression of how theory development could unfold along the categories of 'worldview and international system' 'actor and agency', and 'modes of global governance' (see Table 5.1).

Table 5.1 Continuum of Holocene/Anthropocene IR theory

	Holocene IR	Anthropocene IR
International system	Separation between man and nature	Ecosystem
	Anarchy – from neorealist, institutionalist, constructivist viewpoints	Anarchical ecosystem based on loops and self-regulation
Actor	Mankind (Man)	Post-humanism, involving human and non-human actors
	Focus on states/institutions as actors	Actor proliferation far beyond the state
	Competition between actors	Solidarity among actors
Motivations for agency	Expansion of power & interests	System transformation
		Work on complex 'wicked problems'
	Normative orientations	
	System preservation = political system	System preservation = Earth stewardship
Modes of global governance	Multi-level governance	Glocal governance
	Polycentric governance	
	Regime complexes	
	Stakeholder governance, deliberation representing plural actors	

Conclusion

International theory seems to be on the move, yet the direction is still open. Indeed, Young (2016) speaks of the 'twilight' currently overshadowing the Westphalian Order. It is not yet clear which kind of transformative pressure the Anthropocene as a concept puts on schools of thought and how strong the forces of inertia are. As Earth faces climate change, climate migration and biodiversity loss, a failure of the international system – which also implies a *realpolitik* failure of IR theories – seems quite imaginable. At the same time Young identifies potentials for rapid and not just incremental change, if only climate change was taken as a window of opportunity that would allow for a more fundamental transition of the international system. So far, the Anthropocene concept has been successful in provoking the roll-out of a debate that seeks to reformulate the epistemological and ontological grounds of International Relations theory facing planetary crisis. Some authors have been quick in claiming that IR had failed in offering a theory of collective, post-human survival. However, while manifestos and the echoes that follow certainly make way for discussion, the time has come for a more solid stocktaking of IR theory and its potentials. A fruitful strategy for making sense of the Anthropocene would lie in a closer observation of IR's potentials and pitfalls. This would allow identifying seeds for a yet-to-be-developed theory of IR in the Anthropocene within different IR schools of

thought, as well as in approaches outside the discipline that focus on green political thought, such as political ecology. This kind of interdisciplinary resonance
seems to be happening at the points where global environmental governance,
social/political ecology, normative political theory and postcolonial studies
meet IR's 'theoryscape'. Their crosspollination might offer possibilities for
moving beyond a Holocene understanding of the international system and
would contribute to a theory of survival in the Anthropocene.

Notes

1 Subcommission on Quarternary Stratigraphy (2016) https://quaternary.stratigraphy.org/
 workinggroups/Anthropocene/ Accessed 27 December 2017.
2 The indicators of the planetary boundaries are atmospheric carbon dioxide concentration, species extinction rate, nitrogene/phosphor concentration, ocean acidification,
 land surface converted to cropland, human consumption of water, stratospheric ozone
 concentration, aerosols in the atmosphere and chemical pollution.
3 In the history of International Relations as a discipline, the understanding of the international system, its shape and structure is one of the most central questions. As there is currently no world state, but rather a flexible, polycentric governance structure with various
 international organisations, traditional and 'emerging powers', IR understands the international system as an anarchical structure without central leadership. State anarchy can –
 according to neorealist theories – result in power games, a competition for hegemony
 and an uni-, bi- or multipolar system. According to institutionalist schools, anarchy can
 also be 'tamed' due to the creation of international organisations.
4 The Westphalian Order refers to certain principles of international law that have been
 introduced into European politics as a result of the Peace of Westphalia signed in
 1648, which have since then set a foundational structure for the international system.
 Every nation-state enjoys sovereignty over its territory and agrees to principle of non-
 interference in another country's domestic affairs. Each state (no matter how large or
 small) is considered equal in international law.
5 The 6th mass extinction, climate migration, old and new resource wars, green geopolitics (centred around green resources such as sand for solar cells, lithium for hybrid
 cars, genetically modified climate-resistant crops), new pandemics, deep-sea resources,
 power games in the arctic and antarctic sphere, to name the most pressing ones.
6 Robin Eckersley has outlined an interesting concept for extending the responsibility to
 protect, so that crimes against nature – 'ecocides' – can be persecuted by the law of
 nations. As soon as there are signs of an ecocide happening in a state the community
 of nations should be legitimised to intervene in order to prevent further harm to
 nature (Eckersley 2007; Dalby 2007; Duffy 2015).
7 See the collection of "good Anthropocene" examples by a joint research collaboration
 led by McGill University in Canada, the Stockholm Resilience Centre at Stockholm
 University in Sweden, and the Centre for Complex Systems in Transition (CST) at Stel-
 lenbosch University in South Africa. https://goodanthropocenes.net.

References

Abbot, K.W., Genschel, P., Snidal, D. and Zangl, B. (2016) "Two logics of indirect governance: Delegation and orchestration" *British Journal of Political Science*, 46(4), 719–729.
Andonova, L. and Chelminski, K. (2016) "Emergence of a regime complex for clean
 energy: The critical role of legitimation", Paper presented at the International Workshop

on "Enhancing legitimacy in polycentric climate governance: Opportunities and challenges" European University Institute, Florence, 19–20 May 2016.

Appadurai, A. (2006) "The right to research" *Globalisation, Societies and Education*, 4(2), 167–177.

Biermann, F. (2007) "Earth system governance' as a crosscutting theme of global change research" *Global Environmental Change*, 17, 326–333.

Biermann, F. (2014) *Earth System Governance: World Politics in the Anthropocene* MIT Press, Cambridge, MA.

Biermann, F., Abbot, K., Andresen, S., Bäckstrand, K., Bernstein, S., Betsill, M.M., . . . Zondervan, R. (2012) "Transforming governance and institutions for global sustainability: Key insights from the Earth System Governance Project" *Current Opinion in Environmental Sustainability*, 4, 51–60.

Biermann, F., Bei, X., Bondre, N., Broadgate, W., Chen, C.T.A., . . . Seto, K.C. (2015) "Down to Earth: Contextualizing the Anthropocene" *Global Environmental Change*, OnlineFirst, 1–10.

Braidotti, R. (2010) "The politics of 'life itself' and new ways of dying" in Coole, D. and Frost, S. eds., *New Materialisms: Ontology, Agency and Politics* Duke University Press, Durham, 201–218.

Braidotti, R. (2013) *The Posthuman* Polity Press, Cambridge.

Bullard, R. (1994) "The legacy of American apartheid and environmental racism" *St. Johns Journal of Legal Commentary*, 9, 445–474.

Bullard, R. (2000) "Environmental justice in the 21st century" in Bullard, R., *People of Color Environmental Groups: Directory 2000* Environmental Justice Resource Center, Atlanta, 1–21.

Burke, A., Fishel, S. and Dalby, S. (2016) "Planet politics: A manifesto from the end of IR" *Millennium: Journal of International Studies*, 44(3), 499–533.

Chandler, D. (2015) "A world without causation: Big data and the coming of age of posthumanism" *Millennium*, OnlineFirst, 1–19.

Chakrabarty, D. (2012) "Postcolonial studies and the challenge of climate change" *New Literary History*, 43(1), 1–18.

Chandler, D., Cudworth, E. and Hobden, S. (2018) "Anthropocene, capitalocene and liberal cosmopolitan IR: A response to Burke et al.'s 'planet politics'" *Millennium*, 46(2), 190–208.

Churchman, C.W. (1967) "Wicked problems" *Management Science*, 14(4), B141–B142.

Coward, M. (2009) *Urbicide: The Politics of Urban Destruction* Routledge, London.

Crutzen, P.J. (2002) "Geology of mankind" *Nature*, 415, 23.

Cudworth, E. and Hobden, S. (2011) *Posthuman International Relations* Zed Books, London.

Dalby, S. (2007) "Ecological intervention and Anthropocene ethics" in Rosenthal, J.H. and Barry, Ch. eds., *Ethics & International Affairs* Georgetown University Press, Washington, [Online Edition] (www.ethicsandinternationalaffairs.org/fall-2007-issue-21-3/) Accessed 15 June 2016.

Dalby, S. (2013) "Biopolitics and climate security in the Anthropocene" *Geoforum*, 49, 184–192.

Duffy, R. (2015) "Responsibility to protect? Ecocide, interventionism and saving biodiversity" Paper presented at Political Studies Association Conference, Sheffield, 30 March–1 April 2015.

Eckersley, R. (2007) "Ecological intervention" in Rosenthal, J.H. and Barry, C. eds., *Ethics & International Affairs* Georgetown University Press, Washington, [Online Edition] (www.ethicsandinternationalaffairs.org/fall-2007-issue-21-3/) Accessed 15 June 2016.

Finnemore, M. and Sikkink, K. (1998) "International norm dynamics and political change" *International Organization*, 52(4), 887–917.

Fishel, S., Burke, A., Mitchell, A., Dalby, S. and Levine, D. (2018) "Defending planet politics" *Millennium*, 46(2), 209–219.

Freyberg-Inan, A. (2004) *What Moves Man: The Realist Theory of International Relations and Its Judgment of Human Nature* State University of New York Press, New York.

Hamilton, S. (2016) "The measure of all things? The Anthropocene as a global biopolitics of carbon" *European Journal of International Relations*, OnlineFirst. DOI: 10.1177/1354066116683831.

Haraway, D. (2016) "Anthropocene, capitalocene, plantationocene, chthulucene: Making kin" *Environmental Humanities*, 6, 159–165.

Harrington, C. (2016) "The ends of the world: International relations and the Anthropocene" *Millennium: Journal of International Studies*, 44(3), 478–498.

Keohane, R.O. and Victor, D.G. (2010) "The regime complex for climate change" *Harvard Kennedy School, Belfer Center for Science and International Affairs, Harvard University, Discussion Paper 10–33*.

Levin, K., Cashore, B., Bernstein, S. and Auld, G. (2012) "Overcoming the tragedy of super wicked problems: Constraining our future selves to ameliorate global climate change" *Policy Sciences*, 45(2), 123–152.

Lewis, S.L. and Maslin, M.A. (2015) "Defining the Anthropocene" *Nature*, 519, 171–180. DOI: 10.1038/nature14258.

Ling, L.H.M. (2013) *The Dao of World Politics* Routledge Interventions, London.

Lövbrand, E., Beck, S. and Chilvers, J. (2016) "Who speaks for the future of Earth? How critical social science can extend the conversation of the Anthropocene" *Global Environmental Change*, 32, 211–218.

Lövbrand, E., Stripple, J. and Wiman, B. (2009) "Earth system governmentality: Reflections on science in the Anthropocene" *Global Environmental Change*, 19, 7–13.

Masco, J. (2010) "Bad weather: On planetary crisis" *Social Studies of Science*, 40(1), 7–40.

Mayer, P. (2003) "Die Epistemologie der Internationalen Beziehungen: Anmerkungen zum Stand der 'Dritten Debatte'" in Hellmann, G., Wolf, K.-D. and Zürn, M. eds., *Die neuen Internationalen Beziehungen. Forschungsstand und Perspektiven in Deutschland* Nomos, Baden-Baden, 47–98.

McDonald, M. (2017) "Ecological security" in Eroukhmanoff, C. and Harker, M. eds., *Reflections on the Posthuman in International Relations* E-International Relations Publishing, Bristol, 62–72.

McNeill, J.R. and Engelke, P. (2016) *The Great Acceleration: An Environmental History of the Anthropocene since 1945* Belknap Press, Harvard.

Mitchell, A. (2015) "Decolonising the Anthropocene" (https://worldlyir.wordpress.com/2015/03/17/decolonising-the-Anthropocene/) Accessed 27 December 2017.

Mitchell, A. (2017) "Is IR going extinct?" *European Journal of International Relations*, 23(1), 3–25.

Moravcsik, A. (1997) "Taking preferences seriously: A liberal theory of international politics" *International Organization*, 51(4), 513–553.

Müller, F. (2016) "'Save the planet, plant a tree!': REDD+ and global/local forest governance in the Anthropocene" *Resilience*, 5(3), 182–200.

Müller, F. (2017) "Produktive Wälder: Diffusionsmuster klimapolitischer Verantwortung am Beispiel von REDD+-Projekten" *Politische Vierteljahresschrift*, 335–358.

Ogden, L., Heynen, N., Oslender, U., West, P., Kassam, K.-A. and Robbins, P. (2013) "Global assemblages, resilience, and Earth Stewardship in the Anthropocene" *Frontiers in Ecology and Environment*, 1(7), 341–347.

Onuf, N.G. (2001) "The politics of constructivism" in Fierke, K.M. and Jørgensen, K.E. eds., *Constructing International Relations: The Next Generation* M.E. Sharpe, Armonk, London, 236–254.

Rockström, J. (2010) "Planetary boundaries" *New Perspectives Quarterly*, 27(1), 72–74.

Rockström, J., Steffen, W. and Noone, K. (2009) "Planetary boundaries: Exploring the safe operating space for humanity" *Ecology and Society*, 14(2), 32.

Sagan, C. (1983) *The Nuclear Winter* Scott Meredith Literary Agency, New York.

Scranton, R. (2015) *Learning to Die in the Anthropocene* City Light Books, San Francisco.

Steans, J., Pettiford, L. and Diez, Th. (2005) *Introduction to International Relations*, Chapter 8 "Green Perspectives" Person, Edinburgh, 203–228.

Steffen, W., Crutzen, P. and McNeill, J. (2007) "The Anthropocene: Are humans now overwhelming the great forces of nature?" *AMBIO*, 36, 614–621.

Steffen, W., Grinevald, J., Crutzen, P. and McNeill, J. (2011) "The Anthropocene: Conceptual and historical perspectives" *Philosophical Transactions of the Royal Society*, 369, 842–867.

Swyngedouw, E. (2014) "Anthropocenic politicization: From the politics of the environment to politicizing environment" in Bradley, K. and Johan, H. eds., *Green Utopianism: Perspectives, Politics and Micro-Practices* Routledge, London, 23–37.

Tickner, A.B. (1988) "Hans Morgenthau's principles of political realism: A feminist reformulation" *Millennium: Journal of International Studies*, 17(3), 429–444.

Tickner, A.B. and Blaney, D.L. eds. (2013) *Claiming the International: Worlding beyond the West* Routledge, London.

Vince, G. (2014) *Adventures in the Anthropocene: A Journey to the Heart of the Planet We Made* Vintage Books, London.

Waters, C.N., Zalasiewicz, J., Summerhayes, C. and Barnosky, A.D. (2016) "The Anthropocene is functionally and stratigraphically distinct from the Holocene" *Science*, 351, 6269.

Wendt, A. (2016) "Anarchy is what States Make of it: The Social Construction of Power Politics" *International Organization*, 46(2), 391–425.

Whyte, K. (2016) "The roles for indigenous peoples in Anthropocene dialogues: Some critical notes and a question" (https://inhabitingtheAnthropocene.com/2017/01/25/the-roles-for-indigenous-peoples-in-Anthropocene-dialogues-some-critical-notes-and-a-question/) Accessed 27 December 2017.

Whyte, K. (2017) "Indigenous climate change studies: Indigenizing futures, decolonizing the Anthropocene" *English Language Notes*, 55(1–2), 153–162.

Wimmer, A. and Schiller, N.G. (2002) "Methodological nationalism and beyond: Nation-state building, migration and the social sciences" *Global Networks*, 2(4), 301–334.

Young, O.A. (2016) "International relations in the Anthropocene" in Booth, K. and Erskine, T. eds., *International Relations Theory Today* Polity Press, London, 231–252.

Zalasiewicz, J., Waters, C.N., Williams, M., Barnosky, A.D., … Oreskes, N. (2015) "When did the Anthropocene begin?" *Quarternary International*, 383, 196–203.

Ziai, A. (2010) "Post-positivist metatheory and research in international relations: A comparison of neo-gramscian, feminist and post-structuralist approaches" *Hamburg Review of Social Sciences*, 5(1/2), 31–60.

Part II
Governance and practices

6 Security studies and the discourse on the Anthropocene

Shortcomings, challenges and opportunities

Judith Nora Hardt

Introduction

The Anthropocene is mostly discussed in reference to the proposal Paul Crutzen and Eugene Stormer made just after the start of the new millennium (Crutzen and Stoermer 2000). It holds that humans shape the Earth to a degree that we have inscribed ourselves in the Earth's history (Dalby 2013). However, geologists still do not agree upon a specific definition and quarrel over the origins of the Anthropocene. The most prominent approaches date the Anthropocene back to the Industrial Revolution, measured on the basis of the vast increase of carbon dioxide (CO_2) emissions (e.g., Steffen et al. 2007) or alternatively to the measurement of radioactive elements, dated back to 1950s and to the first atomic test (Zalasiewicz et al. 2017; see also Tremmel, in this volume).

Meanwhile, the Anthropocene has become the subject of art exhibitions and magazines and is discussed widely in the community of scientists. The 'Anthropocene debate' basically divides the scientific community into sceptics and supporters. The sceptics argue that the Anthropocene is simultaneously a potpourri and/or an empty shell as an "all-purpose noun, verb and adjective" (Luke 2017, 83). In contrast, the proponents of the concept of the Anthropocene can be grouped in the attempt to establish a new discipline, i.e., Anthropocene studies. These are mostly informed by the Earth system sciences (e.g., Schellnhuber et al. 2004; Steffen et al. 2004; Steffen 2016) and by environmental humanities (e.g., Lövbrand et al. 2015; Neimanis et al. 2015), even though until today both scientific communities mostly articulate their approaches to the Anthropocene separately.

How can we deal with the concept of the Anthropocene from a political science perspective and which key aspects of the concept could offer an additional focus for future research? In order to grasp the full potential of the Anthropocene concept, I attempt to get hold of some major constitutive features in the context of security studies that could help pave the way for the emergence of inter- and transdisciplinary approaches to the Anthropocene. The main argument put forward here is that the way the Anthropocene is referred to in the environmental security literature and the approaches of critical security studies are promising to contribute to the emerging Anthropocene studies. Therefore the major focus lies in discourses of threat-response logic in the Anthropocene.

This chapter contributes to the topic of the edited volume in two ways: first, I analyse how the sub-disciplines of International Relations and of political sciences, security studies and particularly the field of environmental security[1] have acknowledged the Anthropocene. Second, I scrutinise the contribution of critical approaches in security studies to the Anthropocene debate. The specific focus on security is chosen as it resides at the core of our conception of the world and has been ordering, determining and dominating politics from the individual to the international level in the most profound ways. Security is part of the *hard political issues* and stands closely interrelated with power politics, violence, peace, conflict and the domain of development. While several conceptions of security exist, a basic characteristic is that it protects a fundamental and existential value that requires absolute and immediate protection and emergent response to any type of threat. This is how, even though utopian, the core goal of states, people, but also organisations and societies is to reach a state of absence of threat (Kay 2015, 1).

The chapter proceeds in six parts. In the next section, I describe the analytical framework and the methodology of discourse analysis. In the third section, I introduce the reader to the field of security and discuss the literature on environmental security with regard to three major political concepts of security. In the fourth section, I engage in the critical analysis of the conceptions of the Anthropocene articulated in the form of a political concept of security. In the fifth section, I elaborate on how the Anthropocene discourse heavily relies on the threat-response logic. Finally, I draw conclusions and contend that developing an *Anthropocene thinking* of security can open up and foster a research agenda focused on the most fundamental questions for humankind.

Framework for analysis and methodology

The analytical framework is informed by the so-called mainstream approach of critical security studies, the Copenhagen School and by *Anthropocene thinking*. Two of the most important contributions of the Copenhagen School were made in the publication *Security: A New Framework for Analysis* by Buzan et al. (1998). These are above all the securitisation framework and the closely related conception of security as an analytical tool. The securitisation framework explains the difference between the normal level of politics and the security level, and describes the process of securitisation as a speech act, through which certain power holders transform a certain issue into an issue of security. In accordance with this, a successful securitisation is defined by Buzan et al. (1998, 26) as being composed by "existential threats, emergency action, and effects on inter-unit relations by breaking free of rules". After the threat has been successfully defeated, the process of de-securitisation is aimed at, which means that the issue will not be of security concern again (Buzan et al. 1998, 30).The Copenhagen School conceives of security as intrinsically negative and as a failure of normal politics (McDonald 2008, 566).

While I do not share the strictly negative conception of security (see also Hardt 2017) and I am aware of several limitations and criticisms,[2] I nevertheless build upon the theoretical foundations of the Copenhagen School because of the added value of perceiving security as a research category, which I use as a central tool here. The important asset here is that the Copenhagen School conceives of security as holding the basic values and goals, anxieties of certain societies, groups and institutions. As a consequence, security can be used as an analytical tool in the form of a questionnaire. It reveals the referent object, the threat, the causes and the responses which we can thereby more explicitly analyse and thereby uncover the central conceptions of security (Buzan et al. 1998, 32). I describe below how this analytical tool provides important insight into the discourse of the Anthropocene, in spite of the fact that neither the environment nor the Anthropocene have been described as a specific research inquiry or theme of the Copenhagen School so far.

The second pillar of the analytical framework is the *Anthropocene thinking*, originally proposed by Cudworth and Hobden (2011) and defined in contrast to *Holocene thinking*. I chose this contribution because it illustrates well one characteristic that many scientific communities attribute to the Anthropocene. The Anthropocene is regarded as inducing a 'paradigm shift' in our conception of ourselves as being part of the natural world (see e.g., Bennett 2011; Schellnhuber et al. 2004; Hamilton et al. 2015). Our old, outlived vision of the world, called *Holocene thinking*, presumes a stable environment that functions as a background for human action (see also Müller, in this volume).

Anthropocene thinking profoundly challenges this imaginary in the sense that it describes a dynamic relationship between humans and nature and does not allow a differentiation between background and foreground, between *inside* and *outside* (Harrington and Shearing 2017, 95). The fact that our tools and mindsets are still rooted in *Holocene thinking* supposes an important challenge to switch the *thinking*. Therefore, a special effort to think 'out of the box' is required (Bai et al. 2016, 352), such as overcoming the divide of the natural and social sciences, and developing new forms of knowledge that include civil society and other actors in the process (Jahn et al. 2015; Lövbrand et al. 2015). This description of *Anthropocene thinking* clearly stands in contrast to the contemporary situation in which the different scientific communities remain relatively separated from each other, also (as I will show in the sections on security studies, below) when approaching the Anthropocene.

This chapter is informed by a qualitative methodology and its major focus lies in discourse analysis. Discourses are thereby understood as provinding the possibility to analyse different worldviews. At the same time, discourses constitute and shape world affairs, events and processes (Hajer 1995, 44). In order to identify the underlying worldviews present in the Anthropocene discourse, I use the tool of *deconstruction* to critically analyse, problematise and decompose the multiple meanings of security conceptions. I thereby mainly refer to security as a research tool in line with the Copenhagen School that focuses on the most central values and fears (*security*). The second major research focus identifies whether the human-nature relationship is described in form of a dynamic interrelation (*Anthropocene thinking*), or whether it conceives the environment as a background for human activity (*Holocene thinking*). Consequently, the analysis follows a two-step design. The first step consists of a critical inquiry on how the Anthropocene discourse is conceived within security studies. The second step of the analysis evaluates how security as a research category can inform the debate on the Anthropocene.

Political concepts of (environmental) security and the Anthropocene

Security studies lie at the very centre of International Relations and have evolved into a broad realm that also includes peace and conflict studies, development studies and strategic studies (Buzan and Hansen 2009). In all these disciplines, the conceptualisations and ways to study security differ widely. A basic question that divides the study field is the differentiation between the traditional approaches that convey to security a fixed meaning related to the state and the military, and the critical approaches that conceive of security in the absence of a particular meaning. As a result, several interpretations and perspectives on security exist, which can be described in forms of political concepts of security (Brauch 2011, 61).

In this context, it is important to highlight that the varying security concepts share the characteristics of containing a threat-response logic, such as a central value and a central fear. In other terms, a political concept of security describes a central value, a threat and also measures necessary to prevent the threat. A central characteristic of the response is, according to the Copenhagen School, that it 'brakes free of rules' as any kind of measure applies because the basic value needs to be protected under any circumstances and by any means (Buzan et al. 1998, 26). This is a key assumption that also explains why security is such an attractive and heavily debated field. While the literature describes many different political concepts of security, the two most prominent security concepts are the traditional security concept and human security. These are described in a simplified overview in Table 6.1.

Table 6.1 The four dimensions of the traditional concept of security and of human security

Security concept	Reference	Issue	Space	Threat
Traditional concept of state security	State	Military	National	Loss of territory and sovereignty
Human security concept	The vulnerable and powerless Individuals	*Seven dimensions:* economic security; food security; health security; environmental security; personal security; community security; political security	International and regional Global	Vulnerability and risk

Source: Based on UNDP (1994) and Daase (2010).

First, the so-called traditional security concept is the most important and popular approach and constitutes one of the foundations of the discipline of International Relations. It is still the most widely accepted interpretation and guiding principle of the international state system in theory and practice. This understanding is deeply rooted in the Realist worldview of international politics. This classical account conveys a fixed meaning of security to the state system, territoriality and to military measures that minimise the threat and ensure survival of the sovereign state (Mearsheimer 2001). After the disappearance of the imminent threat of nuclear destruction at the end of the Cold War, however, new threat perspectives emerged and alternative conceptualisations of security arose. They have a broader focus and also conceive of the individual, the environment, or also societal/cultural groups as central agents to be secured (see e.g., Buzan et al. 1998).

Second, the concept of human security was initially set-up in the United Nations Development Report published in 1994 (UNDP 1994). The concept of human security represents the most prominent materialisation for the development of the concept of security and aims to function as a guiding principle for politics (see e.g., Burguess and Tadjbakhsh 2010). This revolutionary outline supposedly focuses on the individual and, more specifically, on vulnerable societal groups. It holds seven interrelated dimensions, among others environmental security, which are not understood in terms of threat but as positive and idealist aspirations to secure basic needs (UNDP 1994; Barnett 2007). While both concepts (traditional and human security) include some aspects of the environmental threat dimension, the threat-response logic of environmental issues is most often discussed in the sub-field of environmental security (see e.g., Rothe 2016).

Environmental security

After discussing the two most prominent security concepts, I now turn to the field of environmental security with the major focus on how the Anthropocene has been acknowledged mostly via recent influence from climate scientists and Earth system scientists (Dalby 2013; Rothe 2016). Environmental security is characterised by diffuseness and by the absence of a clear definition of security (in contrast to, e.g., the human security concept). The nexus of environment and security was mainly acknowledged after the end of the Cold War and has grown from the recognition of the threatening effects of environmental destruction and the ways environmental issues relate to the security of the state and of societies. In the threat perception, we can distinguish the focus on the state, which is similar to the traditional security concept and heavily bound to the so-called environmental-conflict thesis. This thesis holds that environmental degradation leads to, for example, armed conflict and remains a major argument and motivation for current research to engage in the field of environmental security (see e.g., Homer-Dixon 1994; Gleditsch 2015). The focus on how environmental phenomena threaten human development and endanger basic human needs can mostly be related to the concept of human security (see e.g., Barnett 2007).

If we look at these trends and motives, we can conclude that the securitisation of environmental issues heavily relies on the threat-response logic that is independent of a negative or positive conception of security and of the referent object (being the state or the vulnerable populations). Moreover, the central argument is that environmental security scholars often argue that environmental destruction and resource scarcity need to be perceived as existential threats, hence elevated into the security realm in order to be effectively handled (e.g., Dalby 2013; Brauch 2011). In simplified terms, one of the basic assumptions is that attributing more importance to environmental degradation via securitisation will lead to a response to the threat and a solution to the problem. An additional motivation for scholars focusing on environmental security are the positive consequences and opportunities linked to such a securitisation move, which can be described in the environmental-cooperation thesis. This thesis holds that the mere act of necessary cooperation on environmental issues will overcome tensions, conflicts and lead to peace; or that responding to environmental threats secures a sustainable living basis, well-being and long-lasting futures (e.g., O'Brien et al. 2010; Matthew 2014).

Several discussions dominate the field of environmental security, mostly dealing with the question of how environmental phenomena are interlinked with cooperation, conflict and development, and with negative and positive conceptions of security. The criticisms and objections to linking environment and security vary a lot in relation to these different conceptions. There are three main points of critique: The first objection is that, if security included environment, it would be too broad and would therefore loose its analytical capacity (e.g., Wæver 1995). The second criticism is that linking environment to security carries the risk of its misuse or militarisation because it could be interpreted as the negative conception of security and become bound to the logic of power, violence and antagonism (e.g., Floyd 2008). The third objection is that the deployment of security politics does not offer an effective solution to ecological processes (e.g., Deudney 1991). The debate for and against linking security and environment remains a defining trait of the literature today.

In the next section, I will show how similar motivations and discourses can be recognised in relation to the Anthropocene discourse. In spite of these discussions, several actors today refer to environmental, climate or even to planetary security. These are mostly the military, think tanks and international organisations, such as the European Union, bodies of the United Nations and the Organisation for Security and Cooperation in Europe (see e.g., Dellmuth et al. 2017; Trombetta 2014). See also Hardt (2017) for a critical assessment and analysis of environmental security practice.

Acknowledgement of the discourse of the Anthropocene in the environmental security literature

An important turning point in the literature of environmental security was the year 2007; from then on the popularisation of the term *climate security* increased dramatically. This development was mainly triggered by the publication of the report of the Intergovernmental Panel on Climate Change (IPCC), the award of the Nobel Peace Prize for the IPCC and Al Gore, and the first discussion about climate change in the United Nations Security Council,[3] which was followed by others in recent years (Brauch 2011). Since then, the influence of climate scientists and the Earth system scientists on the literature of environmental security has been increasing significantly. This is mainly because the scientific reports refer to the central topics of the environmental security literature. In these reports climate change, resilience and vulnerability are related either to peace, cooperation, conflict or to development (e.g., Methmann and Oels 2015; Rothe 2016; Hardt 2017). One example is presented in the following quote:

> Climate change can indirectly increase risks of violent conflicts in the form of civil war and inter-group violence by amplifying well-documented drivers of these conflicts such as poverty and economic shocks (*medium confidence*). Multiple lines of evidence relate climate variability to these forms of conflict.
> (IPCC 2014, 20–21, emphasis in original)

Furthermore, climate change is seen as having the "potential to increase rivalry among states, but robust national and intergovernmental institutions can enhance cooperation and manage many of these rivalries" (IPCC 2014, 20–21).

More recently, Earth system sciences also increasingly relate to the major themes of security studies. At the same time, several authors from the environmental security literature are referencing the new geological era, for example as the necessity to focus on 'sustainable security' (Dalby 2013, 132) and assuring 'the planet's survival' (Burke et al. 2016, 522). The references to the Anthropocene mainly relate to the concept of planetary boundaries, elaborated by Johan Röckstrom et al. (2009) at the Stockholm Resilience Centre. The planetary boundaries concept describes the Earth system on the basis of nine systemic control variables, among others biodiversity, climate change and biogeochemical cycles that each are described as being threatened and pushed to the corresponding thresholds by human activity (Rockström et al. 2009; Steffen 2016). On the basis of these thresholds, the planetary boundaries concepts defines a 'safe operating space' for humanity (Rockström et al. 2009, 2). In order to maintain or reach this safe space, the planetary boundaries need to be secured. This is how the Anthropocene discourse is increasingly described in relation to threat and urgency action, and has entered the literature on environmental security, in a way that fulfils all necessary requirements and the logic of a new political concept of (environmental) security (Hardt 2017, 97). In consequence, next to the two described major concepts of security (traditional and human security), a third political concept of security is described here, called *eco-centred*, as it supposedly holds the environment as a referent object (see Table 6.2).

Before coming to the description, it is important to highlight that this conception lies at the intersection of security studies, Earth system sciences and climate science, and is shaped by these different academic communities. At the same time, I want to stress that this concept has not yet reached the level of security

Table 6.2 The eco-centred concept of environmental security

Referent object	Nature
Formulated goal	Secure the Earth system
Threat	Changes of the status quo and of the biophysical and geophysical environment
Responses	Steering global environmental change and human activity, e.g., along the planetary boundaries Global environmental governance
Agency	Earth System Science, Climate Science and other sciences, states, international organisations Earth System Council
Conception of the Anthropocene	A geological era of insecurity

Source: Based on Hardt (2017, 97–101) and additionally informed by Burke et al. (2016); Brauch et al. (2016); Crutzen (2011); Rockström et al. (2009); Schellnhuber et al. (2004); and Steffen (2016).

politics (as defined by the Copenhagen School), as currently the "emergency action, and effects on inter-unit relations by breaking free of rules" (Buzan et al. 1998, 26) are still mostly absent. Nevertheless, this concept requires special attention because it is pronounced and pushed by scholars and actors who inform politics, global institutions, and the broader public. This is how the planetary boundaries concept is internationally recognised and praised as a unique, visually catchy conceptualisation of the Anthropocene. It also needs to be highlighted that several claims exist to integrate planetary boundaries into international politics, mainly in the form of becoming included in the Agenda 2030 (Hajer et al. 2015, 1652).

In the following, the eco-centred security concept is presented in Table 6.2 on the basis of the deconstruction tool of security that helps to grasp the threat-response logic in the form of several categories. The presentation of the eco-centred security concept shows that the underlying goal and major concern are to maintain stability of the Earth system. Humans are seen as disturbing and threatening this stability via the exhaustive impacts on ecological processes, measured for example in CO_2 emissions and ocean acidification. Therefore, the necessary measures to confront these threats lie in reducing the ecological footprint and steering human societies to respecting the different planetary boundaries. In order to avoid (at any price) exceeding the defined thresholds or tipping points, the responses to the threat range from technological, scientific, policy or institutional fixes to more generally speaking, actions of regaining control. The agency in charge of defining the responses to the threat entails scientists, states and institutions. This also includes the proposal to establish new institutions. Burke et al. "suggest the creation of an 'Earth System Council' with the task of action and warning – much like the current UN Security Council – that would operate on the basis of majority voting with representation of Earth system scientists, major ecosystems, species groups, and states" (Burke et al. 2016, 516). A fundamental assumption of this eco-centred security concept is that via the "wise application of gained scientific knowledge" (Crutzen 2011, 4), humanity can be steered back into a 'Holocene-like state' (Steffen 2016, 24). In contrast to the above outlined security concepts (traditional and human security) conflict, war, underdevelopment and poverty are not threats as such, but are seen as secondary effects of a changing biophysical and geophysical environment.

On a first note, it can be stated that the field of environmental security lies at a transdisciplinary juncture that focuses on some of the central concerns of humankind, and vary from relating environmental phenomena to conflict, cooperation, health, development and well-being. The Anthropocene discourse, however, is mostly acknowledged in the form of planetary boundaries, whereas a transdisciplinary approach or conception is missing. Furthermore, it seems that the discussion in the geological sciences has received less attention in this field. An additional insight is that a general debate on the Anthropocene, in the sense of being accepted or rejected, remains relatively absent from the field.

Anthropocene discourse in the (environmental) security literature: shortcomings and challenges

In the following, I engage in a critical analysis of the Anthropocene discourse in the political concepts of (environmental) security, and I highlight their shortcomings and challenges. As described above, there are three main political concepts of security, which either focus on securing the state, the vulnerable and powerless, or the Earth system. The responses are presented in terms of military action, development cooperation, compliance of global environmental governance, and steering of humanity along different planetary boundaries. Applying the critical deconstruction tool of security and the *Anthropocene thinking*, the following shortcomings become apparent.

The state-centred security concept and the human security concept have not yet included the Anthropocene discourse and are limited to the traditional foci of International Relations, being the state and the North-South relation. In consequence, both ignore the dynamic world entangled with human-nature and are still strongly limited to the international relations' *Holocene thinking* that describes 'a world that is not of this Earth' (Burke et al. 2016, 504). I will therefore focus in the following on the eco-centred concept. The critical analysis of the eco-centred security concept also reveals important limitations and even dangerous implications, which I will highlight in relation to maintaining stability, maintaining power, falling back into a *Holocene thinking*, and the lack of a clear referent object, fear and central value.

First, the underlying concern and goal of this conception is to maintain stability and a resilient Earth system, which therefore does not focus on substantive change and does not put the contemporary system in question. As maintaining the status quo is impossible and leads to the perpetuation of the challenges and fostering the loop of injustice, destruction and violence, this approach also clearly falls short on the paradigm change and the dynamic interrelation between humans and nature, described as central features of *Anthropocene thinking*.

Second, the focus on (non-existent) stability via the *securitisation of science* does not question power relations, structural injustices, or violence and is likely to maintain power where it is and even increase it. If the planetary boundaries concept was securitised, it would be turned into, what Neocleous has called in reference to Foucault 'a technique of power' that reorders and reshapes "society in the name of security" (Neocleous 2008, 4–5). In a similar vein, Luke highlights that the Anthropocene is likely to be misused as a new 'mantra' for 'global eco-managerialism' for supposing specific plans for "managing the Anthropocene to create specific outcomes for those who are the managers as well as the managed" (Luke 2017, 91). Furthermore, the call for subordinating human interests to ecology would endanger democratic reasoning, decision-making and debate (Chandler et al. 2018, 197). Another important limitation of this concept lies in articulating security for a non-human agent (in this case the Earth system), as this raises suspicion because it can be misused as a cover for pursuing underlying power interests. Informed by the Coxian (1981, 128) insight that theory is always '*for* someone and *for* some purpose', Buzan et al. (1998, 175) therefore prescribe the important analytical questions of 'who influences the security discourse?' and 'who will benefit?'. Applying these questions to the securitising moves of the Anthropocene raises the important concern of being very cautious in the light of possible power politics, being articulated at the level of the Earth system.

Third, this approach still heavily rests on *Holocene thinking* of a manageable, stable environment and steerable Earth system conditions. Instead of a dynamic interrelation of humans as part of nature, this security concept portrays nature "as an object external to society with 'natural' limits and tipping points that can be discerned, quantified and managed with some degree of scientific objectivity" and thereby inserts and re-elevates humankind above nature (Baskin 2014, 4; Lövbrand et al. 2015, 213).

Fourth, this concept excludes the focus on humans as social beings and assumes that a "top-down steering by governments and intergovernmental organizations alone can address global problems" (Hajer et al. 2015, 1652) and revives 'liberal global cosmopolitanism' (Chandler et al. 2018, 200). Furthermore this generalisation and simplification of humans and humanity into a '*universal* we or *global* us' (Chaturvedi and Doyle 2016, 206, emphasis in original) fails to account for "the multiplicity and unequal social values, relations and practices of power that accompany actual humans" (Baskin 2014, 8) and ignores that the particular forms of social organisation cause the impacts on the rest of nature (Chandler et al. 2018, 201).

Fifth, as stated above, the referent object is described as a non-human entity (the Earth system) and therefore rests short of presenting a clear referent object, a central value and fear, articulated *by* humans *for* humans.

Thus, I conclude that the literature on (environmental) security is currently not well tuned to *Anthropocene thinking* as it rests on depoliticised and problem-solving approaches, and is possibly being turned into or misused as an instrument for power politics. The further development of security studies and the inclusion of the environmental humanities into the field are therefore a fundamental necessity, precisely *because* the Anthropocene is not debated, but is already articulated in the literature in a reduced form with possible dangerous implications.

Opportunities: applying the security prism on the Anthropocene discourse

The critical approaches to security studies can contribute to the debate on the Anthropocene in several ways (see e.g., Harrington and Shearing 2017). Due to the limited amount of space, I am focusing here on how the security prism can bring an alternative description of the Anthropocene (as the geological sciences or the planetary boundaries concept) into focus. In the following, I will show that the security prism reveals (1) the threat-response logic inherent in the Anthropocene discourses, and (2) the underlying conceptions of fear, threat and basic values.

Threat-response logic in the Anthropocene discourse

Security studies are primarily based on a so-called 'threat-response logic', which is conceptualised as a political concept of security. Essentially, it contains an existential threat and a response to the threat. When applying this lens to the emerging Anthropocene studies literature, this threat-response logic can also be recognised in two major discourses that describe the future of humankind as peaking between catastrophism and positive change (see e.g. Schellnhuber et al. 2004; Hamilton et al. 2015; Bai et al. 2016). The first narrative is mostly described in relation to survival, existential threat, fear, mass extinction, collapse and destructive imaginations – all of which are however not clearly specified in terms of consequence (e.g., Steffen 2011, 32; Harrington and Shearing 2017, 97). In other words, the Anthropocene portrays a fundamentally dystopian future (Chernilo 2017, 45) with a possible *endpoint* that is associated with destruction, violence and irreversibility.

The second narrative can be understood as response to the implications of the threat narrative. It is synthesised here as *hope for positive change* and is often also associated with the first discourse, as being the chance to finally change course by navigating away from critical tipping points of the Earth system (see Hickmann et al., in the introduction of this volume) by taking *correct*, effective and *immediate* action and 'assure the planet's survival' (Burke et al. 2016, 522). Accordingly, the Anthropocene is described as 'a normative guide to action' (Baskin 2014, 3) or as an opportunity "to channel the transformative and creative potentials of human society towards desirable and novel futures" (Bai et al. 2016, 360). The concept of planetary boundaries can also be categorised here because it captures the dimensions of status quo, threat and solution, which consist in respecting the defined thresholds for human activity.

These discourses and motivations are similar to the above described environmental security literature. Yet, an important difference is that this underlying threat-response logic is located at several crossroads of all approaches to the Anthropocene studies and therefore not necessarily connected to securitisation logic. Nevertheless, more research is warranted to further analyse the interrelations between the two fields and of the possible implications and shortcomings of this threat-response logic inherent in the Anthropocene discourse.

The main point here is that this threat-response logic is seen as a major underlying constitutive feature and therefore an alternative defining characteristic of the Anthropocene discourse. In other words, I argue that one of the major reasons why the Anthropocene gains as much attention (in spite of a missing definition) is the profoundly threatening dimension it carries. Therefore, I propose that exploring more explicitly the nature of different interpretations and conceptions of the threat-response logic in relation to human-nature entanglement is an important future research avenue. Furthermore, I contend that becoming aware of this basic logic applied by the different scientific communities, these pillars could further orient and synthesise the research of the emerging Anthropocene studies. These axes of research could also help to offer a point of encounter for fostering further transdisciplinary approaches.

Basic values and fears in the Anthropocene discourse

In the following, I will argue that the security prism can help to approach the diffuse threat-response logic inherent in the Anthropocene discourse more precisely and better focus and articulate its great potential. Based on this assumption, I propose an experiment by placing the detected threat-response discourse of the Anthropocene into the security prism. Most importantly, these descriptions are not to be misinterpreted as a securitising move – rather they present a deconstruction of discourses. In technical terms, I refill the questionnaire of the security research category of the Copenhagen School and the scenarios of threat and hope in the Anthropocene context with *Anthropocene thinking*. The result is presented in a simplified manner in Table 6.3 and is based on the deconstruction tool and therefore lacks specific references in the following description.

In the security prism, humanity and its entangled world lie at the centre of concern. Threat is described in relation to the discourse of *the end of the human species*, such as by violence, injustice and death. Following the security logic, the response to these threats is described in the paradigmatic change itself, which makes the rethinking of all basic values and structures of the contemporary international society and system necessary. Furthermore, it takes as a reference the discourse of *hope for positive change* with moral and responsible impetus and therefore closely connects the response to socio-ecological change and transformation. The agents are described as a broad alliance of actors, which actively engage in the effort to rethink our basic ethical set of the most valuable features, objects and issues we need to secure. The responsible and accountable agents are scientists, politicians, society and especially decision makers and power holders, as they most directly (intentionally or not) decide,

Table 6.3 De-constructing the threat-response logic of the Anthropocene discourse

Referent object	Humankind
Formulated goal	Secure humanity with its entangled world
Threat	Human extinction, injustice and violence
	Maintenance of status quo, short-term politics
Response	Rethink basic foundations of knowledge and values
	Imply profound change towards better futures
Agency	Alliance of scientists (social and natural scientists), society, politicians, social movements and local group

Source: Based on Bai et al. (2016); Baskin (2014); Chernilo (2017); Hamilton et al. (2015); Harrington and Shearing (2017); Jahn et al. (2015); Lövbrand et al. (2015); Neimanis et al. (2015); Schellnhuber et al. (2004); and Steffen (2011, 2016).

shape and form what is to be secured. A basic understanding of the human-nature relationship hereby consists in accepting the incapacity to control and steer the Earth system and humans.

This experiment confirms that the emerging Anthropocene studies do heavily rely on the underlying threat description of the *end of the human species* and that they are motivated by the search for responses. Nevertheless, it can be observed that the central issue of concern remains an underlying motivation but is rarely explicitly addressed. This can also be seen in referring back to the three political concepts of security described above, especially the eco-centred concept (see Table 6.2 and Table 6.3), which do not include the extinction of humankind as a threat nor as a possibility (Hardt 2017, 271), in spite of being strongly informed by the Anthropocene narrative. Instead, the eco-centred security concept, which is heavily informed by the planetary boundaries concept, focuses on maintaining a stable Earth system. Also Mitchell (2017) recently described a similar research result by stating that, surprisingly, human extinction is not a core concern of International Relations.

An additional insight I would like to highlight is that the very tendency to assume that a possible solution to the *end of the human species* exists, which is characteristic of the Anthropocene discourse, requires future critical reflection. I argue that the assumption of an existing remedy might itself present a central obstacle to change. In the same vein, Chandler et al. (2018, 207) assess the expectations to save the planet as a mere dream that will lead to maintaining the current system. Mitchell (2017) and Harrington and Shearing (2017) point out that accepting and embracing finality of humankind is a fundamental precondition to conceiving of life on Earth.

In summary, critical security studies contribute to the debate on the Anthropocene in two major ways. First, the Anthropocene discourse is characterised as heavily relying on the threat-response logic, which could therefore present an alternative definition and approach to engage with the Anthropocene studies. Second, the emerging Anthropocene studies need to focus more explicitly, in critical and transdisciplinary ways, on the central fears and existential threats that constantly haunt humanity.

Outlook

Here, I would like to suggest some specific future research foci that are likely to occupy scholars operating at the crossroads of security studies and the Anthropocene studies and that will have important impacts on both fields. The first focus should be on relations, structures and processes of power, injustice, violence and militarisation. Here a special critical inquiry will have to focus on the role of the sciences, the responsibility and even power that is gained via narrating possible future scenarios, and on appropriate responses, changes or measures to be taken. The second will lie on the ethical dimension and the role of cosmologies and values (e.g., Harrington and Shearing 2017). The third will need to engage with the ontological and epistemological challenges that *Anthropocene thinking* reveal in security studies and in the study of security (including within the Copenhagen School) (e.g., Harrington and Shearing 2017).

Conclusions

This chapter has analysed how security studies refer to the Anthropocene, and aimed at providing additional insights to the Anthropocene debate. A major assumption for this research was that the Anthropocene concept needs to be further developed and clearly articulated; I also assumed that security studies can help detect major constitutive and defining features of the Anthropocene discourse.

I would like to outline three major conclusions from the analysis. First, the Anthropocene discourse is already acknowledged in a very specific form within security studies and can be described by the political concept of eco-centred security. It relates strongly to the planetary boundaries (Rockström et al. 2009) and is heavily informed by the discourses of the Earth system sciences, as well as by environmental security scholars. The critical inquiries of environmental humanities remain mostly absent from the field. A debate on the Anthropocene within the security studies is currently missing. Precisely because of this fact, I present it as fundamentally important to engage in a critical assessment on how the Anthropocene is articulated. This is a crucial task, as the critical analysis presented here has shown that the securitisation of the planetary boundaries can have dangerous implications, such as falling back into *Holocene thinking* and having repercussions on questions of power politics. This is important as the actors that shape this securitisation trend (among others Earth system scientists and climate scientists) influence the discourses and descriptions of our conceptions of the world and us (within and as part of it) and inform public policies. Therefore, I argue that the different scientific communities need to develop *Anthropocene thinking* further, whereby they could importantly benefit from the lessons learnt in the environmental security literature.

Second, I conclude that critical approaches of security studies can contribute to revealing some defining additional features of the Anthropocene that are not tied to the definition of geological sciences, and that could be described as clear markers of a transdisciplinary approach inherent in the threat-response logic. Especially the severe quality of the threat dimension is a central reason for which the Anthropocene concept gains so much attention and is adopted in spite of lacking a definition. Therefore, I argue that this threat-response logic can be seen as a major pillar, which could be turned into focus areas for synthesised future research of transdisciplinary scope and present an important starting point for structuring the emerging Anthropocene studies. An important precondition to further engage with the Anthropocene is, however, that the focus needs to be directed more explicitly on the central concerns, being the fear of human extinction and the descriptions of central values, which are currently not articulated well enough by the Anthropocene studies. At the same time, the threat-response logic requires further critical inquiry as the very assumption of an existing remedy might present a central obstacle to engage in paradigmatic change of *Anthropocene thinking*.

Finally, connecting the Anthropocene to security enables a centring of the research on the condition of humankind and the central *values* and *fears* in human-nature entanglement. I therefore evaluate the Anthropocene as carrying the important potential to synthesise the issues that have constantly haunted humanity, and presenting a great chance to better understand ourselves in and as part of the world.

Acknowledgements

I would like to express my deep gratitude for the financial support of this publication from the Fondation Maison des Sciences de l'Homme (FMSH), Paris, the Wissenschaftszentrum Berlin für Sozialforschung (WZB), Berlin and particularly from the Cluster of Excellence 'Integrated Climate System Analysis and Prediction' (CliSAP) from the Hamburg University. In addition, I particularly thank the four editors of this volume for their dedication and the important recommendations and challenging criticism. I also thank Jody Westwood for his wholehearted editorial support.

Notes

1 For space reasons, I refer to environmental security and security in the following with the abbreviation of (environmental) security.
2 McDonald (2008, 568) describes several shortcomings of the Copenhagen School along a negation to a positive conception of security, the limited focus on possible emancipation and of "potentially reifying traditional security discourses and practices in the process".
3 United Nations Security Council Press Release, SC/9000 17 April 2007 "Security Council holds first-ever debate on impact of climate change on peace, security, hearing over 50 speakers. At: www.un.org/press/en/2007/sc9000.doc.htm Accessed 18 March 2018.

References

Bai, X., Van der Leuw, S., O'Brien, K., Berkhout, F., Biermann, F., Bronfizio, E.S., Cuden-
nec, C., Dearing, J., Duraiappah, A., Glaser, M., Revkin, A., Steffen, W. and Syvitski,
J. (2016) "Plausible and desirable futures in the Anthropocene: A new research agenda"
Global Environmental Change, 39, 351–362.
Barnett, J. (2007) "Environmental security" in Collins, A. ed., *Contemporary Security
Studies* Oxford University Press, Oxford, 182–203.
Baskin, J. (2014) "The ideology of the Anthropocene?" in *MSSI Research Paper 3* Mel-
bourne Sustainable Society Institute, University of Melbourne, Melbourne, 1–19.
Bennett, J. (2011) *Living in the Anthropocene: A 100 thoughts* Documenta 13 Hatje Cantz,
Ostfildern.
Brauch, H.G. (2011) "Concepts of security threats, challenges, vulnerabilities and risks" in
Brauch, H.G., Oswald Spring, Ú., Mesjasz, C., Grin, J., Kamerie-Mbote, P., Chourou,
B., Dunay, P. and Birkmann, J. eds., *Coping with Global Environmental Change in the
Anthropocene* Springer-Verlag, Berlin, Heidelberg, New York, 61–106.
Brauch, H.G., Oswald Spring, U., Grin, J. and Scheffran, J. (2016) *Handbook on Sustain-
ability Transition and Sustainable Peace* Springer International Publishing, Heidelberg.
Burguess, P.J. and Tadjbakhsh, S. (2010) "The human security tale of two Europes" *Global
Society*, 24, 447–465.
Burke, A., Fishel, S., Mitchell, A., Dalby, S. and Levine, D.J. (2016) "Planet politics: A man-
ifesto from the end of IR" *Millennium: Journal of International Studies*, 44, 499–523.
Buzan, B. and Hansen, L. (2009) *The Evolution of International Security Studies* Cam-
bridge University Press, New York.
Buzan, B., Wæver, O. and De Wilde, J. (1998) *Security: A New Framework for Analysis*
Linnie Rienner Publishers, Boulder, London.
Chandler, D., Cudworth, E. and Hobden, S. (2018) "Anthropocene, capitolocene and
liberal cosmopolitan IR: A response to Burke et al.'s 'planet politics'" *Millennium*,
46, 190–208.
Chaturvedi, S. and Doyle, T. (2016) *Climate Terror: A Critical Geopolitics of Climate
Change* Palgrave Macmillan, New York.
Chernilo, D. (2017) "The question of the human in the Anthropocene debate" *European
Journal of Social Theory*, 20, 44–60.
Cox, R. (1981) "Social forces, states and world orders: Beyond international relations
theory" *Millennium*, 10, 126–155.
Crutzen, P.J. and Stoermer, E.F. (2000) "The 'Anthropocene'" *Global Change Newsletter*,
41, 17–18.
Crutzen, P. (2011) "The Anthropocene: Geology by mankind" in Brauch, H.-J., Oswald
Spring, Ú., Mesjasz, C., Grin, J., Kameri-Mbote, P., Dunay, P., Chourou, B. and Birk-
mann, J. eds., *Coping with Global Environmental Change, Disasters, and Security-
threats, Challenges, Vulnerabilities and Risks* Springer-Verlag, Berlin, Heidelberg,
New York, 3–4.
Cudworth, E. and Hobden, S. (2011) *Posthuman International Relations: Complexity, Eco-
logism, and Global Politics* Zed Books, London.
Daase, C. (2010) "Wandel der Sicherheitskultur" *Aus Politik und Zeitgeschichte (APUZ)*,
50, 13. Dezember, 9–16.
Dalby, S. (2013) "Environmental dimensions of human security" in Floyd, R. and
Matthew, R. ed., *Environmental Security: Approaches and Issues* Routledge, New
York, Oxon, 121–138.

Dellmuth, L.M., Gustafsson, M.-T., Bremberg, N. and Mobjörk, M. (2017) "Intergovernmental organizations and climate security: Advancing the research agenda" *Wiley Interdiscip Rev Clim Chang*, 1–13, e-publication ahead of print, e496. DOI: 10.1002/wcc.496.

Deudney, D. (1991) "Environment and security: Muddled thinking" *The Bulletin of Atomic Scientists*, 47, 22–28.

Floyd, R. (2008) "The environmental security debate and its significance for climate change" *The International Spectator*, 43, 51–65.

Gleditsch, N.P. (2015) "Climate change, environmental stress, and conflict" in Chester, A.C., Osloer Hamposon, F. and Aall, P. eds., *Managing Conflict in a World Adrift* United States Institute of Peace Press, Washington, DC, 147–168.

Hajer, M.A. (1995) *The Politics of Environmental Discourse: Ecological Modernization and the Policy Process* Oxford University Press, Oxford.

Hajer, M.A., Nilsson, M., Raworth, K., Bakker, P., Berkhout, F., de Boer, Y., Rockström, J., Ludwig, K. and Kok, M. (2015) "Beyond cockpit-ism: Four insights to enhance the transformative potential of the sustainable development goals" *Sustainabilty*, 7, 1651–1660.

Hamilton, C., Bonneuil, C. and Gemenne, F. (2015) *The Anthropocene and the Global Environmental Crisis* Routledge, Oxon, New York.

Hardt, J.N. (2017) *Environmental Security in the Anthropocene: A New Framework for Analysis: Assessing Theory and Practice* Routldedge, London.

Harrington, C. and Shearing, C. (2017) *Security in the Anthropocene: Reflections on Safety and Care* Transcript Verlag, Bielefeld.

Homer-Dixon, T.F. (1994) "Environmental scarcities and violent conflict: Evidence from cases" *International Security*, 19, 5–40.

IPCC – Intergovernmental Panel on Climate Change (2014) "Climate change 2014: Impacts, adaptation, and vulnerability-IPCC WGII AR5 summary for policymakers" in Stocker, T.F., Qin, D., Plattner, G.-K., Tignor, M., Allen, S.K., Boschung, J., Nauels, A., Xia, Y., Bex, V. and Midgley, P.M. eds., *Contribution of Working Group II to the Fifth Assessment Report of the Intergovernmental Panel on Climate Change* Cambridge University Press, Cambridge, New York.

Jahn, T., Hummel, D. and Schramm, E. (2015) "Nachhaltige Wissenschaft im Anthropozän" *GAIA*, 24, 92–95.

Kay, S. (2015) *Global Security in the Twenty-First Century: The Quest for Power and the Search for Peace* 3rd ed. Rowman & Littlefield, Lanham, Boulder, New York, London.

Lövbrand, E., Beck, S., Chilvers, J., Forsyth, T., Hedrén, J., Hulme, M., Lidskog, R. and Vasileiadou, E. (2015) "Who speaks for the future of Earth? How critical social science can extend the conversation on the Anthropocene" *Global Environmental Change*, 32, 211–218.

Luke, T.W. (2017) "Reconstructing social theory and the Anthropocene" *European Journal of Social Theory*, 20, 80–94.

Matthew, R. (2014) "Integrating climate change into peacebuilding" *Climatic Change*, 123, 89–93.

McDonald, M. (2008) "Securitization and the construction of security" *European Journal of International Relations*, 14, 563–587.

Mearsheimer, J.J. (2001) *The Tragedy of Great Power Politics* W.W. Norton, New York.

Methmann, C. and Oels, A. (2015) "From 'fearing' to 'empowering' climate refuges: Governing climate-induced migration in the name of resilience" *Security Dialogue*, 46, 51–68.

Mitchell, A. (2017) "Is IR going extinct?" *European Journal of International Relations*, 23, 3–25.

Neimanis, A., Asberg, C. and Hedren, J. (2015) "Four problems, four directions for environmental humanities: Toward a critical posthumanities for the Anthropocene" *Ethics and the Environment*, 20, 67–97.

Neocleous, M. (2008) *Critique of Security* Edinburgh University Press, Edinburgh.

O'Brien, K., St. Clair, A.L. and Kristoffersen, B. (2010) *Climate Change, Ethics and Human Security* Cambridge University Press, Cambridge.

Rockström, J., Steffen, W., Noone, K., Persson, A., Chapin, F.S., Lambin, E., Lenton, T.M., Scheffer, M., Folke, M., Schellnhuber, H.-J., Nykvist, B., De Wit, C.A., Huges, T., Van Der Leuw, S., Rodhe, H., Sölin, S., Snyder, P.L., Costanza, R., Svedin, R.U., Falkmark, M., Karlberg, L., Corell, R.W., Fabry, V.J., Hansen, J., Walker, B., Liverman, D., Richardson, K., Crutzen, P. and Foley, J. (2009) "Planetary boundaries: Exploring the safe operating space for humanity" *Ecology and Society*, 14 (2), Art 32.

Rothe, D. (2016) *Securitizing Global Warming: A Climate of Complexity* Routledge, London, New York.

Schellnhuber, H.-J., Crutzen, P., Clark, W. and Hunt, J. (2004) "Earth system analysis for sustainability" *Environment*, 47, 11–24.

Steffen, W. (2011) "A truly complex and diabolical policy problem" in Dryzek, J.S., Norgaard, J.B. and Schlosberg, D. eds., *The Oxford Handbook of Climate Change and Society* Oxford University Press, Oxford, 21–37.

Steffen, W. (2016) "The planetary boundaries framework: Defining a safe operating space for humanity" in Magalhaes, P., Steffen, W., Bosselmann, K., Aragao, A. and Soromenho-Marques, V. eds., *The Safe Operating Space Treaty: A New Approach to Managing Our Use of the Earth System* Cambride Scholars Publishing, Newcastle, 23–46.

Steffen, W., Crutzen, P. and McNeill, J.R. (2007) "The Anthropocene: Are humans now overwhelming the great forces of nature?" *AMBIO*, 36, 614–621.

Steffen, W., Sanderson, A., Tyson, P., Jäger, J.J., Matson, P., Moore, B., III, Oldfield, F., Richardson, K., Schellnhuber, H.-J., Turner, H.-J., II and Wasson, H.J. (2004) *Global Change and the Earth System: A Planet under Pressure* Springer-Verlag, Berlin, Heidelberg.

Trombetta, M.J. (2014) "Linking climate-induced migration and security within the EU: Insights from the securitization debate" *Critical Studies on Security*, 2, 131–147.

UNDP – United Nations Development Program (1994) *Human Development Report* Oxford University Press, New York.

Wæver, O. (1995) "Securitization and desecuritization" in Lipschutz, R.D. ed., *On Security* Columbia University Press, New York, 46–86.

Zalasiewicz, J., Waters, C.N., Summerhayes, C.P., Wolfe, A.P., Barnosky, A.D., Cearreta, A., Crutzen, P., Ellis, E., Fairchild I.J., Galuszka, A., Haff, P., Hajdas, I., Head, M.J., Ivar do Sul, J.A., Jeandel, C., Leinfelder, R., McNeill, J.R., Neal, C., Odada, E., Oreskes, N., Steffen, W., Syvitski, J., Vidas, D. Wagreich, M. and Williams, M. (2017) "The Working Group on the Anthropocene: Summary of evidence and interim recommendations" *Anthropocene*, 19, 55–60.

7 Global climate governance as boundary object

Making the meaning of the Anthropocene

Lukas Hermwille

Introduction

The advent of the Anthropocene raises the question whether humanity is willing or able to take its fate into its own hands, not only individually but also collectively. There is no turning back, there is no way of return to the 'pure' Holocene. However, it is in the hands of humanity what to make out of the Anthropocene. The Anthropocene implies a necessity for transformative governance (Hermwille 2016a; Pattberg and Zelli 2016). In fact, the very notion of the Anthropocene suggests that we are already transforming the world at the grandest imaginable scale. Avoiding (or at least minimising) a catastrophic transformation by (natural) disaster and instead building a 'good Anthropocene' (Bennett et al. 2016) will require a fundamental transformation of global economies and societies, i.e., the transformation of a vast patchwork of socio-technical systems of various scales.

To date, large parts of the literature on (global) governance of the Anthropocene does not properly take into account the patterns and dynamics of socio-technical change at the level of sectoral systems. This chapter aims to close that gap by building a bridge between the burgeoning transition research literature – an academic field that is dedicated to the study of transitions of individual socio-technical systems (Geels and Schot 2010) – and global governance research. As such, the chapter seeks to contribute to a "deeper understanding of the interplay between networks, institutions and Earth system complexity (including human – environmental – technological interconnections)" as called for by Victor Galaz (2014, 126). It aims to explore how and what environmental governance at the global level can contribute to advance and facilitate the required transformation(s). The chapter specifically examines the field of global climate governance, as anthropogenic climate change is probably the most salient geophysical dimension in the Anthropocene debate. This is true both in terms of the public attention it receives as well as the extent and sophistication of global governance approaches responding to it.

The key insight of this chapter is that global climate governance can make a particular contribution by shaping and institutionalising the Anthropocene (and climate change in particular). I propose to view global climate governance as a 'boundary object' that can help anchor the geophysical pressures of climate change in the socio-political environment of day-to-day decision-making within socio-technical systems. "Boundary objects are a sort of arrangement that allow different groups to work together without consensus" (Star 2010, 602). They do so by being

> both plastic enough to adapt to local needs and the constraints of the several parties employing them, yet robust enough to maintain a common identity across sites. ... They have different meanings in different social worlds but their structure is common enough to more than one world to make them recognisable, a means of translation.
>
> (Star and Griesemer 1989, 393)

So what are the boundaries that need to be overcome in order to make the Anthropocene an amenable concept? And how can it be established as a salient context for day-to-day decision-making in all fields and at levels of governance? The Anthropocene connects a wide range of geophysical changes, which have mostly been treated as isolated environmental problems, and combines them into one transformative challenge. Global governance can help to frame and institutionalise this problem statement as a new paradigm. Global governance can further help decision makers to build their expectations by formulating goals and indicating corresponding pathways/trajectories. The *United Nations Framework Convention on Climate Change* (UNFCCC) and its 2015 Paris Agreement are prime examples of this phenomenon. Finally, global governance can provide a forum to reflect changes in values and interests that may occur as the transformation of societies and economies unfolds.

To unfold this argument, this chapter integrates theoretical perspectives of transition research, in particular the multi-level perspective (MLP) (Geels and Schot 2010), with theories of International Relations (IR). The transformative ambition of global governance in the Anthropocene essentially requires a purposeful and simultaneous transition of a vast patchwork of interdependent socio-technical systems that collectively constitute our economies and societies; governing these transformations may require tools and institutions, and face distinct barriers and limitations that are different from those for governing more confined environmental problems. Traditional governance approaches that focussed on conservation and/or restoration of environmental systems may come to their limits (Dryzek 2016). Understanding the patterns and dynamics of socio-technical transitions at the national and/or sectoral level will hopefully inspire innovative thinking on how to foster and guide these transitions through forms of inter- and transnational governance.

This chapter first reviews key publications from transition research and pays special attention to the politics of and governance approaches for socio-technical transitions. It then integrates global climate governance architecture in the MLP and develops the concept of global climate governance as a boundary object. Subsequently, the chapter discusses the compatibility of the MLP and the concept of global climate governance as a boundary object with various theoretical advances in IR including rationalist approaches that focus on the 'collective action' problematic of climate change (Snidal 2013), liberal IR theory (Moravcsik 1997; Biermann 2014), and constructivist approaches (Wendt 1987; Arts 2000; Miskimmon et al. 2013; Hermwille et al. 2017). Building on these theoretical advances, I suggest that a key function of the global climate governance architecture is to discursively perpetuate the physical challenges of climate change across socio-technical systems. This should contribute to an erosion of the social license of unsustainable technologies and practices. A practical implication is that inter- and transnational climate governance should begin to explicitly address the destabilisation, demise and ultimate discontinuation of incumbent regimes and the systemic change resistance that can be expected from this.

Insights of socio-technical systems analysis

This section provides an introduction to the multi-level perspective (MLP) framework for socio-technical analysis (Geels and Schot 2010) discusses the relationship between transition research and IR, and briefly reviews key publications in the transition research literature with a view to identifying patterns of socio-technical change and the role of politics and governance in socio-technical transformation processes.

Key concepts: landscape, regime, niche

One of the key tools of transition research is the multi-level perspective (MLP) framework for socio-technical analysis. The MLP separates three levels of analysis: regime, niche and landscape. These levels do not refer to specific spatial or organisational locations, but rather to a more theoretical idea of virtual levels characterised by different degrees of structuration. The landscape embodies the highest degree of, or 'deepest' structuration. It cannot be influenced directly by individuals or groups of actors. The 'regime' level embodies structures that co-determine the stability and path dependency of socio-technical systems, and can explain their basic functional logic. Socio-technical 'niches' allow for the emergence of new technologies and practices precisely because many dominant logics that structure the regime level do not apply (Hermwille et al. 2016; Geels and Kemp 2012).

The socio-technical regime is the central unit of analysis. Note that transition researchers have defined the socio-technical regime as "the rule-set or grammar embedded in a complex of engineering practices, production process technologies, product characteristics, skills and procedures, ways of handling relevant artefacts and persons, ways of defining problems; all of them embedded in institutions and infrastructure" (Rip and Kemp 1998, 338). In contrast, the regime term in transition research is not directly compatible with the classic definition of 'international regimes' formulated by Stephen Krasner: "Regimes can be defined as sets of implicit or explicit principles, norms, rules and decision-making procedures around which actors' expectations converge in a given area of international relations" (Krasner 1982, 186). More recently, the concept has been widened to extend beyond intergovernmental arrangements. Consequently, it is now widely

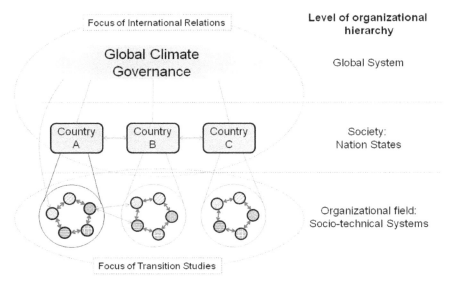

Figure 7.1 Schematic illustration of embedded systems, different levels of organisational hierarchy and complementary perspectives of transition research and IR

Notes: The small circles at the lower section of the figure represent individual (sectoral) socio-technical systems. These systems interact with various other socio-technical systems within one country, but also across borders. Please note that global climate governance is, of course, not a monolithic block but a complex patchwork of inter- and transnational institutions and organisations.

recognised that the global (climate) governance landscape is more adequately described as a 'regime complex' rather than a monolithic (climate) regime (e.g., Keohane and Victor 2011; Orsini et al. 2013; Abbott 2012).

The two regime concepts in transition research and IR are similar to the extent that they focus on institutions in terms of the 'rules of the game' (cf. North 1990), but the socio-technical regime also comprises material components in the form of technological artefacts and infrastructures. Even more important is the fact that the two regime concepts focus on very different levels of organisational hierarchy and hence presuppose different types of actors (see Figure 7.1). IR is typically interested in the highest levels of organisational hierarchy, the global system and the system level of societies (see also Müller, in this volume). Agency is usually assumed to lie with national governments, international organisations and to some extent with transnational corporations and civil society groups (Fearon and Wendt 2002).

In some cases, political actors are considered at the national level (Putnam 1988; Moravcsik 1997). Only recently have IR scholars developed a more pronounced interest in transnational governance, i.e., forms of governance that extent beyond national governance and include, for example, private actors (companies or civil society organisations) and/or (networks of) subnational authorities (e.g., Bulkeley et al. 2014; Hickmann 2016; Hickmann 2017; Roger and Dauvergne 2016; Bäckstrand et al. 2017). In Figure 7.1, this transnational relationship is depicted as the arrow pointing from the global climate governance level directly to the specific socio-technical systems level, bypassing the level of nation-states.

In comparison, transition studies focus on the level of the organisational field. The relevant unit of analysis usually is an individual sectoral system mostly at national or subnational level.[1] The relevant actors include "those organizations that, in the aggregate, constitute a recognized area of institutional life: key suppliers [i.e., firms], resource and product consumers, regulatory agencies, and other organizations that produce similar services or products" (DiMaggio and Powell 1983, 148) for a given socio-technical system (see also Geels and Schot 2010; Hoffman 2001). Well established organisational fields often display a high degree of homogeneity among actors which, in turn, suggests a certain degree of resistance and/or resilience to change in the respective field (DiMaggio and Powell 1983).

While a socio-technical regime comprises the core system that is supposed to be transformed, the other two levels – socio-technical niche and socio-technical landscape – are the co-determinants of transformation. Niches "are spaces where networks of actors experiment with, and mutually adapt, greener organizational forms and eco-friendly technologies" (Smith 2007, 427). In these niches, outside or at the fringe of the socio-technical regime, novelties and innovations can emerge and mature under protected conditions (Smith and Raven 2012). The socio-technical landscape level "forms a broad exogenous environment that as such is beyond the direct influence of regime and niche actors" (Geels and Schot 2010, 23). In other words, the landscape is a container for all kinds of external drivers, structures and global trends that cannot be controlled by even the most powerful actors within the regime. Depending on the respective socio-technical system being studied and its relative importance, most developments at international level and to some extent even at national level could be considered as exogenous developments from a transition researcher's perspective and hence fall into the landscape category.

A necessary condition for a successful socio-technical transformation in a given field is the existence of both successful innovation activities in niches and external pressure on the socio-technical regime coming from the landscape level:

> In a nutshell, the core logic is that niche-innovations build up internal momentum (through learning processes, price/performance improvements, and support from powerful groups); changes at the landscape level create pressures on the regime; and destabilization of the regime creates windows of opportunity for the diffusion of niche-innovations.
>
> (Geels 2014, 23)

Patterns and dynamics: transition phases

Socio-technical transitions typically do not follow a linear development path. Instead, successful transitions typically experience four transition phases: In the first *predevelopment* phase, the status quo of the socio-technical regime still seems to be relatively stable. Subtle changes occur in niches only. When these changes become noticeable and are recognised as potentially significant, the next phase, *take off*, is approaching. The transformation experiences a "*breakthrough* [original emphasis] phase where visible structural changes take place through an accumulation of socio-cultural, economic, ecological and institutional changes that react to each other" (Rotmans et al. 2001, 17). Finally, the speed of change begins to slow down as the new socio-technical regime *stabilises*.

The way in which socio-technical transitions unfold is co-determined by the way in which developments at the niche, regime and landscape levels interact. Different transformation-pathways may emerge depending on the maturity of niche innovations and their disruptive potential, and in relation to that the timing and intensity (e.g., shock vs. slow onset stresses) of external pressure from the landscape level (Geels and Schot 2007; Geels et al. 2016). The different pathways range from a complete substitution of incumbent actors (think of the Kodak Company that used to dominate consumer photography but was almost completely replaced by a host of other companies, including many new entrants as digital imaging became the new standard) to a much more subtle reconfiguration in which incumbent actors built alliance and/or usurp innovative new entrants (Geels et al. 2016, 900).

Moreover, socio-technical transitions do not come about over night. Although rapid changes may be observable during the breakthrough phase, particularly the early phases of a transition may take years, even decades, and changes may be barely noticeable for contemporary observers during this period (Geels and Schot 2010). The German 'Energiewende', for example, sped up considerably after the final decision was made to phase out nuclear power after the nuclear catastrophe in Fukushima. Yet, the term 'Energiewende' itself was coined by a group of authors from the Öko-Institut as early as 1980 (Krause et al. 1980), the first wind park was commissioned in 1987 and the first feed-in tariff was introduced in 1991 (Carbon Brief 2016). A plethora of empirical case studies suggest that, much like the German 'Energiewende', most historic cases of socio-technical transitions took between 30 and 50 years to complete (Markard et al. 2012).

However, this view has recently been challenged by Benjamin Sovacool (2016), who presents 10 case studies of energy-related socio-technical transitions that took only between 1 and 16 years to complete (see also Sovacool and Geels 2016). This suggests that there may be room to accelerate transitions by means of effective governance. Commenting on the work of Sovacool, Kern and Rogge posit: "One key difference between historic energy transitions and the ongoing low carbon transition is that historic transitions have not been planned or governed but were emergent processes" (Kern and Rogge 2016, 14).

Politics and approaches to governance

Early work in the transition research literature has been criticised for a lack of attention to politics in socio-technical transitions (for a brief review of these criticisms see Avelino and Grin 2016). Critics highlighted that the lack of attention is in sharp contrast to any attempts to manage or govern imminent transitions: "The very idea of deliberate transition management supposes some kind of orienting vision" (Shove and Walker 2007, 765). But how is the vision generated and by whom? These questions are inherently political (see Stirling 2014). Critics proposed that transition studies should acknowledge the political nature of transitions (Meadowcroft 2011; Patterson et al. 2017; Scoones et al. 2015), the inherent uncertainty and the fact that the governors of transitions are always part of the systems to be governed and "being part of a system necessarily limits actors' capacities to conceive and understand the dynamics of the whole" (Shove and Walker 2007, 765; see also Avelino and Grin 2016). Meadowcroft highlights that "politics plays a potentially powerful role (defining the landscape, propping up or destabilising regimes, protecting or exposing niches)" (Meadowcroft 2011, 73).

Moreover, socio-technical transitions are also inherently political as they typically entail a refinement or redefinition of societal preferences and interests (Göpel 2016; Meadowcroft 2011) or in the words of Avelino and Grin:

> it is futile to aim to steer a system to a particular equilibrium state, chosen from a range of possible 'attractors' identified on basis of an analysis of the system 'as is'. Rather, novel attractors are to be *(re)constructed (!)* in multi-actor, deliberative practices, so as then, on their turn, provide orientation to further collective action.
>
> (Avelino and Grin 2016, 21,
> emphasis in original)

Creating universally accepted targets/goals is an integral part of transformative governance as these help to align expectations and hence can alter the short-term preferences and ultimately longer-term interests of the affected actors (see also Bornemann, in this volume). These will require constant reflections and updating as the governing values, expectations and interests will necessarily evolve in the course of the ongoing transformation. To this end, coordination of various forms and levels of governance and decision-making is required (Scoones et al. 2015).

The lack of attention of early contributions to the transition research literature may derive from the fact that particularly the more historically oriented studies in the field typically focus on *successful* transitions. This perspective may cause bias in that it excludes cases where, despite emerging innovations, no transition took place due to systemic and political resistance in early transition phases (cf. Shove and Walker 2007). Another reason may be that many applications of the MLP framework focus on innovations and view the incumbent regime only as a background (Geels 2014). As a result, the destabilisation and demise of incumbent (unsustainable) regimes as the consequence of successful transition, let alone the purposeful discontinuation or exnovation of socio-technical systems, remains understudied. Only recently this has started to change (Heyen et al. 2017; David 2017; Stegmaier et al. 2014; Turnheim and Geels 2013; Heyen 2017).

Geels (2014) proposes to explicitly include politics into the MLP framework by conceptualising "relations between policymakers and incumbent firms as a core regime level alliance, which often resists fundamental change" (Geels 2014, 27). Note that this resistance, i.e., power and counter-power, is active and not merely a passive form of inertia, lock-in or path dependency. In order to study the destabilisation of the socio-technical regime, Turnheim and Geels (2013) suggest considering three interactive processes: accumulation of external pressures, strategic responses of incumbent regime actors with respect to the economic and socio-political pressures, and ultimately a weakening of commitment to the institutions of the socio-technical regime on the part of the very regime actors.

However, this framework should not be considered as a general theory, since "destabilisation is a multi-faceted process, it may follow different patterns, depending on interactions between external pressures (speed, size, directionality, spillovers), response strategies (beliefs, resource allocation decisions) and degrees of commitment" (Turnheim and Geels 2013, 1766). Kivimaa and Kern (2016) take this further by discussing how such rigid structures can be mobilised by effective policy intervention. They develop an analytical framework for policy mixes with the aim of achieving sustainability transitions. They argue that the right policy interventions can "shak[e] the regime" (Kivimaa and Kern 2016, 207) so that room becomes available for innovative practices and potentially even incumbent actors become active promoters of the transformation instead of resisting it. The right policy mix, in their view, entails not only policies that promote sustainable innovation but includes both dimensions of the Schumpeterian axiom: 'creation' and 'destruction' (Kivimaa and Kern 2016; Schumpeter 2003).

A stronger focus on destabilisation of socio-technical regimes may be particularly warranted in more advanced transition phases. Mersmann and Wehnert assign Mahatma Ghandi's famous bon mot to the four transition phases introduced above: "First they ignore you [pre-development], then they laugh at you [take-off], then they fight you [breakthrough], then you win [stabilisation]" (Mersmann and Wehnert 2014, 34). They further suggest that different types of intervention may be necessary for the various transition phases. The focus on destabilisation and mechanisms of resistance of the socio-technical regime may be particularly fruitful when a transition approaches a breakthrough and niche innovations for the first time start to challenge the core of what Unruh (2000) has termed the 'techno-institutional complex'. In other words: when the 'fighting' begins. With these perspectives in mind, we can now turn back to the highest level of organisational hierarchy – the world system – and ask how inter- and transnational governance relate to change of specific socio-technical systems and what it can contribute to foster and guide socio-technical transitions.

Where to place global climate governance in the multi-level perspective?

Meadowcroft (2011) argues that politics play a part on all levels of the MLP. When global politics, and in particular global climate governance, is supposed to live up to its transformative ambition (Pattberg and Zelli 2016), it must not focus on managing individual transitions but foster and guide a great transformation (at the level of organisational hierarchy of societies and world systems) as the co-evolution of a patchwork of interrelated socio-technical systems (at the organisational field level). Therefore, conceptually, inter- and transnational governance initiatives should be located at the level of the socio-technical landscape (see Newell and Bulkeley 2017).

However, I do not argue that such governance initiatives are entirely beyond the sphere of influence of particularly the more powerful incumbent actors of the socio-technical regime. While even multinational corporations may have relatively limited direct influence on the UNFCCC there are other cases where there is much more direct influence. This is, for example, true for the United Nations International Civil Aviation Organisation (ICAO), on which industry representatives have traditionally had a very strong influence. It is even more true for transnational governance initiatives in which private corporations are the prime actors.

I therefore suggest to conceptualise global governance initiatives not as elements of the socio-technical landscape per se, but as boundary objects. As such, they translate physical and socio-political developments into terms that are recognisable at the level of socio-technical systems (see Figure 7.2). Global governance initiatives do not determine the socio-technical landscape but they define it in the sense that they cast it into political goals, targets and in some instances policies that immediately resonate with the institutions and practices

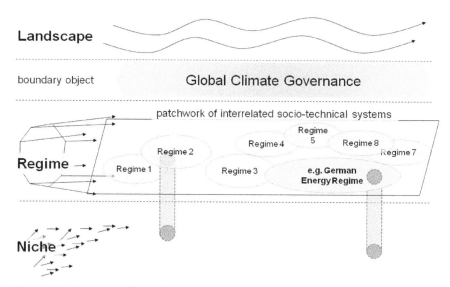

Figure 7.2 Schematic illustration of inter- and transnational governance initiatives in relation to the multi-level perspective

Source: Own illustration based on Geels (2010) and Rotmans et al. (2001).

of socio-technical regimes. The governance initiatives differ in the degree of ambiguity they leave and with respect to the specificity for certain types of socio-technical systems. After having adopted this perspective, the next question is which IR theories are compatible with this view and what we can learn from it to underpin this theoretical conceptualisation.

Compatible perspectives? Theories of IR and the MLP

This sections briefly discusses three major IR theories in view of their compatibility with the ontological and epistemological foundations of transition research: rationalist IR theory (Snidal 2013), liberal IR theory (Moravcsik 1997; Biermann 2014), and most extensively constructivist approaches (Adler 2013; Fearon and Wendt 2002; Hasenclever et al. 2000; Arts 2000; Miskimmon et al. 2013; Wendt 1987; Hermwille et al. 2017). The subsequent section discusses practical implications for governance in the Anthropocene in view of the more applied and/or policy-oriented literature which implicitly rest on the theoretical foundations of liberal IR theory (Biermann et al. 2015; Biermann et al. 2012; Pattberg and Zelli 2016; Galaz 2014) or constructivism (Dryzek 2016; Göpel 2016; Milkoreit 2017; Hermwille et al. 2016).

There seems to be much mutual interest between transition research and IR. Frank Biermann, Chairman of the Earth System Governance Project, was keynote speaker at the2015 International Sustainability Transitions conference in Brighton. And by the same token Frank Geels, one of the leading transition scholars, held a keynote speech at the 2016 Berlin Conference on Global Environmental Change that was held under the topic of Transformative Global Climate Governance 'après Paris'. Yet, there is relatively little work that crosses the disciplinary borders and brings the two fields into conversation with each other. Arguably, this is not only because the two fields have very different perspectives (with little overlap) as illustrated in Figure 7.1, but also because not all of the two fields' ontological and epistemological foundations are easily compatible with each other.

For example, rationalist approaches in IR that conceptualise climate change as a collective action problem and often apply game-theoretic models to analyse climate governance are of limited value, at least to the extent that they presuppose fixed interests/preferences on the part of the actors analysed (e.g., Snidal 2013). As Meadowcroft noted: "The politics of sustainability transitions requires a redefinition of societal *interests*" (Meadowcroft 2011, 73, italics in the original). Furthermore, transition research demonstrates that there is never one set of interests amongst actors but a continuous struggle of competing interests and actors may change their perspectives and interests over time due to successful 'transition governance' (Avelino and Grin 2016). Theories that conceptualise "states, treated as unitary utility maximizers, engag[ing] in interactive decision making in which there are also incentives for individual participants to defect" (Young 1997, 190) are therefore not compatible with the logic of developing or reconfiguring interests in the course of socio-technical transitions.

Liberal IR theory may be more appropriate as a complement to transition theory as it posits that "the fundamental actors in international politics are individuals and private groups" (Moravcsik 1997, 516). The state is a 'representative institution' and state preferences are the result of competing identities, interests and powers of individuals and groups, only a subset of which can be advanced in the international realm (Moravcsik 1997, 518). In other words, state preferences are co-determined by the relative salience and dominance of the interests of particular groups within a given country. That does not, however, explain how these individual or collective interests are shaped in the first place. Nor can it explain any influence that international governance may have on the development of expectations and interests.

Biermann (2014) similarly recognises the diversity of actors relevant for global governance beyond nation-states. He even contends that international bureaucracies such as the UNFCCC Secretariat can have an impact "by helping countries to implement international agreements, which reshapes national interests" (Biermann 2014, 66). Yet, he primarily sees this influence by way of capacity building and does not explicitly address their role in making and institutionalising collective meaning.

In this regard, constructivist approaches may be the most promising to explore. They have served well to understand how preferences and beliefs change and how such preferences and beliefs structure the behaviour of different types of actors change – nation-states as well as unsustainable business corporations (Adler 2013; Fearon and Wendt 2002). Constructivist approaches are also promising because of their sociological foundations (Adler 2013) which may resonate well with the ontological foundations of transition research. In the remainder of this section, I will discuss two approaches that seem to fit particularly well with the theoretical foundations of transition research outlined above.

The first approach discussed here is by Miskimmon et al. and focuses on 'strategic narratives' as core analytical entity and has been described as 'agential constructivism' (Miskimmon et al. 2013, 108). The approach centres on the concept of strategic narratives as "frameworks that allow humans to link apparently unconnected phenomena around some causal transformation. The endpoint of this transformation bestows meaning upon all parts of the whole as a sequence of human actions is given connection and an overall sense" (Miskimmon et al. 2013, 5).

Miskimmon et al. pursue strategic narratives as the political means by which collective meaning is produced. The long-term effect of successful strategic narratives is that "getting others at home and abroad to buy in to your strategic narrative can shape their interests, their identity, and their understanding of how international relations works and where it is heading" (Miskimmon et al. 2013, 2). In the context of the Anthropocene, this means that establishing a shared meaning of the Anthropocene, embedding it in political narratives will allow political actors across all levels of decision-making to (re)formulate their interests and preferences in order to take the geophysical implications seriously which otherwise would be intangible under most circumstance.

The strategic narrative approach also highlights the temporal dimension: "Leaders cannot create a narrative out of nothing, off the cuff. The parameters of a state's strategic narratives are bounded by prevailing domestic and international understandings and expectations of that state, readings of its history, and evaluations of its reputation" (Miskimmon et al. 2013, 8). What follows from this is that any newly constructed narratives are bound to past interpretations of collective meaning, even if power structures and/or dominant actors change over time (see Marquardt, in this volume). In order to contest dominant narratives it is therefore necessary not only to silence rival narratives but to deconstruct "the conditions that make alternative narratives plausible, communicable and intelligible" (Miskimmon et al. 2013, 104).

The second approach that helps relating international governance to socio-technical transitions can in fact be considered as a more general version of the strategic narrative approach described above. Miskimmon et al. do not refer to it explicitly but their conceptualisation of narratives as "vehicle[s] for change as well as the vessel[s]" (Miskimmon et al. 2013, 72) of collective meaning almost perfectly aligns with one of three dimensions of structure introduced by Giddens' (1984) structuration theory: the structure of signification.

A structurationist approach to International Relations was first advanced by Wendt (1987). Structuration theory, much like the strategic narrative approach, argues for a duality of agency and structure, "agents and structures are not kept apart but ... are mutually constitutive of each other" (Stones 2005, 21). Individual behaviour is co-determined by the structures in which all agents operate and in turn actions change or reproduce structures. These structures are defined as rules and resources: rules are the cognitive, interpretive frames and cultural norms within which actors operate and resources are economic resources as well as authoritative and allocative power (Stones 2005). In order to analyse the prevailing structures in more detail, Giddens develops a more fine-grained terminology that differentiates resources and rules: Resources stand for *domination* (control/power) and rules represent *legitimation* (norms) and *signification* (meaning) (Giddens 1984). In acting, the given agent reproduces these structures of *domination, legitimation* and *signification* and hence closes the cycle of structuration.

Building on these sociological foundations, Bas Arts (2000) developed a structurational regime model that allows analysis of international regimes in ways that offer "a plural view on international regime formation and implementation ... without ... neglecting structure, domination, stability and change in international politics" (Arts 2000, 537). Hermwille et al. (2017) apply this framework to the UNFCCC, discussing, on a generic level, the limitations of international governance, and develop recommendations for effective climate governance under the UNFCCC. In essence, they find that the UNFCCC would have the biggest leverage if it were to focus more actively on providing signification and legitimation. In other words, its ability to establish and institutionalise a new discourses (Hajer and Wagenaar 2003; Dryzek 2013; Dryzek 2016).

Like the strategic narrative approach, the structurationist approach provides a nuanced conceptualisation of temporality. It theorises structure and agency as mutually constitutive in an iterative, morphogenetic structuration cycle (Okereke et al. 2009; Sewell 2005). This focus on temporality aligns well with the temporal conceptualisations, including the concepts of transition phases as well as the idea of co-evolution that are at the core of the theoretical foundations of transition theory (Grin et al. 2010). The two approaches also lend themselves to integration with the theoretical framework of transition research because, alongside evolutionary economics, structurational interpretivism is one of two key ontological foundations of the MLP (Geels 2010). Particularly the focus on narratives as vehicles for signification (and indirectly legitimation) has been productively applied in the context of socio-technical transitions (Bosman et al. 2014; Gruszka 2016; Hermwille 2016b; Leach et al. 2010; Leipprand et al. 2017; Luederitz et al. 2016).

Implications for governance in the Anthropocene

Pattberg and Zelli suggest that the Anthropocene "is a substantial challenge but also an opportunity ... for environmental governance research in particular to reorient itself in light of fundamental transformations" (Pattberg and Zelli 2016, 1–2). Yet, the rich literature on socio-technical transitions makes one thing clear: socio-technical systems are themselves complex adaptive systems that cannot be governed by a mode of steering or control (see Hickmann et al., Conclusions, in this volume). They feature their own path dependencies and change is often even actively resisted by powerful incumbent actors within the core of the socio-technical regime. Thus, the actual potential for global climate governance to spur the required transformations may be rather limited.

Yet transition research also shows that governance interventions can have an effect. In order for fundamental socio-technical transformations to succeed it is not sufficient to develop and mature technological alternatives, but it is also required that the incumbent socio-technical systems are challenged by external forces. This is where global climate governance can make a contribution. The consequences of action or inaction in the face of the Anthropocene do not necessarily resonate within the socio-technical systems. It is a legacy of the Holocene that ecological concerns are typically marginalised in the daily business of decision makers in (unsustainable) socio-technical systems. The Anthropocene and its socio-ecological consequences need to be translated and institutionalised in order to shift this cognitive bias (Göpel 2016; Milkoreit 2017). As a boundary object, global climate governance can make an important contribution to establishing and institutionalising the Anthropocene as a salient discourse (also see Dryzek 2016).

The UNFCCC and the 2015 Paris Agreement establish a transformative paradigm, at least on a very general level (Hermwille 2016a). Instrumental for this are the agreement's long-term goals expressed in Article 2 (UNFCCC 2016):

i   To limit global warming 'well below 2°C' and make efforts towards limiting it to 1.5°C;

ii   To promote climate resilient and low greenhouse gas emissions development; and

iii   To make global financial flows consistent with the former two objectives.

Particularly the first objective was further operationalised in Article 4.1 which calls for a net balance of anthropogenic emissions and reductions by sink (climate neutrality) in the second half of the century (UNFCCC 2016, Art. 4.1). Just how transformative these goals are is aptly summarised by Kuramochi et al. (2018). Focussing on the technological implications they determine ten short-term benchmarks for a 1.5°C consistent trajectory. These include that current annual growth rates of 25–30 percent for renewables and other zero and low-carbon electricity generation needs to be sustained until 2025 and a share of 100 percent must be attained by 2050, no new coal power plants can be built and emissions from existing fleet of coal plants must be reduced by 30 percent by 2025, and the production of fossil fuelled cars must cease no later than 2035–2050. Despite this, various scholars question whether or not the Paris Agreement long-term temperature goal is actually adequate (see for example Knutti et al. 2016; Schellnhuber et al. 2016; Geden 2016) or whether a single numerical target is overly simplistic or not, and may instead distract and mask uncertainty and complexity (Galaz 2014).

However, there is some anecdotal evidence that the Paris Agreement did have an immediate effect. The immediate reaction of Brian Ricketts, Secretary-General of the European Association for Coal and Lignite (Euracoal) is a 'smoking gun' example. In a letter sent to the members of his association, Brian Rickets stated that "fossil fuels are portrayed by the UN [United Nations] as public enemy number one" and added that the sector "will be hated and vilified, in the same way that slave traders were once hated and vilified" (cited by Euractiv 2015). Similarly, the Chief Executive Officer of Royal Dutch Shell, Ben van Beurden, commented: "I do think trust has been eroded to the point that it is becoming a serious issue for our long term future. If we are not careful, broader public support for the sector will wane" (cited by Reuters 2017).

Of course, the narratives perpetuated by the Paris Agreement do not resonate as strongly in all sectors and socio-technical systems as they do in the fossil fuel industry. That is why further operationalisation of the long-term goals of the Paris Agreement and the associated governance challenges for the respective socio-technical systems are required. This is where transnational initiatives and other issue-specific international organisations and regimes can and must play a role. Coordination or 'orchestration' among them could be greatly beneficial (Biermann et al. 2012; Hale and Roger 2014; Abbott et al. 2015).

Reflecting the idea of global climate governance as a boundary object, one could argue that the Paris Agreement has effectively made the first step in translating the landscape pressure of a changing climate into the language of socio-technical regimes, but it has only translated the very headlines. A much more nuanced transcription or rather 'contextualization' (Biermann et al. 2015) that is specific to sectors and individual socio-technical systems may help foster the required transitions (Oberthür et al. 2017; Oberthür, Hermwille, Khandekar, Obergassel, et al. 2017).

Dryzek highlights "ecosystemic reflexivity as the first virtue for political institutions in the Anthropocene" (Dryzek 2016, 953). This pretension is in line with key insights from transition research: socio-technical transformations necessarily imply changing values, interests and expectations, both with respect to the social dimensions as well as to the ecological dimensions as a corollary of improved natural science research about the feedbacks and potential tipping points within the geophysical systems (Meadowcroft 2011; Galaz 2014; Avelino and Grin 2016; Göpel 2016). For global climate governance this means being reflexive about socio-economical and socio-ecological implications of the transformation visions as well as connecting and ensuring consistency of transformation visions within the patchwork of interdependent socio-technical systems.

Reflexivity will be extremely important also, when socio-technical transformations, particularly in highly carbon intensive industries, approach the later stages of the transformation process. Although the issue of regime destabilisation and discontinuation of socio-technical regimes has only recently been studied (Turnheim and Geels 2013; Stegmaier et al. 2014; Heyen et al. 2017), this emerging area of research suggests that a focus on regime resistance and contestation in the later transition phases is particularly promising. This issue has been understudied in not only transition research but also in International Relations (a relatively rare exemption is for example Piggot et al. 2017).

Conclusions

> Our failure to grasp the complexity of the Earth system, and the tight interconnectedness of global environmental and technological change, is not only of academic interest. It also leads us to continuously restore a sociopolitical infrastructure – including institutions, organizations, and governance processes – inapt to the challenges posed by the Anthropocene.
>
> (Galaz 2014, 121–122)

This chapter has argued that bringing transition research and global (climate) governance research into conversation with each other can help to remedy the gap to which Galaz attests, above. Transition research can help to shed light on the *interconnectedness of global environmental and technological change* which, in turn, can help to improve governance institutions across multiple levels but particularly on the global governance level (international as well as transnational). Transition research does suggest that the type of deep and fundamental socio-technical transformations required for a 'good Anthropocene' (Bennett et al. 2016) can be governed, although not in terms of a steering or controlling mode of governance. Socio-technical transformations seem to follow a rather general pattern. Paraphrased from Geels (2014), two necessary conditions need to come together: (1) (sustainable) niche innovation must be sufficiently developed to challenge unsustainable regime practices and (2) forces from the socio-political and socio-economic landscape must exert pressure on and consequently destabilise the incumbent socio-technical system.

Under these conditions, niche innovations can break through and either replace or fundamentally reconfigure the incumbent regime. This chapter has proposed to view inter- and transnational governance initiatives as boundary objects. As such they help to institutionalise the landscape pressures of geobiophysical changes of the Anthropocene so that they become tangible across socio-technical regimes. In that sense, the argument complements the many calls for transformative and or disruptive innovation – the first necessary condition for transformative change – with a focus on global governance as a means to support the second necessary condition by translating and amplifying geophysical changes so that it can resonate within the very socio-technical systems that must be transformed.

Following this train of thought, global governance in the Anthropocene would have the biggest impact if it focused on its ability to provide signification and legitimation, i.e., when it focuses on its discursive power. It could make a particular contribution by seeking to formulate, to hone and to institutionalise ever more specific transformative visions that are context-specific in social, spatial and sectoral terms. That is why I consider this view especially fruitful for research perspectives in which the reconfiguration of societal expectations and interests is of particular interest. In particular, I surmise that the conceptual perspective advanced in this chapter will become ever more relevant as we draw closer to, and in some regions even surpass, the breakthrough phase of (energy) transitions.

A number of interesting research questions are likely to emerge from this perspective. What are the international spill-over effects of accelerating domestic transitions and the related governance interventions? How can the grand global transformation challenge be broken down into sectorial or socio-technical system-specific governance challenges? And how can global governance (inter- and transnational) help to escape systemic change resistance, coordinate decarbonisation efforts and mitigate socio-economic impacts in view of the structural changes that deep decarbonisation entails?

Note

1 One exemption to this is the seminal paper by Frank Geels that first introduced the MLP in order to discuss the transition from sail to steam ships in international shipping (Geels 2002).

References

Abbott, K.W. (2012) "The transnational regime complex for climate change" *Environment and Planning C: Government and Policy*, 30(4), 571–590.
Abbott, K.W., et al. (2015) *International Organizations as Orchestrators*, Cambridge University Press, Cambridge, New York.
Adler, E. (2013) "Constructivism in international relations: Sources, contributions, and debates" in *Handbook of International Relations* Sage Publications, London, 112–144.

Arts, B. (2000) "Regimes, non-state actors and the state system: A 'structurational' regime model" *European Journal of International Relations*, 6(4), 513–542.

Avelino, F. and Grin, J. (2016) "Beyond deconstruction: A reconstructive perspective on sustainability transition governance" *Environmental Innovation and Societal Transitions*, 22, 15–25.

Bäckstrand, K., et al. (2017) "Non-state actors in global climate governance: From Copenhagen to Paris and beyond" *Environmental Politics*, 26(4), 561–579.

Bennett, E.M., et al. (2016) "Bright spots: Seeds of a good Anthropocene" *Frontiers in Ecology and the Environment*, 14(8), 441–448.

Biermann, F. (2014) *Earth System Governance: World Politics in the Anthropocene*, MIT Press, Cambridge, MA.

Biermann, F., et al. (2012) "Transforming governance and institutions for global sustainability: Key insights from the Earth System Governance Project" *Current Opinion in Environmental Sustainability*, 4(1), 51–60.

Biermann, F., et al. (2015) "Down to Earth: Contextualizing the Anthropocene" *Global Environmental Change*, 341–350.

Bosman, R., et al. (2014) "Discursive regime dynamics in the Dutch energy transition" *Environmental Innovation and Societal Transitions*, 13, 45–59.

Bulkeley, H., et al. (2014) *Transnational Climate Change Governance*, Cambridge University Press, Cambridge.

Carbon Brief (2016) "Timeline: The past, present and future of Germany's Energiewende" *Carbon Brief* (www.carbonbrief.org/timeline-past-present-future-germany-energie wende) Accessed 12 February 2018.

David, M. (2017) "Moving beyond the heuristic of creative destruction: Targeting exnovation with policy mixes for energy transitions" *Energy Research & Social Science*, 33, 138–146.

DiMaggio, P.J. and Powell, W.W. (1983) "The Iron cage revisited: Institutional isomorphism and collective rationality in organizational fields" *American Sociological Review*, 48(2), 147–160.

Dryzek, J.S. (2013) *The Politics of the Earth: Environmental Discourses*, 3rd ed., Oxford University Press, Oxford.

Dryzek, J.S. (2016) "Institutions for the Anthropocene: Governance in a changing Earth system" *British Journal of Political Science*, 46(4), 937–956.

Euractiv (2015) "Coal lobby chief: COP21 means 'we will be hated like slave traders'" *EURACTIV.com* (www.euractiv.com/section/energy/news/coal-lobby-chief-cop21-means-we-will-be-hated-like-slave-traders/) Accessed 20 March 2017.

Fearon, J. and Wendt, A. (2002) "Rationalism v. constructivism: A skeptical view" in *Handbook of International Relations* Sage Publications, London, 52–72.

Galaz, V. (2014) *Global Environmental Governance, Technology and Politics: The Anthropocene Gap*, Edward Elgar Publishing, Cheltenham.

Geden, O. (2016) "The Paris agreement and the inherent inconsistency of climate policymaking" *Wiley Interdisciplinary Reviews: Climate Change*, 7(6), 790–797.

Geels, F.W. (2002) "Technological transitions as evolutionary reconfiguration processes: A multi-level perspective and a case-study" *Research Policy*, 31(8–9), 1257–1274.

Geels, F.W. (2010) "Ontologies, socio-technical transitions (to sustainability), and the multi-level perspective" *Research Policy*, 39(4), 495–510.

Geels, F.W. (2014) "Regime resistance against low-carbon transitions: Introducing politics and power into the multi-level perspective" *Theory, Culture & Society*, 31(5), 21–40.

Geels, F.W., et al. (2016) "The enactment of socio-technical transition pathways: A reformulated typology and a comparative multi-level analysis of the German and UK low-carbon electricity transitions (1990–2014)" *Research Policy*, 45(4), 896–913.

Geels, F.W. and Kemp, R. (2012) "The multi-level perspective as a new perspective for studying socio-technical transitions" in Geels, F.W., et al. eds., *Automobility in Transition? A Socio-Technical Analysis of Sustainable Transport* Routledge, Abingdon, 49–79.

Geels, F.W. and Schot, J. (2010) "The dynamics of transitions: A socio-technical perspective" in Grin, J., Rotmans, J. and Schot, J. eds., *Transitions to Sustainable Development: New Directions in the Study of Long Term Transformative Change* Routledge, New York, 11–104.

Geels, F.W. and Schot, J. (2007) "Typology of sociotechnical transition pathways" *Research Policy*, 36(3), 399–417.

Giddens, A. (1984) *The Constitution of Society: Outline of the Theory of Structuration* University of California Press, Berkeley.

Göpel, M. (2016) *The Great Mindshift* Springer International Publishing, Cham.

Grin, J., Rotmans, J. and Schot, J. (2010) *Transitions to Sustainable Development: New Directions in the Study of Long Term Transformative Change* Routledge, New York, London.

Gruszka, K. (2016) "Framing the collaborative economy: Voices of contestation" *Environmental Innovation and Societal Transitions*, 23, 92–104.

Hajer, M.A. and Wagenaar, H. eds. (2003) *Deliberative Policy Analysis: Understanding Governance in the Network Society* Cambridge University Press, Cambridge, et al.

Hale, T. and Roger, C. (2014) "Orchestration and transnational climate governance" *The Review of International Organizations*, 9(1), 59–82.

Hasenclever, A., Mayer, P. and Rittberger, V. (2000) "Integrating theories of international regimes" *Review of International Studies*, 26(1), 3–33.

Hermwille, L. (2016a) "Climate change as a transformation challenge: A new climate policy paradigm?" *GAIA: Ecological Perspectives for Science and Society*, 25(1), 19–22.

Hermwille, L. (2016b) "The role of narratives in socio-technical transitions: Fukushima and the energy regimes of Japan, Germany, and the United Kingdom" *Energy Research & Social Science*, 11, 237–246.

Hermwille, L., et al. (2017) "UNFCCC before and after Paris: What's necessary for an effective climate regime?" *Climate Policy*, 17(2), 150–170.

Hermwille, L., Obergassel, W. and Arens, C. (2016) "The transformative potential of emissions trading" *Carbon Management*, 6(5–6), 261–272.

Heyen, D.A. (2017) *Governance of Exnovation: Phasing Out Non-Sustainable Structures* Öko-Institut, Berlin (www.oeko.de/fileadmin/oekodoc/WP-Exnovation-EN.pdf).

Heyen, D.A., Hermwille, L. and Wehnert, T. (2017) "Out of the comfort zone! Governing the exnovation of unsustainable technologies and practices" *GAIA: Ecological Perspectives for Science and Society*, 26(4), 326–331.

Hickmann, T. (2016) *Rethinking Authority in Global Climate Governance: How Transnational Climate Initiatives Relate to the International Climate Regime* Routledge, Oxon, New York.

Hickmann, T. (2017) "The reconfiguration of authority in global climate governance" *International Studies Review*, 19(3), 430–451.

Hoffman, A.J. (2001) "Linking organizational and field-level analyses: The diffusion of corporate environmental practice" *Organization & Environment*, 14(2), 133–156.

Keohane, R.O. and Victor, D.G. (2011) "The regime complex for climate change" *Perspectives on Politics*, 9(1), 7–23.

Kern, F. and Rogge, K.S. (2016) "The pace of governed energy transitions: Agency, international dynamics and the global Paris agreement accelerating decarbonisation processes?" *Energy Research & Social Science*, 22, 13–17.

Kivimaa, P. and Kern, F. (2016) "Creative destruction or mere niche support? Innovation policy mixes for sustainability transitions" *Research Policy*, 45(1), 205–217.

Knutti, R., et al. (2016) "A scientific critique of the two-degree climate change target" *Nature Geoscience*, 9(1), 13–18.

Krasner, S.D. (1982) "Structural causes and regime consequences: Regimes as intervening variables" *International Organization*, 36(2), 185–205.

Krause, F., Bossel, H. and Müller-Reißmann, K.-F. (1980) *Energie-Wende: Wachstum und Wohlstand ohne Erdöl und Uran* S. Fischer, Frankfurt am Main.

Kuramochi, T., et al. (2018) "Ten key short-term sectoral benchmarks to limit warming to 1.5°C" *Climate Policy*, 18(3), 287–305.

Leach, M., Scoones, I. and Stirling, A.C. (2010) *Dynamic Sustainabilities: Technology, Environment and Social Justice* Earthscan, Routledge, Oxon, New York.

Leipprand, A., Flachsland, C. and Pahle, M. (2017) "Advocates or cartographers? Scientific advisors and the narratives of German energy transition" *Energy Policy*, 102, 222–236.

Luederitz, C., et al. (2016) "Many pathways toward sustainability: Not conflict but co-learning between transition narratives" *Sustainability Science*, 12(3), 393–407.

Markard, J., Raven, R. and Truffer, B. (2012) "Sustainability transitions: An emerging field of research and its prospects" *Research Policy*, 41(6), 955–967.

Meadowcroft, J. (2011) "Engaging with the politics of sustainability transitions" *Environmental Innovation and Societal Transitions*, 1(1), 70–75.

Mersmann, F. and Wehnert, T. (2014) *Shifting Paradigms: Unpacking Transformation for Climate Action* Wuppertal Institute, Berlin.

Milkoreit, M. (2017) *Mindmade Politics: The Cognitive Roots of International Climate Governance* MIT Press, Cambridge, MA.

Miskimmon, A., O'Loughlin, B. and Roselle, L. (2013) *Strategic Narratives: Communication Power and the New World Order* Routledge, Taylor & Francis Group, New York, London.

Moravcsik, A. (1997) "Taking preferences seriously: A liberal theory of international politics" *International Organization*, 51(4), 513–553.

Newell, P. and Bulkeley, H. (2017) "Landscape for change? International climate policy and energy transitions: Evidence from sub-Saharan Africa" *Climate Policy*, 17(5), 650–663.

North, D.C. (1990) *Institutions, Institutional Change and Economic Performance* Cambridge University Press, Cambridge [etc.].

Oberthür, S., Hermwille, L., Khandekar, G. and Obergassel, W. (2017) *Strengthening International Climate Governance: The Case for a Sectoral Approach*, Vrije Universiteit Brussels, Institute for European Studies, Brussels (www.cop21ripples.eu/resources/pb-strengthening-international-climate-governance-the-case-for-a-sectoral-approach/) Accessed 14 November 2017.

Oberthür, S., Hermwille, L., Khandekar, G., Obergassel, W., et al. (2017) *Key Concepts, Core Challenges and Governance Functions of International Climate Governance* COP21 RIPPLES Project (Horizon2020), Brussels (www.cop21ripples.eu/wp-content/uploads/2017/02/Deliverable-4.1-Ripples-Final2.pdf) Accessed 23 October 2017.

Okereke, C., Bulkeley, H. and Schroeder, H. (2009) "Conceptualizing climate governance beyond the international regime" *Global Environmental Politics*, 9(1), 58–78.

Orsini, A., Morin, J.-F. and Young, O. (2013) "Regime complexes: A buzz, a boom, or a boost for global governance?" *Global Governance: A Review of Multilateralism and International Organizations*, 19(1), 27–39.

Pattberg, P. and Zelli, F. (2016) "Global environmental governance in the Anthropocene: An introduction" in Pattberg, P. and Zelli, F. eds., *Environmental Politics and Governance in the Anthropocene: Institutions and Legitimacy in a Complex World* Routledge, London, 1–12.

Patterson, J., et al. (2017) "Exploring the governance and politics of transformations towards sustainability" *Environmental Innovation and Societal Transitions*, 24, 1–16.

Piggot, G., et al. (2017) *Addressing Fossil Fuel Production under the UNFCCC: Paris and beyond*, Stockholm Environment Institute, Stockholm (www.sei-international.org/med iamanager/documents/Publications/SEI-2017-WP-addressing-fossil-fuel-production. pdf) Accessed 27 October 2017.

Putnam, R.D. (1988) "Diplomacy and domestic politics: The logic of two-level games" *International Organization*, 42(3), 427–460.

Reuters (2017) "Shell CEO urges switch to clean energy as plans hefty renewable spending" *Reuters.com* (www.reuters.com/article/us-ceraweek-shell-shell-idUSKBN16G2DT) Accessed 14 March 2017.

Rip, A. and Kemp, R. (1998) "Technological change" in Rayner, S. and Malone, E.L. eds., *Human Choice and Climate Change: An International Assessment* Batelle Press, Columbus, OH, 327–399.

Roger, C. and Dauvergne, P. (2016) "The rise of transnational governance as a field of study" *International Studies Review*, 18(3), 415–437.

Rotmans, J., Kemp, R. and van Asselt, M. (2001) "More evolution than revolution: Transition management in public policy" *Foresight*, 3(1), 15–31.

Schellnhuber, H.J., Rahmstorf, S. and Winkelman, R. (2016) "Why the right climate target was agreed in Paris" *Nature Climate Change*, 6, July, 649–653.

Schumpeter, J.A. (2003) *Capitalism, Socialism and Democracy*, 5th Revised ed. Routledge, London, New York.

Scoones, I., Leach, M. and Newell, P. eds. (2015) *The Politics of Green Transformations* Routledge, Oxon, New York.

Sewell, W.H.J. (2005) "A theory of structure: Duality, agency, and transformation" in *Logics of History: Social Theory and Social Transformation* Chicago Studies in the Practices of Meaning. University of Chicago Press, Chicago, 124–151.

Shove, E. and Walker, G. (2007) "Caution! Transitions ahead: Politics, practice, and sustainable transition management" *Environment and Planning A*, 4(39), 763–770.

Smith, A. (2007) "Translating sustainabilities between green niches and socio-technical regimes" *Technology Analysis & Strategic Management*, 19(4), 427–450.

Smith, A. and Raven, R. (2012) "What is protective space? Reconsidering niches in transitions to sustainability" *Research Policy*, 41(6), 1025–1036.

Snidal, D. (2013) "Rational choice and international relations" in *Handbook of International Relations* Sage Publications, London, 85–111 (http://sk.sagepub.com/reference/ hdbk_interntlrelations/n4.xml) Accessed 1 December 2015.

Sovacool, B.K. (2016) "How long will it take? Conceptualizing the temporal dynamics of energy transitions" *Energy Research & Social Science*, 13, 202–215.

Sovacool, B.K. and Geels, F.W. (2016) "Further reflections on the temporality of energy transitions: A response to critics" *Energy Research & Social Science*, 22, 232–237.

Star, S.L. (2010) "This is not a boundary object: Reflections on the origin of a concept" *Science, Technology, & Human Values*, 35(5), 601–617.

Star, S.L. and Griesemer, J.R. (1989) "Institutional ecology, 'translations' and boundary objects: Amateurs and professionals in Berkeley's Museum of Vertebrate Zoology, 1907–39" *Social Studies of Science*, 19(3), 387–420.

Stegmaier, P., Kuhlmann, S. and Visser, V.R. (2014) "The discontinuation of socio-technical systems as governance problem" in S. Borrás and J. Edler eds., *The Governance of Socio-Technical Systems: Explaining Change* Edward Elgar Publishing, Cheltenham, UK, Northampton, MA, 111–131.

Stirling, A.C. (2014) *Emancipating Transformations: From Controlling 'the Transition' to Culturing Plural Radical Progress* STEPS Centre, Brighton (http://steps-centre.org/wp-content/uploads/Transformations.pdf) Accessed 14 January 2015.

Stones, R. (2005) *Structuration Theory* Palgrave Macmillan, Basingstoke.

Turnheim, B. and Geels, F.W. (2013) "The destabilisation of existing regimes: Confronting a multi-dimensional framework with a case study of the British coal industry (1913–1967)" *Research Policy*, 42(10), 1749–1767.

UNFCCC (2016) *Paris Agreement* United Nations Convention on Climate Change (UNFCCC), Bonn (http://unfccc.int/files/meetings/paris_nov_2015/application/pdf/par is_agreement_english_.pdf) Accessed 3 March 2016.

Unruh, G.C. (2000) "Understanding carbon lock-in" *Energy Policy*, 28(12), 817–830.

Wendt, A. (1987) "The agent-structure problem in international relations theory" *International Organization*, 41(3), 335–370.

Young, O.R. ed. (1997) *Global Governance: Drawing Insights from the Environmental Experience* MIT Press, Cambridge, MA.

8 From 'talking the talk' to 'walking the walk'?

Multi-level global governance of the Anthropocene in Indonesia

Chris Höhne

Introduction

At the 2009 Copenhagen Conference of the United Nations Framework Convention on Climate Change (UNFCCC), Indonesia's President Susilo Bambang Yudhoyono declared: "This is not a time for dogma and confrontation. This [is] a time for solution and consensus. The only dogma that binds us here is: human survival" (Yudhoyono 2009). His statement indicates what is at stake in the Anthropocene, which recognises humans as a geological force that are changing the Earth system since the 'Great Acceleration' of socio-economic and Earth system trends, starting in 1950 (Steffen et al. 2015; Zalasiewicz et al. 2017). He refers to humanity's negative impact on the planet and, in response, strives for global cooperation on climate change, which is one of the prime examples of the Anthropocene.

Interestingly, since 2007, Indonesia has shown increasing domestic engagement on climate mitigation despite not being obliged to do so under the UNFCCC (UNFCCC 1998; UNFCCC 1992). Rational choice scholars would therefore not expect any domestic actions, due to the free rider problem (Keohane and Victor 2016). For that reason, it is puzzling that Indonesia started actions eight years prior to the Paris Agreement, where Nationally Determined Contributions (NDC) to climate mitigation became an obligation for each UNFCCC party (UNFCCC 2015, Article 4.2).

Why did Indonesia not choose to free ride, or to exclusively focus on adaptation? In the context of negotiating a Post-Kyoto framework, since 2005, UNFCCC parties have developed new governance arrangements, such as Nationally Appropriate Mitigation Actions (NAMAs), which, for the first time, comprise the norm of climate mitigation actions by developing countries in 2007. To understand the implications of this, I shed light on *how and why developments in the UNFCCC have triggered institutional and policy changes for mitigating climate change in Indonesia*. This question points to two issues which this chapter addresses: the important role of emerging economies in the Anthropocene, and the dynamics between the global and the domestic governance of the Anthropocene.

Firstly, emerging economies need to become more central to the Anthropocene discussion, as they themselves have become strong drivers of global environmental change. Indonesia is the fifth largest greenhouse gas (GHG) emitter in the world with historical emissions of 2.47 Gt CO_2eq in 2014. Historical GHG per capita emissions of 9.69 t CO_2eq in Indonesia are already higher than in the European Union (7.19 t CO_2eq). The land use sector accounts for 68 percent of these emissions (World Resources Institute 2018), but by 2027 is expected to be surpassed by the energy sector (Chrysolite et al. 2017). While Earth system scientists show that "most of the human imprint on the Earth System is coming from the OECD world" (Steffen et al. 2015, 91), they also acknowledge that this is starting to change due to growing middle classes in emerging economies. But emerging economies have not been in the focus of the Anthropocene debate and questions of how they address Anthropocene issues are still mostly unanswered (Lederer 2015; Purdon 2015).

Secondly, we need to focus more on the dynamics between the global and domestic Anthropocene governance by combining approaches from International Relations (IR) and comparative politics. So far, comparative politics has remained absent from the Anthropocene debate, while IR has contributed to it in two ways. One strand of literature focuses on bringing IR and governance research into Anthropocene perspectives (Biermann 2007; Pattberg and Zelli 2016, 2), while the other claims that IR is ill-suited for the challenges of the Anthropocene, and strives to bring in post-humanist thinking into IR (Harrington 2016; Burke et al. 2016, 504; Chandler et al. 2018). I contribute to the former community, acknowledging that international institutions are important in addressing global environmental change (Biermann et al. 2012). As one of these international institutions, the UNFCCC has been criticised for its failures to produce an effective international agreement (Victor 2011; Keohane and Victor 2016). Consequently, much research has focused on polycentric or transnational governance outside of the UNFCCC (Hoffmann 2011; Jordan et al. 2015).

Recently, scholars have recommended studying the governance of the Anthropocene from the global down to the local level (Biermann et al. 2016; Lederer 2015, 10). I take this suggestion seriously, and mainly use a 'second image reversed' perspective to focus on the effects of the global level on the domestic level (Gourevitch 1978). I open the 'black box' nation-state (Purdon 2015), apply a multi-level global governance perspective (Zürn 2012; Hooghe and Marks 2003), and integrate a rationalist and a constructivist framework to specify the mechanisms of influence (Börzel and Risse 2009; Risse and Ropp 2013). While the Anthropocene literature has acknowledged norm research (Biermann et al. 2010, 204–205) as well as approaches integrating constructivism with rationalism, we still lack studies in this regard (Young 2013, 100–101). Therefore, I shift the spotlight to the UNFCCC and to national governments. In addition, I include comparative politics insights on institutional and policy change (Hall 1993).

In the next section, I discuss the IR debate concerning the Anthropocene, followed by my framework for analysis of multi-level global governance of the Anthropocene. In the subsequent sub-chapter, I apply this framework to Indonesia, the case study country, to analyse to what extent the Indonesian government was 'talking the talk' of the climate mitigation norm (i.e., referring mostly rhetorically to the meaning of the norm) or was 'walking the walk' of the norm (i.e., taking actions which are concordant with the norm) in the period from 2005 (i.e., when global discussions on NAMAs started) until 2016. There, I use process tracing "to uncover what stimuli the actors attend to" (George and McKeown 1985, 35), based on primary and secondary sources, including 15 semi-structured interviews with experts from donors, NGOs, research institutions and ministries in Indonesia in August 2016 (see appendix). I show that developments in the UNFCCC have already had impacts on domestic climate politics in Indonesia, even though they remain limited as regards domestic institutional and policy changes. This perspective has been neglected and points to the importance of global multi-level interactions for the governance of the Anthropocene; but also to its limitations. I draw these conclusions in the last section.

The Anthropocene: IR perspective(s)

In the first part of this sub-chapter, I trace the work of IR researchers on the Anthropocene to highlight current views and to explain my own contribution. Based on that, I lay out my conceptual framework in the second part of this section.

IR and the Anthropocene: the end of Holocene IR or fruitful insights from it?

IR researchers have reacted differently to the Anthropocene thesis (see also Müller, in this volume). One group of IR scholars wants to bring radical political theory thinking on the Anthropocene into IR (Harrington 2016; Burke et al. 2016). The other research community rather focuses on bringing IR and governance perspectives into Anthropocene research (Biermann 2007; Pattberg and Zelli 2016, 2).

Bringing political theory in: the end of Holocene IR?

IR approaches on 'new materialism' and 'post-humanism' address the Anthropocene by incorporating insights from political theory. Some political theorists claim that the Anthropocene represents the end of the division between the human and the natural sphere as rooted in Enlightenment philosophy (see also Weißpflug, in this volume). One group regards the Anthropocene as a signal of the 'humanization' and the 'conquest of the natural world' (Lövbrand et al. 2015, 213). They even proclaim the "end of nature [as] . . . neither nature nor humanity . . . exists with any kind of independence" (Wapner 2014, 43). In response, 'new materialists' recognise 'agentic capacities' (Coole 2013, 459) of non-human beings and 'post-humanists' acknowledge that 'the world is more than human' (Cudworth et al. 2018, 4), including the agency of non-human beings. These IR researchers call for an 'end of Holocene IR' (Harrington 2016, 484), and an 'interspecies conception of politics' (Youatt 2014, 207). They argue that IR is ill-suited for the Anthropocene (Harrington 2016; Burke et al. 2016, 504; Chandler et al. 2018), and mostly reject Anthropocene governance by international institutions. For example, Chandler et al. (2018) claim that the Anthropocene indicates the end of global liberalism and of problem-solving through international institutions in general.

These approaches have been criticised for running the risk of subsuming nature under society or society under nature, and for misrepresenting natural-human interactions (Hamilton 2017, 56; Corry 2017, 111). Political theorist Clive Hamilton argues that "rather than dying, nature as the Earth System has in fact come alive" (Hamilton 2017, 47) as the Anthropocene represents the destabilisation of the Earth system through the 'Great Acceleration' and not the millennia-long human impact on nature. He rather proposes a 'new anthropocentrism' which reflects "[human] agency ... as a force always constrained by its embeddedness in the process of nature" (Hamilton 2017, 51). Complementarily, Olaf Corry argues that there may be more benefits for IR in studying the 'dialectics between humans and nature' (Corry 2017, 111) as both categories are distinct, but increasingly linked. One solution may be to consider the changing Earth system as a dynamic structure which is driven by human agency and which impacts humans' activities as well.

Bringing governance in: fruitful insights for IR research on the Anthropocene?

Another group of IR researchers addressing the Anthropocene is not concerned with questions of the human-nature divide, but pose the question of "how [we] can ... steer towards socio-natural co-evolution and a resulting safe operating space" (Pattberg and Zelli 2016, 3). They focus on the global governance of the Earth system and use insights from Holocene IR. They argue that '[t]raditional notions of environmental policy' (Biermann et al. 2010, 203) are insufficient in the Anthropocene due to increasing interdependence, extreme effects (Biermann 2007, 331–335), urgency to act, and material and governance complexity (Pattberg and Zelli 2016, 5–6). They call for the analysis of "institutions and agents that cause global environmental change" (Biermann 2007, 328) and propose to focus on 'Earth System Governance' to analyse the rules and actors which are steering societies' engagements with global environmental change (Biermann et al. 2010, 203).

These researchers note the "emergence of a patchwork of governance arrangements at all levels" (Pattberg and Zelli 2016, 7), which queries their legitimacy, effectiveness and resulting reconfiguration of authority. Most of these scholars focus on agency, architecture, adaptive governance, accountability and allocation (Biermann 2007, 335; Biermann et al. 2010). Interestingly, architecture, agency beyond the state, and accountability of non-state governance have also been at the centre of much Holocene IR research on globalisation (Rosenau 1992; Keohane 1988), which contradicts claims from post-humanists that IR concepts are of little use in the Anthropocene.

Contrary to post-humanists, these governance researchers embrace international cooperation due to the interdependence of nation-states in the Anthropocene

(Young 2013, 99; Biermann et al. 2012). Recently, researchers of this community have emphasised that a development of "effective multilevel and polycentric governance solutions" (Biermann et al. 2016, 342) is needed. However, they argue that "for local and national action to be effective, the global institutional framework must be supportive and well designed" (Biermann et al. 2012, 1307). I agree that "much more integration of both strands of research is needed" (Biermann et al. 2016, 348), and that instead of calling for the end of Holocene IR, we must rather apply IR governance approaches to the analyses of the Anthropocene, while also accounting for the insights of comparative politics. In the following section, I sketch out my multi-level global governance perspective which connects the global with the domestic level.

Multi-level global governance of the Anthropocene: a framework for analysis

Multi-level global governance

The multi-level global governance approach is based on the concept of Hooghe and Marks (2003), while integrating the global governance dimension, i.e., the role of international institutions, more comprehensively (Zürn 2012). It acknowledges that 'spheres of authority' exist which are beyond the nation-state, such as international regimes (Hooghe and Marks 2003, 237–239), even though the consensus principle continues to exist (Zürn 2012, 731 with a different perspective). It opens the 'black box' of the nation-state and allows for the study of interactions between domestic governmental actors and with non-state actors (Stephenson 2013, 820–821). Finally, this perspective integrates the 'second image reversed' perspective by narrowing it down to the UNFCCC and its governance arrangements (Gourevitch 1978), comprising a set of related norms and rules (Duffield 2007, 2). While norms are defined as 'standard[s] of appropriate behavio[u]r for actors' (Finnemore and Sikkink 1998, 891), rules are 'well-defined guides to action' (Young 1989, 16). For specifying how norms and rules of governance arrangements travel from the global to the domestic level, I integrate social mechanisms from constructivism and rationalism, which "often work simultaneously or dominate different phases of the ... process" (Börzel and Risse 2009, 13; see also Risse and Ropp 2013). As we lack such integrated approaches for the study of global environmental governance (Young 2013, 100–101), I start by testing simultaneously one constructivist and one rationalist hypothesis to look for signs of patterns and scope conditions to build synthesis between them.

Constructivism

The *first hypothesis* builds upon constructivism. It assumes that actors are driven by a 'logic of appropriateness' (March and Olsen 1998, 951). They are "guided by collective understandings of what constitutes proper, i.e., socially accepted behavio[u]r in a given rule structure" (Börzel and Risse 2009, 10). Global governance arrangements thus constitute "new rules, norms, practices and structures of meaning to which member states [of an international institution] are exposed" (Börzel and Risse 2009, 10). The following conditions support successful norm socialisation. Firstly, strong norm entrepreneurs can help to advance norms domestically by using consensual knowledge of epistemic communities of experts (Haas 1992, 2), ideas, moral arguments and strategic constructions to induce a persuasion or learning process of the socialisation (Börzel and Risse 2009, 11; Finnemore and Sikkink 1998, 899). Secondly, it is conducive when powerful domestic actors care about their social reputation in the international community (Risse and Ropp 2013, 20), and strive to show appropriate behaviour in an international institution, which derives from a notion of identity, a sense of obligation or responsibility or from peer pressure due to the desire for esteem, legitimate behaviour, conformity and belongingness (Finnemore and Sikkink 1998). Finally, global norms need to resonate well with pre-existing domestic norms and culture as well as institutions (Checkel 1999, 87). The first hypothesis states that:

1 *Domestic politicians will introduce the norms and rules of the global governance arrangement of the Anthropocene and will induce the corresponding institutional and policy changes, if the governance arrangement is supported by strong norm entrepreneurs, if powerful domestic actors care about their social reputation in the international community, and if the domestic cultural and institutional resonance is high.*

Recent norm research argues that socialisation research has been concentrating on norm adoption or rejection only. In the case of partial adoption, we may also see a local reshaping of global norms and rules in the domestic discourse, law and implementation (Zimmermann 2016), as local actors usually follow a pre-existing institutional path (Börzel and Risse 2009, 15; March and Olsen 1998). I follow this suggestion by distinguishing between full adoption, partial adoption (including potential local adjustments), and no adoption of norms and rules.

Rationalism

The *second hypothesis* builds upon rationalism. It assumes that public bodies are acting as self-interested actors trying to gain more resources and power based on their fixed set of preferences (Sprinz and Vaahtoranta 1994, 78). They are thus following a 'logic of expected consequences' (March and Olsen 1998, 949). New incentives from international institutions can shift the interests of key domestic actors to take actions domestically (Keohane 1988, 387). Global governance arrangements can thus be "conceived as an emerging political opportunity structure which offers some actors additional resources to exert influence" (Börzel and Risse 2009, 7). The following conditions support the domestic advancement of global governance arrangements. Firstly, decision makers need to see the opportunity to increase the amount of income or power of their institution. Secondly, it requires sufficient capacities of domestic institutions (Risse and Ropp 2013, 15). Finally, veto players – i.e., "decisionmakers whose agreement is required for the change of the status quo" (Tsebelis 2000, 442) – must not oppose it. The second hypothesis states that:

2   *Domestic politicians will introduce the norms and rules of the global governance arrangements of the Anthropocene and will induce corresponding institutional and policy changes, if the anticipated domestic financial and power benefits for their institutions exceed the costs, if their institutions possess sufficient capacities, and if domestic veto players do not oppose it.*

Scholarship on 'varieties of capitalism' argues that we observe continuing cross-national divergence of rules despite the influence of international regimes (Hall and Soskice 2001, vi, 9, 54, 60). I accept their suggestion that domestic actors aim to continuously organise their behaviour around pre-existing institutions and policies and thus distinguish again between full adoption, partial adoption (including potential local adjustments), and no adoption of norms and rules.

Institutional and policy changes

From a public policy perspective, institutional change as a reconfiguration of public authority can occur horizontally between organisations at one governmental tier or vertically between governmental tiers (Hickmann et al. 2017). Here, I focus on the horizontal redistribution of competences at the national level. A high-scale or transformational institutional change would include the establishment of powerful and large ministerial departments, and the creation of a strong inter-ministerial body. A medium-scale institutional change can be found when new (mostly temporary) agencies or councils, or new (permanent) ministerial units are created which lack implementation power. Finally, small-scale institutional changes are characterised by the establishment of temporary working groups or by a small increase in staff in a pre-existing ministerial unit. Following Hall (1993, 278–279), I distinguish between first, second and third order policy changes. A first order change is characterised by a change at the level of instruments. A second order change encompasses the replacement of the instrument itself, or the introduction of a new one. Only when a policy's hierarchy of goals changes, can we witness a third order or transformational policy change. Institutional and policy changes can still occur at the highest degrees despite a partial norm adoption, as long as they are triggered by the global governance arrangements, while in the process domestic actors adjust it to local circumstances.

UNFCCC's NAMAs and climate politics in Indonesia

In the first part of this sub-chapter, I introduce NAMAs as an Anthropocene governance arrangement, while the second part of this section provides background information on Indonesia. NAMAs are at the centre of the framework application to the case Indonesia in the subsequent parts of this sub-chapter. There, I look for signs of significance of the conditions of the constructivist hypothesis H1 (norm entrepreneurs, social reputation, resonance) and of the rationalist hypothesis H2 (benefits, capacities, veto players) for the adoption of NAMAs climate mitigation norm (no, partial, full) and corresponding institutional changes (small, medium, high) and policy change (first order, second order, third order) in Indonesia. I also indicate if these conditions had a positive (rated as +), very positive (++), neutral (+/−; some positive, some negative), negative (−), very negative (− −), or no effect at all (0) on norm and rule adoption and institutional and policy change. I do this in four different phases: 'agenda-setting (2005–2007)' in part three of this section, 'towards international promises (2008–2009)' in part four of this sub-chapter, 'following up on international promises (2010–2014)' in part five of this section, and 'adherence to the governance arrangement under a new presidency (2014–2016)' in part six of this sub-chapter (see Table 8.1).

UNFCCC's Anthropocene governance arrangement: NAMA(s)

NAMA(s) were mentioned for the first time in the Bali Action Plan of the Conference of the Parties (COP) in 2007, although climate mitigation actions by developing countries had been debated under another term since 2005. They were informally acknowledged at the COP in Copenhagen in 2009 and formally recognised at the COP in Cancun in 2010. NAMAs have two definitions, as both National Level NAMA(s) (i.e., being a communication to the UNFCCC by developing countries about the planned GHG emissions) and as Individual NAMA(s) (i.e., as a supported or unilateral project, programme or policy) (UNFCCC Secretariat 2017). NAMAs represent a reinterpretation of the principle of "common but differentiated responsibilities and respective capabilities", which had previously excluded developing countries from any GHG commitments (UNFCCC 1998; UNFCCC 1992), as they acknowledge the norm that developing countries will also deliver voluntary mitigation actions (UNFCCC 2008, 3). Fifty-eight countries have submitted their NAMAs to the UNFCCC (Energy Research Centre of the Netherlands 2016, 36), ranging from GHG emission (intensity) targets to programmes and projects (UNFCCC Secretariat 2015). NAMAs only incorporate some underspecified rules regarding their measurement, verification and reporting (UNFCCC 2011, 11). Since 2013, countries have communicated their planned GHG emissions in their 'Intended Nationally Determined Contributions' (INDCs). But even there, 46 countries have referred to NAMAs. For their implementation, international registries were set-up and financial resources have been provided by UNFCCC members through funds, such as the NAMA Facility (Energy Research Centre of the Netherlands 2016, 36).

Background information on Indonesia

Indonesia is a presidential republic with a three tier political system that was democratised and decentralised in 1999 after the end of the autocratic Suharto regime (Bünte 2008, 26, 38). As a large economy of South-East Asia with 250 million inhabitants, Indonesia is a G20 member. It has the third largest tropical forests in the world, but from 1990 to 2015, Indonesia's total forest cover declined from 65 to 50 percent of land (World Bank 2016). Indonesia also heavily relies on coal and faces very high urbanisation rates. Indonesia is an archipelagic country, hence being highly vulnerable to climate change, but is also the fifth largest GHG emitter. It only ratified the Kyoto Protocol in 2004 and has not participated much in the Clean Development Mechanism (Sari 2010, 66).

Phase 1: agenda-setting (2005–2007)

Norm entrepreneurs (H1)

Indonesia did not engage domestically in climate change issues in 2005 or 2006. Climate change was only put high on the national agenda in 2007 when Indonesia was approached by the UNFCCC secretariat for the purpose of hosting the COP in 2007, and when a report by the PEACE research institute financed by DFID and World Bank argued that Indonesia was the third highest GHG emitter in the world (nowadays it is the fifth highest GHG emitter in the world). The report compiled existing research results of the epistemic community. Thus, DFID and World Bank acted as early agenda setters and norm entrepreneurs, and were joined by foreign governments and international and domestic NGOs, such as WWF, Pelangi and Walhi, in pressuring the Indonesian government to reduce its GHG emissions (Sari 2010, 67; Resosudarmo et al. 2013, 74).

Social reputation (H1)

These activities helped to raise public awareness when Indonesia, as incoming host of the COP of 2007, was socially highly vulnerable (Sari 2010, 67; Resosudarmo et al. 2013, 74). This was not in the interest of then-President Yudhoyono (in power 2004 until 2014) who aspired to change Indonesia's tarnished international image (Fitriani 2015, 73). He quickly showed interest in climate change issues, and together with then-minister Rachmat Witoelar aspired to make this COP a success for the government (Sari 2010, 67; DI-02082016, see appendix; DI-12082016). Driven by the desire to be recognised as a respectable member of the international community (Fitriani 2015, 73), Yudhoyono wished to establish the country as a frontrunner (DI-02082016; DI-12082016). He facilitated the adoption of the Bali Action Plan, which for the first time, mentioned NAMAs and which presented a timetable for an international agreement at the COP in 2009. Even before the 2007 COP, Yudhoyono presented the 'National Action Plan Addressing Climate Change' and 'Indonesia's Response to Climate Change' by the Ministry of National Development Planning (BAPPENAS) (Indrarto et al. 2012, 50) to showcase Indonesia's engagement. However, both documents were only stocktaking exercises of different sectors.

Resonance (H1)

The resonance with the NAMA norm was initially rather low. Climate change was not a development priority for Indonesia's government, which was focused on economic growth and poverty alleviation. Climate policy had not emerged as a bottom-up issue by subnational actions (Hickmann et al. 2017, 335), as Indonesia was still characterised by a top-down development planning culture (DI-18082016). Furthermore, the Ministry of Environment was unsatisfied with the publication of the PEACE report, indicating its low resonance (Sari 2010, 67; Resosudarmo et al. 2013, 74). Also, Yudhoyono was not known to be an environmentalist prior to his presidency (Anderson et al. 2015, 275). However, the organisation of the COP in Bali in 2007 resonated very well with his goal to improve Indonesia's global image and to present himself and his country as part of the global community (Fitriani 2015, 73).

Benefits (H2), capacity (H2), veto players (H2)

No indications for their relevance were found (e.g., Sari 2010).

Sum up of phase 1 results

Phase 1 shows how pressure by norm entrepreneurs (++) and the desire of the president to be a respected part of the international community (++) helped to put climate change high on the domestic agenda, even though the climate mitigation norm did not resonate well (−). Phase 1 supports the hypothesis 1. While no policy or institutional change occurred, the Indonesian government began to partially adopt the NAMA norm rhetorically. No indications for the relevance of hypothesis 2 (benefits, capacity, veto players) were found (0).

Phase 2: towards international promises (2008–2009)

Norm entrepreneur (H1)

Following the COP in 2007, BAPPENAS began a process which led to the publication of the 2009 'Indonesian Climate Change Sectoral Roadmap'. GIZ acted as a norm entrepreneur as it supported BAPPENAS in the consultation process with other ministries to develop sectoral mitigation actions and to integrate climate change in development planning in response to the NAMA governance arrangement (Indrarto et al. 2012, 50; DI-12082016).

Social reputation (H1)

In 2008, Yudhoyono followed up on the NAMA governance arrangement of the Bali Action Plan by establishing the National Council on Climate Change (DNPI) as an extra-governmental body for the coordination among ministries and, in 2009, the Indonesian Climate Change Trust Fund (ICCTF) for channelling international finance (Sari 2010, 68). These medium-scale institutional changes resemble the conventional habit of UNFCCC parties of that time to set-up new councils and funds, which points to the president's increasing international socialisation. However, the president only very occasionally led the council and ICCTF's operational rules have not yet been clarified (TI-02082016). Internationally,

Yudhoyono showed growing aspirations for his international reputation. In accordance with his foreign policy principle of making 'a million friends and zero enemies' (Fitriani 2015, 74, 84), Indonesia was striving towards international agreements within the UNFCCC (Anderson et al. 2015, 264), where Yudhoyono "wanted to be seen as a true leader on climate issues" (NI-02082016). In September 2009, two months before the Copenhagen COP, he decided while on a plane to the G20 meeting in Pittsburgh to come up with the 'magic number' (MI-05082016) of 26 percent GHG emission reduction compared to business as usual (BAU) by 2020 in order to beat the pledge of Japan, which put 25 percent on the table (MI-05082016; RI-01082016). He declared this goal at the Pittsburgh meeting and re-stated it at the Copenhagen COP (Sari 2010, 70–71). There, he rhetorically showed his aspiration to be part of the global climate community by stating with regard to Indonesia's GHG target: "As a non-Annex 1 country, we did NOT [sic] have to do this. … [W]e set our new reduction target, because we wanted to be part of [the] global solution" (Yudhoyono 2009). This figure was submitted as Indonesia's National Level NAMA to the UNFCCC secretariat. It was underlined by promised actions in the waste, transport, forest, peat land and energy sector (ROI 2010), and the development of a national climate action plan (Sari 2010, 71). As one of the first developing countries to announce the restriction of GHG emissions, Yudhoyono had recognised the NAMA norm. This announcement was quite surprising to the Indonesian public, and even to national ministries, as it had not been debated domestically before (Anderson et al. 2015, 263; Resosudarmo et al. 2013, 72).

Resonance (H1)

While the establishment of the DNPI resonated well with Yudhoyono's preference for the establishment of special units, it did not correspond well with the existing ministries, which contributed to a lack of policy integration. The DNPI was regarded as a rival coordinating institution by the ministries of development planning, forestry, environment and finance. Furthermore, most of DNPI's staff had no government background, undercutting its authority vis-à-vis the ministries (Sari 2010, 68; NI-02082016; Resosudarmo et al. 2013, 76–78).

Benefits (H2)

Attracting international funding was part of the move of Yudhoyono to pledge even 41 percent GHG emission reduction by 2020 compared to BAU when global support would be delivered (Yudhoyono 2009). Initially, line ministries were shocked by the high target, but as it became clear that financial support could be forthcoming, they tried to attract donor money by presenting some project ideas (TI-02082016; DI-01082016). While the establishment of the ICCTF indicates Yudhoyono's increasing international socialisation, it also shows his interest in international funds. But the creation of the DNPI and the ICCTF contributed to an institutional turf war with several ministries which wanted to control the incoming funding and were eager to keep or increase their powers (Sari 2010, 68; Resosudarmo et al. 2013, 75–78).

Capacity (H2), veto players (H2)

No indications for their importance were found (e.g., Sari 2010; Resosudarmo et al. 2013).

Sum up of phase 2 results

In phase 2, we see how Yudhoyono's aspiration to achieve international reputation led him to make international promises and to realise two medium-scale institutional changes (++). Benefits were also important for the formulation of Indonesia's conditional GHG target and the development of new projects in ministries (+). Norm entrepreneurs supported the advancement of Indonesia's sectoral climate action planning (+). In this phase we see initial signs of full norm adoption, which, in the process, was limited by a lack of institutional resonance (−) and the quest for benefits by ministries to a partial norm adoption. Phase 2 mostly supports hypothesis 1 and to a lesser extent hypothesis 2. No indications for any importance of capacity (H2) and veto players (H2) were found (0).

Phase 3: following up on international promises (2010–2014)

Norm entrepreneur (H1)

Following the submission of the National Level NAMA to the UNFCCC, project development for Individual NAMA projects started (e.g., 'Green Chillers NAMA', 'Sustainable Transport NAMA'). These were often initiated and developed by norm entrepreneurs such as GIZ and UNDP in cooperation with ministries (DI-10082016; DI-12082016, DI-15082016; DI-18082016). Furthermore, parts of the Roadmap which had been prepared by BAPPENAS with support of GIZ (from 2007 until 2009) were included in the subsequent mid-term development plan of 2010–2014. This mid-term plan was then the basis for the 'National Action Plan for Greenhouse Gas Emissions Reduction' (RAN-GRK) of 2011 (DI-12082016), which was developed without much involvement of donor agencies (DI-12082016).

Social reputation (H1)

Shortly after the Copenhagen COP in 2009, the national government began to work on the national climate action plan. It appears that the president wanted to show internationally that he was sticking to his promises and the NAMA norm. The RAN-GRK was adopted as a Presidential Instruction in 2011 and represented on paper a second order policy change. The targeted sectors were mostly the same as those mentioned in the 2009 roadmap and the National Level NAMA submission to the UNFCCC (Indrarto et al. 2012, 50; ROI 2010): agriculture, forestry and peat land, energy and transportation, industry and waste management. It also included the GHG emission reduction pledge made at the COP in Copenhagen in 2009 (ROI 2011, Article 2, Attachment 1).

Resonance (H1)

While the RAN-GRK partly built upon the roadmap of 2009, it did not comprise of many new policy initiatives to reach Indonesia's new GHG targets and mostly included actions of the ongoing mid-term development plan (RI-10082016). Furthermore, the RAN-GRK stipulates that mitigation actions have to be in accordance with development targets (ROI 2011, Article 1). In the same year, BAPPENAS issued a plan for economic development until 2025, which was fully detached from the RAN-GRK (Anderson et al. 2016, 37), showing the lack of norm resonance with the development norm, the missing transformational policy change, and an overall partial norm adoption with local adjustments.

Benefits (H2)

Indonesian ministries were especially attracted by the promised international funding at the COPs in Copenhagen in 2009 and in Cancun in 2010. Until 2014, Indonesian ministries participated or supported the development of several individual NAMA projects in cooperation with donors (DI-12082016). However, almost all of these were aiming for the preparation rather than the implementation of Individual NAMA Projects and thus were not leading to domestic changes.

Capacity (H2), veto players (H2)

No indications for their relevance were found (e.g., MI2–05082016; Resosudarmo et al. 2013).

Sum up of phase 3 results

In phase 3, the aspiration for international recognition led to the adoption of Indonesia's national climate action plan of 2011 (++), which represented a second order policy change and a partial norm adoption with adjustments to local circumstances. Individual NAMA Project developments were driven by norm entrepreneurs (+), and the desire of ministries for international climate funding (+). Limited norm resonance with the economic growth norm resulted in a lack of transformational policy change (− −). Overall, we can see some support for both hypotheses, while hypothesis 1 clearly prevails over hypothesis 2. No indications for any importance of capacity (H2) and veto players (H2) were found (0).

Phase 4: adherence under new presidency (2014–2016)

Norm entrepreneurs (H1)

No indications for their importance were found (e.g., TI-02082016; DI-03082016).

Social reputation (H1)

Even though the new President Joko Widodo (in power since 2014) has not been known to be driven by his international appearance (TI-02082016; DI-03082016; MI2–05082016), he still showed an aspiration to be part of the global climate community. He reaffirmed at the COP in Paris in 2015 Indonesia's 2020 GHG target and pledged to reduce, unconditionally, GHG emissions by 29 percent compared to BAU by 2030 (ROI 2015, 5; Widodo 2015, 2). In this context, Widodo pointed out that: "I expect all [of] us to be part of the solution, [and] to make this [E]arth a comfortable place for our future generation to live in" (Widodo 2015). The commitment to the NAMA norm can also be found in the INDC, in which Indonesia has committed itself to a 'transition to a low carbon future' (ROI 2015, 1) to prevent global warming of 2°C.

Resonance (H1)

Domestically, the resonance of the NAMA norm is still limited. At the Paris COP, Widodo emphasised the actions Indonesia is taking, such as first and second order policy changes in the energy, transport and forest sector (i.e., fossil fuel transport subsidy cuts, renewable energy target of 23 percent by 2025, one map policy, peat land moratorium), to support his claim that his country is committed to the NAMA norm (Widodo 2015, 2–3). However, these activities are not directly linked to the RAN-GRK process or the NAMA norm (DI-10082016). Widodo has also been described as a politician who focuses on development priorities first (MI2–05082016), indicating a limited norm resonance. Accordingly, the current review of the RAN-GRK is not aiming for an increase of ambition of RAN-GRK actions (BAPPENAS 2015, 14). Widodo also abandoned the DNPI, but set-up a Directorate-General (DG) for Climate Change in the newly merged Ministry of Environment and Forestry as a move to streamline the bureaucracy. This adjustment to local circumstances represents a medium-scale institutional change as DNPI staffs were not integrated into the ministry, which resulted in an initial decrease in capacities. Furthermore, the new DG does not possess implementation powers and is now in a weaker power position than the previous DNPI to influence other line ministries (MI1–05082016; MI2–05082016). Additionally, institutional changes in line ministries are mostly missing.

Benefits (H2)

Widodo's Paris speech and Indonesia's INDC call for the provision of international finance to achieve the conditional target of 41 percent GHG emission reduction compared to BAU by 2030 (Widodo 2015, 2; ROI 2015, 6). The 'Sustainable Transport NAMA', financed by the bilateral NAMA Facility, is the only NAMA focusing on implementation so far. However, it still has not started on the ground (MI2–05082016). Consequently, policy and institutional changes have not occurred out of the implementation of individual NAMA projects, as all the other NAMA projects only focus on the development of financeable projects.

In 2015, 15 Individual NAMA Projects were still seeking external financial support of 870 million USD until 2020 (BAPPENAS 2015, 13). Due to the lack of international funding, the commitment of national ministries to the development of individual NAMA projects is currently low (RI-16082016).

Capacity (H2), veto players (H2)

No indications for their importance were found (e.g., MI1–05082016; MI2–05082016).

Sum up of phase 4 results

Widodo showed the desire to be part of the global community when announcing Indonesia's INDC targets (+). However, the lack of norm resonance prevented transformative policy change (− −). While this supports hypothesis 1, the ongoing demand for financial assistance and the lack of NAMA project implementation rather supports hypothesis 2 (−). Widodo initiated with the establishment of the DG Climate Change a medium-scale institutional change. However, a lack of policy integration continued in the aftermath. Overall, this indicates a partial norm adoption with adjustments to local circumstances. No indications for any importance of norm entrepreneurs (H1), capacity (H2) and veto players (H2) were found (0).

Discussion and conclusion: global and domestic Anthropocene governance

In this chapter, I have shown that the involvement of Indonesia in the UNFCCC has led to the domestic introduction of the UNFCCC governance arrangement NAMA, to partial norm adoption and to several domestic changes. My results indicate that the constructivist hypothesis 1 is more relevant for explaining the case than the rationalist hypothesis 2. But the rationalist hypothesis 2 adds some additional explanatory richness in phases 2 to 4, showing the importance of integrated approaches of rationalism and constructivism. International socialisation processes (i.e., norm entrepreneurs, social reputation) have very much supported the adoption of norms and domestic change (++/+, see Table 8.1). Financial benefits were mostly supportive of norm adoption and domestic change (+), but sometimes also a hindering factor (−). In all phases, limited resonance prevented more ambitious norm adoption and domestic change (− −/−). Capacity and veto players have not been found to shape the adoption of norms or domestic change (0). However, in the rivalry between the different governmental institutions and the lack of policy integration of climate actions, I see hints for both. All these conditions resulted in partial norm adoption with adjustments to local circumstances, three medium-scale institutional changes and one second order policy change. Most important for the lack of full norm adoption and of transformational domestic change are limited norm resonance (− − /−), and to a lesser extent institutional struggles over power benefits as well as the lack of financial benefits (−).

Regarding patterns or scope conditions, my interpretation is that social reputation remains broadly very important, with positive peaks when global high-level events are occurring. Norm entrepreneurs are very decisive in the beginning of the process (see Finnemore and Sikkink 1998), but loose importance over time, indicating their lack of influence on implementation and policy integration. When implementation becomes more important in the final two phases, the significance of low norm resonance (phase 3 and 4) and of missing financial benefits (phase 4) appears to increase. Both mechanisms contributed to an overall partial norm adoption, to adjustments to local circumstances and to only limited institutional and policy changes. This indicates that Indonesia is still much more 'talking the talk' of climate change than 'walking the walk' of climate actions. Thus, a full-fledged internalisation and adoption of the NAMA norm is still missing in Indonesia.

Overall, multi-level global governance research permits us to scrutinise the effects of international developments in the UNFCCC on the evolution of domestic climate politics. It shows that the UNFCCC, through its governance arrangement NAMA, has already impacted domestic climate politics far more than previously suspected (Victor 2011), pointing to the importance of global multi-level interactions for the governance of the Anthropocene. However, in the case of Indonesia, much more 'talking the talk' than 'walking the walk' was found, indicating the limitations of previous global-domestic dynamics. Nevertheless, the Paris Agreement brings even more momentum for domestic climate actions: my research findings indicate that international high-level meetings contribute to the aspiration for social reputation of nation-state leaders, which in turn leads to an increase in the promised climate ambition level, and to a domestic advancement of climate policy-making in the aftermath. This very much shows the importance of constructivist insights on global-domestic dynamics. These findings are good news for the pledge and review mechanism of the Paris Agreement, which aims to progressively increase the ambition level of UNFCCC parties. This mechanism will strengthen the opportunities for norm entrepreneurs to shame governments into taking actions, and will increase the desire of governments to take actions to remain a respected part of the global community. However, the low norm resonance, and to a lesser extent the lack of international funding, must eventually be overcome for full norm adoption and transformational changes to be unleashed. This strongly supports the importance of studying domestic reshaping and contestation of global norms. Further comparative research with other countries will grant more insights into these dynamics. This conceptual framework may also be useful for the study of other environmental issues in order to broaden our understanding of the governance of the Anthropocene. Finally, my findings show that international institutions are much more important for the governance of the Anthropocene than post-humanist researchers acknowledge, as they contribute to domestic institutional and policy change. However, their role is also limited to overcome a low norm resonance, to

Table 8.1 Compilation of results: UNFCCC's NAMAs in Indonesia

Phase	Relevance of hypotheses and their direction of effect	Norm adoption	Domestic change
Agenda-setting (2005–2007)	$^{++}$ norm entrepreneur (H1) $^{++}$ social reputation (H1) $^{-}$ resonance (H1) ^{0} benefits (H2) ^{0} capacity (H2) ^{0} veto players (H2)	partial adoption (rhetorically)	no institutional and policy changes
International promises (2008–2009)	$^{+}$ norm entrepreneur (H1) $^{++}$ social reputation (H1) $^{-}$ resonance (H1) $^{+}$ benefits (H2) ^{0} capacity (H2) ^{0} veto players (H2)	partial adoption, while initial indications of full adoption	2 medium-scale institutional changes
Domestic follow-up (2010–2014)	$^{+}$ norm entrepreneur (H1) $^{++}$ social reputation (H1) $^{--}$ resonance (H1) $^{+}$ benefits (H2) ^{0} capacity (H2) ^{0} veto players (H2)	partial adoption with adjustments to local circumstances	1 second order policy change
Adherence under new presidency (2014–2016)	^{0} norm entrepreneur (H1) $^{+}$ social reputation (H1) $^{--}$ resonance (H1) $^{-}$ benefits (H2) ^{0} capacity (H2) ^{0} veto players (H2)	partial adoption with adjustments to local circumstances	1 medium-scale institutional change

Source: Own compilation. The second column indicates how important (if at all) the six different conditions of the two hypotheses have been for the adoption of norms and rules and corresponding institutional and policy change:

$^{++}$very positive effect of the condition on norm and rule adoption and institutional and policy change,

$^{+}$positive,

$^{+/-}$overall neutral (some positive, some negative),

$^{-}$negative,

$^{--}$very negative,

^{0}no effect at all.

provide sufficient funding or to resolve domestic power struggles. Overall, for analysing the significance of international institutions and global-domestic dynamics, IR governance research still has much to offer.

Acknowledgements

I thank Markus Lederer and colleagues from Potsdam, Münster and Darmstadt for valuable discussions on the topic, Lena Partzsch and Philipp Pattberg for their enriching comments on this chapter, all editors for their support, all interviewees for sharing their insights, and Katharina Fietz and Edward Atkinson-Clark for proofreading. Funding has been provided by the German Research Foundation (DFG); reference number: LE 2644/4–1.

References

Anderson, P., et al. (2015) "Big commitments, small results: Environmental governance and climate change mitigation under Yudhoyono" in Aspinall, E., Mietzner, M. and Tomsa, D. eds., *The Yudhoyono Presidency: Indonesia's Decade of Stability and Stagnation* Institute of Southeast Asian Studies, Singapore, 258–278.

Anderson, Z.R., et al. (2016) "Green growth rhetoric versus reality: Insights from Indonesia" *Global Environmental Change*, 38, 30–40.

BAPPENAS (2015) "Developing Indonesian Climate Mitigation Policy 2020–2030", through RAN-GRK Review, Jakarta 61.

Biermann, F. (2007) "'Earth system governance' as a crosscutting theme of global change research" *Global Environmental Change*, 17, 326–337.

Biermann, F., et al. (2012) "Navigating the Anthropocene: Improving Earth System Governance" *Science*, 335, 1306.

Biermann, F., et al. (2016) "Down to Earth: Contextualizing the Anthropocene" *Global Environmental Change*, 39, 341–350.

Biermann, F., et al. (2010) "Navigating the Anthropocene: The Earth System Governance Project strategy paper" *Current Opinion in Environmental Sustainability*, 2, 202–208.

Börzel, T.A., et al. (2009) "Conceptualizing the domestic impact of Europe" Manuscript prepared for Featherstone, K. and Radaelli, C. eds., *The Politics of Europeanisation* Oxford University Press, Oxford, 1–23.

Bünte, M. (2008) "Dezentralisierung und Demokratie in Südostasien" *Zeitschrift für Politikwissenschaft*, 18, 25–50.

Burke, A., et al. (2016) "Planet politics: A manifesto from the end of IR" *Millennium*, 44, 499–523.

Chandler, D., et al. (2018) "Anthropocene, capitalocene and liberal cosmopolitan IR: A response to Burke et al.'s planet politics" *Millennium*, 46(2), 190–208.

Checkel, J.T. (1999) "Norms, institutions, and national identity in contemporary Europe" *International Studies Quarterly*, 43, 84–114.

Chrysolite, H., et al. (2017) "Evaluating Indonesia's progress on its climate commitments" (www.wri.org/blog/2017/10/evaluating-indonesias-progress-its-climate-commitments) Accessed 4 October 2017.

Coole, D. (2013) "Agentic capacities and capacious historical materialism: Thinking with new materialisms in the political sciences" *Millennium*, 41, 451–469.

Corry, O. (2017) "The 'nature' of international relations: From geopolitics to the Anthropocene" in Eroukhamanoff, C. and Harker, M. eds., *Reflections on the Posthuman in International Relations: The Anthropocene, Security and Ecology* E-International Relations Publishing, Bristol, UK, 102–118.

Cudworth, E., et al. (2018) "Introduction: Framing the posthuman dialogues in international relations" in Cudworth, E., Hobden, S. and Kavalski, E. eds., *Posthuman Dialogues in International Relations* Routledge, Oxon, UK, New York, USA, 11–24.

Duffield, J. (2007) "What are international institutions?" *International Studies Review*, 9, 1–22.

Energy Research Centre of the Netherlands, et al. (2016) "Annual Status Report on Nationally Appropriate Mitigation Actions (NAMAs)", (http://www.mitigationmomentum.org/downloads/Mitigation-Momentum-Status-Report-NOV2016.pdf) Accessed 29 June 2018.

Finnemore, M., et al. (1998) "International norm dynamics and political change" *International Organization*, 52, 887–917.

Fitriani, E. (2015) "Yudhoyono's foreign policy: Is Indonesia a rising power?" in Aspinall, E., Mietzner, M. and Tomsa, D. eds., *The Yudhoyono Presidency: Indonesia's Decade of Stability and Stagnation* Institute of Southeast Asian Studies, Singapore, 73–90.

George, A.L., et al. (1985) "Case studies and theories of organizational decision making" *Advances in Information Processing in Organizations*, 2, 21–58.

Gourevitch, P. (1978) "The second image reversed: The international sources of domestic politics" *International Organization*, 32, 881–912.

Haas, P.M. (1992) "Introduction: Epistemic communities and international policy coordination" *International Organization*, 46, 1–35.

Hall, P.A. (1993) "Policy paradigms, social learning, and the state: The case of economic policymaking in Britain" *Comparative Politics*, 25, 275–296.

Hall, P.A., et al. (2001) "An introduction to varieties of capitalism" in Hall, P.A. and Soskice, D. eds., *Varieties of Capitalism: The Institutional Foundations of Comparative Advantage* Oxford University Press, Oxford, UK, 1–70.

Hamilton, C. (2017) *Defiant Earth: The Fate of Humans in the Anthropocene* Polity Press, Cambridge, UK, Malden, MA, USA.

Harrington, C. (2016) "The ends of the world: International relations and the Anthropocene" *Millennium*, 44, 478–498.

Hickmann, T., et al. (2017) "Carbon governance Arrangements and the nation-state: The reconfiguration of public authority in developing countries" *Public Administration and Development*, 37, 331–343.

Hoffmann, M.J. (2011) *Climate Governance at the Crossroads: Experimenting with a Global Response after Kyoto* Oxford University Press, Oxford, UK.

Hooghe, L., et al. (2003) "Unraveling the central state, but how? Types of multi-level governance" *The American Political Science Review*, 97, 233–243.

Indrarto, G.B., et al. (2012) "The context of REDD+ in Indonesia: Drivers, agents and institution's" in *CIFOR Working Paper 92* Bogor, Indonesia.

Jordan, A.J., et al. (2015) "Emergence of polycentric climate governance and its future prospects" *Nature Climate Change*, 5, 977–982.

Keohane, R.O. (1988) "International institutions: Two approaches" *International Studies Quarterly*, 32, 379–396.

Keohane, R.O., et al. (2016) "Cooperation and discord in global climate policy" *Nature Climate Change*, 6, 570–575.

Lederer, M. (2015) "Global governance" in Bäckstrand, K. and Lövbrand, E. eds., *Research Handbook on Climate Governance* Edward Elgar Publishing, Cheltenham, UK, Northampton, USA, 3–13.

Lövbrand, E., et al. (2015) "Who speaks for the future of Earth? How critical social science can extend the conversation on the Anthropocene" *Global Environmental Change*, 32, 211–218.

March, J.G., et al. (1998) "The institutional dynamics of international political orders" *International Organization*, 52, 943–969.

Pattberg, P., et al. (2016) "Global environmental governance in the Anthropocene: An introduction" in Pattberg, P. and Zelli, F. eds., *Environmental Politics and Governance in the Anthropocene: Institutions and Legitimacy in a Complex World* Routledge, Abingdon, UK, New York, USA, 1–12.

Purdon, M. (2015) "Advancing comparative climate change politics: Theory and method" *Global Environmental Politics*, 15, 1–26.

Resosudarmo, B.P., et al. (2013) "The dynamics of climate change governance in Indonesia" in Held, D., Roger, C. and Nag, E.-M. eds., *Climate Governance in the Developing World* Polity Press, Cambridge, UK, Malden, MA, USA, 72–90.

Risse, T., et al. (2013) "Introduction and overview" in Risse, T., Ropp, S.C. and Sikkink, K. eds., *The Persistent Power of Human Rights: From Commitment to Compliance* Cambridge University Press, Cambridge, UK, 3–25.

ROI (2010) "Indonesia voluntary mitigation actions" (http://unfccc.int/files/meetings/cop_15/copenhagen_accord/application/pdf/indonesiacphaccord_app2.pdf) Accessed 31 August 2016.

ROI (2011) Presidential Regulation of the Republic of Indonesia No. 61 Year 2011 on the National Action Plan for Greenhouse Gas Emissions Reduction, Jakarta.

ROI (2015) "Intended nationally determined contribution" (www4.unfccc.int/submissions/INDC/Published%20Documents/Indonesia/1/INDC_REPUBLIC%20OF%20INDONESIA.pdf) Accessed 9 May 2016.

Rosenau, J.N. (1992) "Governance, order and change in world politics" in Rosenau, J.N. and Czempiel, E.O. eds., *Governance without Government: Order and Change in World Politics* Cambridge University Press, Cambridge, UK, 1–29.

Sari, A.P. (2010) "The politics of climate change in Indonesia" in Green, M.J., Freeman, C.W., III and Searight, A. eds., *Green Dragons: The Politics of Climate Change in Asia* Center for Strategic and International Studies, Washington, DC, 56–73.

Sprinz, D., et al. (1994) "The interest-based explanation of international environmental policy" *International Organization*, 48, 77–105.

Steffen, W., et al. (2015) "The trajectory of the Anthropocene: The Great Acceleration" *The Anthropocene Review*, 2, 81–98.

Stephenson, P. (2013) "Twenty years of multi-level governance: 'Where does it come from? What is it? Where is it going?'" *Journal of European Public Policy*, 20, 817–837.

Tsebelis, G. (2000) "Veto players and institutional analysis" *Governance*, 13, 441–474.

UNFCCC (1992) *United Nations Framework Convention on Climate Change*, FCCC/INFORMAL/84. GE.05-62220 E 200705 (https://unfccc.int/resource/docs/convkp/conveng.pdf) Accessed 29 June 2018.

UNFCCC (1998) *Kyoto Protocol to the United Nations Framework Convention on Climate Change*, (https://unfccc.int/resource/docs/convkp/kpeng.pdf) Accessed 29 June 2018.

UNFCCC (2008) *Report of the Conference of the Parties on Its Thirteenth Session*, held in Bali from 3 to 15 December 2007, 1–59.

UNFCCC (2011) *Report of the Conference of the Parties on Its Sixteenth Session*, held in Cancun from 29 November to 10 December 2010 UNFCCC Secretariat, 1–30.

UNFCCC (2015) *Paris Agreement*, UNFCCC Secretariat, Paris.

UNFCCC Secretariat (2015) *Compilation of Information on Nationally Appropriate Mitigation Actions to Be Implemented by Developing Country Parties*, revised note by the secretariat, 1–60.

UNFCCC Secretariat (2017) *FOCUS: Mitigation-NAMAs, Nationally Appropriate Mitigation Actions* (http://unfccc.int/focus/mitigation/items/7172.php) Accessed 15 March 2017.

Victor, D.G. (2011) *Global Warming Gridlock: Creating more Effective Strategies for Protecting the Planet* Cambridge University Press, Cambridge.

Wapner, P. (2014) "The changing nature of nature: Environmental politics in the Anthropocene" *Global Environmental Politics*, 14, 36–54.

Widodo, J. (2015) "Statement: The President of the Republic of Indonesia H.E. Joko Widodo at the Leaders's Event" 21th Conference of the Parties to the UNFCCC Paris, France, 30 November 2015.

World Bank (2016) "Forest area (% of land area)" (http://data.worldbank.org/indicator/AG.LND.FRST.ZS) Accessed 6 January 2016.

World Resources Institute (2018) "CAIT climate data explorer: Historical emissions" (http://cait.wri.org/historical/) Accessed 29 January 2018.

Youatt, R. (2014) "Interspecies relations, international relations: Rethinking Anthropocentric politics" *Millennium*, 43, 207–223.

Young, O.R. (1989) *International Cooperation: Building Regimes for Natural Resources and the Environment* Cornell University Press, Ithaca.

Young, O.R. (2013) "Sugaring off: Enduring insights from long-term research on environmental governance" *International Environmental Agreements: Politics, Law and Economics*, 13, 87–105.

Yudhoyono, S.B. (2009) "Speech by H.E. Dr. Susilo Bambang Yudhoyono" President of the Republic of Indonesia, COP-15, Copenhagen.

Zalasiewicz, J., et al. (2017) "The working group on the Anthropocene: Summary of evidence and interim recommendations" *Anthropocene*, 19, 55–60.

Zimmermann, L. (2016) "Same same or different? Norm diffusion between resistance, compliance, and localization in post-conflict states1" *International Studies Perspectives*, 17, 98–115.

Zürn, M. (2012) "Global governance and multi-level governance" in Levi-Faur, D. ed., *Oxford Handbook of Governance* Oxford University Press, Oxford, UK, New York, USA, 730–744.

Appendix
List of incorporated interviews

- RI-01082016: research interviewee, 1 August 2016
- DI-01082016: donor interviewee, 1 August 2016
- DI-02082016: donor interviewee, 2 August 2016
- TI-02082016: think tank interviewee, 2 August 2016
- NI-02082016: NGO interviewee, 2 August 2016
- DI-03082016: donor interviewee, 3 August 2016
- MI1–05082016: ministry interviewee, 5 August 2016
- MI2–05082016: ministry interviewee, 5 August 2016
- DI-10082016: donor interviewees, 10 August 2016
- RI-10082016: research interviewee, 10 August 2016
- DI-12082016: donor interviewee, 12 August 2016
- DI-15082016: donor interviewee, 15 August 2016
- RI-16082016: research interviewee, 16 August 2016
- DI-18082016: donor interviewee, 18 August 2016
- NI-18082016: NGO interviewee, 18 August 2016

9 Agricultural governance in the Anthropocene

A research agenda

Sandra Schwindenhammer

Introduction

The concept of the Anthropocene suggests that humanity has become a 'geological superpower' that influences Earth's ecosystems and geology (Barry and Maslin 2016, 8). The Anthropocene is, however, not just a new geological epoch. It has also significant political and normative implications. The complex and dynamic co-evolutionary relationship between nature and society (see Weißpflug, in this volume) is both a challenge and an opportunity for political scientists to critically engage with. This chapter sheds light on how International Relations (IR) research as one of the major sub-disciplines of political science can contribute to the Anthropocene debate. Since the constructivist turn in IR with its fundamental initial premise of the codetermination of structure and agency (Wendt 1987), IR scholars have increasingly focused on norm-driven regime analysis (Finnemore and Sikkink 1998), the formation and diffusion of norms (Keck and Sikkink 1998), the contestation of global norms (Wiener 2009, 2008), and the role of public and private norm entrepreneurship in International Relations (Schwindenhammer 2017; Flohr et al. 2010).

The chapter connects findings from (critical) constructivist IR research with recent theoretical works on environmental governance and politics in the Anthropocene. It conceives the Anthropocene not only as a condition of nature, but also as a social construction that is "a means by which contemporary societies interpret their place in the world in light of major shifts in experience" (Delanty and Mota 2017, 30). Conceiving the Anthropocene not only as an objective state of planetary change, but also as an interpretative category draws our attention to societal interpretations and reflections about the present and future of the Earth (Delanty and Mota 2017, 19). However, these reflections are also material since normative interpretations have major implications for what institutions do (Dryzek 2014, 949). Today, technological innovations, e.g., in synthetic biology, enable the rethinking and redesign of entire biological systems. The key argument of the chapter is that conceiving the Anthropocene as a social construction requires more nuanced conceptions of agency, norms and technological innovations.

The empirical focus of the chapter is on global agricultural production and governance in the Anthropocene. This focus is attractive for several reasons. Since most studies of global environmental governance today concentrate on climate change, they risk crowding out analyses of other important environmental issues (Dauvergne and Clapp 2016, 8). Hence, the focus on global agriculture broadens the empirical perspective. The global agri-food system reveals complex interdependencies between global food supply chains and non-linear environmental change. While modern agriculture is a major cause of environmental pollution, including large-scale nitrogen- and phosphorus-induced environmental change (Rockström et al. 2009, 474), the consequences of climate change, such as floods, droughts and rising sea levels, significantly impact agricultural production systems (FAO 2016). Global food and agricultural governance organisations do not form part of legal governance structures among states as environmental treaties do. They rather *inform dialogue* at the international level (Clapp 2017, 508). Agricultural governance in the Anthropocene reveals the importance of ideas, discursive structures and processes and, thus, substantiates "the discursive realm in social-ecological affairs" (Dryzek 2014, 949). Global agricultural governance is fragmented and patchy (Clapp 2017) and rests on the interplay of public and private sources of political authority (Schwindenhammer 2017, 2016). Agricultural governance schemes increasingly involve normative reflections about agricultural production in the light of shifts in experience with the Anthropocene. Focusing on the underlying normative and discursive dynamics in agricultural governance in the Anthropocene allows what Dryzek (2014, 950) postulates: "Rather than rush to conclusions about appropriate institutional configurations for the Anthropocene, the prior task is surely to establish more secure foundations for institutional analysis, design and experimentation".

The chapter is structured as follows: It starts with discussing the material implications of the rise of anthropogenic agricultural systems in the history of the Anthropocene. The chapter then outlines a constructivist research agenda including three main dimensions and related areas for future research. The *dimension of agency* deals with the material and normative embeddedness of norm entrepreneurship in the Anthropocene and discusses who is conceived as an agent in charge of governing agricultural systems and why. The *dimension of norms* highlights the (conflictive) normative foundations and interpretations of societal problems in the agri-food system in the Anthropocene. The *dimension of technological innovations* discusses the rise of transformative technologies in light of normative debates about agricultural governance in the Anthropocene. Finally, the chapter draws conclusions and discusses potential contributions of constructivist IR research to the Anthropocene debate.

The development of anthropogenic agricultural production systems

The precise moment when the human footprint on Earth became so influential to indicate the onset of the Anthropocene is a matter of ongoing debate. The original definition of the Anthropocene refers to data retrieved from glacial ice cores that indicate a growth in the atmospheric concentrations of several greenhouse gases, in particular CO_2 (carbon dioxide) and CH_4 (methane) (Crutzen and Stoermer 2000, 17). These changes in the atmospheric composition coincide with the early Industrial Revolution in Europe (around 1800).

Proponents of the early Anthropocene hypothesis argue that anthropogenic greenhouse gas elevation began much earlier, in the mid-Holocene (Fuller et al. 2011; Ruddiman et al. 2008; Ruddiman 2003). They state that the beginnings of agriculture and subsequent technological innovations in human farming marked the onset of the Anthropocene thousands of years ago (Ruddiman 2003). Human alterations of Eurasian landscapes began at a small-scale during the late Stone Age (8000 to 6000 BCE) and then grew significantly during the subsequent Bronze and Iron Ages (Ruddiman 2003, 262). Especially early agriculture in Asia influenced major increases in prehistoric atmospheric CH_4 concentrations (Fuller et al. 2011). The early farming activities involved irrigating rice paddies, tending methane-emitting livestock, burning seasonal (grass) biomass, and generating human waste (Ruddiman et al. 2008, 1292). While the final assessment of the onset of the Anthropocene is not the aim of this chapter, looking back at the historical development of anthropogenic agriculture systems reveals that the Anthropocene is not an inevitable outcome of human existence. It is the result of conscious choices made by humans (Harrington 2016, 483).

The power of human agency continued to increase, especially when the methods of agricultural production changed through the application of science and technology (Perry 2016, 127). In 1840, Justus von Liebig presented his vision of a rational system of agriculture that should be based on the application of principles from the natural sciences. He emphasised that "this knowledge we must seek from chemistry" (Liebig 1840, vi–vii; cited in Paull 2009, 16). In 1909, Fritz Haber and Carl Bosch gave impetus to the use of chemicals in agriculture through their discovery of the conversion of nitrogen and hydrogen into ammonia (Paull 2009, 16). This discovery and its commercialisation by the chemical company BASF fundamentally transformed global agricultural production by providing ready access to cheap synthetic fertilisers (Smil 2001). The rapid post-1950 diffusion of nitrogenous fertiliser applications increased their worldwide use to nearly 80 million tonnes by the late 1980s and to just above 85 million tonnes by the late 1990s (Smil 2002, 126).

Advances in biology since the 1960s have led to the development of biotechnologies to enhance crop production, breeding and gene mapping (Perry 2016). In the 1990s, the world experienced the first on-field applications of biotechnology to crop production, e.g., crops with resistance to herbicides, pest attacks and glyphosate (Perry 2016). The rise of transformative technologies, such as precision farming technologies, drone technology, or genetically modified (GM) insect technology, paves the way for visions of high-tech food systems in the Anthropocene.

The very short (and, thus, necessarily incomplete) summary of key developments in the history of anthropogenic agricultural production systems reveals both negative and positive effects of increased human control over nature. On the one hand, achievements in science and technology have significantly increased the amount of agricultural outputs. The post-1950's increase in fertiliser application and the spread of intensified large-scale agricultural production systems relying on monoculture contributed considerably to the raising of high-yield varieties of grains and agricultural productivity (Lu and Tian 2017, 181). They are thus credited for reducing hunger worldwide (Holt-Giménez 2011, 316). On the other hand, intensified large-scale agricultural production has caused a number of negative environmental and social impacts, such as air pollution, soil acidification and degradation, water eutrophication, the loss of 90 percent of the Global South's agricultural biodiversity, the monopolisation of seed and chemical inputs by companies from the Global North, and the displacement of millions of peasants to fragile hillsides, shrinking forests, and urban slums (Lu and Tian 2017, 181–182; Holt-Giménez 2011, 316). The material impacts of anthropogenic agricultural production on the ecosystems of the planet seem to be evident. However, the notion of the Anthropocene not only as a material reality but also as social construction implies that the history of anthropogenic agricultural production systems embodies a normative dimension regarding the question whether human agents should further advance their influence to manage the Earth or respect their natural limits.

The dimension of agency and the embeddedness of norm entrepreneurship

The notion of the Anthropocene as a material reality assumes that "humanity itself has become a global geophysical force" (Steffen et al. 2011, 741). However, the ecological markers used to assess the impact of humanity in environmental history, such as atmospheric concentrations of CO_2 and CH_4, can be called 'politically naïve' since they equate the pure existence of humans with the Anthropocene (Harrington 2016, 483). The conceptualisation of human agency in the Anthropocene as an undifferentiated whole runs the risk of depoliticising the Anthropocene (Delanty and Mota 2017, 23), since it attributes no temporal or spatial variability, no differentiated history, culture or politics to humans (Lidskog and Waterton 2016, 401). The centrality of human agency in the concept of the Anthropocene as a condition of nature also involves the risk of 'Anthropocentrism', which is a reductionist view of the planet as shaped by human agents who have become its masters (Delanty and Mota 2017, 22). This view neglects the important aspects of different types, roles, identities and interests of agents (public and private), power relations and different responsibilities.

There is a need to re-conceptualise political agency in the Anthropocene, that is, to differentiate forms of agency and also to assess the contextual factors (material and normative) that form agency in the Anthropocene. Human agency in the Anthropocene is always part of larger cultural and material flows, exchanges and interactions (Dürbeck et al. 2015, 119). It is constructed and shaped in the co-evolution with nature, and based on reflections and re-evaluations of the position of human agents in the world (Delanty and Mota 2017, 19). In this regard, agency in the Anthropocene can also be seen as a paradox. While human beings have established themselves as the agents of change over nature, they are at the same time slaves to nature. They cannot entirely master it since they are part of it (Delanty and Mota 2017, 22).

To develop a more nuanced conceptualisation of agency, the Anthropocene debate can benefit from constructivist IR research on the role of norm entrepreneurs in global governance, which regards a broad range of public and private actors as entrepreneurs with the potential for discursive and normative change, e.g., non-governmental organisations (NGOs), activist networks, epistemic communities, international organisations (IOs), governments or business actors (Schwindenhammer 2016, 105–106). Entrepreneurs are defined as 'meaning managers' that create new 'cognitive frames', thus establishing "new ways of talking about and understanding issues" (Finnemore and Sikkink 1998, 897). Entrepreneurs establish political authority to influence other actors. Political authority exists when an organisation "has decision-making power over a particular issue and is regarded as exercising that power legitimately" (Cutler et al. 1999, 5). Entrepreneurs give emphasis to certain ideas and, thus, prioritise certain governance solutions while neglecting concepts deemed inappropriate and unimportant.

With the increase in human power through scientific and technological innovations, some entrepreneurs in the global agri-food system today even have the power to intervene in the natural evolutionary process, e.g., through the application of GM insect technology in agricultural production (as discussed in detail later in the chapter). However, entrepreneurial involvement in agricultural governance in the Anthropocene needs to be seen in context. It is determined by specific material and cultural circumstances that shape human actions (Dürbeck et al. 2015, 119). The Anthropocene creates, changes or reinforces multiple interdependent relations within and among societies (Biermann 2014a, 58). Recent governance efforts are characterised by a multitude of layers and clusters of rule-making, fragmented both vertically between supranational, international, national and subnational layers of authority, and horizontally between parallel rule-making systems, often comprising different sets of public and private actors (Biermann 2014b, 25).

Normative change in this context is no longer exclusively associated with the political authority of agents from the public sector. It rests on the interaction of public and private sources of political authority (Schwindenhammer 2016). Sources of legal, moral and technical authority increasingly interact in a blurred functional division of labour between the public and the private sector (Flohr et al. 2010, 210). Legal authority refers to the constitutionally institutionalised delegation of competencies by democratic procedures and is exercised by public actors. Moral authority is based on the credibility with which actors pursue goals in the public interest. Technical authority rests on the promise of more rational governance solutions by providing knowledge-based expertise or financial means (Flohr et al. 2010, 210). The search for sound governance solutions in agricultural governance in the Anthropocene directs our analytical attention to the interplay of agency *and* structural factors, that is, the interplay of public and private sources of political authority, rule-making institutions, as well as their interconnections. There are three related research tasks in particular.

Identifying norm entrepreneurs

The first task is to assess who qualifies as an entrepreneur in agricultural governance; with the political authority to formulate, disseminate and represent future visions, and with the ability to motivate others to invest in them (Berenskoetter 2011, 663). The most important IO in charge of food and agriculture politics is the Food and Agriculture Organisation of the United Nations (FAO) and its associated institutions, such as the Committee on World Food Security and the World Food Programme. Due to the inter-sectoral nature of food and agricultural politics, other United Nations (UN) organisations also deal with food-related issues, such as the World Health Organisation (WHO), the World Trade Organisation, and the UN Special Rapporteur on the Right to Food. These organisations are increasingly interacting and building inter-institutional arrangements, e.g., the Codex Alimentarius Commission within the framework of the Joint FAO/WHO Food Standards Programme. Regional public agents, such as the European Union, also engage in entrepreneurial activities. Entrepreneurs from the private sector are also increasingly playing a role in global agriculture governance. Transnational NGOs, such as La Via Campesina or the International Foundation for Organic Agriculture Movements (IFOAM), have gained political influence by promoting new normative frames, such as food sovereignty or organic agriculture. The organic movement, for example, has grown from local activism to representation in commonly used food labelling and on the shelves of major supermarket chains (Liverman and Kapadia 2010, 20). Another important trend is the entrepreneurial involvement of transnational agri-food corporations, such as Bayer, Monsanto or Nestlé. The rise of corporate power has put business actors in a position to influence the broad lines of agricultural research and development and to make governance decisions themselves (Clapp and Fuchs 2009, 9). This list of entrepreneurs is still far from complete. Given the different types of actors on different governance levels with different resources and interests, there is a need to further analyse which entrepreneurs engage in agricultural governance when, why and with what effects in the Anthropocene.

Assessing the attribution of political authority

The second task is to assess how political authority is attributed to entrepreneurs in agricultural governance in the Anthropocene. The general claim of entrepreneurs contributing to governance is based on their moral commitment to universally accepted norms, knowledge-based professional expertise, or problem-solving resources (Flohr et al. 2010; Cutler et al. 1999). The entrepreneurial involvement of NGOs is allegedly based on ideas that relate to commonly accepted social and environmental norms and is thus closely linked to moral authority. Business actors claim knowledge-based expertise based on technical authority. The exercise of legal authority by states and IOs promises added value regarding the legitimacy of governance processes (Schwindenhammer 2016, 108). However, the Anthropocene faces the risk of becoming an all-purpose projection screen and amplifier for everyone's preferred version of 'taking responsibility for the planet' (Purdy 2016, 1). Hence, there is a need to uncover where the concept of the Anthropocene requires and thus privileges specific sources of political authority in agricultural governance. Stories of inevitability and constraints posited in a time of resource scarcity might for instance help powerful agents from the Global North dominate the political discourse and disadvantage small-scale farmers from developing countries (Buck 2015, 371).

Identifying different responsibilities

The third task is to identify different responsibilities and to assess how they can be implemented. Critical scholars interpret the Anthropocene as a result of the expansion of global capitalism (Altvater 2016, 144) and the (quasi-) imperialistic domination of the rest of the world by Western agents (Chakrabarty 2009, 216). They argue that nature has been incorporated into capitalist rationality and reduced to something that can be valued and traded just as any other business asset (Altvater 2016, 145). From a critical perspective, the question of entrepreneurship in agricultural governance in the Anthropocene implies the attribution of different responsibilities. Smallholder farmers face specific barriers, such as limited access to global food markets, loans, risk management tools, and social protection (FAO 2016, xii). In the words of Chakrabarty (2009, 216),

> why should one include the poor of the world ... by use of such all-inclusive terms as species or mankind when the blame for the current crisis should be squarely laid at the door of the rich nations in the first place and of the richer classes in the poorer ones?

The dimension of norms and the role of norm contestation and discourse

The notion of the Anthropocene as an interpretative category implies that contemporary societies reflect upon themselves and upon life (Delanty and Mota 2017, 24). From a constructivist perspective, analysis and discourse about what we can save and what we most want to save on Earth are needed (Purdy 2016, 1).

The academic debate on the Anthropocene has brought about two competing narratives of the Anthropocene as either a crisis for sustainability or an opportunity to increase human well-being (for an excellent overview see Lundershausen, in this volume). The two narratives represent the extreme ends of different descriptions of the Anthropocene based on very different interpretations of past and contemporary Earth system changes and the concomitant development of human civilisations.

The first narrative refers to the Anthropocene as a crisis of human development on a finite planet. Rockström et al. (2009, 472) present the vision that overstepping the planetary boundaries has "consequences that are detrimental or even catastrophic for large parts of the world". Large-scale industrial, mono-cropped landscapes are a main reference for Anthropocene horror stories (Buck 2015, 374). Geophysical processes inevitably constrain human conduct and, thus, bring about instability, uncertainty and the risk of unsustainability. The Anthropocene as a crisis-narrative rests on the assumption that leaving the safe space of the Holocene entails the risk to permanently overthrow the current strategies of human development (see Lundershausen, in this volume).

The second narrative points to the Anthropocene as an opportunity to achieve long-term sustainability. It highlights the ability of human agents to determine natural processes and, thus, to navigate environmental changes. The Anthropocene as an opportunity-narrative regards planetary thresholds as not fixed. It involves a managerialist approach in which human agents do not only react to global changes but act as designers of the Earth through improved technology and planetary stewardship (Dürbeck et al. 2015, 120).

The notion of the Anthropocene as a social construction points to the relevance of interpretative and reflexive processes, e.g., about imagining future possibilities and redefining the present in light of such possibilities (Delanty and Mota 2017, 24). Dryzek (2014, 950) identifies 'ecosystemic reflexivity' as the primary desideratum for institutions in the Anthropocene. This differs from simple reflexivity in at least two ways: the incorporation of better ways to listen to ecological systems that have no voice into human institutions; and an ability to rethink core values in the context of an active and unstable Earth system. The core challenge of agricultural governance in the Anthropocene might thus not be institutional fragmentation, but rather determining the relative weight of different discourses; notably, the subordination of the sustainability discourse to the economic discourse (Dryzek 2014, 950).

To shed more light on the role of discursive processes, interpretations and conflicts over norms, scholars of agricultural governance in the Anthropocene can benefit from (critical) constructivist norm research in IR, which provides a considerable amount of knowledge on the role of ideas, norms and discourses. Intersubjective knowledge and ideas have constitutive effects on social reality (Adler 2002, 102). Norms are standards of appropriate behaviour for actors with a given identity (Finnemore and Sikkink 1998, 891). While classical approaches of norm research conceptualise the spread of norms as a rather simple dichotomy between adaptation and rejection (Wiener 2009, 179), critical approaches conceptualise norms as dynamic social constructions. They argue that norms can be shaped in political discourses and that normative understandings can vary with different discursive settings or cultural practices (Wiener 2008). Building upon key findings from critical IR research, this section identifies norm contestation and its settlement as two related research tasks.

Assessing guiding norms and their contestation

The first task is to assess the guiding norms in global agricultural governance in the Anthropocene and to analyse how far these norms are contested. The formal adoption of norms is often lacking because norms are interpreted in different ways by differently socialised actors with different socio-cultural traditions (Wiener 2008). Although there might be formal agreement on the importance of a norm, the meaning of the norm can vary with local structures and agents promoting different normative understandings (Wiener 2008, 33). This is particularly instructive regarding the Sustainable Development Goals (SDG) adopted in 2015. SDG 2 aims to end hunger, achieve food security and improved nutrition, and promote sustainable agriculture (UN 2015). Although at first glance, SDG 2 provides a commonly accepted normative reference, global agricultural governance reveals norm contestation. Many of the norms that substantiate agricultural governance in the Anthropocene are polarised and open to different conflicting and sometimes mutually exclusive interpretations (Clapp 2017; Schwindenhammer et al. 2017). Given the plurality of norms in the global agri-food regime, norm contestation, defined as "the range of social practices which discursively express disapproval of norms" (Wiener 2014, 1), is expected to be rather the rule than the exception. Norm contestation can range from the reinterpretation of global norms to fit with regional or domestic contexts (norm localisation) (Acharya 2004) to the creation of new regional norms to preserve regional autonomy (norm subsidiarity) (Acharya 2011), or it can even result in ongoing norm conflicts (Schwindenhammer et al. 2017).

The *food security norm*, for instance, implies that "all people, at all times, have physical and economic access to sufficient safe and nutritious food to meet their dietary needs and food preferences for a healthy and active life" (FAO 1996). However, there are two contradictory paradigms for mitigating food insecurity with regard to agricultural production (Freyer et al. 2015, 82–85): The high-input paradigm promotes reliance on crop biotechnology, large-scale farms, and corporate concentration in processing, marketing and distribution. The low-input paradigm focuses on small-scale farms, incorporates socio-cultural concern, and is driven by ethical, ecological and social reasoning. For a long time, global agricultural governance followed the high-input paradigm and, thus, ignored the interrelation between global environmental change and processing, distributing, retailing and consuming food (Liverman and Kapadia 2010, 21).

The spread of the *sustainability norm* gave the impetus for the concept of sustainable food systems. Although there is general agreement on the importance of the sustainability norm, varying normative understandings and weightings of the economic, ecological and social pillars of sustainable development give rise to entrepreneurs' different preferences for high-input or low-input agricultures (Schwindenhammer et al. 2017). The FAO (2016, xii) promotes the use of nitrogen-efficient and heat-tolerant crop varieties, zero-tillage, and integrated soil fertility management to boost agricultural productivity. Entrepreneurs from the agri-food industry, such as Bayer CropScience, promote integrated crop solutions made up of high-value seeds, chemical and biological crop protection products, and tailored services (Bayer CropScience 2017). In January 2017, the CEOs of Bayer and Monsanto met with newly elected US President Trump "to share their view on the future of the agriculture industry" (Bayer 2017). They declared that the merged company expected to spend approximately $16 billion for research and development over the next six years to drive their vision of innovation in agriculture with geneticists, roboticists, satellite imagery specialists, engineers, data scientists, advanced breeders, and statisticians (Bayer 2017). Other entrepreneurs reject high-input agricultures because of the adverse impacts of synthetic fertilisers on human health and the environment. While the WHO's cancer agency, the International Agency for Research on Cancer, classifies the key ingredient in Monsanto's Roundup herbicide, glyphosate, as probably carcinogenic, many governments regard glyphosate as unlikely to pose a cancer risk to humans (Rosendahl and Forsell 2017). The UN Special Rapporteur on the Right to Food criticises the assertion promoted by entrepreneurs from the agrochemical industry that pesticides are necessary to achieve food security as being "not only inaccurate, but dangerously misleading" (UN 2017, 19).

In contrast, the *food sovereignty norm* is a normative counter-frame to food security. Food sovereignty relates to cultural aspects of food production, supports the right to seek self-sufficiency, and intends to strengthen local agricultures with a special focus on the needs of smallholder farmers. Agriculture is reconceptualised as part of a movement to protect local values from the dominance of corporate interests (Buck 2015, 375). Transnational NGOs from the food sovereignty movement, such as La Via Campesina, emphasise the social component of sustainable development and criticise the food security norm for treating "food as a problem of insufficient trade rather than hunger by privileging *access* to food rather than *control over* systems of production and consumption" (Wittman 2011, 91).

Analysing the potential of agricultural governance schemes to settle norm contestation

From a critical constructivist perspective, a key element of dealing with norm contestation is to institutionalise ways that facilitate mutual normative understanding and allow for bottom-up participation in processes of negotiating normativity (Wiener 2014, 42–43). Agricultural governance schemes that have – implicitly or explicitly – already begun to deal with the issue of norm contestation provide valuable empirical cases for further research. Global benchmarking (Broome and Quirk 2015) and standardisation (Ponte et al. 2011) schemes are especially interesting from a critical norm research perspective because they develop indicators for assessing the implementation of global norms and thereby attribute expertise, responsibility and political authority to different entrepreneurs.

Global benchmarking involves the classification and numerical translation of relative performance or value and enables a comparative assessment of the quality of conduct, design and outcomes (Broome and Quirk 2015, 815). Global benchmarking includes a "normative agenda" (Broome and Quirk 2015) since it strengthens the legitimacy of certain practices, while marginalising or delegitimising others. Benchmarking is a recursive process whereby complex and contested normative values are translated into simplified numerical representations (Broome and Quirk 2015, 815). It transmits particular normative frames and influences the design of subsequent governance interventions. The Sustainability Assessment of Food and Agriculture Systems (SAFA) is the first holistic global benchmarking framework for the understanding and assessment of sustainability along food and agriculture value chains (FAO 2013, v). SAFA builds on existing sustainability tools and assists public and private organisations in demonstrating their level of sustainability performance. SAFA assessments include adaptation to geographic, sector-specific, and individual conditions of the assessed organisation and the comprehensive use of existing documentation, standards and tools (FAO 2013, vi).

Standardisation in agricultural governance has emerged on different regulatory levels in response to globalised flows of food trade and consumer demand for healthy products (Ponte et al. 2011). Standards "tell us what is relevant, what is valued, what is important; and, by implication, they tell us what is not important" (Busch 2011, 3248). Food and agricultural standards vary as to whether they are product, process or management standards (Ponte et al. 2011) and can either make global claims or have a regional, national or individual regulatory reach (Schwindenhammer 2016, 104). Global organic agricultural governance through standards provides an interesting field for assessing norm contestation. IFOAM, FAO and the UN Conference on Trade and Development established two global public-private-partnerships (International Task Force on Harmonisation and Equivalence in Organic Agriculture (2002–2008) and Global Organic Market Access Project (2009–2012)) to improve standard harmonisation, recognition and equivalence. The entrepreneurs reached a common understanding of regional standard-setting as an appropriate strategy to facilitate global organic trade (Schwindenhammer 2016). At first sight, regional organic standards create a wide constituency of insider norm proponents and adapt to different cultural-normative understandings. However, they also increase the influence of ideas about efficiency and growth from the business world, make organic agriculture more capital and management skill dependent and, thus, further marginalise smallholder farmers (Schwindenhammer 2017).

All in all, the open research question remains whether benchmarking and standardisation schemes provide inclusive settings and allow for bottom-up participation in processes of negotiating normativity and thereby avoid privileging specific normative understandings at the expense of others.

The dimension of technological innovations

Interpretative and reflexive processes in agricultural governance in the Anthropocene do not only serve entrepreneurs as means of self-reflection and re-evaluation, they also inform the development and application of technological innovations. Normative debates about whether entrepreneurs should further advance their influence on the direction of global agricultural change or restraint themselves to stay within the natural limits of the Earth system go hand in hand with advances in science and technology. Especially the rise of new transformative technologies paves the way for visions of high-tech agricultural systems. Visions can be an empowering force, since visions motivate agents to realise or prevent possibilities of being in the world (Berenskoetter 2011, 648). By laying out a future path, a vision stimulates, mobilises and directs entrepreneurial activities towards decreasing or increasing the distance between what is and what could be (Berenskoetter 2011, 663). Against this background, this section highlights two related research areas.

Assessing the role of transformative technologies

The development and application of *GM insect technology* provides an illustrative example (see in what follows Schwindenhammer 2019). As part of the next generation of agricultural biotechnology, GM insect technology offers an alternative vision for insect pest control in global agricultural production. It promises a significant future reduction of the use of chemical insecticides. There are two potential ways of GM insect use: self-sustaining and self-limiting strategies (Leftwich et al. 2015; Mumford and Carrasco 2014). In self-sustaining strategies wild insect populations are replaced by new populations with modified behaviour or physiology that reduces their impact as vectors or plant feeders (Mumford and Carrasco 2014, 306). Self-limiting strategies suppress local insect populations by using the natural mating system to introduce genetic traits that will ultimately lead to their demise (Leftwich et al. 2015, 212).

Oxitec Limited (located in the United Kingdom) is the most influential business entrepreneur in the field of GM insect technology. As one of the five subsidiaries of the transnational biotechnology company Intrexon Corporation (USA), Oxitec has successfully developed, patented and tested self-limiting strategies for several insect species. The company succeeded in presenting GM insect technology as an approach to serving the public goods of health and sustainable agriculture. Oxitec paved the way for GM insect field trials and deliberate releases. Self-limiting strategies are already being assessed and applied in different parts of the world, e.g., in Brazil, the United States and the Caribbean. Oxitex's GM insect 'products' include genetically modified strains of the yellow fever mosquito, the olive fly, the diamondback moth, and the pink bollworm.

The company has also successfully managed to become a source of exclusive expert knowledge political representatives draw on. The collaboration with public officials has allowed Oxitec to influence political discussions and emerging regulatory frameworks at national and international levels (Schwindenhammer 2019). From a normative perspective, Oxitec's entrepreneurial involvement seems to confirm the observation that giving political authority to business corporations from the Global North because of their supposed expert knowledge values the rationality of professional expertise – and market interests – over that of democratic checks and balances (Flohr et al. 2010, 236).

Dealing with risks and the burden of uncertainty

The application of GM insect technology in agricultural production also serves as an illustrative example of how the application of transformative technologies challenges agricultural governance in the Anthropocene. Transformative technologies promise benefits for future agricultural production systems but pose risks at the same time. GM insect technology raises human and environmental safety issues. Unintended effects may include new or more vigorous pests, harm to other species, and disruption of ecological communities and ecosystem processes (Convention on Biological Diversity 2016, 84–86). GM insect technology also poses new governance challenges, e.g., regarding the attribution of responsibility, the liability for potential damage, the role of complex scientific assessments relying on specific knowledge, the transparency and legitimacy of knowledge generation, the compensation for context-specific knowledge gaps, and conflicts between the aim of independent scientific evaluation and the protection of proprietary data and patent rights (Schwindenhammer 2019).

Most of these challenges point to another core feature of the Anthropocene – the burden of uncertainty. Some degree of uncertainty is an inherent element of scientific and technological innovations. However, even if humans achieved discursive consent about the use of transformative technologies and related visions of agricultural systems, we do not know if nature would follow that path.

Constructivist research is equipped to engage with the question of uncertainty, even though constructivists have, so far, widely neglected the subsequent question how entrepreneurs deal with uncertainty, that is, how they claim to know the future and how this affects their discourse behaviour (Berenskoetter 2011, 648). Sustainability assessments and an increased level of scientific, technical, environmental and legal information might, at least theoretically, put societies in a better position to engage in public discourses about what people are willing to risk and about potential trade-offs between innovation and precaution in the Anthropocene.

The Cartagena Protocol's guidance on risk assessment of living modified organisms (LMOs) that possess novel genetic material obtained through the use of modern biotechnology suggests including information on national and international standards and guidelines as well as knowledge and experience of farmers, growers, scientists, regulatory officials, indigenous peoples and local communities in the risk assessment of GM insects (Convention on Biological Diversity 2016, 17). However, context-specific knowledge gaps prevail, especially in developing countries. These gaps derive from "information-poor environments" (Mol 2009, 118). Information-poor environments can result from a variety of causes: economic constraints can restrict the collection of or access to information or there can be political constraints on information collection, processing, spreading, access and use. They can be related to poor organisational conditions and capacities or can be an implication of specific cultural or ideological contexts where dominant interpretative frames of information or hegemonic institutional practices limit the meaning of information (Mol 2009, 115). In the latter case of norm contestation, even high levels of information flow may become irrelevant. There is thus a need to further analyse the conditions that enable independent and transparent knowledge production, sharing and assessment (Galaz 2014, 46).

Conclusion

The chapter aimed at connecting findings from (critical) constructivist IR research with recent theoretical debates on environmental governance and politics in the Anthropocene. This perspective provides a valuable approach for analysing the underlying social dynamics in agricultural governance in the Anthropocene. The key argument of the chapter is that the Anthropocene is more than an objective condition of planetary change. It is also a social construction that requires more nuanced conceptions of agency, norms and technological innovations. The chapter has outlined a constructivist research agenda including three main research dimensions (namely agency, norms and technological innovations) and several related areas for future research.

The *dimension of agency* reveals the material and normative embeddedness of norm entrepreneurship in the Anthropocene. From a constructivist perspective, human agency in the Anthropocene is more than a simple case of instrumental domination. It is shaped in co-evolution with nature, and based on reflections and re-evaluations of the position of human agents in the world (Delanty and Mota 2017, 19–21). The chapter has identified three tasks for future research on agency in agricultural governance in the Anthropocene – the identification of who qualifies as an entrepreneur, with the political authority to formulate, disseminate and represent visions of agricultural governance; the assessment of how political authority is attributed to norm entrepreneurs; and the identification of different responsibilities.

The *dimension of norms* highlights the (conflictive) normative foundations of agricultural governance in the Anthropocene. The chapter has shown that seeing the Anthropocene as a social construction involves the need to pay more analytical attention to the role of ideas, discursive structures and processes underlying agricultural governance in the Anthropocene instead of focusing exclusively on institutional interaction and fragmentation. The chapter has identified two research tasks related to the dimension of norms – the assessment of guiding norms and their contestation and the analysis of the potential of agricultural governance schemes to settle norm contestation. Referring to the Anthropocene as an interpretative category, future research on norm contestation should find out 'how meaning is enacted' (Wiener 2009, 176) in agricultural governance arrangements. What are the appropriate mechanisms for addressing norm contestation? And how can we prevent governance institutions from marginalising alternative normative frames?

The *dimension of technological innovations* discusses the rise of new technologies in light of normative debates about agricultural governance in the Anthropocene. It identifies the role of transformative technologies and the development of political strategies to deal with risks and the burden of uncertainty as future research areas. Constructivist research on the role of visions (Berenskoetter 2011) and findings from research on technological innovations in the Anthropocene (Galaz 2014) provide a starting point for analysing transformative technologies. Some pending questions are: How do entrepreneurs claim to know the future and how does this affect their behaviour? Who has the scientific knowledge and legitimacy to assess technological innovations in agricultural production?

The research agenda offers manifold opportunities for (critical) IR scholars to engage with the Anthropocene debate. While constructivist IR research can add comprehensive knowledge on the formation and diffusion of global norms and the role of norm entrepreneurs, critical constructivist IR research directs our attention to norm contestation and the marginalisation of non-Western normativity in the Anthropocene. Looking at global governance in the Anthropocene through the lens of critical constructivist IR research enables, inter alia, the analysis, rethinking and renegotiation of global norms and the dismantling of practices and political institutions of Western domination. (Critical) constructivist IR research has the potential to widen the focus of the Anthropocene debate empirically and normatively. To do so, we clearly face a lot of research tasks – so, let us begin!

Acknowledgements

I thank Per-Olof Busch, Thomas Hickmann, Sabine Weiland, the members of the Working Group Environmental Politics and Global Change of the German Political Science Association, and Farhood Badri for insightful comments on earlier drafts of this chapter.

References

Acharya, A. (2004) "How ideas spread: Whose norms matter? Norm localization and institutional change in Asian regionalism" *International Organization*, 58(2), 239–275.

Acharya, A. (2011) "Norm subsidiarity and regional orders: Sovereignty, regionalism, and rule-making in the Third World" *International Studies Quarterly*, 55(1), 95–123.

Adler, E. (2002) "Constructivism and international relations" in Carlsnaes, W., Risse, T. and Simmons, B.A. eds., *Handbook of International Relations* Sage Publications, New York, 95–118.

Altvater, E. (2016) "The capitalocene, or, geoengineering against capitalism's planetary boundaries" in Moore, J.W. ed., *Anthropocene or Capitalocene? Nature, History, and the Crisis of Capitalism* PM Press, Oakland, 138–152.

Barry, A. and Maslin, M. (2016) "The politics of the Anthropocene: A dialogue" *Geo: Geography and Environment*, 3(2), e00022.

Bayer (2017) "Joint statement: Monsanto, Bayer CEOs meet with new administration" (www.advancingtogether.com/en/ir-media/press-releases/joint-statement-monsanto-bayer-ceos-meet-with-new-administration/) Accessed 20 March 2018.

Bayer CropScience (2017) "Three basic components: Sustainable agriculture in practice" (www.cropscience.bayer.com/en/crop-science/forwardfarming) Accessed 20 March 2018.

Berenskoetter, F. (2011) "Reclaiming the vision thing: Constructivists as students of the future" *International Studies Quarterly*, 55(3), 647–668.

Biermann, F. (2014a) "The Anthropocene: A governance perspective" *The Anthropocene Review*, 1(1), 57–61.

Biermann, F. (2014b) *Earth System Governance: World Politics in the Anthropocene* MIT Press, Cambridge, MA.

Broome, A. and Quirk, J. (2015) "The politics of numbers: The normative agendas of global benchmarking" *Review of International Studies*, 41(5), 813–818.

Buck, H.J. (2015) "On the possibilities of a charming Anthropocene" *Annals of the Association of American Geographers*, 105(2), 369–377.

Busch, L. (2011) "Food standards: The cacophony of governance" *Journal of Experimental Botany*, 62(10), 3247–3250.

Chakrabarty, D. (2009) "The climate of history: Four theses" *Critical Inquiry*, 35(2), 197–222.

Clapp, J. (2017) "Food" in Pattberg, P.H. and Zelli, F. eds., *Encyclopedia of Global Environmental Governance and Politics* Edward Elgar, Cheltenham, 504–512.

Clapp, J. and Fuchs, D. (2009) "Agrifood corporations, global governance, and sustainability: A framework for analysis" in Clapp, J. and Fuchs, D. eds., *Corporate Power in Global Agrifood Governance* MIT Press, Cambridge, MA, 1–25.

Convention on Biological Diversity (2016) *Guidance on Risk Assessment of Living Modified Organisms and Monitoring in the Context of Risk Assessment*, UNEP/CBD/BS/COP-MOP/8/8/Add.1, submitted to the Eighth Meeting of the Conference of the Parties to the Convention on Biological Diversity, 14 September 2016, Cancun.

Crutzen, P.J. and Stoermer, E.F. (2000) "The 'Anthropocene'" *Global Change Newsletter*, 41, 17–18.

Cutler, A.C., Haufler, V. and Porter, T. (1999) "Private authority and international affairs" in Cutler, A.C., Haufler, V. and Porter, T. eds., *Private Authority and International Affairs* State University of New York Press, Albany, 3–28.

Dauvergne, P. and Clapp, J. (2016) "Researching global environmental politics in the 21st century" *Global Environmental Politics*, 16(1), 1–12.

Delanty, G. and Mota, A. (2017) "Governing the Anthropocene: Agency, governance, knowledge" *European Journal of Social Theory*, 20(1), 9–38.

Dryzek, J.S. (2014) "Institutions for the Anthropocene: Governance in a changing earth system" *British Journal of Political Science*, 46(4), 937–956.

Dürbeck, G., Schaumann, C. and Sullivan, H. (2015) "Human and non-human agencies in the Anthropocene" *Ecozon@*, 6(1), 118–136.

FAO (1996) *Rome Declaration on World Food Security* FAO, Rome.

FAO (2013) *SAFA Guidelines: Version 3.0* FAO, Rome.

FAO (2016) *The State of Food and Agriculture: Climate Change, Agriculture, and Food Security* FAO, Rome.

Finnemore, M. and Sikkink, K. (1998) "International norm dynamics and political change" *International Organization*, 52(4), 887–917.

Flohr, A., Rieth, L., Schwindenhammer, S. and Wolf, K.D. (2010) *The Role of Business in Global Governance: Corporations as Norm-Entrepreneurs* Palgrave Macmillan, Basingstoke.

Freyer, B., Bingen, J., Klimek, M. and Paxton, R. (2015) "Feeding the world: The contribution of the IFOAM principles" in Freyer, B. and Bingen, J. eds., *Re-Thinking Organic Food and Farming in a Changing World* Springer, Dordrecht, et al., 81–106.

Fuller, D.Q., van Etten, J., Manning, K., Castillo, C., Kingwell-Banham, E., Weisskopf, A., Qin, L., Sato, Y.-I. and Hijmans, R.J. (2011) "The contribution of rice agriculture and livestock pastoralism to prehistoric methane levels: An archaeological assessment" *The Holocene*, 21(5), 743–759.

Galaz, V. (2014) *Global Environmental Governance, Technology and Politics: The Anthropocene Gap* Edward Elgar, Cheltenham.

Harrington, C. (2016) "The ends of the world: International relations and the Anthropocene" *Millennium: Journal of International Studies*, 44(3), 478–498.

Holt-Giménez, E. (2011) "Food security, food justice, or food sovereignty? Crises, food movements, and regime change" in Alkon, A.H. and Agyeman, J. eds., *Cultivating Food Justice: Race, Class, and Sustainability* MIT Press, Cambridge, MA, 309–330.

Keck, M.E. and Sikkink, K. (1998) *Activists beyond Borders: Advocacy Networks in International Politics* Cornell University Press, Ithaca.

Leftwich, P.T., Bolton, M. and Chapman, T. (2015) "Evolutionary biology and genetic techniques for insect control" *Evolutionary Applications*, 9(1), 212–230.

Lidskog, R. and Waterton, C. (2016) "Anthropocene: A cautious welcome from environmental sociology?" *Environmental Sociology*, 2(4), 395–406.

Liebig, J. (1840) *Organic Chemistry in Its Applications to Agriculture and Physiology* Taylor and Walton, London.

Liverman, D. and Kapadia, K. (2010) "Food systems and the global environment: An overview" in Ingram, J., Ericksen, P. and Liverman, D. eds., *Food Security and Global Environmental Change* Earthscan, London, 3–24.

Lu, C. and Tian, H. (2017) "Global nitrogen and phosphorus fertilizer use for agriculture production" *Earth System Science Data*, 9, 181–192.

Mol, A.P.J. (2009) "Environmental governance through information: China and Vietnam" *Singapore Journal of Tropical Geography*, 30(1), 114–129.

Mumford, J.D. and Carrasco, L.R. (2014) "Economics of transgenic insects for field release" in Benedict, M.Q. ed., *Transgenic Insects* CABI, Wallingford, 306–318.

Paull, J. (2009) "A century of synthetic fertilizer: 1909–2009" *Elementals: Journal of Bio-Dynamics Tasmania*, 94, 16–21.

Perry, M. (2016) "Sustaining food production in the Anthropocene: Influences by regulation of crop biotechnology" in Kennedy, A. and Liljeblad, J. eds., *Food Systems Governance: Challenges for Justice, Equality and Human Rights* Routledge, New York, 127–142.

Ponte, S., Gibbon, P. and Vestergaard, J. eds. (2011) *Governing through Standards: Origins, Drivers and Limitations* Palgrave Macmillan, Basingstoke.

Purdy, J. (2016) "Surviving the Anthropocene: What's next for humanity?" (www.abc.net.au/religion/articles/2016/03/01/4416386.htm) Accessed 20 March 2018.

Rockström, J., Steffen, W., Noone, K., Persson, Å., Chapin, F.S., Lambin, E.F., Lenton, T.M., Scheffer, M., Folke, C., Schellnhuber, H.J., Nykvist, B., de Wit, C.A., Hughes, T., van der Leeuw, S., Rodhe, H., Sörlin, S., Snyder, P.K., Costanza, R., Svedin, U., Falkenmark, M., Karlberg, L., Corell, R.W., Fabry, V.J., Hansen, J., Walker, B., Liverman, D., Richardson, K., Crutzen, P. and Foley, J.A. (2009) "A safe operating space for humanity" *Nature*, 461, 472–475.

Rosendahl, J. and Forsell, T. (2017) "EU chemical agency says weed killer glyphosate not carcinogenic" (www.reuters.com/article/us-health-eu-glyphosate/eu-chemical-agency-says-weed-killer-glyphosate-not-carcinogenic-idUSKBN16M1KM) Accessed 20 March 2018.

Ruddiman, W.F. (2003) "The anthropogenic greenhouse era began thousands of years ago" *Climatic Change*, 61(3), 261–293.

Ruddiman, W.F., Guo, Z., Zhou, X., Wu, H. and Yu, Y. (2008) "Early rice farming and anomalous methane trends" *Quaternary Science Reviews*, 27, 1291–1295.

Schwindenhammer, S. (2016) "Authority pooling and regional organic agriculture standard-setting: Evidence from East Africa" *Journal of Environmental Policy & Planning*, 18(1), 102–120.

Schwindenhammer, S. (2017) "Global organic agriculture policy-making through standards as an organizational field: When institutional dynamics meet entrepreneurs" *Journal of European Public Policy*, 24(11), 1678–1697.

Schwindenhammer, S. (2019) "The rise, regulation, and risks of genetically modified insect technology in global agriculture" *Science, Technology and Society*, forthcoming.

Schwindenhammer, S., Breitmeier, H. and Kirf, B. (2017) "Die Norm der Nachhaltigkeit im globalen Regimekomplex für Ernährung. Anerkannt und doch umstritten" *Zeitschrift für Außen-und Sicherheitspolitik*, 10(3), 353–371.

Smil, V. (2001) *Enriching the Earth: Fritz Haber, Carl Bosch, and the Transformation of World Food Production* MIT Press, Cambridge, MA.

Smil, V. (2002) "Nitrogen and food production: Proteins for human diets" *AMBIO*, 31(2), 126–131.

Steffen, W., Persson, Å., Deutsch, L., Zalasiewicz, J., Williams, M., Richardson, K., Crumley, C., Crutzen, P., Folke, C., Gordon, L., Molina, M., Ramanathan, V., Rockström, J., Scheffer, M., Schellnhuber, H.J. and Svedin, U. (2011) "The Anthropocene: From global change to planetary stewardship" *AMBIO*, 40(7), 739–761.

UN (2015) *Transforming Our World: The 2030 Agenda for Sustainable Development*, A/Res/70/1, Resolution adopted by the General Assembly on 25 September 2015, New York.

UN (2017) *Report of the Special Rapporteur on the Right to Food*, submitted to the Human Rights Council Thirty Fourth Session, 24 January 2017, A/HRC/34/48, Geneva.

Wendt, A.E. (1987) "The agent-structure problem in international relations theory" *International Organization*, 41(3), 335–370.

Wiener, A. (2008) *The Invisible Constitution of Politics: Contested Norms and International Encounters* Cambridge University Press, Cambridge.

Wiener, A. (2009) "Enacting meaning-in-use: Qualitative research on norms and international relations" *Review of International Studies*, 35(1), 175–193.

Wiener, A. (2014) *A Theory of Contestation* Springer, Heidelberg.

Wittman, H. (2011) "Food sovereignty: A new rights framework for food and nature?" *Environment and Society: Advances in Research*, 2, 87–105.

Part III
Critical perspectives and implications

10 Sustainability impact assessment of land use changes in the Anthropocene

Till Hermanns and Qirui Li

Introduction

Around the world, changes in land use are not only driven by natural developments such as climate change but also by various societal developments, for example demands and policies of land use (Foley et al. 2005). As a major geological force of the Earth system (Zalasiewicz et al. 2010; Crutzen and Stoermer 2000), humankind produces its own specific space (Lefebvre 1991), disturbing the previous equilibrium of the Holocene (Rockström et al. 2009). Land use changes driven by human space production frequently place a burden on the environment, irreversibly altering atmospheric and biospheric processes of the Earth system. Leaving the 'safe operating space' and crossing the bio-geophysical thresholds of these Earth systems will have disastrous consequences for humankind (Rockström et al. 2009). Such notions are behind the debate on the Anthropocene as a new geological era as well as its political implications. Within the debate, we note a dichotomy between descriptions of the Anthropocene as a 'crisis' and an 'opportunity' (Lundershausen, in this volume). Although both highlight the underlying normative dimension of land use decisions, the 'crisis' description emphasises that, by satisfying the land use claims of current generations, we are undermining the safety of operating space. In contrast, the description of the Anthropocene as an 'opportunity' focuses on the benefits of satisfying land use claims by human-driven environmental alteration and changes to the ecosystem. In this chapter, we adopt the perspective of the 'Anthropocene as a crisis for sustainability', given the irreversible impact on Earth system processes.

The 'Great Acceleration' (Steffen et al. 2014) in the geological era of the Anthropocene is characterised by socio-economic pressures such as increased production and consumption by a growing global population, especially in emerging economies, e.g., China and India. These changes manifest themselves in the increased exploitation of natural resources and intensified land use patterns (Zalasiewicz et al. 2010). The boundaries of the 'safe operating space' are being crossed by global societal challenges such as climate change and an acceleration in biodiversity loss and environmental pollution (Rockström et al. 2009). A key requirement to help us cope with these pressures is to integrate knowledge of bio-geophysical thresholds of the Earth system with a sustainability assessment of human space usage (Hossain et al. 2017; Moldan et al. 2012) and governance (Jordan and Lenschow 2010). Further, a vital and ever more complex task in supporting political decisions about future land use patterns is to assess the impacts of land use changes.

Sustainability impact assessment (SIA) is an integrative approach to measuring the impacts of land use changes on environmental, economic and social systems (Helming et al. 2008). Hence, SIA can serve as a tool to promote the sustainable transition of society (Markard et al. 2012; Pope et al. 2004). It adopts the 'triple-bottom-line' model of sustainability, defined as the equal consideration of environmental, economic and social aspects of sustainable development (SD) (Paracchini et al. 2011; Hacking and Guthrie 2008). Moreover, integrative SIA approaches that include economic, environmental and social considerations must be spatially explicit. This enables the application of SIA to specific regions and helps policymakers make decisions while weighing the various unintended impacts of land use changes (Bennett et al. 2015). To this end, objectives-led SIA approaches are particularly useful in introducing societal benchmarks for the state of environmental, economic and social aspects regarding SD, such as 'improving water quality' or 'creating new jobs' (Pope et al. 2004). In contrast to a broad and non-specific orientation along the triple bottom-line, objectives-led SIA approaches help to give direction to the decision-making process (Pope et al. 2004). Quantitative SIA approaches based on impact models are available to measure the impacts of land use changes (Li et al. 2016; Böhringer and Löschel 2006). On the other hand, there also exist qualitative approaches that explicitly consider societal values (Schindler 2017; Uthes et al. 2010).

In the context of the Anthropocene debate, however, there is a dearth of studies that operationalise space production through objectives-led SIA approaches. Here, therefore, we intend to present a framework for assessing the impacts of land use changes in the Anthropocene. The framework allows the matching of region-specific supply with societal demand in terms of functions and services related to land use. Land use related functions and services are those benefits provided to humankind by land, while land use claims reflect human demands on land use in a region in the broadest sense. The proposed framework links the supply of land use related functions and services in the environmental, economic and social systems to societal demands on land use. To achieve this, the framework enables the analysis of manifold targets and normative values from stakeholder strategies at different scales. Thus, it can operationalise the field of tension around space production and reproduction as characterised by contemporary use (e.g., agricultural and forestry harvests and regional value creation) and the logics of conservation (e.g., conserving water quality, soil fertility and valuable habitats) from current and future generations in global human space usage.

The objective of our chapter is to contribute to the overarching Anthropocene debate by presenting an analytical framework for the SIA of land use changes as well as to discuss conceptual implications for social and political science by addressing the following research questions:

1 Which analytical-methodological implications for sustainable land use changes can be derived within the perspective of the 'Anthropocene as a crisis for sustainability'?

2 What are the (conceptual) implications of the Anthropocene debate for social and political science regarding the SIA of land use changes?

The rest of this chapter is structured as follows: In the second section, we describe theoretical principles of space production and reproduction as related to the societal discourse of SD as well as the challenge of environmental policy integration. Subsequently, we present an analytical framework for the SIA of land use changes. In the third section, we discuss a case study in northeast Germany in order to illustrate an analysis of human space usage to identify land use claims. In the fourth section, we consider the analytical framework of SIA in the context of the Anthropocene debate, thereby exploring analytical and methodological challenges. Finally, we draw conclusions regarding the future role of SIA under conditions of the proclaimed Anthropocene.

Framework for sustainable land use changes in the Anthropocene

In this section, we explain the area of tension between space production and reproduction as well as governance challenges regarding changes in sustainable land use. Together, these provide the theoretical principles required to build the analytical framework for the SIA of land use changes in the Anthropocene.

Theoretical principles

Space production and reproduction

Changes in global land use are driven by various forces. These can be natural aspects such as climate change or societal aspects such as government policies and land use demands. The resulting patterns of space production have an impact on future space reproduction (e.g., an area contaminated by coalmining activities cannot be used for other purposes such as a habitat or to produce drinking water for a longer period without renaturation). The debate on humanity as a geological force at planetary scale explores this area of tension in the Anthropocene. In particular, the exceeding of planetary boundaries by natural resource extraction will lead to future sustainability deficits and scarcities. This can be seen as an example of the perspective 'Anthropocene as a crisis for sustainability' (Lundershausen, in this volume). The implication is that an anthropogenic Earth system is not only unprecedented but also unsustainable (Crutzen and Steffen 2003).

In terms of sustainable changes in land use, demands for land are related to the supply of services of both private goods (e.g., renewable raw materials for construction, energetic use, or food production) and public goods (e.g., for a good quality of life, recreational values). Hence, there exist different societal (private and political) claims to future land use with a plurality of spatial relevant impacts. Regarding the needs of future generations, the societal negotiation process on the intensities of current land use systems is intended to ensure the developmental capacity of regional land use systems (see Table 10.1). Warnings about the overshooting of sustainable limits due to exponential global population growth as well as the depletion of natural resources (Meadows et al. 1972) have provoked societal debates and initiatives to ensure greater sustainability in the production systems of private goods and consumption styles. Within the Anthropocene debate, Rockström et al. (2009) have emphasised the environmental limits to atmospheric and biospheric Earth systems by identifying nine planetary systems as critical boundaries. Against this background, it is essential to apply SIA to reveal the impacts of land use changes on these planetary boundaries (Hossain et al. 2017). The nature and extent of space reproduction will take further depend on the endogenous potentials (bio-geophysical, socio-cultural, and socio-economic) in a specific region. In the context of the Anthropocene, the SIA assessment should be conducted under the hypothesis that humankind has the tendency to overuse these endogenous potentials of Earth system processes.

Governance challenges for sustainable land use changes in the Anthropocene

In the following, we introduce governance challenges regarding the Anthropocene, highlighting the necessity of operationalising the SD discourse and the governance of environmental policy integration for SIA approaches. Integration of

Table 10.1 Factors influencing the area of tension between space production and reproduction for the sustainability impact assessment of land use changes

Space production	• Different and partially contradicting political, societal and private use demands persist for current land use and related private goods as well as public goods and services. • Different governance levels (supranational, national and federal state level).
Space reproduction	• Demands and values related to future private and public goods as well as services provision. • Different governance levels (supranational, national and federal state level). • For sustainable development in a region, permanent space reproduction is fundamental → Long-term nature and path dependencies of spatial planning and land use decisions.

Objectives for sustainable land use changes:
→ Permanent discourse among multiple stakeholders and other societal actors for sustainable development.
→ Avoidance of overuse of environmental resources and maintenance of planetary boundaries.

Source: Adapted from Hermanns (2017).

the environmental dimension is a precondition for the long-term SD of global human space usage in the Anthropocene (Pintér et al. 2012). Arguably, SD implies that the bio-geophysical thresholds of the Earth system represent limits which should be maintained even at the expense of human development. Furthermore, it must be remembered that decisions about land use are made at different administrative levels.

As described above, regional human space usage in the Anthropocene is in conflict between the range of contemporary uses and protection logics. By affecting policy fields, land use sectors and involved stakeholders, this leads to land use disputes and land use competition at various scales (Söderberg and Eckerberg 2013; Harvey and Pilgrim 2011). As an example, the provision of bioenergy is influenced by different sectoral policies such as the EU Water Framework Directive (Söderberg and Eckerberg 2013). In urban areas the conflict is, for instance, between preserving open space for groundwater recharging, on the one hand, and soil sealing for infrastructure or settlements, on the other. Such conflicts arise through diverging stakeholder targets and normative values on the relative importance of the factors of sustainability related to a specific research region (Lange et al. 2015).

Sustainable land use is characterised as a multi-level governance issue with manifold and contradicting stakeholder targets for current and future land use. Mostly, the land use demands in a region such as northeast Germany are established by policymakers at European and national level. Hence, the SIA of land use changes needs both (1) to upscale the impacts of regional land use changes to supra-regional SD targets and (2) to regionalise superior policy priorities and stakeholder targets. To avoid unintended impacts on other policy fields, the horizontal and vertical integration of sector-oriented policy actions have to be considered. The concept of environmental policy integration was established to reconcile seemingly incompatible goals of economic competitiveness, social development, and environmental viability (Söderberg and Eckerberg 2013; Jordan and Lenschow 2010). This political concept can be transferred to the land use assessment framework in the form of a representation of land use demands at different governance levels, serving as a conceptual basis for transferring environmental limits into the SIA of land use changes.

Analytical framework

Based on the theoretical principles mentioned above, we present an analytical framework to operationalise the tension field of space production and reproduction in the Anthropocene epoch (see Table 10.1). Hermanns et al. (2015, 2017) have developed an analytical framework for the *ex-ante* SIA of land use scenarios at regional level. This is designed to match the supply and demand of functions and services related to land use and to condense SD targets of multi-level stakeholder strategies into land use claims as 'objectives-led sustainable development benchmarks'. In this process, the authors have adapted and integrated the concepts of 'driver-pressure-state-impact-response' (DPSIR) (OECD 1993), the three-dimension model of SD (UN 2005), land use functions (LUFs) (Pérez-Soba et al. 2008), multifunctional land use (Mander et al. 2007), and environmental policy integration. Multi-level stakeholder strategies have been integrated into land use claims through frame analysis (Söderberg and Eckerberg 2013; Rein and Schön 1996).

The 'DPSIR' concept and the three-dimension model of SD (UN 2005) were adopted as the basis of the analytical framework. The 'DPSIR' concept gives a better understanding of causal chains in social-ecological systems (Pires et al. 2017; Sun et al. 2016; Gari et al. 2015) by identifying decision-relevant indicators at regional level (Pires et al. 2017) and communicating the sustainability assessment of policies and land use scenarios to stakeholder groups (Tscherning et al. 2012). The 'DPSIR' concept served to structure the assessment of the future impacts of land use changes. It structured driving forces ('drivers') on possible land and water use options ('pressures') and their effects on sustainability-relevant topics ('states'). The region-specific effects on sustainability were measured by indicators representing the three SD dimensions of environment, economy and society. Furthermore, it was used to derive SD targets that were condensed to land use claims ('impacts').

The authors applied the LUFs approach to operationalise the supply and demand for region-specific goods and services. This approach has been applied in several case studies of sustainable land use changes to reveal their impacts on regional stakeholder groups (Schindler 2017). LUFs define goods and services provided by different land uses, summarising the most relevant social, economic and environmental aspects of a region (Pérez-Soba et al. 2008). Multi-level stakeholder strategies have reflected future societal demand and normative values. The analytical framework was designed to match the supply, in the form of sustainability-relevant topics and indicators, with the societal demand for region-specific LUFs in terms of land use claims specified in main- and side-use claims (see Figure 10.1). For instance, the environmental LUF 'Provision of abiotic resources' can be specified in the sustainability-relevant topic 'water quality'. The corresponding land use claim is 'improving water quality'.

Hermanns and others (2015) and (2017) have used the concepts of multifunctional land use and environmental policy integration as a theoretical basis to operationalise the above described field of space production and reproduction as well as corresponding contemporary use and protection logics in the Anthropocene. The concept of multifunctional land use can accommodate the plurality of societal demands on land use and the production of public goods and services. This resonates with the statement of O'Farrell and Anderson (2010) that the sustainability of land use is endangered only if certain functions predominate. For the assessment of the SD of land use systems, it is therefore important to manage land use in a multifunctional way (Helming and Pérez-Soba 2011; Mander et al. 2007). In addition, Hermanns and others (2015, 2017) applied the concept of environmental policy integration to the analytical framework in order to address trade-offs and synergetic effects among the identified environmental, economic and social targets relating to the societal demand for LUFs

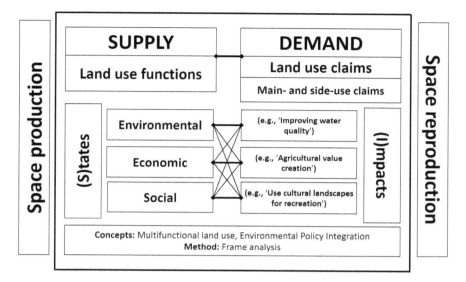

Figure 10.1 Analytical framework for *ex-ante* sustainability impact assessment of land use changes

Note: The framework is designed to match the region-specific supply of land use functions with the societal demand in terms of land use claims. The land use claims, in turn, are the driving forces of the supply of land use functions (adapted from Hermanns et al. 2015, 2017). The original works were published under the CC BY 4.0 license (https://creativecommons.org/licenses/by/4.0/).

at different governance levels. Based on this, the authors have undertaken a frame analysis of the underlying action logics of SD targets to identify stakeholder targets and to condense land use claims at different scales (Hermanns et al. 2015).

In addition, Hermanns and others (2017) have adapted the 'Framework for Participatory Impact Assessment' approach in a case study on the *ex-ante* SIA of peatland-use scenarios. This methodological approach matched the region-specific LUFs with land use claims in participatory assessment workshops of land use scenarios. For participatory impact assessments of land use changes, it is vital to involve balanced (along the SD dimensions) and relevant stakeholder groups in the assessment process. Options for multifunctional land use can be developed and presented to stakeholders by designing land use scenarios. This qualitatively measure so-called 'LUF and land use claim budgets', which identify sustainability gains and deficits of land use changes.

A case study of human space usage in northeast Germany

In this section, we present a case study to illustrate the analysis of land use demands. The study aimed to identify land use claims that, in the context of the Anthropocene, are the driving forces of humankind in shaping the Earth system.

The analytical framework for the *ex-ante* SIA of land use changes presented above links the endogenous potentials of a specific region with external driving forces and multi-level stakeholder targets (policy, actors and planning concepts). Thus, it can match region-specific portfolios of LUFs with land use claims.

To determine societal demand and to identify SD targets for region-specific LUFs, Hermanns et al. (2015) conducted a cross-strategy analysis of relevant stakeholder documents. The analysis considered various documents covering different policy fields and land use sectors at different governance levels. Thereby, the normative implications for SD and human well-being in northeast Germany and the selected area-types *peatlands* and *irrigation fields* were derived from policy strategies (e.g., National Biodiversity Strategy, Strategy for Sustainable Development of the Federal State of Brandenburg, Biomass Strategy of the Federal State of Brandenburg) as well as actor strategies, planning concepts and federal state laws. Criteria for selecting the stakeholder strategies were legal bindingness and the 'Nomenclature des unites territoriales statistiques' levels.

Stakeholder strategies were analysed at the European, national and federal state level of Berlin and Brandenburg, in addition to considering strategies at the regional and district level. The case study focused on national policy strategies as well as supra-regional and regional planning concepts. The goal was to condense region-specific main- and side-use claims for LUFs. The authors adapted the main-use and side-use claims according to the identified policy frames in policy-making on the European bioenergy sector (Söderberg and Eckerberg 2013). Moreover, the authors carried out a demand analysis by adopting the integrative 'sustainability rules' (Grunwald and Rösch 2011). According to Grunwald and Rösch (2011), the fundamental goals of SD can be specified as securing mankind's existence, upholding society's productive potential, and keeping options for development and action open. These can facilitate the operationalisation of space production and reproduction, and assist in finding solutions for sustainable human space usage.

As a result, the authors pinpointed land use claims in terms of main- and side-use claims. From the cross-strategy analysis, they identified six main-use claims for human space usage in northeast Germany (see Table 10.2). These were the societal core demands for LUFs in rural and semi-rural areas in this region. Consequently, the authors defined main-use claims as the substantial paradigms of society in the negotiation process of future land use and the normative spatially specific land use demands and values. They also defined side-use claims to underline why the respective main-use claims should be implemented by the future society, as well as to promote the achievement of the main-use claims. The identified side use claims were, for instance, 'valorisation of alternative land use systems' or 'reducing eutrophication and pollution of running waters'. Within the 'DPSIR' concept, the identified land use claims represent the 'impacts' of land use scenarios on the regional SD. In later assessment steps, sustainability indicators such as water quality or landscape aesthetic can be derived from the identified land use claims related to SD of human space usage in a specific region, such as northeast Germany.

Table 10.2 Main-use claims for human space usage in northeast Germany

Main-use claims: Land and water management for	Definition
1. Sustainable Intensification	Agricultural and forestry land use in rural areas for (green) growth, while maintaining non-provisioning ecosystem services (e.g., global climate regulation)
2. Environment, resource and nature protection	Sustainable use of renewable and non-renewable resources
3. Climate adaptation and protection	Averting climate change and mitigating negative impacts
4. Regional and rural development	Regional value chains for (green) growth and provision of public service tasks
5. Rural-urban interdependencies	Exchange of public and private goods between agglomerations and rural areas. Embedding land use in the spatial context to reduce disparities
6. Quality of life	Soft location factors affecting human well-being

Source: Adapted from Hermanns et al. (2015).

To match the six main-use claims, it is important for the SIA of land use changes and the achievement of sustainable human space usage in the Anthropocene to prioritise land use systems with multifunctional management (Helming and Pérez-Soba 2011; O'Farrell and Anderson 2010). However, according to Bennett et al. (2009) and Burkhard et al. (2012), trade-offs frequently arise in multifunctional land use systems because the extension of one societally desired provisioning (e.g., food) or non-provisioning (e.g., global climate regulation) ecosystem service results in the decline of other ecosystem services. This also seems to be the case for the assessment of region-specific 'LUF and land use claim budgets' at regional level (Hermanns et al. 2017). Nevertheless, attention still needs to be paid to trade-offs in land use decision support and sustainability assessment approaches (Inostroza et al. 2017; Gibson 2006). The transfer of the concept of environmental policy integration to the assessment framework can help decision makers handle trade-offs between environmental, economic and social development targets at different governance levels. A frame analysis can condense manifold stakeholder targets at these various governance levels into spatially explicit land use claims, specified as main- and side-use claims.

Discussion

Based on the findings of the case study to identify land use claims, we here discuss analytical and methodological challenges for the SIA of land use changes in the Anthropocene. The case study highlights the fact that human activities represent a geological force at planetary scale. Since SIA is located in a field of tension between space production and reproduction, we propose combining land use claims and knowledge about planetary boundaries in order to address analytical and methodological challenges.

Political and social dimension of the Anthropocene for SIA of land use changes

The Anthropocene thesis has several implications for the integrative and spatially explicit SIA of land use changes. Analytical and methodological challenges persist regarding the integration of environmental limits (Hossain et al. 2017; Kates 2001) into sustainability assessment as well as in the identification of appropriate and relevant SD targets, topics and indicators at different scales (Laedre et al. 2015; Helming and Pérez-Soba 2011). Finding appropriate SD targets and indicators for the SIA of land use changes in a specific region is complicated by changing land use demands and normative values due to shifting policy targets and emerging policy fields. Examples are the transition to renewable forms of energy and corresponding multi-level land use demands such as climate change adaptation and renewable energy creation from biomass (Petit and Frederiksen 2011). Such changing of direction hampers the development of corresponding sustainability indicators (Petit and Frederiksen 2011).

Consequently, 'objectives-led sustainable development benchmarks' are vital for the SIA of land use changes in a specific region and to operationalise the field of tension between space production and reproduction. Hermanns and others (2017) have derived region-specific SD targets and sustainability indicators from multi-level stakeholder strategies. Stigson and others (2009) have presented 'Strategies for Sustainable Development' as plans for trans-sectoral policy targets at national and federal level in Germany. In addition, the Sustainable Development Goals (SDGs) (Kanie and Biermann 2017) have to be considered in the future SIA of land use changes as a global stakeholder strategy for the governance of sustainable human space usage. SD principles derived from political guidelines (e.g., the Brundtland Report), and the 'sustainability rules' (e.g., Grunwald and Rösch 2011) can be used for the SIA of land use changes in the Anthropocene. This is an alternative to the adoption of societal targets derived from stakeholder documents.

Despite advances in research, it is still a challenging task to operationalise the political and normative concept of SD of human space usage in a region (Grunwald and Rösch 2011). This is due to the fact that human space usage and the production of space (Lefebvre 1991) arises through an ongoing societal process of negotiating land use in a specific region. According to Pahl-Wostl et al. (2013), deciding, governing and managing land use towards SD is a continual learning process for stakeholders. The negotiation process regarding future land use is influenced by various power resources of involved actors. In these struggles, we find different and partly opposing societal demands for use within multi-level stakeholder strategies for future land use. Thereby, human space usage in the Anthropocene lies in an area of conflict between various forms of contemporary use and protection logics. This may lead to an overuse of the environment. To steer global human space usage and land use systems in the Anthropocene towards SD, therefore, we must analyse and determine the societal demand for region-specific LUFs by including the governance of environmental policy integration in an SIA to create an expanded assessment dimension.

While the natural sciences focus on exploring environmental limits (Reid et al. 2009), the objectives of political and social sciences here should be to analyse the societal demand for region-specific LUFs in stakeholder strategies, actor constellations (Schäfer and Kröger 2016), and policy fields (Rein and Schön 1996) at different scales. This can help to achieve sustainable human space usage in the Anthropocene. Thereby, a distinction needs to be made between short-term and long-term goals in stakeholder strategies at various scales (Bai et al. 2015). Given the growing body of evidence that humankind is exceeding environmental thresholds, goal-setting in global land use governance should focus on implementing environmental SD targets. However, the socio-economic dimension of SD should be considered in research approaches so as not to neglect socio-economic injustices and inequalities in developed and non-developed countries.

Implications of the debate on planetary boundaries for the SIA of land use changes

As a geological era with region-specific institutional settings and intensities of human space usage, the Anthropocene affects the vision of SD and the global governance of sustainable human space usage. Geological and natural sciences provide mounting evidence that humankind is the major driver behind shifts in Earth systems, whereby planetary boundaries to such systems are already being exceeded (Rockström et al. 2009). A core principle of sustainability assessment is to investigate the impact of land use changes on the state of the environment (Pintér et al. 2012). Consequently, sustainable land management has the normative goal of ensuring the viability of land use systems (Rückert-John et al. 2013).

Societal land use demands with unbalanced use and protection logics can endanger the SD of land use systems in a specific region. To ensure SD in the Anthropocene and to locate sustainable long-term solutions, global forms of space reproduction are required that satisfy the need of future generations for goods and services but which do not exceed planetary boundaries and leave the 'safe operating space' (Steffen et al. 2011; Rockström et al. 2009). In particular, the globally predominant frame of societal development that foresees unlimited and continual economic growth (Soetebeer 2015) against a backdrop of limited natural resources (e.g., phosphorus cycle) will endanger the SD of regional land use systems. This frame is a specific issue for sustainable land use changes in the Anthropocene because it is a core driver behind the 'Great Acceleration' and the constant overuse of natural resources and further intensified land use patterns. Therefore, we must urgently strike a balance between satisfying current human needs and preserving ecosystem services (MEA 2005) as well as other functions and services related to land use for future generations (Steffen et al. 2011). Further research on SIA frameworks should thus integrate evidence from natural science on the impacts of land use changes on planetary boundaries (Rockström et al. 2009) and environmental limits (Moldan et al. 2012) in bio-geophysical Earth systems. The planetary boundaries and environmental limits should be integrated as thresholds into the SIA (Hossain et al. 2017; Kates 2001).

Conclusion

SIA is a tool to support political decision-making concerning the SD of human space usage. The debate on the Anthropocene calls for new social science approaches for an integrative and spatially explicit SIA of land use changes. It also influences scientific approaches to the SIA of land use changes due to increasing evidence that planetary boundaries are being exceeded by humankind and that societal value systems are changing. For the SIA of land use changes, an analytical framework is needed to operationalise the area of tension between space production and reproduction, which is characterised by corresponding use and protection logics of current and future generations. This framework needs to match a region-specific supply portfolio of LUFs with a demand portfolio of land use claims. In particular, to correctly identify land use claims, we require SIA approaches that include a representation of humankind as a major geological driver of land use changes. Moreover, future research must integrate land use claims and thresholds into bio-geophysical Earth systems.

Specifically, our reflections on conceptual implications suggest that social science approaches should focus on the analysis of value systems of stakeholders and other societal actors. Subsequently, political science can contribute to the SIA of land use changes by analysing land use demands as well as different and potentially contradicting societal targets at different governance levels. Trans-sectoral and cross-policy SD targets and indicators are vital for the SIA of land use changes at regional level that concern local decision makers and stakeholders. The resulting implications for political decision-making and governance can be related to the Anthropocene hypothesis. Alongside global governance approaches such as the SDGs, region-specific SD targets need to be identified and integrated in impact assessment approaches in order to link top-down and bottom-up goal-setting for sustainable human space usage. In addition, a multi-scale and multi-sector governance approach is required to ensure SD of human space usage. The governance of sustainable land use changes needs to consider knowledge about thresholds in the bio-geophysical Earth systems in order to avoid overuse in human space. In future SIA research, we suggest that anthropogenic land use claims and patterns are linked with the boundaries of bio-geophysical thresholds of the Earth system. This will help to integrate the knowledge base on sustainability gains and deficits of land use changes when addressing issues of global governance.

References

Bai, X., et al. (2015) "Plausible and desirable futures in the Anthropocene: A new research agenda" *Global Environmental Change*, 39, 351–362.

Bennett, E.M., Peterson, G.D. and Gordon, L.J. (2009) "Understanding relationships among multiple ecosystem services" *Ecology Letters*, 12(12), 1394–1404.

Bennett, E.M., et al. (2015) "Linking biodiversity, ecosystem services, and human well-being: Three challenges for designing research for sustainability" *Current Opinion in Environmental Sustainability*, 14, 76–85.

Böhringer, C. and Löschel, A. (2006) "Computable general equilibrium models for sustainability impact assessment: Status quo and prospects" *Ecological Economics*, 60, 49–64.

Burkhard, B., et al. (2012) "Solutions for sustaining natural capital and ecosystem services" *Ecological Indicators*, 21(Supplement C), 1–6.

Crutzen, P.J. and Steffen, W. (2003) "How long have we been in the Anthropocene era? An editorial comment" *Climatic Change*, 61(3), 251–257.

Crutzen, P.J. and Stoermer, E. (2000) "The Anthropocene" *IGBP Newsletter*, 41, 17 Accessed 22 April 2018.

Foley, J.A., et al. (2005) "Global consequences of land use" *Science*, 309(5734), 570.

Gari, S.R., Newton, A. and Icely, J.D. (2015) "A review of the application and evolution of the DPSIR framework with an emphasis on coastal social-ecological systems" *Ocean & Coastal Management*, 103(Supplement C), 63–77.

Gibson, R.B. (2006) "Sustainability assessment: Basic components of a practical approach" *Impact Assessment and Project Appraisal*, 24(3), 170–182.

Grunwald, A. and Rösch, C. (2011) "Sustainability assessment of energy technologies: Towards an integrative framework" *Energy, Sustainability and Society*, 1:3.

Hacking, T. and Guthrie, P. (2008) "A framework for clarifying the meaning of triple bottom-line, integrated, and sustainability assessment" *Environmental Impact Assessment Review*, 28, 73–89.

Harvey, M. and Pilgrim, S. (2011) "The new competition for land: Food, energy, and climate change" *Food Policy*, 36(Supplement 1), S40–S51.

Helming, K. and Pérez-Soba, M. (2011) "Landscape scenarios and multifunctionality: Making land use impact assessment operational" *Ecology and Society*, 16(1), 50.

Helming, K., Pérez-Soba, M. and Tabbush, P. eds. (2008) *Sustainability Impact Assessment of Land Use Changes* Springer, Berlin, Heidelberg, 507.

Hermanns, T. (2017) "Sustainability impact assessment of land use scenarios in the area of tension between space production and reproduction: Development of an analytical framework at the regional level" PhD thesis Department of Geography, Georg-August-University Göttingen, Göttingen.

Hermanns, T., et al. (2017) "Sustainability impact assessment of peatland-use scenarios: Confronting land use supply with demand" *Ecosystem Services*, 26, 365–376.

Hermanns, T., et al. (2015) "Stakeholder strategies for sustainability impact assessment of land use scenarios: Analytical framework and identifying land use claims" *Land*, 4(3), 778–806.

Hossain, Md.S., et al. (2017) "Operationalizing safe operating space for regional social-ecological systems" *Science of The Total Environment*, 584(Supplement C), 673–682.

Inostroza, L., et al. (2017) "Putting ecosystem services into practice: Trade-off assessment tools, indicators and decision support systems" *Ecosystem Services*, 26, 303–305.

Jordan, A. and Lenschow, A. (2010) "Environmental policy integration: A state of the art review" *Environmental Policy and Governance*, 20(3), 147–158.

Kanie, N. and Biermann, F. eds. (2017) *Governing through Goals: Sustainable Development Goals as Governance Innovation* (assisted by Young, R.O.) MIT Press, Cambridge, MA, London.

Kates, R.W. (2001) "Environment and development: Sustainability science" *Science*, 292 (5517), 641–642.

Laedre, O., et al. (2015) "Determining sustainability impact assessment indicators" *Impact Assessment and Project Appraisal*, 33(2), 98–107.

Lange, A., Siebert, R. and Barkmann, T. (2015) "Sustainability in land management: An analysis of stakeholder perceptions in rural northern Germany" *Sustainability*, 7(1), 683–704.

Lefebvre, H. (1991) *The Production of Space* (translated by Nicholson-Smith, D.) Blackwell Publishing, Malden, Oxford, Carlton.

Li, Q., et al. (2016) "Sustainability of smallholder agriculture in semi-arid areas under land set-aside programs: A case study from China's Loess Plateau" *Sustainability*, 8(4), 395.

Mander, Ü., Wiggering, H. and Helming, K. (2007) "Multifunctional land use: Meeting future demands for landscape goods and serivces" in Mander, Ü., Wiggering, H. and Helming, K. eds., *Multifunctional Land Use: Meeting Future Demands for Landscape Goods and Services* Springer, Berlin, Heidelberg 1–13.

Markard, J., Raven, R. and Truffer, B. (2012) "Sustainability transitions: An emerging field of research and its prospects" *Research Policy*, 41(6), 955–967.

Millennium Ecosystem Assessment (MEA) (2005) *Ecosystems and Human Well-Being: Millennium Ecosystem Assessment* Island Press, Washington.

Meadows, D.L., et al. (1972) *Die Grenzen des Wachstums. Bericht des Club of Rome zur Lage der Menschheit* Deutsche Verlags-Anstalt, München.

Moldan, B., Janoušková, S. and Hák, T. (2012) "How to understand and measure environmental sustainability: Indicators and targets" *Ecological Indicators*, 17(Supplement C), 4–13.

O'Farrell, P.J. and Anderson, P.M.L. (2010) "Sustainable multifunctional landscapes: A review to implementation" *Current Opinion in Environmental Sustainability*, 2(1), 59–65.

Organization for Economic Co-operation and Development (OECD) (1993) *OECD Core Set of Indicators for Environmental Performance Reviews: A Synthesis Report* Environment Monographs, 83. ed., Paris.

Pahl-Wostl, C., et al. (2013) "Transition towards a new global change science: Requirements for methodologies, methods, data and knowledge" *Environmental Science & Policy*, 28, 36–47.

Paracchini, M.L., et al. (2011) "An aggregation framework to link indicators associated with multifunctional land use to stakeholder evaluation of policy options" *Ecological Indicators*, 11(1), 71–80.

Pérez-Soba, M., et al. (2008) "Land use functions: A multifunctionality approach to assess the impact of land use changes on land use sustainability" in Helming, K., Pérez-Soba, M. and Tabbush, P. eds., *Sustainability Impact Assessment of Land Use Changes* Springer, Berlin, Heidelberg, 375–404.

Petit, S. and Frederiksen, P. (2011) "Modelling land use change impacts for sustainability assessment" *Ecological Indicators*, 11(1), 1–3.

Pintér, L., et al. (2012) "Bellagio STAMP: Principles for sustainability assessment and measurement" *Ecological Indicators*, 17(Supplement C), 20–28.

Pires, A., et al. (2017) "Sustainability assessment of indicators for integrated water resources management" *Science of The Total Environment*, 578(Supplement, C), 139–147.

Pope, J., Annandale, D. and Morrison-Saunders, A. (2004) "Conceptualising sustainability assessment" *Environmental Impact Assessment Review*, 24(6), 595–616.

Reid, W.V., Bréchignac, C. and Tseh Lee, Y. (2009) "Earth system research priorities" *Science*, 325(5938), 245.

Rein, M. and Schön, D. (1996) "Frame-critical policy analysis and frame-reflective policy practice" *Knowledge and Policy*, 9(1), 85–104.

Rockström, J., et al. (2009) "A safe operating space for humanity" *Nature*, 472–475.

Rückert-John, J., et al. (2013) "Verständnis Nachhaltigen Landmanagements im Verbundprojekt ELaN" in Weith, T., Besendörfer, C., Gaasch, N., Kaiser, D.B., Müller, K., Repp, A., Rogga, S., Strauß, C. and Zscheischler, J. eds., *Nachhaltiges Landmanagement: Was Ist Das?* ZALF, Müncheberg, Germany, 16–17.

Schäfer, M. and Kröger, M. (2016) "Joint problem framing in sustainable land use research: Experience with constellation analysis as a method for inter-and transdisciplinary knowledge integration" *Land Use Policy*, 57(Supplement C), 526–539.

Schindler, J. (2017) "Sustainability impact assessment for improved food security: The benefit of local stakeholder participation: The case of four villages in Dodoma and Morogoro Region, Tanzania, PhD thesis Faculty of Life Science, Humboldt University Berlin, Berlin.

Söderberg, C. and Eckerberg, K. (2013) "Rising policy conflicts in Europe over bioenergy and forestry" *Forest Policy and Economics*, 33(Supplement C), 112–119.

Soetebeer, I. (2015) "Well-being and prosperity beyond growth: Discursive struggles in the German *Enquete Commission on Growth, Prosperity and Quality of Life*" *GAIA: Ecological Perspectives for Science and Society*, 24(3), 179–187.

Steffen, W., et al. (2014) "The trajectory of the Anthropocene: The Great Acceleration" *The Anthropocene Review*, 2(1), 81–98.

Steffen, W., et al. (2011) "The Anthropocene: From global change to planetary stewardship" *AMBIO*, 40(7), 739–761.

Stigson, B., et al. (2009) "Peer review on sustainable development policies in Germany. peer review der deutschen Nachhaltigkeitspolitik" *German Council for Sustainable Development Texte*, 29.

Sun, S., et al. (2016) "Sustainability assessment of regional water resources under the DPSIR framework" *Journal of Hydrology*, 532(Supplement C), 140–148.

Tscherning, K., et al. (2012) "Does research applying the DPSIR framework support decision making?" *Land Use Policy*, 29(1), 102–110.

United Nations (UN) General Assembly (2005) *World Summit Outcome: resolution/ adopted by the General Assembly*, 24 October 2005, A/RES/60/1.

Uthes, S., et al. (2010) "Policy relevance of three integrated assessment tools: A comparison with specific reference to agricultural policies" *Ecological Modelling*, 221, 2136–2152.

Zalasiewicz, J., et al. (2010) "The new world of the Anthropocene" *Environmental Science & Technology*, 44(7), 2228–2231.

11 The nuclear legacy in the Anthropocene

Interrelations between nature, technology and society

Dörte Themann and
Achim Brunnengräber

Introduction

The Working Group on the Anthropocene in the International Commission on Stratigraphy (WGA-ISC) is examining whether a new geological time span, the 'Anthropocene', should be declared. Meanwhile, there is ample evidence for the 'geology of mankind' (Jahn et al. 2015). On this account, humans as a 'planetary force' have left traces on the Earth that will remain 'readable' in 40,000 (!) generations time. One example is the highly radioactive waste produced by humans over just half a century, which must be kept away from people and the environment in the most secure manner possible for very long periods of time. Against this backdrop the crucial question is not so much when the Anthropocene started or by which markers it can be measured. Hamilton speaks rightly of a 'golden spike fetish' (Hamilton 2015, 103). To us it seems far more important to scrutinise which dynamics in the relationship between nature, technology and society have led to these vestiges and how strong their impact is for current and future generations.

Being aware of the incalculable dynamics within the process of storing and disposing nuclear waste, this chapter seeks to address the socio-technical dimension within the process of finding a repository for nuclear waste. Our aim is to find argumentative evidence that the Anthropocene is 'just' the expression of such incalculable dynamics as these are caused for example through the 'wicked problem' connected with nuclear waste. Therefore, the Anthropocene maybe is a new geological time span, but is also a manifestation of new traces in the Earth system, caused by a changed relationship between human beings, nature and technology. This relationship is characterised by incalculable timescales, socio-ecological crises and the increasing inability to control the process of regulation.

In this chapter, we are not concerned with quantitative evidence or with a deconstruction of the term Anthropocene. We rather wish to highlight that the term Anthropocene is an expression of the 'multiple crises' that confront today's societies (Demirovic et al. 2011; Brand and Wissen 2013). It is imperative to explore the opportunities offered by such an understanding of the term in order to tackle the various forms of crisis. In particular, we wish to discuss whether the characteristics of the Anthropocene call for new governance structures. We demonstrate the key characteristics of this changed relationship – of which the Anthropocene is an expression – using the example of the handling of the remnants of the nuclear age and the unresolved global issue of the final disposal of radioactive nuclear waste (Brunnengräber et al. 2015, 2018). The high-level of danger associated with this type of waste and society's approach to it shape this relationship in a very specific manner.

To support our argument, in section 2 the theoretical background regarding the critical relationship between nature, technology and society will be presented. In section 3 we outline how nature, technology and society interact in the specific case of the storage and disposal of nuclear waste and argue that there is no ground for optimism regarding the implementation of possible technical solutions. In section 4 we discuss the need for new forms of governance that take into account uncertainties and uncontrollable dynamics and can overcome unequal power relations. Finally, section 5 presents the conclusion, namely that the term Anthropocene points to the fact that all current and future decisions regarding the development and use of technologies need to be measured against the extent to which the consequences of these decisions can be controlled by current and future generations from a planetary perspective.

Theoretical background – nature, society and technology

Describing the relationship between society, nature and technology is a complex task. Different combinations of this relationship will be presented as well as their interactions. There are strong interactions between society and nature that manifest themselves in the ecological crisis. Also, socio-technical processes become more and more interesting when talking about path dependencies and lack of control. In this section we argue that since the start of the processes of the 'Great Acceleration' (Steffen et al. 2015) or the 'rupture' of industrialisation (Hamilton 2016a) – which are often understood as the beginning of the Anthropocene – interactions between nature, society and technology have progressed gradually. In the Anthropocene "the social contract to hold nature, society and technology separate, as if each were originally independent of each other" (Edwards 2002, 186), can no longer be maintained.

The socio-ecological crisis

In tracing back the growing incalculable dynamics and interrelations between nature, humans and technology and the growing materialisation of 'golden spikes', we build upon authors such as Hamilton (2016a) and Steffen et al. (2015). Hamilton describes the beginning of industrialisation and the large-scale burning of fossil fuels as the first major intervention and 'rupture' in the history of the world (Hamilton 2016a). Steffen et al. introduce the concept of a 'Great Acceleration' and interpreted it as the beginning of the

Anthropocene (Steffen et al. 2015). The authors present different socio-economic trends (e.g., fertiliser consumption, population increase, water use, etc.) and corresponding Earth system trends (e.g., ocean acidification, the accumulation of carbon dioxide in the atmosphere and the related rise of surface temperatures) that have experienced exponential growth. Closely linked to this is power generation, which has enabled economic growth since the Industrial Revolution. Power generation started with burning wood and coal, and was followed by oil, gas and the use of nuclear energy, which is the reason why we can also refer to a fossil-nuclear age. Linked to this is the question of military power through the existence of nuclear weapons and access to resources for power generation and therefore invariably power structures, hegemony and geo-strategies. Wars over energy and energy resources were and are still fought, with negative consequences for the environment. Herein we see the multi-faceted nature of the crisis in the relationship between humankind, nature and technology – a social power relationship which has been installed to facilitate the constant pursuit of economic growth.

Therefore, we argue that the concept of Anthropocene encompasses the contradiction between social prosperity on the one hand and destructive growth on the other, which has led to uncertainty and unknown risks as well as the so-called socio-ecological crisis. The relationship between society and nature is not only paradoxical but also in a state of crisis (e.g., externalisation, extractivism). As Craig explains, this relationship is characterised by an

> expanding production and rising ecological impacts under capitalism (which) is, however, a complex one. This is because technological and organisational changes in capitalist production have historically shaped the 'impact profile' of individual capitalist industries and capitalist production as a whole.
>
> (Craig 2017, 20)

The physical impact that the capitalistic production has on the biosphere, becomes a threat for the "reproduction of human societies" (Craig 2017, 12). One example for this is the "fossil fuel use in the global energy infrastructure. The symptom associated with this aspect of crisis is the accumulation of greenhouse gases in the atmosphere(...)" (ibid.).

This 'socio-ecological crisis' or 'Great Acceleration' can be ascribed to a specific kind of economic activity and the use of a specific technology, which is related to the battle over finite resources and (unequal) relations between humans. Society-technical-nature relationships, thus, have to be understood as closely tied to social power relations. We are not only concerned with the considerable impact of humans on the Earth system, observed since the beginning of the Industrial Revolution. We also want to demonstrate that the Anthropocene can be viewed as a specific expression of power relations and as an issue of inter- and intra-generational justice.

The lack of control and 'unknown unknowns' in the interaction with the technosphere

Technology plays a major role in enabling the 'Great Acceleration'. Therefore, humankind's relationship with technological objects (or artefacts) has to be considered both as an innovation and a solution to the crises as well as their cause. In the case of the former, it could be that humankind is controlled or forced into path dependencies by the technosphere – the nuclear remnants with their strict safety requirements force humankind into a permanent state of action for hundreds and thousands of years (Kersten 2016, 285). Socio-technical innovations are often considered as societal progress. This applies to for example coal and nuclear power generation, mobility via combustion engines, modern agriculture (relying on huge quantities of pesticides/herbicides and fertilisers) or geo-engineering. The changes and negative impacts resulting from this progress can however no longer be controlled by socio-technological practices, especially since they have assumed planetary dimensions. Bruno Latour concludes that humans are embedded in a complex network of interactions between human and non-human actors (Latour 1996, 2007). Technology, nature and humans cannot be considered independently of one another, let alone can their relationship be shaped independently of one another.

Regarding control and path dependencies, Haff goes one step further by stressing the autonomy and thereby the inability to control technological artefacts in their totality, i.e., as a systemically large-scale technosphere:

> we abandon the apparently natural assumption that the technosphere is primarily a human-created and controlled system and instead develop the idea that the workings of modern humanity are a product of a system that operates beyond our control and that imposes its own requirements on human behaviour. The technosphere is a system for which humans are essential but, nonetheless, subordinate parts. As shorthand we can say that the technosphere is autonomous. This does not mean that humans cannot influence its behaviour, but that the technosphere will tend to resist attempts to compromise its function.
>
> (Haff 2014, 127)

This leads Haff to the conclusion that we should speak of a 'quasi-autonomous technosphere' (130). With an increasing complexity within technological systems also the risks rooted in those systems are increasing. Control and technology enter a strong interaction. "Increasingly complex technical systems induce ... increasingly complex control systems, a vicious circle results" (Joerges 1996, 9). As a consequence, with the usage and upcoming dynamics of new technologies there exist high levels of uncertainty and invariably residual risk to society. These unknown factors, called 'unknown unknowns' (Eckhardt and Rippe 2016), are factors that we do not even know that we do not know about them. The technosphere plays a special role within these dynamics and the production of 'unknown unknowns'. It is producing deep uncertainties and we cannot foresee if the innovative solutions of today are pre-problems of tomorrow. But by focusing on the technosphere, it may be also possible to uncover the underlying dynamics within the relationship between humankind, nature and technology and provide input for new forms of governance.

The Anthropocene debate itself shows a highly positive belief in technology as a solution for the imbalanced nature-society relationship. Technological solutions have from the outset featured prominently in the discourse on the Anthropocene, right from the time Crutzen and Stoermer dated the start of the Anthropocene back to the beginning of the Industrial Revolution (Steffen et al. 2015, 82; Wissenburg 2016). Furthermore, Crutzen explicitly calls on engineers and academics to search for solutions:

> to guide society towards environmentally sustainable management during the era of the Anthropocene. This will require appropriate human behaviour at all scales, and may well involve internationally accepted, large-scale geo-engineering projects, for instance to 'optimize' climate.
>
> (Crutzen 2002, 23)

The Ecomodernist Manifesto, launched by scholars, scientists, campaigners and citizens, builds precisely upon these ideas that "technologies have made humans less reliant upon the many ecosystems that once provided their only sustenance, even as those same ecosystems have often been left deeply damaged".[1] Also this points to the dialectic in the relationship between humans and nature in which humans use technology to emancipate themselves from nature and a decoupling of human advancement and nature takes place (Grunwald 2015).[2] Thereby the manifesto refers to the 'Good Anthropocene' and the belief in future scientific and technological solutions.

But the handling of both nuclear remnants and climate change point to strong political and economic interests and to the limits to the promises of global engineering (Stirling 2015). To put it bluntly, the interplay between politics, science and technology has failed, as illustrated by the dilapidated temporary nuclear storage structures or the increase in greenhouse gases and progress of climate change. Nevertheless, through the ecomodern interpretation of the Anthropocene, the motif of people subduing the Earth is experiencing a renaissance. Similarly the often questioned growth paradigm is also being justified and legitimised anew via a 'green growth' concept (Fatheuer et al. 2016), which is desirable from an ecomodernist perspective (Grunwald 2015).

With regard to the case of nuclear remnants, Görg finds on the one hand that such a decoupling of nature and humankind makes little sense (Görg 2016). Rather the use of nuclear technology points to a typical artefact of modernity,[3] i.e., that humans are not always able to control their influence on the Earth system or the dynamics between humans and technological artefacts. On the other hand, Görg also points out that the specific characteristics of human behaviour also have to be included in the analysis. These include social, economic and political motives and interests and underlying power structures that have been, and continue to be, inherent to the use of nuclear technologies. From this perspective the Anthropocene is an expression of a potential crisis in the interaction between society and nature (Bonneuil 2015). The separation of human progress, risk-technology and the destruction of nature is no longer possible.

The nuclear legacy

In this section the implications of the complex relationship between nature, technology and society will be applied to the case of nuclear power and nuclear waste. The legacy of half a century nuclear activities is also a consequence of the 'Great Acceleration' and of the dictate of a continuous economic growth. Therefore, this issue helps to understand, in an inductive way, which dynamics within the nature-technology-society relationship occur within the Anthropocene. Political decisions to utilise a specific technology (in this case nuclear power) thereby relying on nature as the supplier of raw materials (uranium) and as a shelter (in the Earth crust for nuclear waste) can be seen as the cause of the waste disposal crisis which society is facing today.

Many political, legal and technical problems associated with the handling of nuclear remnants remain unsolved. Instead, extensive debates about individual sub-problems are taking place, which in their entirety show the state of crisis. In the following we will present considerations about (1) the lack of permanent nuclear repositories, (2) safety and security, (3) the debate on low-level radiation and thresholds and (4) the presumed contribution of nuclear energy to climate protection efforts. We reiterate that there is substantial room for discourse. The nature of this powerful discourse and the narratives that dominate it determine not least how problems are dealt with. The background to this is that whatever measures are taken there can be no guarantee that the results of human activity (in this case the use of nuclear energy) can be controlled. Doubts within society, technical problems and challenges and geological uncertainties remain and interact in complex ways.

First, to the lack of permanent repositories: Regarding highly radioactive waste, over 370,000 tonnes of heavy metal (tHM) of spent fuel have been discharged of which approximately 120,000 tHM have been reprocessed until today (World Nuclear Association 2018). Spent fuel is being stored in temporary facilities – usually located next to nuclear power plants – on or close to the Earth's surface, which are not designed for long-term storage (Di Nucci et al. 2015; Budelmann et al. 2017). Despite the existence of several permanent repositories for low and intermediate-level radioactive waste, no permanent repository for highly radioactive waste has entered into operation yet. Locations for such permanent repositories have been identified in Finland, Sweden and France and construction is already underway. A part from these sites, the global search for suitable locations has yielded only poor results (Brunnengräber et al. 2015; Di Nucci et al. 2015). Meanwhile the amount of highly radioactive waste is growing by 12,000 tonnes per year. According to prevailing academic opinion, these dangerous substances should be stored several hundred metres below the Earth's surface. We cannot however determine in advance and in detail which technical or geological changes to the host rock may occur in these permanent repositories over the course of the coming centuries. This fact has led to a discussion about whether provisions should be made for the retrieval of highly radioactive waste for a certain period of time or whether the fast closure of permanent repositories may be a better option.

In addition, in many countries a proof of safety for over one million years must be provided for the final disposal (Endlager-Kommission 2016). This proof should be supported by scientific evidence that the safety of the final repository's barriers can be guaranteed for the one million year period. These barriers include the geological conditions, geotechnical measures (for example, the chambers and closing devices) as well as technical components for sealing off the waste. Most calculations are based on computer-aided modelling as laboratory testing over such a long time period is not possible. For that reason, there still exist high levels of uncertainty and invariably residual risk to society (e.g. the stability of society and democracy itself over such a long time periode or unknown factors in the geological conditions). This shows that the 'wicked problem' of nuclear waste disposal contains the already mentioned 'unknown unknowns' (Eckhardt and Rippe 2016). Therefore, political considerations are required, which cannot only be based on scientific findings but have to take into account societal discourses.

Second we turn to the concepts of safety and security. Protecting humans and the environment from the dangers resulting from the storage of nuclear waste is summed up by the term 'safety'. The population, operating staff and the environment should be protected from exposure to radioactive and chemotoxic substances. It is not only human health that could be affected by the release of radiation from a final repository, long-term implications for the functioning of ecosystems may also arise. In order to illustrate these implications we rely, however, solely on analogies. The biologists Mousseau and Møller investigated the regions surrounding Chernobyl and Fukushima and they point out that "a careful observer will quickly become aware of the peculiar distortions of tree growth …, numerous abnormalities in insects, and tumours and cataracts in birds (Møller et al. 2012), all caused by genetic mutations induced by exposure to the radiation in the region" (Møller and Mousseau 2013, 551). They identified a decline in pollinators in selected regions surrounding Chernobyl which has impacted the fruit yielded by fruit trees, thereby affecting the population of fruit-eating birds which in turn also has a long-term impact on the reproduction of fruit trees and other plants (Møller et al. 2012). Modelling and worst-case scenarios provide examples of the impact that the potential discharge of radioactive materials from the final repository could have on the environment, for example, on groundwater. And yet considerable uncertainties remain about the impact on humans, animals and ecosystems of a discharge that takes place in several hundred years' time.

In contrast to 'safety', 'security' refers to the need to prevent criminal proliferation, i.e., the illegal accessing of residual, potentially weapons-grade material;

sabotage by employees; or external attacks, leading to a two-sided potential hazard. The concepts of safety and security point, in different ways, to the fact that there is no guarantee of the safe storage of waste according to absolute benchmarks. Rather the use of nuclear power is accompanied by perpetual risk (Eckhardt and Rippe 2016).

The limits or thresholds for considering a dose of radiation as a risk to health and ecosystems which are often agreed upon in political negotiations offer a third example of the state of crisis:

> Although the technical definition of low-dose radiation is set by international policymaking panels (e.g., the International Council for Radiation Protection, ICRP) and as such is to a large extent arbitrary, it is generally characterized as the dose below which it is not possible to detect adverse health effects. No figure for this dosage has ever been calculated, and the so-called threshold theory assumes that there is dosage of low-level radiation below which no damage occurs. The theory is comforting, but it has never been shown to be true, nor has any safe 'threshold' been established.
>
> (Møller and Mousseau 2013, 551–552)

Nevertheless, thresholds are interpreted in very different ways. Thresholds offer a false sense of security which can politically neutralise the unpredictability and uncontrollability that would accompany a major contamination: 'but we are under the threshold!' However, they also provide an important indication of the potential dangers and appropriate countermeasures as well as offering orientation for technological innovation (see also Kalmbach and Röhlig 2016).

Climate change offers a fourth example of the existence of a space for discourse. According to this discourse, nuclear energy makes a substantial contribution to the clean generation of energy as it is portrayed as a CO_2-neutral technology. This viewpoint continues to be supported by many powerful actors from government, business and international organisations. For example, the Intergovernmental Panel on Climate Change (IPCC) has lent support to this ongoing debate, calling nuclear energy "a zero and low-carbon energy technology, which 'does not contribute to direct GHG emissions'" (IPCC 2014, chapter 7, 23). Independent of the fact that nuclear energy is also responsible for considerable levels of emissions, especially when the overall life cycle is included in the calculations (Öko-Institut 2007), the unsolved problem of final storage is once again being ignored. A technology implemented as an innovation, turns out to be a new problem. The technical problem associated with coal-fired power generation is simply replaced with another risk-technology, that of nuclear fission.

This leads us to two far-reaching considerations. Firstly, that public behaviour has long been, and continues to be, influenced by a strong belief in our ability to control technology and nature. Secondly, that the Anthropocene should not be viewed with the unquestioned optimism displayed by supporters of the ecomodernism. Rather the Anthropocene is a term that covers precisely this, i.e., whatever the measures taken to fight the symptoms of crisis or to increase wealth, in several cases there can be no guarantee that the results of human activity (in this case the use of nuclear energy) can, due to the dangers of nuclear waste and the length of timescale involved, be controlled. Uncertainties and incalculable time-scales remain and interact and characterise the Anthropocene.

Humankind is controlled or forced into path dependencies by the techno-sphere. Even after a final repository is closed, a specific period of monitoring is still advisable. If the strategy of making the final repository as undetectable as possible is not followed, then permanent signage is required. The same applies to the case of greenhouse gases which will remain in the Earth's atmo-sphere for centuries to come, even if the burning of fossil fuels stopped tomor-row. We observe here again, what has been described by Latour – humans and the nuclear remnants are embedded in a complex network of interactions (see above).

These examples clearly show that the discussion about the one and only 'golden spike'[4] misleads the debate about the Anthropocene, which appears in fact to be a sum of several 'spikes' and also includes impacts that have not been discussed as spikes until now. The Anthropocene can be interpreted as an expression of 'unknown unknowns' or rather a short phase of human activ-ity – in this case the period of civilian use of nuclear energy – which can result in serious repercussions, path dependencies, uncertainties and risks that will be detectable far into the future. Scientific-technological research has so far not enabled highly radioactive substances to be entirely neutralised nor stored in a totally secure manner anywhere in the world. The traces left by soci-eties on and in the Earth's crust must therefore, in so far as is possible for humans to judge, be viewed as 'eternal burdens' (Brunnengräber 2015). In the Anthropocene it becomes clear that the negative impacts of human actions are accepted from powerful actors and on a large-scale, despite the fact that the major risks and challenges associated with the disposal of nuclear waste were known from the outset of the nuclear age. The small number of politicians, aca-demics or citizens groups who voiced criticism were outnumbered by a clear majority in favour of pushing for nuclear energy (Jungk 1977; Radkau and Hahn 2013).

Governance, equity and sustainability

The regulation of the relationship between humans, nature and technology takes place via institutions, politics, norms, values and normalised practices that often bring to the fore new strategies of growth. The question now is how existing insti-tutions deal on the one hand with uncertainties and the loss of control, which is revealed by the growth in unforeseeable dynamics in natural processes, and on the other whether these institutions in part provide answers to the dynamics created by the technosphere and the loss of equilibrium in the Earth system. To answer these questions, it becomes necessary also to scrutinise social and political inequalities and differences in power created during the 'Great Acceleration'.

The Anthropocene as an expression of power structures

The Anthropocene implies that humankind as a whole has an impact on the Earth system and that all humans are part of the 'Great Acceleration' or the usage of nuclear energy in the same way. Pichler et al. disagree with this, arguing that "(t)he historically and geographically specific expansion of capitalist society-nature relations and the associated social differentiation have led to persistent social inequalities, challenging the assumption of humanity as a homogenous driver" (Pichler et al. 2017, 32). It is therefore the nature of our economy and complex social dynamics and power structures, which determine and drive the use of biophysical resources and their impact on society.[5] In this, Pichler and colleagues see the real reasons for social inequality and significant regional differences, which in turn give rise to doubts that humankind can be defined as the homogenous driver of the Anthropocene. The negative dynamics which led to the Anthropocene and which were caused by "a minority in the capitalist West" (Schwägerl 2014, 45) are being projected on to all of humankind, although the victims of, for example climate change, are above all the already socially disadvantaged inhabitants of the Global South.

When the discourse about desirable developments, innovation and progress takes place, it is however the countries of the Global North that take the lead, thereby causing responsibilities to become blurred. Jahn and colleagues (2015) correctly deduce that a greater focus should be dedicated to the 'anthropos' as should current 'production, gender and power structures'. It is important to understand the role of power and impotence in the 'world order' (Jahn et al. 2015, 94; see also Brunnengräber 2017). To achieve this, we must once again undertake a critical examination of existing institutions which were born out of capitalism or the 'Great Acceleration' and which are to be found in corresponding path dependencies. They are both part of the solution and the cause of the problem. Social inequality and the growth paradigm are directly connected to the destruction of the Earth system. Exactly here we see a gap in the term of the Anthropocene. Addressing the Anthropocene means not only to consider the out-of-control Earth system, but equally the social structures that also define the relationship between nature, technology and society.

The nuclear remnants, which we identified as part of the 'Great Acceleration', also point to these social inequalities. Approaches to dealing with these remnants are associated with risks and benefits for different regions or social groups. Therefore, Isidoro Losada points out from an international perspective that the selection of a location for highly radioactive waste replicates persistent quasi-colonial structures, which were already created in the field of nuclear energy by the extraction of uranium and during atomic bomb tests. As a result, in many countries the "control and decision-making powers" continue to lie with the state or a strong nuclear industry, whereby "environmental racism in the sense of discrimination and the conscious exposure of certain groups of the population to risks" continues to be practiced in the context of the nation-state (Isidoro Losada 2016, 314). Consequently, in several cases the (planned) storage facilities for radioactive waste often overlap with the living space of ethno-cultural minorities or indigenous groups (e.g., Yucca Mountain in the United States or Muckaty Station in Australia). In addition, Losada makes clear how tangible the "economic structures of exploitation and dependency" (314) are. Blowers follows a similar argument when he views the Gorleben salt dome in the German state of Lower Saxony from the perspective of his concept of *peripheralisation*, which, however, does not exclude the transforming of a "peripheral community from weakness into strength". "Gorleben, initially on the periphery, moved eventually to the centre of a broader conflict over the future of nuclear policy in Germany" (Blowers 2017, 202). The impacts of the 'Great Acceleration' again show that the Anthropocene must be considered alongside questions of inequality and power.

The need for new forms of governance in the Anthropocene

The Anthropocene is the result of governance[6] structures that both led to the crisis and that were unable to stop it. They are the outcome of strongly asymmetrical relations of power. Pichler et al. point out that "current governance initiatives tend to focus on existing institutions and established response measures in addressing the inherent unsustainability of the Anthropocene. They thereby reinforce the drivers of epochal environmental change" (Pichler et al. 2017, 34). Put differently, hitherto governance was designed for the Holocene and not for the Anthropocene with its accompanying dynamics in the sphere of humankind, nature and technology as outlined above. For that reason, several scientists speak of the need for new governance structures and a total rethink of current institutions. Noteworthy examples include Biermann's concept of Earth System Governance (Biermann 2012; Biermann 2015) or Dryzek (2016) who argues that the Anthropocene is "a highly dynamic era" (p. 10) and due to this global governance structures cannot continue to remain static. He searches for global governance criteria that would offer greater dynamism. This criterion could for example be the 'reflexivity' of governance institutions (p. 11). The concept of reflexive governance was introduced by Voß et al. (2006) and describes governance structures which, while facing uncertainties, non-linear and uncontrollable dynamics and complexity, are able to produce robust paths and decisions regarding future developments (Voß et al. 2006). Tremmel (in this volume) calls for the establishment of 'future councils' as a new (fourth) branch of the political system to ensure that the interests of future generations be taken into account within today's decision-making process.

We think that such considerations of how to reorganise society and make its institutions and regulations more resilient and reflexive are highly important. Based on the analysis in this chapter, we do not wish to provide a new concept; rather we offer our reflections on initial attempts made by Voß or Dryzek and Biermann in order to enhance their promising concepts. In the view of the challenges associated with the Anthropocene, it is necessary to make radical changes to political institutions and the related potential solutions. In addition, the socio-ecological crisis – and so the Anthropocene – is the expression of unequal power relations both on different political levels and between countries. Overcoming this power inequality must be the first goal of new governance structures, regulations and institutions.

Regarding the search for a final repository for example, it is important to examine current forms of governance with respect to their multi-level processes. Up until now, decisions on nuclear energy and disposal policy have been made in a top-down manner, with little societal involvement. However, in the last decade there have been signs for a "participatory turn in radioactive waste management" (Bergmans et al. 2014). Another problem associated with existing governance structures is that the local populations in the majority of countries[7] that are searching for a site for a final repository have up until now been underrepresented and barely included as decisive actors in the process (Di Nucci et al. 2017). But it is precisely at the local level that the population incurs significant burdens in dealing with the problems resulting from the direct and concrete actions being taken (see case studies in Blowers 2017), i.e., the risk of radiation being released into their immediate surroundings. Resulting from this, a new configuration of governance should be formed, such as one in which all levels are taken into account during the creation of regulation to deal with this problem. We also think that these realisations regarding current governance deficits are applicable to other symptoms of the socio-ecological crisis.

Political decisions on the final storage of nuclear waste have both major ethical, in particular inter and intra-generational implications resulting from the incalculable timescales and dynamics of the technosphere. In Germany, the Federal Constitutional Court has not awarded future generations constitutional protection against irretrievable radioactive waste (BVerfG 2011, cited in Kersten 2016, 271). The court argues that due to unforeseeable timescales and future developments over the next hundred thousand years, a reference to the subjective legal rights of those people living now is ruled out, which thereby also rules out the right of future generations to bring action (Kersten 2016, 272). The difficult balancing act in decision-making, which covers both current and future generations (or not), becomes apparent in the question of the disposal of nuclear waste. In this context Ott and Semper argue that

> today [we face] a contradiction between the demands to reverse all measures and the avoidance of a continuous pressure to act for future generations. There is no simple solution. The interests of future human beings must be considered in current processes, while at the same time humans living today must also be able to put a solution into effect.
>
> (Ott and Semper 2017, 100)

In this argument we also see the links with the discourse on sustainability, which is closely connected with the discourse on equity. Gardiner states a "primary moral task in this environmentally precarious later stage of the Anthropocene is to ensure that future generations inherit a liveable world" (Gardiner 2011, quoted in McMichael 2014, 54).

On the basis of the elaborated example of nuclear remnants and following on from our discussion of the technosphere, an appropriate handling of what we do not know and what we cannot control would be the first step in a new, responsible form of governance. Here the natural sciences and engineering have a major role to play in communicating more clearly the uncertainties and things we do not know to the political system than has been the case up until now. Recognition of the uncontrollability and lack of temporal clarity must also be taken into greater account in the political decision-making process. Society must discuss whether this approach should be underscored by an ethic such as Hans Jonas' 'heuristic of fear'. According to Jonas, when a new technology is introduced the impact of which cannot be predicted, we must assume the worst consequences for humans and the environment. If it would be untenable for society if this scenario were to become a reality the technology would be rejected (Jonas 1979).

Barnosky and Hadly demand a broad societal approach to solving environmental problems in order to avoid risks to society. They emphasise a stronger interaction "between scientists, policy makers, the business community, technological innovators, thought leaders and the public-at large about the key issues" in spite of "the technological advances that characterize the Anthropocene" (Barnosky and Hadly 2014, 76). This means that it is not only up to science and politics to add substance to the Anthropocene. Answers to the challenges of the term must also come from societies themselves. In light of this, the Anthropocene offers a potential for a socio-ecological transformation – one which however has yet to manifest itself.

Conclusion

Nuclear waste creates a wicked legacy and constitutes a permanent risk to the entire globe. This waste is a manifestation of our imperial mode of living (Brand and Wissen 2013) and our understanding of the Anthropocene. Moreover, it represents a world of interaction, with human practices creating arrangements that are a combination of technological and natural elements. In this way, the Anthropocene enables a new understanding of the relationship between humans, nature and technology and how unforeseeable dynamics and timescales become produced out of this configuration. Against this background, it is particularly important to be aware of the possible irreversibility of interventions. Science and political decisions were at the root of this crisis to occur first. However, in cases where the know-how provided by natural scientists and engineers is embedded in a deliberative political process an inclusive search and implementation of the final disposal of the waste is possible. Such a complex and critical perspective on technological optimism could enrich and broaden the discourse on the Anthropocene. It also becomes clear from the theoretical background and analysis why the Anthropocene should not be identified and analysed on the basis of selected 'golden spikes' and also not purely within the academic context of Earth system science as, for example, Hamilton (2016b) demands.

Instead, the Anthropocene as term extends far beyond the mere diagnosis of humankind as the primary agent of a new geological epoch. The Anthropocene includes not only the upsetting of the Earth system's equilibrium by humankind, but exposes power relations as well as the interdependencies between a radically transformed nature, the man-made technosphere with its resulting path dependencies and internal dynamics, and societies which are both driving forces of the Anthropocene and are affected by it. According to our argument, societies' actions have led to interdependencies between humans, nature and technology, which over time can lead to both expected and unexpected outcomes. These occurrences are no longer fully controllable (Brunnengräber and Görg 2017) and due to their complexity are difficult to describe. Furthermore, society's relationship with nature is not only paradoxical but equally in a state of crisis.

As we have illustrated, the use of a specific technology can undermine the basic rights to safety and health of current and future generations, which could result in major socio-spatial inequalities. This kind of undermining can occur during several possible 'golden spikes'. As explained above, the Anthropocene must be the starting point for finding new forms of governance that connect and include all levels equally and give power to those actors that are currently powerless. The Anthropocene can be seen as a synonym for the loss of control, but the insight of the increase of unforeseeable dynamics could help to overcome old governance structures and embark on a sustainable path based on a more detailed examination of the impacts for the Earth's history in the current decision-making process than was the case in the past.

In sum, more deliberative and reflexive politics and less static institutions to avoid path dependencies are urgently needed. The Anthropocene narrative could at least push sustainability to go beyond piecemeal policies by genuinely integrating economy, ecology and society with equity, i.e., inducing the will to overcome inequality. A productive impulse to recognise the complexity of the relationship between nature, technology and society can then emanate from the Anthropocene. This could pave the way for new forms of governance and related political institutions which do justice to the complexity of this relationship or, as Dalby succinctly puts McAfee's blog text: "Nature is ever more a matter of politics" (Dalby 2016; McAfee 2015).

Acknowledgements

This chapter is a contribution by the Environmental Policy Research Centre (Forschungszentrum für Umweltpolitik, FFU) at Freie Universität Berlin to the project "Methods and measures to deal with socio-technical challenges in storage and disposal of radioactive waste management – SOTEC-radio". The project is funded by the Federal Ministry for Economic Affairs and Energy (Grant Number: BMWi, FK 02E11547C). The authors would like to thank Rosaria Di Nucci for her valuable comments.

Notes

1 The Ecomodernist Manifesto is a statement of different authors with mostly scientific background, www.ecomodernism.org/manifesto-english/ Accessed 24 April 2018.
2 In contrast, the European interpretation contains a reconciliation and coexistence with nature (Grunwald 2015).
3 Therefore Zalasiewicz et al. also highlight that:

> As humans have colonised and modified the Earth's surface, they have developed progressively more sophisticated tools and technologies. These underpin a new kind of stratigraphy, that we term technostratigraphy, marked by the geologically accelerated evolution and diversification of technofossils.
>
> (Zalasiewicz et al. 2014, 34)

4 The WGA-ISC decided that radioactive elements from atomic bomb tests, which expelled particles into the stratosphere, landing across the entire planet as nuclear fallout, represent the very 'golden spike' through which we can determine the Anthropocene: "The radionuclides are probably the sharpest – they really come on with a bang", stated Jan Zalasiewicz, Chair of the WGA (*The Guardian* 2016). An exact date of the start of the Anthropocene was also given, July 16 1945 – the date of the first explosion of an atomic bomb in Alamogordo, New Mexico. This decision did not take into account the role of the civilian use of nuclear energy to generate electricity and its resulting highly radioactive waste, nor catastrophes such as Chernobyl (1986) and Fukushima (2011) or other nuclear accidents during which ever higher levels of radionuclides were released. After Fukushima, for example, radioactive caesium escaped into the North Pacific (Kumamoto et al. 2014). However, the WGA-ISC only attaches importance to the military use of nuclear energy.
5 The Anthropocene literature has identified 'humanity' or 'mankind' as the driving force of epochal ecological and geological change without further elaborating on the societal drivers ... particular emphasis is on the complex societal dynamics and power relations that drive the use of biophysical resources and the related societal impacts on the Earth System. These drivers have led to 'persistent social inequalities and vast regional differences' [Biermann et al. 2016] which challenge the assumption of humanity as a homogenous driver.

(Pichler et al. 2017, 32)

6 In general, governance can be interpreted as a further development to government. Governance includes a certain actor setting, new forms of regulation, new institutions and new forms of cooperation through which societal development is governed. Governance can also be defined as the "characteristic processes by which society defines and handles its problems" (Voß et al. 2006, 8).
7 Initial attempts to involve the local and regional levels have taken place in, for example, Belgium, Sweden, Finland and Great Britain. Their participation, consultation or public participation procedures during the search for a final repository site have been attempted.

References

Barnosky, A.D. and Hadly, E.A. (2014) "Problem solving in the Anthropocene" *The Anthropocene Review*, 1(1), 76–77.
Bergmans, A., Kos, D., Simmons, P. and Sundqvist, G. (2014) "The participatory turn in radioactive waste management: Deliberation and the social-technical divide" *Journal of Risk Research*, 18(3), 347–363.

Biermann, F. (2012) "Navigating the Anthropocene: Improving Earth system governance" *Science*, 335, 1306–1307.

Biermann, F. (2015) "Erdsystem-governance: Ein neues Paradigma der globalen Umwelt-politik" *ZFAS Zeitschrift für Außen-und Sicherheitspolitik*, 8(1), 1–8.

Biermann, F., Bai, X., Bondre, N., Broadgate, W., Chen, C.-T.A., Dube, O.P., Erisman, J.W., Glaser, M., van der Hel, S., Lemos, M.C., Seitzinger, S. and Seto, K.C. (2016) "Down to Earth: Contextualizing the Anthropocene" *Global Environmental Change*, 39, 341–350.

Blowers, A. ed. (2017) *The Legacy of Nuclear Power* Routledge, London.

Bonneuil, C. (2015) "The geological turn: Narratives of the Anthropocene" in Hamilton, C., Gemenne, F. and Bonneuil, C. eds., *The Anthropocene and the Global Environmental Crisis: Rethinking Modernity in a New Epoch* Routledge, New York, 17–31.

Brand, U. and Wissen, M. (2013) "Crisis and continuity of capitalist societynature relationships: The imperial mode of living and the limits to environmental governance" *Review of International Political Economy*, 20(4), 687–711.

Brunnengräber, A. ed. (2015) *Ewigkeitslasten. Die 'Endlagerung' radioktiver Abfälle als soziales, politisches und wissenschaftliches Projekt* edition sigma in der Nomos, Baden Baden.

Brunnengräber, A. (2017) "Warum sich die Klimaforschung mit harten Machtverhältnissen beschäftigen muss" *GAIA*, 26(1), 13–15.

Brunnengräber, A., Di Nucci, M.R., Isidoro Losada, A.M., Mez, L. and Schreurs, M.A. eds. (2015) *Nuclear Waste Governance: An International Comparison* (Vol. 1) Springer VS, Wiesbaden.

Brunnengräber, A., Di Nucci, M.R., Isidoro Losada, A.M., Mez, L. and Schreurs, M.A. eds. (2018) *Challenges of Nuclear Waste Governance: An International Comparison* (Vol. 2) Springer VS, Wiesbaden.

Brunnengräber, A. and Görg, C. (2017) "Nuclear waste in the Anthropocene: Uncertainties and unforeseeable time scales in the disposal of nuclear waste" *GAIA*, 26(2), 96–99.

Budelmann, H., Di Nucci, M.R., Isidoro Losada, A.M., Köhnke, D. and Reichhardt, M. (2017) "Auf dem Weg in die Endlagerung. Die Notwendigkeit der langfristigen Zwischenlagerung hoch radioaktiver Abfälle" *GAIA*, 26(2), 110–113.

Bundesverfassungsgericht (Federal Constitutional Court) (2011) "Beschluss vom 10.11.2009–1 BvR 1178/07" in Verein der Richter des Bundesverfassungsgerichts eds., *BVerfGK. Kammerentscheidungen des Bundesverfassungsgerichts* C.F. Müller, Heidelberg, 370–389.

Craig, M.P.A. (2017) *Ecological Political Economy and the Socio-Ecological Crisis* Building a Sustainable Political Economy: SPERI Research & Policy Series Palgrave Macmillan, Cham.

Crutzen, P.J. (2002) "Geology of mankind" *Nature*, 415, 23.

Dalby, S. (2016) "Framing the Anthropocene: The good, the bad and the ugly" *The Anthropocene Review*, 3(1), 33–51.

Demirovic, A., Dück, J., Becker, F. and Bader, P. (2011) *VielfachKrise im finanzmarktdominierten Kapitalismus* VSA, Hamburg.

Di Nucci, M.R., Brunnengräber, A. and Isidoro Losada, A.M. (2017) "From the 'right to know' to the 'right to object' and 'decide': A comparative perspective on participation in siting procedures for high level radioactive waste repositories" *Progress in Nuclear Energy*, 100, 316–325.

Di Nucci, M.R., Brunnengräber, A., Isidoro Losada, A.M., Mez, L. and Schreurs, M.A. (2015) "Comparative perspectives on nuclear waste governance" in Brunnengräber,

A., et al. eds., *Nuclear Waste Governance: An International Comparison* (Vol. 1) Springer VS, Wiesbaden, 25–43.

Dryzek, J. (2016) "Global environmental governance" in Gabrielson, T., Hall, C., Meyer, J.M. and Schlosberg, D. eds., *The Oxford Handbook of Environmental Political Theory* Oxford University Press, Oxford, 533–544.

Eckhardt, A. and Rippe, K.P. (2016) *Risiko und Ungewissheit? Bei der Entsorgung hochradioaktiver Abfälle* vdf, Zürich.

Edwards, P.N. (2002) "Infrascructure and modernity: Force, time and social organization in the history of sociotechnical systems" in Misa, T.J., et al. eds., *Modernity and Technology* MIT Press, Cambridge, MA.

Endlager-Kommission (2016) *Verantwortung für die Zukunft. Ein faires und transparentes Verfahren für die Auswahl eines nationalen Endlagerstandortes, Abschlussbericht der Kommission Lagerung hochradioaktiver Abfallstoffe* Deutscher Bundestag, Berlin.

Fatheuer, T., Unmüßig, B. and Fuhr, L. (2016) *Inside the Green Economy: Promises and Pitfalls* Heinrich Boell Foundation and Green Books, Cambridge.

Gardiner, S. (2011) *"A Perfect Moral Storm: The Ethical Tragedy of Climate Change"* Oxford University Press, Oxford.

Görg, C. (2016) "Zwischen Tagesgeschäft und Erdgeschichte. Die unterschiedlichen Zeitskalen in der Debatte um das Anthropozän" *GAIA*, 25(1), 9–13.

Grunwald, A. (2015) "Ökomodernismus ist verantwortungsethisch nicht haltbar" *GAIA*, 24(4), 249–253.

The Guardian (2016) "The Anthropocene epoch: Scientists declare dawn of human-influenced age" (www.theguardian.com/environment/2016/aug/29/declare-anthropocene-epoch-experts-urge-geological-congress-human-impact-earth) Accessed 16 April 2018.

Haff, P. (2014) "Humans and technology in the Anthropocene: Six rules" *The Anthropocene Review*, 1(2), 126–136.

Hamilton, C. (2015) "Getting the Anthoropocene so wrong" *The Anthropocene Review*, 2(2), 102–107.

Hamilton, C. (2016a) "The Anthropocene as rupture" *The Anthropocene Review*, 3(2), 93–106.

Hamilton, C. (2016b) "The Anthropocene belongs to Earth system science" (http://thecon versation.com/the-anthropocene-belongs-to-earth-system-science-64105) Accessed 11 April 2018.

IPCC (2014) "Climate change 2014: Mitigation of climate change: Prepared by working group III (WG III AR5)" International Energy Agency (http://mitigation2014.org/report) Accessed 11 April 2018.

Isidoro Losada, A.M. (2016) "Nuklearer Kolonialismus. Atommüll und die Persistenz quasi-kolonialer Logiken" in Brunnengräber, A. ed., *Problemfalle Endlager. Gesellschaftliche Herausforderungen im Umgang mit Atommüll* edition sigma in der Nomos, Baden-Baden, 313–336.

Jahn, T., Hummel, D. and Schramm, E. (2015) "Nachhaltige Wissenschaft im Anthropozän" *GAIA*, 24(2), 92–95.

Joerges, B. (1996) "Large technical systems and the discourse of complexity" in Ingelstam, L. ed., *Complex Technical Systems* Affärslitteratur, Stockholm.

Jonas, H. (1979) *Das Prinzip Verantwortung. Versuch einer Ethik für die technologische Zivilisation* Suhrkamp, Frankfurt am Main.

Jungk, R. (1977) *Der Atomstaat: vom Fortschritt in die Unmenschlichkeit* Kindler Verlag, München.

Kalmbach, K. and Röhlig, K. (2016) "Interdisciplinary perspectives on dose limits in radioactive waste management: A research paper developed within the ENTRIA project" *Journal of Radiological Protection*, 36, 8–22.

Kersten, J. (2016) "Eine Million Jahre? Über die juristische Metaphysik der atomaren Endlagerung" in Kersten, J. ed., *Inwastement – Abfall in Umwelt und Gesellschaft* Transcript Verlag, Bielefeld, 269–288.

Kumamoto, Y., Aoyama, M., Hamajima, Y., Aono, T., Kouketsu, S., Murata, A. and Kawano, T. (2014) "Southward spreading of the Fukushima-derived radiocesium across the Kuroshio Extension in the North Pacific" *Scientific Reports*, 4(4276), 1–9.

Latour, B. (1996) "On actor-network theory: A few clarifications" *Soziale Welt*, 47(4), 369–382.

Latour, B. (2007) *Eine neue Soziologie für eine neue Gesellschaft. Einführung in die Akteur-Netzwerk-Theorie* Suhrkamp, Frankfurt am Main.

McAfee, K. (2015) *The Politics of Nature in the Anthropocene* Resource Politics, Centre, ESRC Steps, Sussex (https://resourcepolitics2015.com/2015/09/09/the-politics-of-nature-in-the-anthropocene/) Accessed 11 April 2018.

McMichael, A.J. (2014) "Population health in the Anthropocene: Gains, losses and emerging trends" *The Anthropocene Review*, 1(1), 44–56.

Møller, A.P., Barnier, F. and Mousseau, T.A. (2012) "Ecosystems effects 25 years after Chernobyl: Pollinators, fruit set and recruitment" *Oecologia*, 170, 1155–1165.

Møller, A.P. and Mousseau, T.A. (2013) "Investigating the effects of low-dose radiation from Chernobyl to Fukushima: History repeats itself" *Asian Perspective*, 37, 551–565.

Öko-Institut (2007) *Treibhausgasemissionen und Vermeidungskosten der nuklearen, fossilen und erneuerbaren Strombereitstellung*, Darmstadt (www.oeko.de/oekodoc/318/2007-008-de.pdf) Accessed 25 April 2018.

Ott, K. and Semper, F. (2017) "Nicht von meiner Welt – Zukunftsverantwortung bei der Endlagerung von radioaktiven Reststoffen" *GAIA*, 26(2), 100–102.

Pichler, M., Schaffartzik, A., Haberl, H. and Görg, C. (2017) "Drivers of society-nature relations in the Anthropocene and their implications for sustainability transformations" *Current Opinion in Environmental Sustainability*, 26, 32–36.

Radkau, J. and Hahn, L. (2013) *Aufstieg und Fall der deutschen Atomwirtschaft* Oekom, München.

Schwägerl, C. (2014) "Die menschgemachte Erde" in Bammé, A. ed., *Schöpfer der zweiten Natur-Der Mensch im Anthropozän* Metropolis-Verlag, Marburg, 39–48.

Steffen, W., Broadgate, W., Deutsch, L., Gaffney, O. and Ludwig, C. (2015) "The trajectory of the Anthropocene: The Great Acceleration" *The Anthropocene Review*, 2(1), 81–98.

Stirling, A. (2015) *Time to Rei(g)n Back the Anthropocene? Pathways to Sustainability* Centre Steps, Sussex.

Voß, J., Bauknecht, D. and Kemp, R. eds. (2006) *Reflexive Governance for Sustainable Development* Edward Elgar, Cheltenham.

Wissenburg, M. (2016) "The Anthropocene and the body ecologic" in Pattberg, P.H. and Zelli, F. eds., *Environmental Politics and Governance in the Anthropocene: Institutions and Legitimacy in a Complex World* Routledge, New York, 15–30.

World Nuclear Association (2018) "Radioactive Waste Management" (http://www.world-nuclear.org/information-library/nuclear-fuel-cycle/nuclear-wastes/radioactive-waste-management.aspx) Accessed 26 June 2018.

Zalasiewicz, J., Williams, M., Waters, C.N., Barnosky, A.D. and Haff, P. (2014) "The technofossil record of humans" *The Anthropocene Review*, 1(1), 34–43.

12 Worlds apart?

The Global South and the Anthropocene

Jens Marquardt

Introduction

In times of global climate change, biodiversity loss and threats to other critical planetary boundaries (Rockström et al. 2009), humans have become a primary driver for global environmental change and the main geological force on Earth. Reflecting this development, Crutzen (2002); Gill (2015), Pattberg and Zelli (2016), and many other scholars have used and developed the concept of the Anthropocene to describe the geological era dominated by humankind.

For the sake of analytical clarity, it is useful to distinguish between the Anthropocene's different meanings. On the one hand, the term reflects a highly complex debate about an ecological epoch based on measurable indicators and scientific evidence. On the other hand, the Anthropocene essentially revolves around political and normative questions when action programmes and policies are derived from ecological evidence (see Schwindenhammer, in this volume). For example, Crutzen and Schwägerl's (2011) call for substantial action in the name of the Anthropocene is primarily based on a firm belief in advanced technologies and innovations from the industrialised world. Arguing that "countries worldwide [are] striving to attain the 'American Way of Life'", they propose that the "citizens of the West should ... pioneer a modest, renewable, mindful and less material lifestyle" (Crutzen and Schwägerl 2011). In that sense, the Anthropocene is more than a scientifically grounded definition of a geological epoch – it is also a highly political programme and a call for massive action. Transformations towards sustainability appear without an alternative to save humans and other living beings from extinction. Solutions to the problems caused by the Anthropocene are often considered universal as they shape all aspects of society in all areas of the world. International organisations and donors link their development-related initiatives for climate action, sustainable energy and even good governance to the Anthropocene concept to foster reforms and change in the Global South.[1] Guided by the "principles of inclusivity, universality and resilience" (Nakicenovic et al. 2016, 46), a grand transformation towards global sustainability becomes imperative for all nations, with the Anthropocene representing a highly normative narrative (see Weißpflug, in this volume).

Despite the term's widespread use in academia and increasing popularity at large, there is also considerable critique concerning the consequences and (socio-political) implications from the Anthropocene (Moore 2016). A universalistic understanding of the Anthropocene leads to some fundamental questions: Is the Anthropocene an overarching paradigm for humanity that speaks to all humans in the same way? How does it affect debates around development, lifestyles and global governance (see Bornemann, in this volume)? Who fosters these debates and for whom is it relevant? Regarding humanity or humankind, the Anthropocene demands not less than a global transformation. Such a 'post-social' assumption risks rejection of social diversity and exclusion of alternative perspectives (Lövbrand et al. 2015). Rooted in a firm belief in ecological modernisation, economic development and technological progress, it seems as if solutions can be exclusively found in the West – including not only technological innovations, such as geo-engineering (Crutzen 2006), but also appropriate political institutions and governance mechanisms (Biermann et al. 2012). Scholars like Manemann (2014) criticise the concept's narrow focus on technological progress and free markets as solutions to global (environmental) problems. In addition, the role of global power struggles and scientific knowledge production in defining these solutions to the Anthropocene has rarely been problematised (Görg 2015, 32).

Framing the Anthropocene not only as the 'geology of mankind' (Crutzen 2002), but also as a challenge to all humankind runs the risk of blurring a differentiated perspective on who is historically responsible for the dramatic global change. Scholars from the Global South in the field of global warming have long raised that criticism (Agarwal and Narain 1991). This chapter argues that despite its global aspiration, the concept of the Anthropocene reflects a powerful Western discourse. Voices from the Global South could provide critical reflections on human-nature relations or attitudes towards technologies, but thus far have rarely been acknowledged. This chapter argues that the concept is embedded in a Western way of thinking and largely neglects alternative development paradigms emerging in the Global South, such as *sumak kawsay*, *Ubuntu* or *ecological Swaraj*. The broader social and political consequences derived from the mainstream scientific discourse around the Anthropocene advocated by scholars like Crutzen (2002) seem to be worlds apart from alternative perspectives from the Global South. In asking how voices and ideas from the Global South contribute to the Anthropocene discourse, three aspects are investigated here:

- To what extent are voices from the Global South underrepresented in the Anthropocene debate (representation)?
- What can be learned empirically and theoretically from the Global South (contributions)?
- What are the central narratives that constitute a collective role of the Global South (framing)?

To answer these questions, an extensive literature review was carried out based on the Web of Science™ database. With such an approach we can identify the representation of the Global South, its contributions, as well as some overarching narratives attached to the Global South in the Anthropocene discourse.

Alternative perspectives from the Global South

The potential marginalisation of the Global South is not a particular concern of the Anthropocene discourse. For the field of development studies, Noor (2015) urges the stronger representation and recognition of voices from the Global South to develop nuanced and contextualised solutions distinct from more generalised approaches fuelled by Western experts. Non-Western ways of knowing, learning and understanding the world are often dismissed as relevant contributors to debates around economic growth, natural resource management or development planning (Ottinger et al. 2017, 1035). These deficits in acknowledging traditional forms of knowledge and alternative ideas from the Global South are most striking in discussions related to concepts with global aspirations, such as the Anthropocene.

Yet, the field of sustainable development has witnessed and still encounters a vast diversity of critical reflections concerning the Global South's 'marginalization, voicelessness and dependency' (Fischer 2012). While the World Commission on Environment and Development (WCED, 1987)[2] urged change towards sustainability in all countries, 'large and small, rich and poor', one stream of criticism tackles the concept's failure to challenge a growth-oriented development model and widespread materialism.

> Instead of encouraging the global North to reduce its ecological footprint in order to increase the living standards of the poor without exceeding biophysical limits, the Brundtland Commission extolled the benefits of international trade as ... the solution to poverty and inequality.
>
> (Gonzalez 2015, 149)

Criticism also arose from the WCED report's unidirectional call for aid and assistance in developing countries. Doyle (1998, 782) trenchantly describes it as a Western notion of supremacy where developing countries "do not know how to live; they do not know how to act ...; they do not know how to think: the North must help them think and act in appropriate ways".

Griggs et al. (2013, 306) also criticise the universalistic ambitions behind sustainable development that run similar to those in the Anthropocene: "Growing affluence and the right to development among the world's poor demand that people of all nations make the transition to sustainable lifestyles". Du Pisani (2006, 4) describes sustainable development as a normative, all-encompassing approach of industrialised nations based on 'Western modernity and the belief in progress'. According to Bauriedl (2015), it is even more striking that the ideal of modernisation and industrialisation driven by Western countries is reframed as the primary solution for global environmental threats, although the same industrialised countries are historically most responsible for these problems.

Instead of fundamentally questioning the Western paradigm of modernisation and development, it can be argued that sustainable development as defined by the WCED emphasises adjustments – or transitions – within the existing system rather than inviting more radical systemwide transformations.

Over the years, various scholars have criticised the mainstream notion of sustainable development and thus contributed to a rich and diverse discourse. Post-development thinkers have critically reflected on underlying concepts like modernisation or catch-up development and have taken a sceptical position towards the link between sustainable development, economic growth and poverty alleviation (Escobar 2011, 2015). Similarly, degrowth scholars have criticised green economy concepts and the dominance of growth-oriented development based on fossil fuels and a neoliberal capitalistic system (Latouche 2009). Alternative societal concepts from the Global South have entered the debate – including *sumak kawsay* (Merino 2016), *Ubuntu* (Louw 2002) and *ecological Swaraj* (Kothari 2014). In contrast to the WCED's understanding of sustainable development, these concepts emphasise human mutuality, the importance of the community, autarky, sovereignty, well-being and happiness, instead of technological advancement and consumption. In that sense, a plurality of voices – including major criticism – characterises today's academic discourse and controversies around sustainable development. Such a vibrant debate can hardly be observed for the Anthropocene discourse despite the various calls for a substantial transformation of humankind, the international system, and societies all over the world.

Methodology

This chapter argues that the mainstream Anthropocene discourse reflects a Western way of thinking while neglecting alternative development paradigms from the Global South that differ from modern capitalism. Investigating such a claim requires a closer look at the Anthropocene discourse, which is accomplished here through a literature review based on the Web of Science™. This chapter reveals to which extent voices from the Global South are underrepresented in the Anthropocene discourse (representation), how research on the Global South contributes to that debate (contributions), and how the Global South is being collectively constructed (framing). Going beyond the Web of Science™ context, alternative ideas and concepts related to human-nature relations and development stemming from the Global South are then discussed.

This explorative research is based on a sample of 1,209 articles derived from the Web of Science™ bibliographic database, all published between 2002 and 2016, and each of which mention 'Anthropocene' in the title, keywords, and/or abstract at least once.[3] The starting date is 2002 for pragmatic reasons since by then articles using the term 'Anthropocene' had significantly increased.[4] That same year, Paul Crutzen's (2002) article 'Geology of mankind' also advanced the term's popularity. Such a broad investigation based on a single term also comes with limitations. The sample potentially includes articles that take the Anthropocene as an eye catcher with little added value or reference to the debate while concomitantly it might exclude other contributions that do discuss alternative development concepts from the Global South, but are not doing so under the heading of the Anthropocene. In addition, the scientific debate is taken as a proxy for the overall discourse on the Anthropocene.

Quantitative analysis has been conducted to first acquire a general overview of the articles regarding their languages, author affiliations and case study selection (representation). Subsequently, 119 articles with an explicit reference to the Global South in general, or to specific developing countries, were more deeply investigated through an iterative process of qualitative data analysis (Stake 1995; Suter 2012). A more exploratory research approach (Stebbins 2001) was applied to identify substantial empirical and theoretical contributions related to the Global South (contribution). To further elaborate on how the Global South is perceived and constructed in the mainstream Anthropocene discourse, 15 frequently cited and thus influential articles from social sciences and the humanities were selected to identify overarching narratives on the role of the Global South in the Anthropocene (framing). These were incrementally derived from the texts through a structured content analysis. All references to the Global South were first extracted and compiled before they were grouped into overarching themes and pulled together into four key narratives. Finally, alternative views and concepts from outside the Web of Science™ context were selected to expand the scope of discussion. Figure 12.1 summarises this workflow. In sum, this research combines a systematic overview with a more qualitative approach to investigate the role of the Global South in the Anthropocene discourse.

The Global South in the Anthropocene discourse

Investigating the role of voices from the Global South and their representation in academic Anthropocene discourse can be undertaken in different ways: Measuring representation as the languages used in the articles and authors' affiliations is arguably the simplest. Although a scholar's affiliation should not be understood as equivalent to the representation of actual people from the Global South, it tells us where research related to the Anthropocene is being conducted and hints at the potential dominance of Western institutions. While this might only reflect the dominance of the Global North in academic discourse in general, it is particularly important to highlight Western dominance as a concept with global aspirations. In more qualitative terms, this chapter sheds light on specific empirical and theoretical contributions from the Global South to discuss how ideas and perspectives from outside the Western hemisphere do or do not enter the Anthropocene discourse. Finally, it is asked how the Global South is collectively perceived, described and framed in the mainstream Anthropocene debate.

Representation: voices from the Global South

Based on the articles' languages and the authors' institutional affiliations for all 1,209 relevant articles, scholars from the Global South are massively underrepresented in

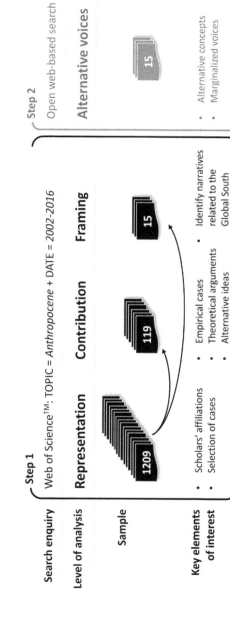

Figure 12.1 Consecutive steps of this literature review

the Anthropocene debate. Unsurprisingly, in the context of Web of Science[TM], the overwhelming majority (97 percent) of all records are written in English (less than 1 percent in German, Spanish and French). Language represents a powerful mechanism of exclusion and a 'major barrier to global science' (Amano et al. 2013) because it excludes voices, views and ideas from non-English speakers from scientific debates and controversies. The language barrier hampers communication and exchange among global communities. Indigenous knowledge and alternative perspectives from the Global South thus face a serious obstacle to be heard in academic debates.

Concerning the authors' affiliations, institutions from the Global North (especially the United States, the United Kingdom and Australia) dominate the field (88.7 percent), whereas research conducted at institutions in the Global South remains a definite minority (11.3 percent). China is an exception here, being the only country from the Global South to appear among the top-ten country affiliations for the sample. In general, the numbers suggest only minor input from researchers working in institutions in the Global South.[5] Figure 12.2 provides an overview of the geographical distribution of author affiliations for the articles investigated here.

For practical reasons, Figure 12.2 defines the Global South as countries receiving Official Development Assistance (ODA) as listed by the Organisation for Economic Co-Operation and Development (OECD 2014).

After mapping the geographical focus of those sample articles, the situation looks slightly different. Based on the articles' titles and abstracts, most research does not refer to a certain country or region (61 percent). This number can be partly attributed to the fact that the field is dominated by natural and applied sciences, largely without a dedicated geographical focus. Although the rest of the sample still shows a significant imbalance between articles referring to the Global North (29 percent of the overall sample) and research dealing with the

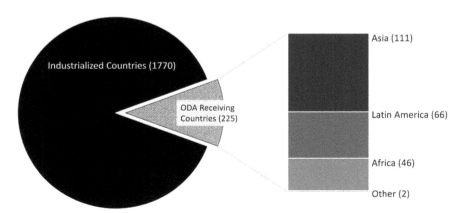

Figure 12.2 Records by country affiliation

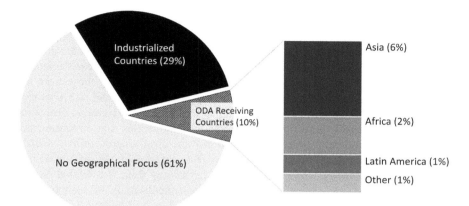

Figure 12.3 Records by geographical focus

Global South or developing countries (10 percent), the picture is not as sharp as it was for authors' affiliations. While these numbers show a particular geographical focus and a relative lack of case and regional studies located in the Global South, it does not hint at the lack of voices from the Global South as such because the studies did not necessarily require a regional empirical focus. Figure 12.3 summarises the geographical focus of the records.

These numbers emphasise that direct input from research institutions in the Global South as well as knowledge from cases and regional studies located in developing countries is extraordinarily limited. This finding stands in contrast to the universalistic claim the Anthropocene concept and its central narratives make.

Contributions: research on the Global South

Empirical contributions derived from research on the Global South are primarily related to environmental policy fields, such as agriculture, water, climate or biodiversity. Examples include effects of anthropogenic behaviour on fish stock (Dudgeon 2011), the effects of climate change on soil and agriculture (Gunatilaka 2009), and the link between biodiversity and resilience (Awiti 2011). In investigating the consequences of dam building and anthropogenic climate change on river fishes, Dudgeon (2011) places his case about fish stock and fishery in the Yangtze and Mekong Rivers directly into the context of the Anthropocene. Although Dudgeon (2011, 1516) mentions the importance of 'Anthropocene Asia', he exclusively references Western scholars like Steffen et al. (2007). Similarly, Awiti (2011) takes for granted Crutzen's (2002) propsed Anthropocene concept when investigating cichlid species in Lake Victoria. He loosely connects his call for a 'new management paradigm' (Awiti 2011, 1) to foster resilience to the idea of the Anthropocene. These cases demonstrate the limits of our quantitative analysis:

Dealing with case studies in the Global South does not automatically mean the inclusion of (critical) voices from the Global South; rather, it can also mean jumping on the mainstream Anthropocene bandwagon.

The sample in general lacks contributions from social sciences and the humanities. While this might be attributed to the Web of Science™ database's selection bias, it also reveals the challenges for social scientists, especially those from the Global South, to enter the mainstream Anthropocene discourse and tackle its narratives. Research from natural and applied sciences focuses on technological solutions, such as geo-engineering or agricultural innovations for environmental and development-related problems, presuming universally applicability. Such a technocentric view tends to prefer solutions from technologically advanced and industrialised countries while overlooking alternatives from the Global South. Summarising the idea of a universalistic conceptualisation of technological problem-solving capacity, Orbach (2011, 1) argues that "technological innovation has the potential to maintain our standard of living while stabilising global temperatures". Similarly, Gunatilaka's (2009) case about the effects of climate change and environmental degradation in Sri Lanka reveals a strong belief in technical solutions. He argues that 'modern science, technology and proven socio-economic policies' are needed "to reverse the negative trends and achieve a sustainable world" (Gunatilaka 2009, 3). These articles exemplify how various contributions dealing with the Global South follow the mainstream Anthropocene discourse as outlined by scholars like Crutzen (2002) or Steffen et al. (2007).

The sample articles' lack of theoretical reflections is even more striking. Articles dealing with the Global South fail to provide any substantive contributions to theoretical or methodological debates. Missing are critical conceptual reflections regarding the Anthropocene not only as a geological term, but also as a universal programme with socio-political implications. While this might be a function of time, it hints at the need for further social science analysis. Only a few exceptions explicitly link the Anthropocene to alternative worldviews or non-Western beliefs. As an example, Schneiderman (2012, 94) draws lines between the Anthropocene and Buddhism, concluding that such a perspective allows us to "begin to extricate ourselves from the cycles of 'slow violence' through a green practice path based both in wisdom and heartfelt ethical conduct". Global South perspectives of *sumak kawsay*, *Ubuntu* or *ecological Swaraj* have not been seriously considered in the sample of the 1,209 articles investigated here.

The selection of articles under review reflects only a fraction of the Anthropocene discourse, namely the one occurring within Web of Science™ journals. A broader and more nuanced discourse outside the Web of Science™ does exist but obviously struggles to find its way into major academic journals. The underrepresentation of the Global South in Web of Science™ listed journals should nevertheless be alarming because these highly ranked and frequently cited sources significantly shape academic discourses and how we understand the world. More in-depth analyses from the Global South, such as a monography about multiple socio-ecological initiatives in Brazil (Liz-Rejane Issberner 2017), does exist, but access to major journals is limited.

Framing: key narratives

Although the Global South becomes increasingly relevant for global environmental concerns the "Anthropocene concept does not fully do justice to the specific position of the global South and its actors" (Isailovic 2016, 199). The brief overview of the literature presented above underlines that position. Vis à vis the questions of representation of and contributions from the Global South, we also investigated how the Global South is framed in the Anthropocene discourse. Based on 15 key publications related to the Anthropocene, at least four different but interlinked central narratives can be described.

Narrative 1: helping the Global South

Countries and regions in the Global South are often considered to be extraordinarily vulnerable to the effects of anthropogenic activities. For example, societies highly vulnerable to ocean acidification are mainly located in developing countries and small island states (Cooley et al. 2012). This leads to a strong normative demand to support the Global South in general, or at least some developing countries, such as poor island nations profoundly affected by climate change. Biermann (2016, 345) stresses that "global solutions are required for reducing carbon dioxide emissions, as well as for the support of particularly affected communities in poorer regions in the South". The Anthropocene is then linked to global climate governance, development cooperation, and financial compensation mechanisms that have been or should be established under a global environmental governance architecture, where "strong financial support of poorer countries remains essential" (Biermann et al. 2012, 1307).

Narrative 2: making the Global South accountable

Despite widespread differentiation between historical and current responsibilities for the global environment, the apparent duality between industrialised and developing countries regarding their commitments has eroded over the last three decades. It is even argued that "the global North's excessive historical use of the atmosphere's absorptive capacity has closed off similar development routes for the global South" (Palsson et al. 2013, 7). The burden of a 'climate debt' or an 'ecological footprint' is discussed not only for North America and Europe, but also countries like Libya or Uganda, which face critical debate concerning their overconsumption of natural resources (Mungai 2015). While the United Nations' earlier Millennium Development Goals (MDGs) largely targeted improving the situation in the Global South (except for goal eight, the call for a global partnership for development), current Sustainable Development Goals (SDGs) "recognize that *all* countries have problems to solve and contributions to make" (United Nations 2016, 2, emphasis in original). High emissions, especially in emerging economies like China or India increase the pressure on the Global South and urge developing countries to take significant action to combat global problems like climate change. While "the Great Acceleration of the 1945–2000 period was almost entirely driven by the OECD countries", Steffen, Grinevald et al. (2011, 853) argue, "the Great Acceleration of the twenty-first century has become much more democratic". This also implies that the Global South has to take substantial measures against anthropogenic environmental change. The Global South's right for (economic) development similar to the industrialised world is being scrutinised and questioned in light of the Anthropocene.

> The pathways of development followed by today's wealthy countries after the Second World War ... cannot be followed by the 75%–80% of the human population who are now at various stages of their trajectories out of poverty, and are beginning to compete with today's wealthy countries for increasingly scarce resources.
>
> (Steffen, Persson et al. 2011, 739)

Ironically, "the global South is denied a similar development path to the global North due to the latter's excessive use of the planet's resources and absorptive capacity" (Isailovic 2016, 211).

Narrative 3: guiding the Global South

High potentials for 'technological leapfrogging' and the ability to 'decouple economic growth from emissions' (Steffen, Persson et al. 2011, 746) are often linked to the Global South. While scientific knowledge, technologies and innovations to solve the problems of the Anthropocene are largely developed in the Global North, developing countries are framed as the main beneficiaries of these innovations. Instead of a critical reflection of the Western development model as such, technology-driven development paradigms, such as ecological modernisation or the Green New Deal with substantial financial flows towards green technologies, are framed as legitimate and promising paths to avoid global environmental degradation. Such a perception leads to overwhelmingly broad and general recommendations that are not exclusively related to the Anthropocene but can be linked to the strong belief in modern technology's problem-solving capacity in broader development concepts or environmental discourses. Thus, the perception of the Global South in the Anthropocene also reflects the strong hegemony of Western concepts at large. For example, Gunatilaka (2009, 10) concludes that improving climate adaptation in Sri Lanka requires "the world's most innovative scientists to tackle the developing crisis". Slaughter (2012) is more sceptical about the problem-solving capacities of technologies and suggests a greater emphasis on global institutions, cultural innovations and massive innovations in education. What is mostly missing in the debate are alternative conceptual ideas from the Global South itself, including insights from debates in environmental justice (e.g., Shiva 2008).

Narrative 4: assimilating the Global South

The concept of the Anthropocene underlines the interdependencies of all nations and the need for a robust global governance framework (Pattberg and Zelli 2016).

Countries and communities of the Global South are thus merging into a 'single human community on a global scale' (Gill 2015, 827) and more integrated into universal efforts to address global environmental crises. Critical questions related to legitimacy and a global democratic foundation are rarely formulated (Isailovic 2016). Instead, for developing countries, becoming inevitably involved in globalisation and economic development becomes a key universal characteristic of the Anthropocene paradigm:

> All regions in the world, irrespective of their past positions in the geographical divisions created by the legacies of colonialism between Global North and Global South, will increasingly participate in globalisation processes and by doing so redefine their positions in the world system.
>
> (Gill 2015, 825)

Nixon (2011) also addresses the negative effects of globalisation and global interdependencies. For example, consumption patterns in countries like the United States are linked to negative externalities exported to production sites in India. As a result, developments in the North impose 'slow violence' (Nixon 2011) on the Global South as they lead to lower life expectancies, increased environmental degradation, and reduced overall quality of life.

These four narratives are neither distinct nor exclusive. They do highlight a more general observation. While scholars discuss Western ideas and technologies as potential solutions to the problems arising from the Anthropocene, the Global South is primarily framed as vulnerable to the effects of anthropogenic environmental effects, passive in terms of its own problem-solving capacity, and dependent on technological, institutional and social innovations from the Global North. Instead of providing alternatives to the growth-based development model, voices from the Global South are marginalised as they are in related academic debates about topics like global environmental governance (Najam 2005) or climate justice (Roberts and Parks 2006).

Linking alternative concepts from the Global South to the Anthropocene

While the Anthropocene discourse within the Web of Science™ mostly seems to marginalise voices and ideas from the Global South, their views can be found elsewhere. To highlight a broader and more diverse debate beyond the scope of this analysis, this section links (1) insights from other schools of thought, such as *sumak kawsay* and post-development, to the Anthropocene discourse and (2) identifies critical reflections about the Anthropocene outside of the Web of Science™ database.

(1) Representing a central principle for indigenous peoples living in the Andes, *sumak kawsay* (often translated as *buen vivir* or *good living*) has become a global social movement driven not only by indigenous peoples and other marginalised groups, but also activists and researchers from the Global North. Instead of

understanding well-being from a merely individual perspective, *sumak kawsay* is more concerned about "the individual in the social context of their community and in a unique environmental situation" (Gudynas 2013). The movement aims "to change our development model, from a growth-oriented and extraction of natural resources oriented model to something that is more holistic" (Escobar 2012) and refuses the notion of material well-being and material consumption as equivalent to prosperity.

> It is a plural concept with two main entry points. On the one hand, it includes critical reactions to classical Western development theory. On the other hand, it refers to alternatives to development emerging from indigenous traditions, and in this sense, the concept explores possibilities beyond the modern Euro-centric tradition.
>
> (Gudynas 2011, 441)

With its emphasis on harmonious and collective development, *sumak kawsay* promotes alternatives to Western modernity and provides a different understanding of human-nature relations in the Anthropocene. Instead of giving nature a monetary value by defining ecosystem services, *sumak kawsay* conceptualises humans as stewards – not owners – of the Earth. Reinforcing cultural identity and merging context-specific forms of indigenous knowledge with Western discourses (e.g., on feminism) *sumak kawsay* acts "as an umbrella for a set of different positions" (Gudynas 2011, 444).

Similar principles can be found in *radical ecological democracy* or *ecological Swaraj*, where human well-being is meant to be achieved through pathways that empower all citizens to participate in decision-making, ensure equitable distribution of wealth, and respect the Earth's limits and the rights of nature (Kothari 2014). Such a radical notion of democratic participation could foster debates around the democratic foundation and the legitimisation of the Anthropocene as a universalistic global governance approach.

Post-development scholars are engaging in a vibrant debate about "biocentrism, 'rights of nature' movements, and non-dualist approaches" (Escobar 2015, 456) over the last decades. They provide another broad and nuanced critique of modernity defined by economic growth, technological development, and ecological modernisation that is often the (tacit) foundation of the Anthropocene discourse. While a much more in-depth investigation into potential links between these concepts and the Anthropocene is needed, post-development scholars offer a variety of arguments for critical controversies, such as human well-being vs. economic development, the dualisms between nature and society, or the role of technological innovations vs. social organisation.

(2) Outside the Web of Science[TM] a few publications already directly link contributions and concepts from the Global South to the Anthropocene. For example, Inoue et al. (2016) investigate the role of indigenous knowledge in the Anthropocene. They conclude that the diverse understandings of nature based on different indigenous knowledge systems could overcome the human-nature divide

encountered in Western thinking and global environmental governance "by bringing a more holistic worldview, so helping to overcome the dichotomies of modernity" (Inoue et al. 2016, 16). In contrast to what others might perceive as progress and development, indigenous peoples might encounter social conflicts, environmental destruction, or the violation of sacred sites (Swift and Cock 2015).

> For many indigenous peoples, other non-human (spiritual) beings and elements of nature have consciousness and culture. In many traditional cultures, the various elements of nature … are each imbued with its corresponding soul, spirit and sacredness. This intense relation with the elements of nature makes a significant difference in human relations with nature, in particular in the greater respect for other beings and how events toward nature are perceived.
>
> (Inoue et al. 2016, 16–17)

According to Briggs and Sharp (2004), indigenous knowledge and alternative visions from the Global South should not simply be integrated into a mainstream Anthropocene discourse. They argue that adding non-Western knowledge to existing universalist approaches – such as a universal global governance architecture for the Anthropocene (Biermann et al. 2012) – will not necessarily lead to a critical reflection. Instead, they call for acknowledging and thoughtfully engaging with alternative worldviews and perceptions vis à vis Western narratives behind the Anthropocene. Voices from the Global South "must be allowed to criticise dominant worldviews, challenge terms of debate and propose alternative agendas, rather than simply being added into an existing way of doing things" (Briggs and Sharp 2004, 668). The Paris Agreement on Climate Change (UNFCCC 2015) is a good example of how indigenous knowledge is not treated on equal terms. According to the agreement, "adaptation action … should be based on and guided by the best available science and, as appropriate, traditional knowledge, knowledge of indigenous peoples and local knowledge systems". Such a notion reflects a hierarchical understanding of concepts, where ideas from the Global South become subordinate to mostly Western science and technology and where globalised scientific facts and expert knowledge become detached from cultural norms and meanings (Jasanoff 2010).

Conclusions

Scholars dealing with the Anthropocene have raised numerous critical questions related to the future of this planet. While Lövbrand et al. (2015) highlight the role of social sciences when asking 'who speaks for the future of Earth?', this could be enhanced by a geographical perspective. Rather than focusing on 'implications for the Global South' (Isailovic 2016) we should also seriously consider voices and concepts from the Global South. While this chapter has revealed how the Global South plays a marginal role in the Anthropocene discourse, further research could explore potential implications from a stronger perspective of the

214   *Jens Marquardt*

Global South. Instead of treating the Global South as an object and simply integrating indigenous knowledge into top-down development approaches (Briggs and Sharp 2004), we should explore and engage with alternative world views, development paradigms, and concepts from the Global South (Hollington et al. 2015) in a more reflexive way. Elaborating on the added value of concepts from the Global South and ethical debates about geo-engineering, or questions related to the legitimacy of global governance arrangements, seems to be a promising avenue for future research and societal debate. While Najam (2005) reveals the challenges for developing countries to move 'from contestation to participation to engagement' in global environmental governance, this can also be investigated for the Anthropocene debate.

This literature review has shown that the concept of the Anthropocene mainly reflects a Western perspective, neglecting or silencing alternative development pathways that differ from modern industrialisation. The Global South is not entirely marginalised in that discourse, but to a large degree is underrepresented despite its increasing relevance for global environmental concerns. A more serious consideration of the Global South when it comes to defining the Anthropocene and deriving socio-political implications could increase the Anthropocene's legitimacy and acceptance. This would help to identify substantial contributions beyond technology- and modernisation-driven solutions. Ideas and concepts from the Global South in opposition to the technocentric perspective of the Anthropocene are rarely discussed, which should be striking in light of the Anthropocene as a universalist political programme used to legitimise action around the world. As a 'boundary concept' (Görg 2015, 32) between scientific knowledge and political action, to date the Anthropocene has seen little critical debates about its functions.

The analysis of the discourse within the Web of Science™ and the brief notes about alternative views from the Global South can act as a starting point to advance the role of the Global South in the Anthropocene debate. Valuable contributions include indigenous forms of knowledge, *sumak kawsay*, *Ubuntu* or *ecological Swaraj*. Inoue et al. (2016) provide a good example when they suggest overcoming the human-nature dichotomy through the lens of indigenous knowledge. And, while Ellis et al. (2016, 192) have argued that social scientists need to be involved in formalising the Anthropocene because 'the causes of Earth's transition are human and social', the social science research agenda should not limit itself to a technocratic understanding of societal transformations in the Anthropocene. Instead,

we must explore how Western thought traditions, hitherto heavily dependent on the dualism of nature and society, can confront their internal limits and intellectual tipping points. Their flexibility needs to be enhanced and adapted to the human condition of the Anthropocene.

(Palsson et al. 2013, 11)

Global collective commitments, such as the Sustainable Development Goals (SDGs) or the Paris Agreement on Climate Change, have blurred the formerly clear distinction between industrialised countries and the developing world. While this development reflects a growing awareness of the need for substantial action towards sustainability in all parts of the world, scholars from the Global South have counterargued and criticised that this also marginalises the industrialised countries' historical responsibilities and whitewashes a distinction between 'luxury emissions' and 'survival emissions' (Narain and Riddle 2007). To do justice to this and other perspectives from the Global South, a truly global topic like the Anthropocene should not only "be treated by scholars from all disciplines with the seriousness it deserves" (Maslin and Ellis 2016), but it should also reflect the world's geographical diversity.

Notes

1 The 'Global South' or 'developing countries' are not understood here as neutral terms. Instead, these are highly contested concepts. Numerous definitions and controversial perceptions of the Global South exist (Hollington et al. 2015). The term does not refer to a homogenous group of countries. Although these countries cannot be easily defined, they are understood here as countries mainly in the geographical south which share a history shaped by "colonialism, a struggle to address widespread poverty, and a predominant policy concern with the process of 'development' over the past few decades" (Dubash and Morgan 2012, 263). For the quantitative part of the analysis, countries receiving Official Development Assistance (ODA) as listed by the Organisation for Economic Co-Operation and Development (OECD) are considered to represent the Global South (OECD 2014).
2 The WCED (1987) broadly defined sustainable development as "development that meets the needs of the present without compromising the ability of future generations to meet their own needs".
3 Publication data was retrieved from the Web of Science[TM] bibliographic database (www.webofknowledge.com).
4 According to Google Ngram Viewer (2008), the frequency of the term was 5.5 times higher in 2008 compared to 2001 in the Google Books text corpora.
5 Calibrating these numbers against the term 'sustainable development' leads to a different picture: Out of a significantly larger sample (49,419 relevant articles with the topic 'sustainable development' and published between 2002 and 2016) derived from the Web of Science[TM] database, more than a quarter is related to institutions based in China (25.7%). In addition, more than 23% come from other non-OECD countries, most notably India (2.8%), Brazil (2.4%), South Africa (1.5%), Malaysia (1.4%) and Turkey (1.4%). While this difference might be attributed to the field's development over time and a much broader scope, it shows that a more diversified and globalised academic discourse can be possible.

References

Agarwal, A. and Narain, S. (1991) *Global Warming in an Unequal World: A Case of Environmental Colonialism* Center for Science and Environment, New Delhi.
Amano, T., et al. (2013) "Languages are still a major barrier to global science" *PLoS Biology*, 14(12), 1–8.
Awiti, A.O. (2011) "Biological diversity and resilience: Lessons from the recovery of cichlid species in Lake Victoria" *Ecology and Society*, 16(1), 1–11.
Bauriedl, S. (2015) *Wörterbuch Klimadebatte* Transcript Verlag, Bielefeld.

216 *Jens Marquardt*

Biermann, F., et al. (2016) "Down to Earth: Contextualizing the Anthropocene" *Global Environmental Change*, 39, 341–350.

Biermann, F., Abbott, K. and Andresen, S. (2012) "Navigating the Anthropocene: Improving Earth system governance" *Science*, 335(6074), 1306–1307.

Briggs, J. and Sharp, J. (2004) "Indigenous knowledges and development: A postcolonial caution" *Third World Quarterly*, 25(4), 661–676.

Cooley, S.R., et al. (2012) "Nutrition and income from molluscs today imply vulnerability to ocean acidification tomorrow" *Fish and Fisheries*, 13(2), 182–215.

Crutzen, P.J. (2002) "Geology of mankind" *Nature*, 415(6867), 23.

Crutzen, P.J. (2006) "Albedo enhancement by stratospheric sulfur injections: A contribution to resolve a policy dilemma?" *Climatic Change*, 77(3–4), 211–219.

Crutzen, P.J. and Schwägerl, C. (2011) "Living in the Anthropocene: Toward a new global ethos" *Yale Environment 360* (http://e360.yale.edu/features/living_in_the_anthropocene_toward_a_new_global_ethos) Accessed 1 April 2017.

Doyle, T. (1998) "Sustainable development and Agenda 21: The secular bible of global free markets and pluralist democracy" *Third World Quarterly*, 19(4), 771–786.

Dubash, N.K. and Morgan, B. (2012) "Understanding the rise of the regulatory state of the South" *Regulation and Governance*, 6(3), 261–281.

Dudgeon, D. (2011) "Asian river fishes in the Anthropocene: Threats and conservation challenges in an era of rapid environmental change" *Journal of Fish Biology*, 79(6), 1487–1524.

Ellis, E., et al. (2016) "Involve social scientists in defining the Anthropocene" *Nature*, 540(7632), 192–193.

Escobar, A. (2011) "Sustainability: Design for the pluriverse" *Development*, 54(2), 137–140.

Escobar, A. (2012) *Alternatives to Development (an interview with Arturo Escobar) Transition Culture* (www.transitionculture.org/2012/09/28/alternatives-to-development-an-interview-with-arturo-escobar/) Accessed 12 September 2017.

Escobar, A. (2015) "Degrowth, postdevelopment, and transitions: A preliminary conversation" *Sustainability Science*, 10(3), 451–462.

Fischer, D. (2012) *Sustainable Development and Governmentality: Marginalization, Voicelessness, Dependency* Aberystwyth University, Aberystwyth.

Gill, B. (2015) "Global development in the Anthropocene" *Globalizations*, 12(5), 824–827.

Gonzalez, C.G. (2015) "Bridging the North-South divide: International environmental law in the Anthropocene" *Pace Environmental Law Review*, 32(2), 407–434.

Görg, C. (2015) "Anthropozän" in Bauriedl, S. ed., *Wörterbuch Klimadebatte* Transcript Verlag, Bielefeld, 29–35.

Griggs, D., et al. (2013) "Policy: Sustainable development goals for people and planet" *Nature*, 495(7441), 305–307.

Gudynas, E. (2011) "Buen vivir: Today's tomorrow" *Development*, 54(4), 441–447.

Gudynas, E. (2013) "Buen vivir: The social philosophy inspiring movements in South America" *The Guardian* (www.theguardian.com/sustainable-business/blog/buen-vivir-philosophy-south-america-eduardo-gudynas) Accessed 12 September 2017.

Gunatilaka, A. (2009) "The Anthropocene: A 200 year record of human driven geological impacts: Prelude to global climate changes and implications for South Asia" *Journal of the National Science Foundation of Sri Lanka*, 37(1), 3–11.

Hollington, A., et al. (2015) *Concepts of the Global South, Voices from around the World* Global South Studies Center Cologne, Cologne.

Inoue, C.Y.A., et al. (2016) "Many worlds, many nature(s), one planet: Indigenous knowledge in the Anthropocene" *Revista Brasileira de Política Internacional*, 59(2).

Isailovic, M. (2016) "The legitimacy and transformation of global climate governance in the Anthropocene: Implications for the global South" in Pattberg, P. and Zelli, F. eds., *Environmental Politics and Governance in the Anthropocene* Routledge, London, 198–211.

Jasanoff, S. (2010) "A new climate for society" *Theory, Culture and Society*, 27(2), 233–253.

Kothari, A. (2014) "Radical ecological democracy: A path forward for India and beyond" *Development*, 57(1), 36–45.

Latouche, S. (2009) *Farewell to Growth* Polity Press, Cambridge.

Liz-Rejane Issberner, P.L. (2017) *Brazil in the Anthropocene Conflicts between Predatory Development and Environmental Policies*, Routledge, London.

Louw, D.J. (2002) *Ubuntu and the Challenges of Multiculturalism in Post-Apartheid South Africa* Expertisecentrum Zuidelijk Afrika, Utrecht.

Lövbrand, E., et al. (2015) "Who speaks for the future of Earth? How critical social science can extend the conversation on the Anthropocene" *Global Environmental Change*, 32, 211–218.

Manemann, J. (2014) *Kritik des Anthropozäns: Plädoyer für eine neue Humanökologie* Transkript Verlag, Bielefeld.

Maslin, M. and Ellis, E. (2016) "Scientists still don't understand the Anthropocene: And they're going about it the wrong way" *The Conversation* (https://theconversation.com/scientists-still-dont-understand-the-anthropocene-and-theyre-going-about-it-the-wrong-way-70017) Accessed 19 March 2018.

Merino, R. (2016) "An alternative to 'alternative development'?: Buen vivir and human development in Andean countries" *Oxford Development Studies*, 44(3), 271–286.

Moore, J.W. (2016) "The rise of cheap nature" in Moore, J.W. ed., *Anthropocene or Capitalocene? Nature, History, and the Crisis of Capitalism* PM Press, Oakland, 78–115.

Mungai, C. (2015) "Which countries are in ecological debt?" *World Economic Forum* (www.weforum.org/agenda/2015/08/which-countries-are-in-ecological-debt/) Accessed 11 September 2017.

Najam, A. (2005) "Developing countries and global environmental governance: From contestation to participation to engagement" *International Environmental Agreements: Politics, Law and Economics*, 5(3), 303–321.

Nakicenovic, N., et al. (2016) "Global commons in the Anthropocene: World development on a stable and resilient planet" *International Institute for Applied System Analysis*, October, 1–53.

Narain, S. and Riddle, M. (2007) "Greenhouse justice: An entitlement framework for managing the global atmospheric commons" in Boyce, J.K., Narain, S. and Stanton, E.A. eds., *Reclaiming Nature: Environmental Justice and Ecological Restoration* Anthem Press, London, New York, 401–414.

Nixon, R. (2011) *Slow Violence and the Environmentalism of the Poor* Harvard University Press, Cambridge.

Noor, R.A. (2015) "Enough with western voices: 'Experts' are fueling dangerous development myths" *The Guardian* (www.theguardian.com/global-development-professionals-network/2015/oct/31/enough-with-western-voices-experts-are-fueling-dangerous-development-myths) Accessed 8 September 2017.

OECD (2014) *DAC List of ODA Recipients, Organisation for Economic Co-Operation and Development* (www.oecd.org/dac/stats/daclist.htm) Accessed 2 April 2017.

Orbach, R.L. (2011) "Our sustainable Earth" *Reports on Progress in Physics*, 74(11), 112801, (1–16).

Ottinger, G., Barandiarán, J. and Kimura, A.H. (2017) "Environmental justice: Knowledge, technology, and expertise" in Felt, U., et al. eds., *The Handbook of Science and Technology Studies*, MIT Press, Cambridge, London, 716–725.

Palsson, G., et al. (2013) "Reconceptualizing the 'Anthropos' in the Anthropocene: Integrating the social sciences and humanities in global environmental change research" *Environmental Science and Policy*, 28, 3–13.

Pattberg, P. and Zelli, F. (2016) *Environmental Politics and Governance in the Anthropocene: Institutions and Legitimacy in a Complex World* Routledge, London.

Du Pisani, J.A. (2006) "Sustainable development: Historical roots of the concept" *Environmental Sciences*, 3(2), 83–96.

Roberts, J.T. and Parks, B. (2006) *A Climate of Injustice Global Inequality, North-South Politics, and Climate Policy*, MIT Press, Cambridge, MA.

Rockström, J., et al. (2009) "A safe operating space for humanity" *Nature*, 461(7263), 472–475.

Schneiderman, J.S. (2012) "Awake in the Anthropocene" *Contemporary Buddhism*, 13(1), 83–97.

Shiva, V. (2008) *Soil Not Oil: Environmental Justice in an Age of Climate Crisis*, South End Press, Brooklyn.

Slaughter, R.A. (2012) "Welcome to the Anthropocene" *Futures*, 44(2), 119–126.

Stake, R. (1995) *The Art of Case Study Research*, Sage Publications, Thousand Oaks.

Stebbins, R.A. (2001) *Exploratory Research in the Social Sciences*, Sage Publications, London.

Steffen, W., Crutzen, P.J. and Mcneill, J.R. (2007) "The Anthropocene are humans now overwhelming the great forces of nature?" *AMBIO*, 36(8), 614–621.

Steffen, W., Grinevald, J., et al. (2011) "The Anthropocene: Conceptual and historical perspectives" *Philosophical Transactions*, 369(1938), 842–867.

Steffen, W., Persson, Å., et al. (2011) "The Anthropocene: From global change to planetary stewardship" *AMBIO*, 40(7), 739–761.

Suter, W.N. (2012) "Qualitative data, analysis, and design" in *Introduction to Educational Research: A Critical Thinking Approach* Sage Publications, Thousand Oaks, CA, 342–386.

Swift, P. and Cock, A. (2015) "Traditional khmer systems of forest management" *Journal of the Royal Asiatic Society*, 25(1), 153–173.

UNFCCC (2015) *Paris Agreement, 21st Conference of the Parties*, United Nations, Framework Convention on Climate Change, Bonn.

United Nations (2016) *From the MDGs to Sustainable Development for All* United Nations Development Programme, New York.

WCED (1987) *Our Common Future* World Commission On Environment and Development, New York.

13 The Anthropocene concept as a wake-up call for reforming democracy

Jörg Tremmel

Introduction

A vast majority of scientists at the 35th International Geological Congress in Cape Town (September 2016) spoke out in favour of changing the classification of geological epochs and of declaring a new world age – the Anthropocene. The first part of this chapter assesses the validity of the term 'Anthropocene' from an empirical point of view. The upshot is that there are sound reasons to proclaim a new phase of geostratigraphy. The human footprint is traceable by, among others, lithostratigraphic, biostratigraphic and chemostratigraphic means. The second part of this chapter delves into the question of what implications the proclamation of the Anthropocene has for the currently relevant concept of democracy. It is argued that responding to the Anthropocene necessitates (and justifies) a substantial reform of democracy. Specifically, the chapter suggests an extension of the centuries-old separation of powers between the legislative, executive and judicial branches. The classic *trias politica* should be supplemented by a new branch which ensures that the interests of future generations be taken into account within today's decision-making processes. The chapter concludes with a discussion about the legitimacy of offices for future generations (OFGs) as the embodiment of the proposed future branch.

Anthropocene and ethics

Classifying the history of Earth in geochronology

The need for designating geological eras first came up when the theological doctrine that the Earth had to be at most 6,000 years old according to biblical sources was refuted during the age of the Enlightenment.[1] This was a turning point in the human conception of self. The grasping of basic geological facts since the end of the 17th century, most notably the insight into the Earth's strikingly old age, rank among the most important achievements of human thought. The invention and refinement of a geological timescale to subdivide 4.6 billion years of Earth history has implications for the self-concept of humanity that can hardly be overstated. For only now do humans know where they stand. Against this background, the significance of the pending proclamation of the Anthropocene becomes clear:

It, too, may significantly alter the human conception of self. It is thus with good reason that the idea of labelling our current age the 'Anthropocene' has attracted wide interest as of late. A Google scholar-search in February 2018 with the term 'Anthropocene' coughs up around 51,500 results; dozens of eminent readings are listed on the 'Anthropocene' article at wikipedia.org, and first academic journals with 'Anthropocene' in the title have been founded.

Literally speaking, the term 'Anthropocene' can be translated as the 'Epoch of Men' or 'Age of Men', with 'anthropos' (Ancient Greek: 'human') connected to the suffix '-cene' used to designate new geological epochs. According to the geological timescale currently in place, we have been living in the Holocene for roughly the past 11,700 years.

The term 'Anthropocene' was coined most notably by Nobel laureate in Chemistry Paul J. Crutzen, the discoverer of the ozone hole.[2] In 2002, for instance, he published a brief article in *Nature* (Crutzen 2002, 23) entitled 'Geology of Mankind,' which inspired a great number of geologists. In the stratigraphic (the science of strata) community, a *Subcommission on Quaternary Stratigraphy* was instituted in 2008 in order to collect evidence in mainly three different areas: lithostratigraphic (novel sediments, minerals and mineral magnetism), biostratigraphic (macro- and micropaleontologic successions and anthropogenic traces of life), and chemostratigraphic (organic, inorganic and radiogenic). The task of the commission is to resolve, by scientific means, the question of whether humankind has become a factor which creates geological changes to an extent which in the past was deemed sufficient for declaring the end of an epoch and the beginning of a new one (Waters et al. 2016).

At the 35th International Geological Congress in Cape Town (September 2016), the members of the subcommission voted almost unanimously in favour of changing the classification of geological epochs and of declaring a new world age – the Anthropocene. This, however, does not mean that the official classification of geological epochs is a done deal or that schoolbook publishers should start rewriting their textbooks.[3] The reason for this is that, within geology, a number of subdisciplines are in charge of geological classification. Chronostratigraphy classifies strata according to their age of origin. Geochronology is more interpretative, and compiles the unfiltered facts into a geological timescale, that is, into a partitioning of Earth history into meaningful stages. Superior committees that are yet to be convinced include the International Commission on Stratigraphy (ICS) and, as a last step, the executive committee of the International Union of Geological Sciences (IUGS). A final vote has not yet been scheduled, but the odds are good that the Anthropocene will formally be proclaimed within the next few years.

Evidence for a shift in the geological epoch

With regard to the lithostratigraphic evidence, one marker is the urban structures that currently cover around 3 to 5 percent of the Earth's land surface. As a result of urbanisation, large areas are by now covered by a mixture of concrete, glass and metals. Even if humankind were to go extinct tomorrow, those structures would remain where they are for millennia to come. If in a few thousand years from now, if intelligent aliens were to visit the place where a large city is standing today, they would discover fragments of concrete, rusted iron, the bitumen of roads, glass from fibre optic cables, and an enormous of amount of aluminium which as such is not found in nature.

Another signature of humankind is visible in the non-decomposing layers of plastic garbage currently floating in the maelstrom of certain ocean drifts. There is evidence suggesting that they create sedimentary deposits after subsiding. In mid-2014, geologists discovered structures formed by plastics, volcanics, coral fragments and sand grains off the coast of Hawai'i which, in view of their solidness, they labelled as a stone of its own kind – as plastiglomerate (Chen 2014). However, humankind also creates new sedimentary structures by ablating mountains, filling up valleys, and impounding huge seas (Smil 2002). Three-quarters of the ice-free mainland are no longer in the state they used to be in when the human species emerged (Leinfelder 2017). The shifting from wilderness to grasslands in particular is an important marker of the enormous changes humanity has brought upon the Earth's surface. While the proportion of non-wilderness was minimal 12,000 years ago, more than a third of the Earth's surface is being used as grassland for livestock even today. If one were to place all mammals on a huge scale, one could figure out that humans and their livestock accounted for 0.1 percent of all biomass at the beginning of the Holocene, while today this share has grown to 90 percent of all biomass (Vince 2011).

Further examples of the unprecedented depth and long-term nature of human interventions include:

1   The harvesting of subterranean forests, that is, the extraction of coal, oil and gas from the lithosphere. If ever, it would take hundreds of millions of years for these resources to regenerate.
2   The anthropogenic contamination by radioactivity, the timescale of which is likewise only measurable in millions of years.
3   The worldwide flora and fauna species extinction caused by the human species. Nature is always in the process of creating new species, so it is indeed only a matter of time until the ramifications of the sixth mass extinction will have been 'processed' by nature. However, this too will run into the low millions of years time-wise.
4   Climate change, by comparison, is reversible within a much shorter time frame, but here too we are dealing with tens of thousands of years.
5   Space debris has been accumulating in the Earth's orbit since the beginning of space travel, and the forces of nature alone will be unable to dispose of it within the next few thousands of years.

When should the beginning of the Anthropocene be set? Points in time that are conceivable but have now been ruled out include the beginning of agriculture as well as the beginning of the industrial revolution. Many researchers argue in favour of the 1950s, since a large number of indicators have been skyrocketing ever since then. Be it urbanisation,[4] primary energy consumption, or international air travel – one can date the beginning of several processes of exponential growth to the time after the Second World War, which for that reason has also come to be known as the 'Great Acceleration' (Steffen et al. 2015). However, some indicators – such as the global population – have been on the rise for a somewhat longer period of time, while other indicators of the Earth system – such as the acidification of oceans – have begun their steep rise only more recently. A preliminary majority decision by the 37-member subcommission declared 16 July 1945 – the day of the first atomic bomb blast – to be the most plausible date for the beginning of the Anthropocene. The signature of long-lived plutonium from mid-20th century bomb blasts in the sediments will remain visible for thousands of years. This is an unambiguously scientific marker of human impact on the environment (see Themann and Brunnengräber, in this volume).

Are there counter-arguments against the proclamation of the Anthropocene? To be sure, the impact of humankind on the *length* of the Earth's history is miniscule. This can be illustrated by a thought experiment by which the history of the planet Earth is converted into one calendar year. The Earth is around 4.6 billion years old. Recalibrated to fit into one calendar year, one hour equals 525,114 years, one minute is 8,752 years and one second is 145 years. In this scale, no humans appeared on the surface of the Earth between 1 January and 30 December. On the first hours of 31 December, the first human-like apes (hominids) showed up. Bipedal walking was still hours (i.e., millions of years) away. Around 20:30 (8:30 pm), members of the species homo erectus managed to exit from Africa. At 48 minutes before midnight, they learnt to tame the fire; some minutes later they started cooking, and again some minutes later they started wearing clothes. Anatomically modern humans appeared around 23:36 and they developed a number of sophisticated languages in different places on the Earth. The first sculptures and paintings were created around 23:54. The Neolithic Revolution (the start of agriculture) took place around 81 seconds before midnight. At 23:59:24 the first big cities in Egypt and the Indus Valley were built; nevertheless, the alphabet and the wheel had still not yet been invented. By 18 seconds before midnight on 31 December, the first states and empires had been established (Classical Greece, Roman Republic, Qin Dynasty, Ashoka Empire), and humankind started to record history. The takeaway of this story: the 'Great Acceleration' in the 1950s happened less than one second before midnight on this timescale!

As the history of the Earth until now is subdivided more or less equally in ages, as indicated by Table 13.1, each of them usually designates a period of several million years. The Pliocene encompasses 2.745 million years, the Pleistocene 2.5763 million years, the Holocene just 0.0117 million years so far. A counterargument to the proclamation of a new age might be that, until much more time has passed, there is simply no vacancy for a new age according to the established nomenclature. But this seems to be an artificial argument. Apart from tradition, there is no problem with 'smaller-amount-of-time' ages. If the real-world phenomena change at a quicker pace than before, the nomenclature employed by geologists can legitimately be adjusted to keep pace with this.

Table 13.1 Excerpt of the currently valid geological timescale

System	Series/Epoch	Stage/Age	Age (million years)
Quaternary	Holocene		0.0117 (– ?)
	Pleistocene	Late Pleistocene (Tarantian)	0.126–0.0117
		Middle Pleistocene (Ionian)	0.781–0.126
		Calabrian	1.806–0.781
		Gelasian	2.588–1.806
Neogene (the newer part of tertiary)	Pliocene	Piacenzian	3.6–2.588
		Zanclean	5.333–3.6
	Miocene	Messinian	7.246–5.333
		Tortonian	11.62–7.246
		Serravallian	13.82–11.62
		Langhian	15.97–13.82
		Burdigalian	20.44–15.97
		Aquitanian	23.03–20.44

Note: For the full picture, including the major events of each epoch, see https://en.wikipedia.org/wiki/Geologic_time_scale. The 'correct' subdivision of Earth history into systems, series and stages in chronostratigraphy or into periods, epochs and ages in geochronology has always been a matter of serious dispute within geology. It took centuries to compare rock formations across the globe and to integrate them into the current framework.

In the debate about the Anthropocene, it is important to separate empirical from evaluative questions. The questions discussed above (If we humans were to perish, would the impact of our existence continue to remain for a long time? Or would everything return immediately to the way it was before our formation?) are, first of all, empirical questions. But these questions also have an evaluative dimension. The notion of the Anthropocene forces us to redefine our place in the world, since it addresses humankind in an entirely new way.

Holocene ethics and Anthropocene ethics

The thoughts of the *Ancients*, particularly in matters of ethics, were considered to be timeless and ever-new for more than two thousand years. That this holds true even today, at least in parts, is expressed by the witticism that "where questions of the right life are concerned, only that which is false can be truly new" (Spaemann 1989, 9). This notion, however, is currently brought into question by the concept of the Anthropocene. The ethics developed in Ancient Greece was concerned with the vicinity, with dealing with neighbours, other estates, the other sex. One might call it an 'ethics of neighbourhood' (Tremmel 2009, 3). In this ethical realm, humans living on the other side of the world were as little an object of ethical considerations as humans living 500 years in the future. To put it pointedly: Plato did not know of plutonium. In his epoch-making book *The Imperative of Responsibility: In Search of Ethics for the Technological*

Age, the philosopher Hans Jonas carved out what was once true, or, as one might say, what used to be true during the Holocene:

> that, for all his boundless resourcefulness, man is still small by the measure of the elements: precisely this makes his sallies into them so daring and allows those elements to tolerate his forwardness. Making free with the denizens of land and sea and air, he yet leaves the encompassing nature of those elements unchanged, and their generative powers undiminished. ... Much as he harries Earth, the greatest of gods, year after year with his plough – she is ageless and unwearied; her enduring patience he must and can trust, and to her cycle he must conform.
>
> (Jonas 1984, 3)

In view of the fact that things changed in the second half of the 20th century, Jonas urged a new ethics which would transcend the spatial and temporal vicinity. The fields of 'global ethics' and 'future ethics' that since have been more and more established as ethical sub-disciplines of their own are therefore distinctly new phenomena.[5] Ethical theories developed *before* the Anthropocene might increasingly become outdated. At any rate, it should be undisputed that the house of ethics stands in need of at least some new rooms.

Hercules in Olympus or Gulliver in Lilliput?

One implication of the proclamation of the Anthropocene evolves around the human conception of self. The narcissism of mediaeval man has suffered two great wounds from scientific progress, as Sigmund Freud famously put it in his *General Introduction to Psychoanalysis* (Freud 1920, 246) The first wound, known as the 'cosmological blow', was the discovery that the Earth is not, in fact, at the centre of the universe (Copernican heliocentrism, since 1543). Humankind thereby lost its central position within the cosmos. Roughly three hundred years later, the so-called 'biological blow' occurred when it was discovered that humankind is embedded in the developmental system of the organisms (evolution by natural selection, since 1859). The species *Homo sapiens* is a product of evolution just as millions of other species are. In both cases, humankind's belief in its central position within the cosmos or within animated nature was deeply shaken by the findings of modern natural science.

The Anthropocene discourse does not add a further blow. On the contrary, the notion of an 'age of men' has the connotation that humankind, as a collective, is much more powerful than previously thought. Human leverage is much bigger than one used to think in the early days of the environmental movement. However, one must be beware of the naturalistic fallacy. The fact that the human species has become a quasi-geological force at its current point of existence surely does not mean that this state of affairs is imperative. This would be the same naturalistic fallacy as if a political philosopher were to infer from the mere existence of a certain form of rule that this particular form of rule *ought* to exist.

What is new about the Anthropocene is not the insight that humankind changes nature in various ways – this much was known in the 20th century. Rather, the concept of an Anthropocene implies that the human species affects its environment in a deeply profound and long-term way through unconscious, almost incidental actions. Consider, by way of example, the ozone hole. As is well known, chlorofluorocarbons (CFCs) used to occur mainly in deodorants, air conditioners and fridges. It is unsettling that a few inventions designed to raise human comfort just by a little should have such grave effects on the stratospheric ozone layer.

Humankind was equally surprised at its degree of impact with regard to the problem of plastic garbage in the oceanic currents. In the 1980s, scientists were still used to assuming that the plastic particles were environmentally irrelevant, since the oceans were thought of as huge and resilient. It was a surprise to our species to find an enormous layer of plastic (some have called it a plastic continent) in the vastness of the Pacific Ocean, and yet more garbage patches in similar out-of-the-way places that are of little interest to humankind and that have hardly ever been visited.

For the self-image of humankind and its view of the environment, there are two possible interpretations of the geological facts. The first is that humankind has become a new Hercules. The other – and, in my view, better – interpretation compares him to the role of Gulliver. Hercules is the great, invincible hero, assertive and often ruthless, someone who is able to perform the most difficult labours with ease. Gulliver, however, has to come to grips with a new environment that only at first sight resembles his familiar environment. In the socio-critical novel by Jonathan Swift published in 1726, the Lilliputians referred to Gulliver as the Man-Mountain. Gulliver himself must quickly learn to move slowly in what is to him the unknown Land of Lilliput. Gulliver knows that there is much he does not know; and he is also aware that, due to his height, every misstep (literally speaking) can have disastrous consequences for his environment. He soon realises that, despite of his size, he himself is in danger, too, precisely because he has troubles adapting to his environment. The story of Gulliver seems perfectly suited to serve as the core narrative of the Anthropocene. This story could represent the idea that the human species increasingly changes its surrounding nature without (yet) being capable of controlling the negative consequences of these changes.

In view of growing insights on the unintended consequences of human actions, fantasies of power and doability – think of climate engineering – should be met with scepticism. Rather than acting as a new Hercules, who masterfully triumphs in one quest after another, humankind should behave and act as a Gulliver.

Reforming democracy

A wake-up call that is overdue

The ecological crisis brings the failure of our current way of living to the fore. All political efforts since the beginning of explicit environmental and sustainability policies in the 1970s have fallen short of what is necessary.

The measures taken, important though they might have been for particular regions and sectors, were unable to impede the great acceleration from a global perspective, and have mostly just led to spatial or temporal relocations. A sustainability science which takes the provocation posed by the Anthropocene seriously ought to be dealing with this skandalon.

(Görg 2016, 10, own translation)

Almost all key indicators for ecological performance are turning bad. Take, for instance, human-made climate change: The curve of global greenhouse gas emissions continues to point steeply upwards, despite enormous efforts to reduce anthropogenic emissions. The only traceable drops occur during wars and economic crises. In 2009, the global financial and economic crisis led to a decrease in global greenhouse gas emissions of 1.3 percent. Already in the following year, however, emissions went back to a growth of 5.9 percent.

One should draw a distinction between indicators which could be seen as more of a direct consequence of government policy and ones whose causes are less directly attributable to government policy, or are more closely related to the power of economics and individual choices. Put differently, there is an important distinction in measuring how certain countries are *governed*, on the one hand, and how certain societies *behave*. While it is true that not all indicators are amenable to the levers of government policy, the rest of this chapter argues the case for improving our political institutions. The fact that far too few people maintain an environmentally sustainable lifestyle can (and should) be influenced by policies.

It is not very controversial any more in philosophy that the 'neighbour ethics' that was very useful in the Holocene is of limited use for the future in this new era. But it is less understood that the ecological crisis is also a crisis of democracy as a form of government. Our political institutions, as we know them, were designed in and for the Holocene. The transition into a new phase of geology necessitates a reform of these institutions, namely parliamentarianism. One should not think of 'the Anthropocene concept' as just another frame, but rather understand it as *the* wake-up call to reform democracy. Before outlining what such a reform might look like, two caveats seem to be necessary: one with regard to the superiority of democracy to all other forms of political rule; the second with regard to the limited use of posterity protection clauses in constitutions.

Democracy as a valuable inheritance for future generations

Reforming democracy, to be sure, does not mean calling its essential value into question. Since the 1970s (e.g., Ophuls 1977), some unnecessary ink has been spilt pleading for an eco-authoritarian 'solution' (for a summary, see Hammond and Smith 2017). Especially after a series of failed international climate conferences between 2009 and 2014 before the success in Paris 2015 (and then again when US president Donald Trump opted out of this accord in 2017), several contributions to the debate asked whether democracy is the best form of government to cope with ecological challenges (Shearman and Smith 2007; Randers 2012).

This provocative question is misleading, whether it is answered in the affirmative or not. It is true that the international community has not yet set up a climate regime that will stabilise the concentration of greenhouse gases in the atmosphere at a level that will keep temperature increase in a safe corridor. But the international climate conferences are a bad case in point, given that not only democratic but also non-democratic nation-states contributed to the failure of the negotiations. Comparative studies have shown that the environmental performance of authoritative regimes is worse than that of democracies (Jänicke 1996). On average, authoritarian regimes display less concern for the future interests of their citizens, and they typically engender patronage and corruption (Boston 2017). So-called epistocrats (proposing rule by those who have knowledge) could reply in return that they do not advocate authoritarianism per se, but an enlightened non-democratic rule. One lesson from history is that there is no way to ensure that an enlightened dictator does not abandon his benevolence eventually. Some 150 years ago, at a time when intellectuals open-mindedly discussed whether or not democracy is better than monarchy or aristocracy, Mill wrote sensible words that are still (or again) worth reading today:

> In no government will the interests of the people be the object, except where the people are able to dismiss their rulers as soon as the devotion of those rulers to the interests of the people becomes questionable.
>
> (Mill 1977, 73)

In the long run, no other form of government but democracy is better suited to solving global environmental problems.

Posterity protection provisions in constitutions do not suffice

The growing acceptance of responsibility for future generations has led to the trend of including posterity protection clauses in constitutions. Insofar as constitutions have been newly adopted – for example, in Eastern Europe and Central Asia after 1989, or in South Africa after the end of apartheid – a regard for generations was inscribed in almost all of these cases. Even well-established constitutions were changed in order to reflect the increasing future-mindedness of citizenries around the world. Five constitutions speak explicitly of 'rights of future generations': Norway (art. 110b), Japan (art. 11), Iran (art. 50), Bolivia (art. 7), and Malawi (art. 13, art. 11). In other constitutional texts, for instance in art. 37 (4) of the Georgian constitution, the 'interests' of future generations are addressed; alternatively their 'needs', e.g., in the constitution of Uganda (Art. XXVII ii).

The number of constitutions with posterity protection clauses is already considerable, and it continues to grow. But does this make any difference? A sobering conclusion seems in order. The establishment of such clauses has resulted neither in the phasing out of nuclear power nor in serious climate action in the respective countries. Constitutional courts are obviously not optimal to serve as the guardians of future generations' interests: they cannot represent such interests with full commitment for the simple reason that they have no mandate to do so.

Paradigm shift from a three-to a four-power-model

What is required in the Anthropocene is nothing less than a paradigm shift. The new paradigm would entail a 'future branch', and regard it as a legitimate and necessary part of a democratically constituted community. The linchpin of this paradigm would be that the age-old separation of powers into legislative, executive and judicial branches is no longer sufficient in the Anthropocene. The present-day demos of the 21st century can affect the living conditions of a future demos far more than in former times. Just as in the 18th century, when in the course of first establishing a democracy in a large territorial state, the *Federalist Papers* considered a system of checks and balances to protect minorities against the 'tyranny of majority' (Tocqueville 1835/1840), so today we are in need of checks and balances against the tyranny of the present over the future.

It seems appropriate to draw on the history of ideas to conceptualise the new 'future branch'. The historical roots of the separation of powers are usually associated with the political theorists John Locke and Charles de Montesquieu. However, even a thinker as early as Aristotle already recommended a mixed constitution or, more specifically, a mixture of democracy and oligarchy, which he called 'politie', designed to prevent an excessive concentration of power. In his *Two Treatises of Government*, published in 1690, John Locke distinguishes between legislative and executive, but leaves no room for an independent third judicial power. Locke introduces a clear hierarchy of powers when he writes that "this *legislative* is not only the *supreme power* of the common-wealth, but sacred and unalterable in the hands where the community has once placed it" (Locke 1823, Chapter XI, § 134).

Montesquieu, the actual father of the tripartite separation of powers doctrine, applies the classical division of legislative, executive and judiciary power in his *De l'esprit des lois* of 1748. In the sixth chapter of the 11th book (Montesquieu 2001), which mainly deals with the English constitution, he is concerned with the sharing and balancing of powers. Montesquieu (2001, 173) writes: "In every government there are three sorts of power: *the legislative; the executive, in respect to things dependent on the law of nations; and the executive, in regard to things that depend on the civil law*". Following this statement, Montesquieu explains that this latter power is to be referred to as the judiciary power of the state. This brings us to the classic tripartite division of legislative, executive and judicial power.

The *trias politica* was conceived by thinkers in the 17th and 18th centuries and is now universally established in Western democracies. The view of our present three-power-model changes when we learn about the evolution from a two-to a three-power-model in the approaches of Locke and Montesquieu. The most important lesson from the history of ideas seems to be that even the supposedly definitive present is only a stage between the past and the future. The tripartite division was sufficient for the past; but at the brink of the 21st century it does not suffice any more.

A few remarks with regard to the 'vertically' directed separation of powers seem appropriate. In federal states like Germany, for example, the federalisation of political systems means the division of labour between a local level, a *Länder* level and a national level, complemented by the European Union (EU). The *Länder* have governments, parliaments and constitutional courts. The European level also has a parliament (the EU parliament), a court (European Court of Justice) and a sort of government (the European Commission). In a four-power system, all such levels should get 'future branches' as well to complement their 'horizontal' separation of powers.

Apart from the horizontal and vertical 'separation of powers', further overloading the term is of little use. The media is also often referred to colloquially as 'the fourth power'. The same applies for interest groups such as trade unions or employers' associations. It is true that the power of the political system does not fully penetrate other autonomous areas such as business, science, media, religion, or private relationships; however, to prevent confusion, the term 'separation of powers' should continue to refer to the organisation of state power. The terminology used here counts only the 'branches of government' (not society) and adds a fourth such branch to the existing three.

The legislative branch passes the laws, the executive branch implements them, and the judiciary controls their abidance. Constitutional courts also check the *constitutionality* of laws after the legislative branch has passed them. Where does the 'future branch' fit in here? This branch *could* be designed as a body which checks the *sustainability* of laws, and quashes them if they harm future citizens. Alternatively, it is quite possible to see the 'future branch' somewhat closer to the legislative than to the judiciary branch, namely as a body with the right to initiate legislation instead of preventing it.

It should not be forgotten that the idea of the *trias politica* currently varies from country to country as a result of different traditions of political thought. With regard to institutions for future generations, there cannot be a *one-size-fits-all* solution; rather, it seems apt to conceive of such a representative body differently for each country. 'Future branch' is thus an umbrella term that does not designate a particular model. Instead, it refers to all institutions for future generations that are powerful enough to credibly represent the needs and interests of future citizens. Throughout the globe, there are now a considerable number of organisations with a mandate for sustainability and intergenerational justice. However, most of these enjoy merely consultative status. They exercise little actual power in a Weberian sense: "Power means every chance in a social relation to realize one's own will even against the resistance of others" (Weber 1922, § 16, own translation).

The legitimacy of a future branch

Repudiating the charge of 'dictatorship'

The idea of a fourth branch is new and has not been aired in political science, philosophy or law so far. As a reaction to the ecological crisis, a number of scholars and institutions (e.g., WBGU 2011) have called for a transformation of our society that goes beyond marginalia, but they have not called for a Four-Power-Model. Nevertheless, the discussion about institutions for the representation of future generations is well underway (Stein 1998; Barry 1999; Eckersley 2004; Thompson 2010; González-Ricoy and Gosseries 2016; Boston 2017; Tremmel 2006; 2015; 2018). These institutions have been given various names. I will call them offices for future generations (OFGs); and I take them as embodiments for the future branch if they are powerful enough – that is, if OFGs are given real power by their statutes and in practice. In this last part of this chapter I will discuss the legitimacy of OFGs in the context of the four-power-model.

OFGs should be unelected bodies. While popular elections would maximise the formal independence of the organisation's members – vis-à-vis the legislative, executive and judicial branches – they would inescapably subject the election candidates to the short-termist pressures of parliamentary elections, thereby defeating the purpose for which the office was created. Given that electorates tend to be biased in favour of the present, those candidates for OFGs who promise to cater for the short-term wishes of their constituencies would be at an advantage. If the candidates for the OFG had to run campaigns and court votes, they would *de facto* turn into politicians. No longer would knowledge and expertise be the decisive qualities, but eloquence and smoothness.

Lacking a popular mandate, OFGs could be criticised as unaccountable, or, more drastically, as a form of 'expertocracy' (which is the same as 'epistocracy', just more negatively connoted). Expertocracy, literally meaning the rule of experts, has been discussed in political theory for a long time, arguably since Plato promoted it for Kallipolis, the utopian city in his dialogue *Politeia*. Here again, terminology is crucial for concept formation. Fischer (1990) highlights the dangers of 'technocracy' but, to be sure, 'technocracy' and 'expertocracy' should not be conflated. It is possible that experts in an OFG might be rather opposed to a technocratic stance. Terminologically, the model proposed here could be criticised as paving the way to a 'future-dictatorship', not a 'technocratic dictatorship', if anything at all.

But such a criticism would be unfounded. To put it into perspective, let us recall the rights of the third branch in the existing Three-Branches-Model. In many countries, constitutional courts exercise enormous power in interpreting if a specific law is compatible with the constitution. The doctrine of a living constitution allows courts to overrule parliament if the court's present interpretation of a constitution's semantics is in contradiction to passed legislation. This is of course country-specific. To this day, popular sovereignty is equated much more closely with parliamentary sovereignty in some countries than in others. But on a global level, the readiness of constitutional courts to challenge legislatures is generally increasing rather than decreasing (Rosanvallon 2011).

The debate between proponents of popular sovereignty and its most important institution, namely parliaments, on the one hand, and proponents of constitutionalism and the power of courts on the other hand, can serve as a blueprint for a debate about the democratic legitimacy of OFGs. To cut a long story short, most scholars agree that courts might be unelected bodies, but they serve democracy quite well. If this is agreed, then the charge of 'dictatorship' cannot reasonably directed against OFGs, as their competencies (if they are well designed) come not even close to those of courts. 'Expertocracy', if this term is intended to be meaningful, always designates an *authoritarian* solution to the environmental crises. As a one-power-model in a Hobbesian sense,[6] such an authoritarian construct is per se incompatible with the Four-Power-Model defended here. After all, all models of power-sharing are aimed at diffusing state power, not concentrating it. This has been formulated in the following terms: "Because man, who has power, has a propensity to misuse power when he is not prevented from doing so by boundaries, it is necessary that power is divided between many authorities, which mutually prevent each other's misuse" (Riklin 2006, 290). *Que le pouvoir arrête le pouvoir!*

OFGs should be proposers, not preventers

I have argued elsewhere (Tremmel 2018) the case for a German Future Council, endowed with a right of initiative, allowing it to introduce proposals for new legislation into the parliament. OFGs, composed of independent appointees, are not at odds with the principle of democratic legitimacy if (and only if) they do not have the power to stop the law-making process of the legislative branch. The key criterion suggested here for the design of OFGs is 'proactiveness', in the sense of a right to *initiate* legislation. Such OFGs would use their power differently than courts, as they would not have the right to suspend laws temporarily or permanently, but only to propose them. We should think of OFGs as proposers, not preventers.

OFGs might be less able to assert themselves, compared to courts, but the power to partake in the agenda-setting of the law-making process should not be underestimated. In order to allow an OFG to place bills on the formal voting agenda, most parliaments would just have to change their rules of procedure. Bills usually have to be signed either by a party fraction or, inter-fractionally, by a certain percentage of all members of the parliament. If an OFG, in its capacity as representative for future citizens, did also get the right to initiate laws, its motions would be treated like inter-fractional motions – the proceedings of which are often shining examples of parliamentarianism.

The strengthening of the scientific and academic elements of parliamentarian debates, as suggested in my proposal, does not imply that the legislators *must* necessarily follow the scholarly advice of an OFG. Indeed, it would be naïve to believe that the legislature would take up and implement each and every proposal made by the Future Council.[7] Rather, past experience with inter-fractional motions would suggest that parliament would pass on most of the Future Council's legislative initiatives to committees, where they would face a silent death by non-treatment.[8] However, there is reasonable hope that at least in some cases the legislative initiatives brought forward by the Future Council might be able to garner the support of future-oriented lawmakers, as well as that of the press and public opinion.

A fourth branch of government, embodied in a Future Council, is not at odds with the principle of democratic legitimacy as long as such a new body does not have the power to stop the law-making process of the legislative branch. By limiting itself to a purely constructive role, the legitimacy of such a Future Council is ensured.

To be sure, the model of a Future Council as presented here transcends the dualist interpretation of science and politics spelled out in their respective binary codes of 'knowledge' and 'power' (see Lundershausen, in this volume). Unlike political advisors, the independent members of a Future Council would not approach politicians as mere supplicants, hoping for a willing ear that may be lent but does not have to be. While on the one hand the power of decision-making fully remains with the politicians, on the other the element of long-term rationality is strengthened by parliament's obligation to at least consider the Future Council's proposals. The endemic problem of politics' resistance to advice is not entirely solved, but mitigated. In times like these, with politicians like US president Trump presenting their own 'alternative facts' by consciously disregarding – or even showing contempt for – scientific insights, there is need for a stronger coupling of politics and science. Knowledge *ought* to play a role in political decision-making.

The prevention of an additional veto player

The logic of proactiveness not only renders the charge of a 'future-dictatorship' (or 'eco-dictatorship') invalid; it also prevents another 'veto player'. Traditionally, institutionalists have examined dichotomous classifications (unitary vs. federalist, parliamentarian vs. presidential etc.). By contrast, Tsebelis's theory of veto players (Tsebelis 2002) asks how many actors must consent to a decision or are able to veto it. Multi-level parliamentarianism already features a high number of veto players, such as the second legislative chamber, the constitutional court, the president (if he or she has to formally sign laws in parliamentary systems), and the people itself, insofar as it makes itself heard through referenda.

There is a risk that creating a fully operational OFG will result in the addition of a new veto player, thereby increasing the chances of gridlock in the political system. In contrast to some theories that advocate slowing democracy down (Clark and Teachout 2012; Ekeli 2009), Political gridlock should be regarded as a drawback in times when problems such as climate change demand urgent action. *Not* slowing down the political system is a strong additional argument for giving OFGs the right to initiate legislation, but not the right to prevent it.

The right to *delay* law-making (for a limited period of time, not indefinitely) seems to lie somewhat in between the input and the output side of the political process. But in fact, postponement rights are not initial or constructive actions; they are part of a reactive capacity. They can be a sharp sword too, as Shlomo Shoham, the one and only Knesset Commissioner for Future Generations in Israel, explains:

> The right to be given enough time to prepare an opinion is an implied author-ity to create a delay in the legislative process. Such a delay may be crucial for the parliamentary work when it comes to bills discussed in the framework of the state's budget. In that case, the time factor is vital since the implication of not voting on the state's budget for the next year ... is that parliament must dissolve itself and go to elections.
>
> (Shoham and Lamay 2006, 248)

While this might be a peculiarity of the political system in Israel, the US-American experience with filibustering highlights that delaying resistance is often difficult to overcome at all.

Independent bodies have been a fundamental part of democratic architecture since classical Athens – just think of scrutineers, auditors, supervisors and later constitutional courts and public ombudsman. The role of such bodies is suppor-tive for democracy as they equip it against the anxieties of the majoritarian prin-ciple. OFGs are democratically legitimised as long as they are granted their status by law – and as long as this status can be revoked by law as well (Rosanvallon 2011). Unelected representatives of future citizens, appointed by elected politi-cians but not for their pleasure (Pettit 2012, 306), are a necessary and legitimate instrument against political presentism.

Conclusion

OFGs are more than just a vision or illusion. The future-orientated *part* of the political class takes a genuine interest in amending the rules of the game so as to engage the self-commitment of the *entire* political class. This nourishes the hope that a special version of OFGs, a Future Council characterised by the right to initiate legislation, will eventually come into existence. An increasing number of experiments with OFGs, and the lessons learnt, alter the political landscapes in more and more countries in a both spirited and innovative way. The problem of political presentism cannot be solved, only alleviated. But limiting the size of this problem would be no small achievement. In fact, it is of paramount impor-tance for the future of humankind.

Notes

1 The 'Six Ages of the World' (Latin: *sex aetates mundi*) doctrine was a Christian period-isation put forward by Church Father *Augustine of Hippo* (354–430), which endured

well into the Middle Ages. It was repudiated during the Enlightenment. The pioneer geological works by Georges-Louis Leclerc, Comte de Buffon (1707–1788) and Charles Lyell (1797–1875) paved the way towards the modern worldview which rests upon scientific insights rather than on assertions from Holy Scriptures.

2 Others have suggested similar terms earlier, such as 'anthropolithic era' (Haeckel 1870), 'anthropozoic era' (Stoppani 1873), and 'Noosphere' (Teilhard de Chardin 1925). But in an overview article, Hamilton and Grinevald (2015) argue that there were no precursors to the conception of the Anthropocene because earlier scientists who commented on 'the age of man' did so in terms of human impact on 'the face of the Earth', not the Earth system. According to Hamilton and Grinevald, the understanding of the changes of the Earth system were not possible until the recent interdisciplinary understanding of the Earth as an evolving planet inaugurated in the 1980s by the International Geosphere-Biosphere Programme and Earth system science.

3 The potential of the following new mission statement would be particularly relevant for school curricula (Crutzen and Schwägerl 2011). The term 'Anthropocene' might help pupils to grasp the idea of the enormous impact of humankind on nature. The pupil who carelessly used to dispose of his candy wrapper in nature, thinking that it would decompose quickly there, might be inspired to change his behaviour by the concept of an Anthropocene.

4 Haber (2016, 29, own translation) describes urbanisation as the constitutive feature of the Anthropocene: "It is due to this development that from an ecological point of view, one can base the Anthropocene on one criterion alone – to wit, on the greatest possible centralisation of the a central system 'nature' – with its transformation into culture – towards its human user who is centred around the city".

5 Here, it must be added that the future is not a moral object (moral patient) in itself, and rather what is of concern here are human beings living in the future – hence for a diachronic, temporal ethics, the notion of 'generational ethics' is more appropriate than the term 'future ethics'.

6 For Hobbes, men only overcome the state of nature when they agree upon a social contract amongst themselves, which subordinates them to the rule and authority of an abstract body. In the *Leviathan* (1651), Hobbes writes: "The only way to erect such a common power, as may be able to defend them from the invasion of foreigners, and the injuries of one another, and thereby to secure them in such sort as that by their own industry and by the fruits of the Earth they may nourish themselves and live contentedly, is to confer all their power and strength upon one man, or upon one assembly of men, that may reduce all their wills, by plurality of voices, unto one will: which is as much as to say, to appoint one man, or assembly of men, to bear their person; and every one to own and acknowledge himself to be author of whatsoever he that so beareth their person shall act, or cause to be acted, in those things which concern the common peace and safety; and therein to submit their wills, every one to his will, and their judgements to his judgement" (2000, 105–106).

7 When I write Future Council, I am referring to the here described specific OFG (with the right to initiate laws but without the right to stop or delay them), using capital letters to distinguish it from the more generic usage of the term *future council*.

8 For a more comprehensive account, including some figures, of the treatment of inter-fractional motions in the German Parliament, see Tremmel (2018).

References

Barry, J. (1999) *Greening Political Theory* Sage Publications, London.

Boston, J. (2017) *Governing for the Future: Designing Democratic Institutions for a Better Tomorrow* Emerald, Bingley.

Chen, A. (2014) "Rocks made of plastic found on hawaiian beach" *Science* 4 June (www.sciencemag.org/news/2014/06/rocks-made-plastic-found-hawaiian-beach) Accessed 16 April 2018.

Clarke, S. and Teachout, W. (2012) *Slow Democracy: Rediscovering Community, Bringing Decision Making Back Home* Chelsea Green Publishing, White River Junction.

Crutzen, P. (2002) "Geology of mankind" *Nature*, 415, 23.

Crutzen, P. and Schwägerl, C. (2011) *Living in the Anthropocene: Toward a New Global Ethos* (http://e360.yale.edu/feature/living_in_the_anthropocene_toward_a_new_global_ethos/2363/) Accessed 16 April 2018.

Eckersley, R. (2004) *The Green State: Rethinking Democracy and Sovereignty* MIT Press, Cambridge, MA, London.

Ekeli, K. (2009) "Constitutional experiments: Representing future generations through submajority rules" *Journal for Political Philosophy*, 17(4), 440–461.

Fischer, F. (1990) *Technocracy and the Politics of Expertise* Sage Publications, London.

Freud, S. (1920) *A General Introduction to Psychoanalysis* Horace Liveright, New York.

González-Ricoy, I. and Gosseries, A. (2016) *Institutions for Future Generations* Oxford University Press, Oxford.

Görg, C. (2016) "Zwischen Tagesgeschäft und Erdgeschichte. Die unterschiedlichen Zeitskalen in der Debatte um das Anthropozän" *GAIA*, 25(1), 9–13.

Haber, W. (2016) "Anthropozän – Folgen für das Verhältnis von Humanität und Ökologie" in Haber, W., Held, M. and Vogt, M. eds., *Die Welt im Anthropozän. Erkundungen im Spannungsfeld zwischen Ökologie und Humanität* Oekom, München, 19–37.

Hamilton, C. and Grinevald, J. (2015) "Was the Anthropocene anticipated?" *The Anthropocene Review*, 2(1), 59–72.

Hammond, M. and Smith, G. (2017) "Sustainable Prosperity and Democracy: A Research Agenda" CUSP Working Paper no. 8. University of Surrey, Guildford.

Hobbes, T. (2000) *Leviathan* (http://socserv.mcmaster.ca/econ/ugcm/3ll3/hobbes/Leviathan.pdf) Accessed 16 April 2018.

Jänicke, M. (1996) "Democracy as a condition for environmental policy success" in Lafferty, W.M. and Meadowcroft, J. eds., *Democracy and the Environment* Edward Elgar, Cheltenham, 71–85.

Jonas, H. (1984) *The Imperative of Responsibility: In Search of Ethics for the Technological Age* University of Chicago Press, Chicago.

Leinfelder, R. (2017) "Die Erde wie eine Stiftung behandeln" *Stuttgarter Zeitung*, (37), 14 February, 16.

Locke, J. (1823) *Two Treatises of Government* (http://socserv.mcmaster.ca/econ/ugcm/3ll3/locke/government.pdf) Accessed 16 April 2018.

Mill, J.S. (1977) *The Collected Works of John Stuart Mill* (Vol. 18) Essays on Politics and Society (edited by Robson, J.) University of Toronto Press, Toronto.

Montesquieu, C. (2001) *The Spirit of Laws* Batoche Books, Kitchener.

Ophuls, W. (1977) *Ecology and the Politics of Scarcity* W.H. Freeman, San Francisco.

Pettit, P. (2012) *On the People's Terms: A Republican Theory and Model of Democracy* Cambridge University Press, Cambridge.

Randers, J. (2012) *2052: A Global Forecast for the Next Forty Years* Chelsea Green Publishing, White River Junction.

Riklin, A. (2006) *Machtteilung: Geschichte der Mischverfassung* Wiss. Buchgesellschaft, Darmstadt.

Rosanvallon, P. (2011) *Democratic Legitimacy: Impartiality, Reflexivity, Proximity* Princeton University Press, Princeton, NJ.

Shearman, D. and Smith, J.W. (2007) *The Climate Change Challenge and the Failure of Democracy* Praeger Publishers, Westport.

Shoham, S. and Lamay, N. (2006) "Commission for future generations in the Knesset: Lessons learnt" in Tremmel, J. ed., *Handbook of Intergenerational Justice* Edward Elgar Publishing, Cheltenham, 244–262.

Smil, V. (2002) *The Earth's Biosphere: Evolution, Dynamics, and Change* MIT Press, Cambridge, MA.

Spaemann, R. (1989) *Glück und Wohlwollen* Klett-Cotta, Stuttgart.

Steffen, W., et al. (2015) "The trajectory of the Anthropocene: The Great Acceleration" *The Anthropocene Review*, (2/1), 81–98 (http://anr.sagepub.com/content/2/1/81) Accessed 16 April 2018.

Stein, T. (1998) "Does the constitutional and democratic system work? The ecological crisis as a challenge to the political order of constitutional democracy" *Constellations*, 4(3), 420–449.

Thompson, D.F. (2010) "Representing future generations: Political 'presentism' and democratic trusteeship" *Critical Review of International Social and Political Philosophy*, 13 (1), 17–37.

Tocqueville, A. (1835/1840) *Democracy in America* (www.gutenberg.org/files/815/815-h/815-h.htm) Accessed 16 April 2018.

Tremmel, J. (2006) "Establishment of intergenerational justice in national constitutions" in Tremmel, J. ed., *Handbook of Intergenerational Justice* Edward Elgar Publishing, Cheltenham, 187–214.

Tremmel, J. (2009) *A Theory of Intergenerational Justice* Earthscan, London.

Tremmel, J. (2015) "Parliaments and future generations: The four-powers-model" in Birnbacher, D. and Thorseth, M. eds., *The Politics of Sustainability: Philosophical Perspectives* Routledge, London, 212–233.

Tremmel, J. (2018) "Zukunftsräte zur Vertretung der Interessen kommender Generationen. Ein praxisorientierter Vorschlag für Deutschland" in Mannewitz, T. ed., *Die Demokratie und ihre Defekte* Springer VS, Heidelberg, 107–142.

Tsebelis, G. (2002) *Veto Players: How Political Institutions Work* Princeton University Press, Princeton.

Vince, G. (2011) "An epoch debate" *Science* 7 October, 32–37.

Waters, C.N., Zalasiewicz, J., Williams, M., Ellis, M.A. and Snelling, A.M. eds. (2016) *A Stratigraphical Basis for the Anthropocene* Geological Society, Special Publication 395 (www.geolsoc.org.uk/sp395) Accessed 16 April 2018.

WBGU (Wissenschaftlicher Beirat der Bundesregierung Globale Umweltveränderungen) (2011) *World in Transition: A Social Contract for Sustainability* (www.wbgu.de/en/flagship-reports/) Accessed 16 April 2018.

Weber, M. (1972) *Wirtschaft und Gesellschaft: Grundriss der verstehenden Soziologie* Mohr-Verlag, Tübingen (first published in 1921/1922).

14 Conclusion

Towards a 'deep debate' on the Anthropocene

Thomas Hickmann, Lena Partzsch,
Philipp Pattberg and Sabine Weiland

Summary

In this edited volume, we explored the contributions that political science as a discipline can offer to the evolving Anthropocene debate. The term *Anthropocene* denotes a new geological epoch in the Earth's history in which humans have become the main drivers of planetary-wide changes (Crutzen 2002). Some authors interpret this as good news, pointing to progress as a result of human ingenuity and the endless possibilities of managing the Earth system for the sake of human benefits (e.g., Ellis 2011; DeFries et al. 2012). Others have argued that the notion of the Anthropocene constitutes a wake-up call for humanity to act in the light of scientific evidence which is indicating fundamental and irreversible state shifts in the various interrelated ecosystems of our planet (e.g., Rockström et al. 2009; Steffen et al. 2015). Against this background, we seek for a 'deep debate' on the Anthropocene in the sense of providing sound disciplinary insights to an interdisciplinary exchange. We have addressed two fundamental questions in this book: (1) *What is the contribution of political science to the Anthropocene debate, e.g., in terms of identified problems, answers and solutions?* (2) *What are the conceptual and practical implications of the Anthropocene debate for the discipline of political science?*

To answer these questions, the edited volume presented a series of original analyses from the field of political science organised along three dimensions: In *Part I* (*Theories and concepts*), we provided novel theoretical and conceptual accounts of the Anthropocene. The chapters in this part dealt with the questions: What is the political dimension of the Anthropocene debate, and how does the human-dominated epoch change the foundations of existing theoretical and conceptual approaches of the discipline? *Part II* (*Governance and practices*) engaged with contemporary politics and policy-making in the Anthropocene. The contributions in this part scrutinised questions of political repercussions of the human age for individual policy domains, such as climate change, agriculture and security. Finally, *Part III* (*Critical perspectives and implications*) offered critical reflections on the Anthropocene debate. The chapters of this part raised questions related to societal responsibilities in the human age and consequences for political procedures, our political-administrative systems, and for future generations.

This concluding chapter proceeds with a summary and review of the results put forth in the individual contributions along the volume's main questions. We then highlight three distinct themes and related challenges emerging from the research presented in this book. Firstly, we refer to the question of *governance*, touching upon the need for improved institutions and practices to avoid planetary disruptions, as well as the in-built limitations of steering and management – both in terms of effectiveness and democratic values. Secondly, we stress the important analytical and normative contribution of *political theory* for the Anthropocene debate. Thirdly, we discuss the challenge of *interdisciplinarity*, in which disciplinary perspectives, such as political science, need to find their adequate role and place with regard to the overarching debate. Finally, we provide an outlook on the ongoing Anthropocene debate and close with some final remarks.

Key findings

This section recapitulates the main findings of this edited volume along the two guiding questions developed at length in the introductory chapter. By referring to the individual chapters, we (1) underscore the contributions of a political science perspective to the Anthropocene debate, and (2) discuss the implications of the Anthropocene for the discipline of political science. We begin with a summary of the chapters' findings along the three parts of the book, *theories and concepts*, *governance and practices* and *critical perspectives and implications*. Thereafter, we identify four broader challenges for political science theory and practice emerging from the Anthropocene debate: *ontological and epistemological foundations*, *human-nature relations*, *concepts and concrete institutional forms* and *governance*.

Contributions from political science to the Anthropocene debate

The authors of this volume provide rich insights into the question of what the contributions of a political science perspective to the Anthropocene debate could be. Regarding the first part of the volume, dealing with *theories and concepts*, the authors carved out theoretical and conceptual findings which emphasise the political dimension of the Anthropocene term.

In chapter 2, Maike Weißpflug illustrates what political theory can contribute to the Anthropocene debate. By inquiring into the political philosophers Hannah Arendt and Theodor Adorno, Weißpflug is able to explain the multiple ways in which the Anthropocene is embedded in ideas about the relationship between human and nature. Weißpflug outlines how the Anthropocene has been framed as a normative narrative from the very beginning, starting with the original article by Paul Crutzen and Eugene Stoermer (2000). Both Arendt and Adorno criticised such 'grand' narratives and, instead, demanded a more nuanced understanding of human-nature relations. Such ideas have developed within the discourse of modernity over a longer period. Arendt's critique of the 'Archimedean point' and her understanding of politics as 'care for the world' and Adorno's 'idea of a natural history', his critical reflections on nature domination, and the question of technology, are vantage points to rethink the philosophical framework for a more resonating Anthropocene narrative. This narrative could reconnect our actions with the consequences for the world we live in.

In chapter 3, Johannes Lundershausen evaluates the Anthropocene as a scientific description of ongoing Earth system transformations. He outlines the dichotomisation of the scientific descriptions of the Anthropocene as 'crisis' or 'opportunity' which opens up the different normative logics underpinning these representations and enables scrutiny of the complex co-constitution of scientific and normative statements. While there might not be concrete policy prescriptions emerging from this line of inquiry, connecting the normative logics of scientific representations to political implications will help analysts and political actors alike to better navigate the complex entanglement of Earth system research and decision-making, for example, with regard to discussions about geo-engineering.

In chapter 4, Basil Bornemann critically reflects upon the relationship between the concept of governance and the Anthropocene. The author demonstrates that the Anthropocene invokes a co-evolutionary, transformation-oriented and temporally extended understanding of governance. Such an understanding of 'anthropocenic governance' revolves around several features: It mediates between the universalistic claims of the Anthropocene concept and particularistic governance interpretations thereof. Moreover, it conceives of collective action as being shaped by, and at the same time shaping, co-evolutionary socio-ecological dynamics. This implies that anthropocenic governance is essentially post-hierarchical, and makes use of diverse ways of thinking and forms of collective action which are beyond human control. Overall, anthropocenic governance is located on a metalevel to allow for both taking account of the diversity of contexts and forms of governance, and referring to the big picture. Yet, anthropocenic governance is still not a sufficient basis for future-oriented governance. It is lacking an element of normative guidance which is crucial for mobilising and perpetuating support for societal transformations of the future.

In chapter 5, Franziska Müller seeks to make sense of the Anthropocene from an International Relations theory perspective. She approaches the debate along the three dimensions of (1) worldviews and research paradigms, (2) analytical categories, especially the understanding of agency, as this category is central for understanding the relation between human agency and man-made ecological crisis, and (3) problem-solving strategies, such as problem definitions and modes of governance. Müller's main contribution is to raise awareness about the incompatibility of current Holocene International Relations theory and the challenges of the Anthropocene, which she describes as 'ecocide'.

In the second part of the volume, engaging with *governance and practices*, the authors underscored the political repercussions of the Anthropocene as a concept and a debate by focusing on different policy domains.

In chapter 6, Judith Nora Hardt analyses how the field of security studies has dealt with the concept of the Anthropocene and scrutinises the contribution of environmental security studies to the Anthropocene debate. Hardt holds that the

current Anthropocene debate is problematic because of the lack of a clear definition of the term Anthropocene. Hence, she suggests that the Anthropocene concept
needs to be further developed and articulated. In this endeavour, security studies
can, according to Hardt, help detect major constitutive and defining features of
the Anthropocene discourse. The particular contribution of the field of environmental security studies to the Anthropocene debate is that it reminds us that
actors shape the current securitisation trend as for example by highlighting and dis-
seminating the planetary boundaries concept. In this regard, the sub-discipline of
critical security studies can reveal (potentially dangerous) securitisation moves in
academic and public discourses.

In chapter 7, Lukas Hermwille aims to build a bridge between two academic
schools of thought concerned with global changes, i.e., the transition research
literature – an academic field that is dedicated to the study of transitions of
socio-technical systems – and the global environmental governance perspective.
Hermwille claims that the field of global climate governance can be regarded as a
'boundary object' or a 'governance laboratory' to explore possible solutions for
addressing human-induced global environmental changes in the Anthropocene.
Reviewing the broad literature on global climate governance and politics, Hermwille argues in favour of a more systemic perspective that takes the interconnectedness of global environmental and technological changes into account. Thus,
the author aims at broadening the narrow perspective on the issue of climate
change and suggests that the various existing governance mechanisms for com-
bating global warming will also have an effect on the responses to other pressing
environmental challenges.

In chapter 8, Chris Höhne contributes to the debate on the Anthropocene by
pointing to the important role of emerging economies in causing and potentially
mitigating environmental changes. His chapter deals with the case of Indonesia
that is showing increasing domestic engagement on climate mitigation. As the
country was not obliged to fulfil any mitigation targets under the Kyoto Protocol,
rational choice scholars would not expect any domestic action. To understand Indonesia's commitment, Höhne hence adds a constructivist perspective to the rationalist approach. He finds that the fact that the Indonesian government has incorporated
global norms of climate mitigation since 2007 can first of all be explained with
norm entrepreneurs (external actors like the World Bank) and the country's concerns of its social reputation (e.g., as host of the Conference of the Parties to the
United Nations Framework Convention on Climate Change held in Bali in 2007).

In chapter 9, Sandra Schwindenhammer analyses the issue of agricultural governance in the Anthropocene. The global agri-food system reveals complex interdependencies between global food supply chains and non-linear environmental
changes and can hence be regarded as an example of the dynamic co-evolutionary
relationship between nature and society. Schwindenhammer adopts a (critical)
constructivist perspective to International Relations research. From that perspective, the Anthropocene is conceived not only as an objective state of planetary
change, but as a social construction. It is an interpretative category that draws
our attention to processes of societal interpretation about the present and future

of the Earth. Consequently, she concludes that more nuanced concepts of norms and actors are needed in the literature concerned with International Relations. While the dimension of norms highlights the normative foundations and interpretations of societal problems in the Anthropocene, the dimension of agency deals with the material and normative embeddedness of norm entrepreneurship in the Anthropocene. Constructivist research can contribute to the Anthropocene debate by adding knowledge on the formation and diffusion of global norms and the role of norm entrepreneurs. It can also direct our attention to processes of norm contestation and the marginalisation of non-Western normativity in the Anthropocene.

With regard to the third part related to *critical perspectives and implications*, the authors identified crucial and future-oriented consequences that are so far underrepresented in the current Anthropocene debate.

In chapter 10, Till Hermanns and Qirui Li focus on land use change in the Anthropocene. Sustainability impact assessment is a tool to measure the impacts of land use changes on environmental, economic and social systems. The authors present an analytical framework for sustainability impact assessment that includes a representation of humans as a major geological driver of land use changes in the Anthropocene. As a result, the authors call for objectives-led sustainability impact assessment approaches, which use societal benchmarks for assessing the state of environmental, economic and social aspects of sustainable development. Political science, and social sciences more generally, have an important contribution to make to these assessments. On the other hand, the integration of knowledge about environmental thresholds of the Earth system into sustainability assessment is a key requirement in order to support political decisions about future land use patterns. Overall, sustainability impact assessment of land use changes in the Anthropocene requires both, knowledge about targets and values of stakeholders and other societal actors at different regional scales and governance levels, and knowledge about thresholds in the bio-geophysical Earth systems to avoid overuse in the human space usage.

In chapter 11, Dörte Themann and Achim Brunnengräber perceive the Anthropocene as a concept to explore the interdependencies between a radically transformed nature, the human-made technosphere with its resulting path dependencies and internal dynamics, and societies (which are both driving forces of the Anthropocene and are affected by it). From a critical theory perspective, the two authors illustrate the unintended consequences of human progress and capitalist accumulation using nuclear power generation and the question of nuclear waste and its storage as an illustrative example. A key finding of the two authors is the necessity for modes of governance that are better suited for the Anthropocene. A central concern in improving governance, according to the authors, should be overcoming unequal power relations both on different political levels and between countries.

In chapter 12, Jens Marquardt examines how the Global South is involved in the Anthropocene debate. Based on an assessment of more than 1,200 articles published in the Web of Science™ database between 2002 and 2016, the chapter looks at representation, contributions and framings, i.e., the involvement of researchers based in the Global South, research on the Global South, and specific non-Western framings of the Anthropocene from a Southern perspective. Marquardt finds that, for a global topic like the Anthropocene to become a legitimate discourse, it is necessary not only to have diversity in terms of disciplines involved, but also in terms of geographic representation and adequate local and regional framings. In this regard, the contribution once again highlights the political nature of the Anthropocene concept.

In chapter 13, Jörg Tremmel, coming from the sub-discipline of political theory, makes a normative argument and recommends an extension of the 300-year-old separation of powers between the legislative, executive and judicial branches. Tremmel claims that in order to make our political system more future-oriented, it is crucial to establish a new (fourth) branch which ensures that the interests of future generations be taken into account within contemporary decision-making processes. In particular, he proposes the establishment of an office for future generations or a 'future council' that should have the right to introduce norms and rules, integrating the competencies of this institution with those of the parliament. Thus, Tremmel points out that political scientists, or more particularly political theorists and philosophers, can contribute to the Anthropocene debate by calling attention to the necessity of rethinking our existing forms of government.

Impacts of the Anthropocene debate on the discipline of political science

In addition to highlighting the distinct contributions made by political science scholarship, our authors also acknowledge the need for the discipline to take seriously the challenge of the Anthropocene. We see four broader challenges emerging here.

First, established political science theories and entire sub-disciplines have to rethink their *ontological and epistemological foundations* in the Anthropocene. Müller's contribution (chapter 5) is most advanced in this regard and clearly underlines the demand for a more in-depth discussion of International Relations theory against the backdrop of the human age. Referring to Adam Burke et al. (2016), she argues that the status of the planet as a whole remains unseen when observed through the theory's epistemological lenses. While other authors have been quick in claiming that International Relations theory has failed in offering approaches to collective, post-human survival, Müller makes suggestions for research strategies that can pave the way towards a theory of Anthropocene International Relations. She argues in favour of a shift away from anthropocentric worldviews. Instead, classical norms have to be redefined in a way that embeds socio-ecological perspectives and leaves space for system transformation. This points to an ecological understanding of mutual solidarity, a redefinition of the responsibility to protect as a directive for 'ecological intervention', or to an inter-species right to clean air.

These findings are mirroring the argument put forward by Hardt (chapter 6). She contends that a broadening of the security norm in terms of 'ecological security' would help to overcome the separation between international anarchy and the ecosystem by emphasising the relationship between humanity and the conditions of our own survival. Hardt further points out that the advent of the Anthropocene challenges existing security conceptions and requires scholars dealing with such concepts to reconsider core assumptions of their particular field. At the same time, Hardt sees great potential for a connection between the Anthropocene to the issue of security as it would allow for a research focus on the condition of humankind and the central values and fears in the human-nature relationship.

Related to that, Schwindenhammer (chapter 9) looks at global agricultural governance from a constructivist International Relations perspective, which focuses on processes of social interpretations of the Anthropocene. She argues that more elaborate concepts of norms and actors in International Relations research are needed, e.g., regarding the normative foundations and interpretations of societal problems in the Anthropocene, and the normative embeddedness of actors. Against various forms of universalist accounts of the Anthropocene, her analysis directs our attention to issues like norm contestation and the marginalisation of non-Western perspectives in the Anthropocene. This is in line with Müller's contribution which demands theory development to deal with post-humanist worldviews that put limitations to human agency, while being aware of anti-democratic and post-political tendencies some post-humanist readings bear. Agency would in this sense be driven by inter-species/trans-species solidarity and empathy for each other's vulnerabilities, as those are everyone's 'Earth others'. Both contributions thus question the existing ontological foundations on which large parts of the current Anthropocene debate rest.

A second theme highlighted as a challenge for political science is the renewed interest in *human-nature relations* revealed by the Anthropocene.

Bornemann (chapter 4), for example, in his analysis of governance in the Anthropocene, states that governance is a concept rooted in the social world and thus comes with a clear social bias. The Anthropocene concept, in contrast, points to the inescapable interconnectedness of the social and natural spheres and highlights their co-evolution. Consequently, the Anthropocene calls for a re-materialisation of politics and political theory. Nature needs to be integrated in the conceptual constructions of political science. For governance analysis and practice, this means to acknowledge that it is deeply entwined with co-evolutionary socio-ecological dynamics, in the sense that governance is limited by socio-ecological dynamics, but also has potential for (reflexive) governance design. This insight should be integrated in environmental and sustainability governance more generally.

The theme of a re-materialisation of societal practices can also be discerned in the analysis by Hermanns and Li (chapter 10). As the two authors argue, the integration of knowledge about ecological thresholds of the Earth system into sustainability impact assessment is a key requirement for sustainable land use. While this is not new but rather a fundamental requirement of any sustainability assessment, the novel twist of sustainability impact assessment in the Anthropocene can be seen in the fact that, even in the 'human age', the material and ecological preconditions of life are not overridden but remain valid. The result is again – as with 'anthropocenic governance' in Bornemann's contribution – hybrid. Meaningful sustainability assessment needs both: knowledge about targets and values of social actors at different regional scales and governance levels as well as knowledge about ecological thresholds of the Earth system.

Another perspective on human-nature relations is offered in the contribution by Weißpflug (chapter 2). She argues that political theory needs to revisit this core discussion in the light of the grand challenges. Weißpflug demonstrates that the Anthropocene narrative is a fruitful stimulus for an updated philosophical discourse of modernity. For this purpose, it might be helpful that scholars of political theory engage in broader debates about the modern lifestyle, the possibility and conditions of cultural change and the experimental search for new life forms. She further argues that who 'we' are and what we 'should do' are political questions depending on and decided by real-world actions. Instead of taking 'god-like' perspectives, scholars should contribute to a plurality of decentralised narratives of the Anthropocene that allow people to actually connect with nature, while not losing sight of the dire and radical global consequences of human lifestyles and actions for the Earth system.

A third theme can be found in the call for revisiting *established concepts and concrete institutional forms* in the Anthropocene.

Höhne (chapter 8) shows that the Anthropocene debate forces International Relations research to open the 'black box' of the nation-state. His contribution stresses the need for studies that bring constructivist norm research together with a rational choice approach in order to understand 'real world' phenomena. Höhne moreover makes a case for overcoming sub-disciplinary boundaries within political science. In particular, he argues that, in order to be able to respond to environmental change, we need to combine insights from the sub-fields of International Relations and comparative politics to better understand the dynamics between the global, the national and the local.

In a similar vein, Hermwille (chapter 7) argues in favour of a combination of transition theory and regime theory to better understand climate change governance as a boundary object. He perceives global climate change as an external pressure to existing (global) governance approaches and contends that the various insights gained from studied concerned with global climate governance should be put in context with broader ideas on societal transformations. By taking advantage of the knowledge of both the literature on global climate governance and the scholarship of transition studies, scholars and policy makers will be able to alter unsustainable routines and deep structure variables that are otherwise difficult to change from within the different socio-technical systems.

Bornemann (chapter 4) takes a more critical view and questions the political science portfolio in that he scrutinises the concept of governance in the Anthropocene. He argues that the underlying problem orientation of governance becomes an issue. Governance thinking in the Anthropocene, oftentimes being pragmatic and solution-oriented, is primarily concerned with attempts to influence ongoing co-evolutionary, socio-ecological dynamics and development trajectories. Notions such as 'navigation', 'adaptation' and 'transformation' bear witness of a loss of control and suggest that actual states have become more fluid and insecure. As a consequence, governance is no longer geared (only) towards problem-solving in the sense of collective negotiation and choice.

Marquardt (chapter 12) calls for exploring and engaging with alternative world-views and development paradigms from the Global South. Instead of asking what impacts the Anthropocene debate might have on the Global South, the author argues for an open debate in which novel conceptualisations originating in the Global South can be taken seriously, for example indigenous forms of knowledge, *sumak kawsay, Ubuntu* or *ecological Swaraj*. This is closely related to Müller's contribution which argues that a careful assessment of our concepts in terms of appropriateness and aptitude for Anthropocene problem constellations is needed, as they may contain anthropocentric limitations, for instance regarding questions of political representation or actor proliferation. Instead, Müller demands Anthropocene governance to limit the role of Eurocentric voices and encourage a greater plurality. The result in all of the above cases is a reinterpretation of established concepts as a reaction to the Anthropocene debate.

A fourth identifiable theme related to the question of how political science needs to react to the Anthropocene debate is *governance.*

Lundershausen (chapter 3) studies scientific descriptions of the Anthropocene 'as crisis' and 'as opportunity' in order to highlight the co-constitution of scientific and normative statements. Scrutinising the normative logics that descriptions of desirable states of the Earth system incorporate, the chapter also illustrates their implications for responses to Earth system change. On this account, governance is influenced by apparently non-political scientific descriptions of the Earth system. This implies that political science research needs to engage more deeply with the normative foundations of the Anthropocene debate. As Bornemann (chapter 4) observes, the Anthropocene is challenging established environmental and sustainability governance theory and practice by promoting 'anthropocenic governance' as a new form of future-oriented governance. Traditionally, governance thinking focuses on current problems and actor constellations to bring about collective action to tackle the issues at stake. The Anthropocene expands this time horizon. Governance arrangements become embedded in 'deep time' (Davies 2016) that includes the challenge of dealing with long-term consequences and effects, which are uncertain or unknown. As mentioned above, this necessitates acknowledgement that governance is deeply entwined with co-evolutionary dynamics of socio-ecological systems.

With regard to global climate governance, Hermwille (chapter 7) argues that the field of political science and particularly the scholarship engaged with the policy domain of climate change need to rethink their narrow approach. Exploring the ontological basis of the two fields of global climate governance and transition research, he calls for a combination of these two literatures that help to develop a more holistic perspective on environmental changes in the Anthropocene. Similarly, Themann and Brunnengräber (chapter 11) highlight the need to overcome established forms of Holocene governance by acknowledging the complex interrelations between nature, technology and society. Here the natural and engineering sciences have a major role to play in communicating uncertainties and 'unknowables' to the political system. Recognition of the fundamental uncontrollability of certain technologies and the related temporal uncertainties should also be taken into greater account in the decision-making process.

Finally, Tremmel (chapter 13) highlights the implications that the proclamation of the Anthropocene has for the currently relevant concept of democracy. He contends that the emergence of a new geological epoch, which is characterised by an increasingly disruptive human impact on the Earth system, requires a further advancement of our form of government. To render our political system more future-oriented, he proposes the introduction of a new fourth branch that represents the interests of future generations, i.e., 'future councils' that should have the right to pass bills, integrating its competences with those of the parliament.

Summing up the various answers to the two guiding questions of this edited volume, it has become apparent that political science as a social science discipline is able to make genuine contributions to the Anthropocene debate, while at the same time the Anthropocene challenges political science scholarship in fundamental ways. We believe that this conclusion is a solid basis for the future engagement of political science with the Anthropocene debate.

Challenges and opportunities

Beyond the findings of the individual chapters summarised and structured above, we identify three broader challenges and opportunities arising from adopting a political science perspective on the Anthropocene debate. First, the question of *governance* is paramount, as both, the protagonists of a 'crisis' reading of the Anthropocene and those that regard the Anthropocene as a chance, develop ideas about how to 'steer' the coupled nature-social system in the right direction. Second, in determining this 'right' direction, *political theory* might offer important normative insights. And third, while disciplinary depth is an important prerequisite for meaningfully engaging in the Anthropocene debate, the complexity of the challenge requires to move beyond disciplinary silos and to practice genuine *interdisciplinarity*.

Governance

If we take the diagnosis contained in the Anthropocene framing serious, we need to urgently change course. As Frank Biermann and colleagues formulate in their Earth System Governance Project, humanity needs to "steer away from critical tipping points in the Earth system that might lead to rapid and irreversible change. This requires fundamental reorientation and restructuring of national and international institutions toward more effective Earth system governance and planetary stewardship" (Biermann et al. 2012, 1306). Insights from political science based governance scholarship are therefore in high demand. There is an opportunity to improve the quality of the often quite technical and non-political governance debate by adding genuine insights from the field of political science, as developed throughout the pages of this book. Against this background, we formulate three important reminders for those interested in the urgent task of devising appropriate governance systems for the Anthropocene.

First, governance is political. The task of governing and the related instruments and approaches of governance are by no means purely a technical issue, a mere implementation of planetary boundaries objectively revealed by natural scientists. Governance is instead a genuinely political activity that involves ethical judgements and that has (often well masked) distributive consequences. The well-known mantra of political science 'who gets what, when and how?' can serve as a welcome reminder that we need to constantly scrutinise the inherent contradictions and contestations manifesting themselves in governance options for the Anthropocene. Throughout this book, we have encountered various contributions engaging with questions of legitimacy and accountability. We believe that this broad theme constitutes an important avenue for future research.

Second, governance is complex. The Anthropocene debate has raised attention to the inherently complex nature of the Earth system and the related tipping points and, more broadly speaking, the issue of non-linearity. Adding to this complexity of coupled social-natural systems, governance in itself has become increasingly complex (Pattberg and Widerberg 2019). The Anthropocene is governed at various levels by myriads of formal and informal systems of rules, involving a broad range of actors, agendas and rationalities. As a result of this governance complexity, we are observing unintended side-effects and emergent properties that are difficult to anticipate. The complexity of existing governance is also an important reminder that rational planning and design for governing the Anthropocene might be a mere fiction.

And third, governance is uncertain. Even when well designed and accurately implemented, the outcomes of different modes of governance entail a high level of uncertainty and ambiguity. Next to the challenge of unintended consequences and non-linear behaviour, governance is also constantly (re-) negotiated and contested. As a consequence, governance efforts might fail. Anticipating, acknowledging and allowing for failure thus becomes an important strategy in the Anthropocene. Political science scholarship concerned with governance and institutions can offer important contributions to this line of thinking, for example, via the concepts of governance experiments (Hoffmann 2011) and experimentalist governance (Zeitlin 2015).

Political theory

One genuine opportunity lies in enriching the Anthropocene debate with insights from political theory. The contributions in this book illustrate that some issues of the Anthropocene debate have been at the core of political theory for several decades, if not centuries. In particular, from a political theory perspective, the Anthropocene debate essentially deals with human-nature relations and 'our place in the world' (Tremmel, chapter 13). Although these issues are not new, we can observe crucial differences and shifts.

Ethical theories developed in the Holocene tend to become increasingly outdated, in particular in terms of scale. They were concerned with the vicinity, with dealing with neighbours, other estates, the other sex or gender. Humans living on the other side of the world were hardly an object of ethical considerations nor were future generations in Ancient Greek philosophy. In this vein, most people continue to prioritise issues in their immediate surrounding to which they are emotionally attached. It is easier to mobilise for local nature conservation than for global climate action.

The Anthropocene implies a shift in political theory as it provokes debates about 'global ethics' and 'future ethics'. Political scientists can make suggestions for reform of our political systems and institutions to realise new normative imperatives (Biermann et al. 2012). For example, Tremmel envisions an office for future generations. However, such suggestions for political reform raise serious concerns. The 'grand' narrative tends to normatively imply even greater human interventions. While present institutions cannot be held accountable by future generations anymore, there is a general tendency that experts replace elected decision makers.

The dichotomy between humans and nature as well as between present and future generations neglects, first, differences and inequalities among the present generations and, second, common interests that past, present and future generations share. Moreover, the dichotomy implies that humans are separate from nature. The volume revealed the need for a more nuanced understanding of human-nature relations in the Anthropocene debate. Besides, again, we need to face the very politics of the undifferentiated Anthropocene concept itself. There is an invisible weight that comes along with this 'grand' narrative; and it implies greater burden for some compared to others.

Interdisciplinarity

The thrust of this volume was to bring political science perspectives to fruition for the Anthropocene debate. Throughout the book, we have shown that the discipline is in the position to meaningfully contribute to the debate. At the same time, it remains challenging to make the political science contributions relevant and accessible for the more natural science-oriented debates. On the one hand, there is request for 'answers' and 'solutions' with regard to how to govern in an age of 'global ethics' (for example, offices for future generations as a fourth branch of government). Political scientists should more intensively engage in a debate on how to reform democracy with regard to Earth system protection and future generations' interests. On the other hand, the vast majority of political scientists might contribute to postponement of this debate by deconstructing the 'grand' narrative and revealing the very politics of the demand for a reform of government. The challenge is to take advantage of political science analytical capacity and to inject the deeper and more meaningful conclusions from political science into the Anthropocene debate – without however making dialogue impossible.

Disciplinary depth is a prerequisite for any meaningful engagement in the Anthropocene debate. At the same time, our aim is not to play off the different (natural and social science) disciplines against each other. The aim is not to find novel, allegedly 'better' definitions and concepts to understand the Anthropocene, or 'superior' policy recommendations to address the global environmental and sustainability problems. We argue that the complexity of the challenge requires to move beyond disciplinary silos and to practice genuine interdisciplinarity. Therefore, we call for a plurality of voices and disciplines in the debate. As Andrew Barry and Marc Maslin put it:

> If a formal definition of the Anthropocene epoch is accepted, this is only one of many equally valid definitions of the Anthropocene and others must be continually explored. It has been exciting to see how the concept of the Anthropocene has engaged different subjects in ways that climate change and sustainability have not.
>
> (Barry and Maslin 2016, 4)

Our plea goes in the same direction: The Anthropocene should be understood as a bridging concept that can help to overcome the gap between natural and social sciences. This requires participation and engagement of a broad range of disciplines to contribute with all their depth. Each disciplinary perspective, such as from the discipline of political science and others, needs to find their adequate role and place in the debate. A challenge also lies in the communication and mutual understanding between the disciplines which are based on radically different ontologies and epistemologies. The various challenges and quandaries of interdisciplinary collaboration have been analysed and discussed elsewhere (e.g., Hix 1994; Barry et al. 2008; Frodeman et al. 2017). These difficulties notwithstanding, we call for a 'deep debate' on the Anthropocene that allows for in-depth *and* interdisciplinary debates of the various topics of the 'human age'.

Outlook and final remarks

The Anthropocene is upon us. However, far from representing a unified and coherent concept, the Anthropocene appears in multiple forms and thereby retains a certain amorphousness. As a basic distinction, the Anthropocene can be on the one hand understood as a scientific debate about the system boundaries of planet Earth, the role of *homo sapiens* in shaping this system and the related indicators to measure human impacts. The discussion about the exact starting point of the Anthropocene, and its related 'golden spike' is emblematic for this part of the debate. On the other hand, the Anthropocene also serves as a metaphor for complex changes and evolving uncertainties in the role and self-perception of humankind as a planetary agent. This is the angle from which political science enters the debate.

As we have seen throughout this book, political science is able to contribute to both of these broader strands of the overall debate. Related to the understanding of the Anthropocene as a warning against crossing important Earth system boundaries, political sciences as a discipline can offer analyses and prescriptions about governance as problem-solving, from suggestions for improved sustainability impact assessments to better future-oriented governance frameworks. However, beyond a focus on problem-solving, political scientists can provide meaningful contributions to a critical discourse about the ethical and normative implications of the Anthropocene and human agency therein. We are therefore convinced of the relevance of political science as one voice in the emerging Anthropocene debate.

Nevertheless, we also acknowledge a need for further learning and cross-fertilisation across disciplinary boundaries. The challenge of the next years will be to make the multiple disciplinary voices of political science heard in the Anthropocene debate, without rejecting the fundamental and possibly transformative meaning of the Anthropocene for studying contemporary politics.

References

Barry, A., Born, G. and Weszkalnys, G. (2008) "Logics of interdisciplinarity" *Economy and Society*, 37(1), 20–49.

Barry, A. and Maslin, M. (2016) "The politics of the Anthropocene: A dialogue" *Geo: Geography and Environment*, 3(2), 1–12.

Biermann, F., Abbott, K., Andresen, S., Bäckstrand, K., Bernstein, S., Betsill, M.M., Bulkeley, H., Cashore, B., Clapp, J., Folke, C., Gupta, A., Gupta, J., Haas, P.M., Jordan, A., Kanie, N., Kluvankova-Oravska, T., Lebel, L., Liverman, D., Meadowcroft, J., Mitchell, R.B., Newell, P., Oberthür, S., Olsson, L., Pattberg, P., Sanchez-Rodriguez, R., Schroeder, H., Underdal, A., Vieira, S.C., Vogel, C., Young, O.R., Brock, A. and Zondervan, R. (2012) "Navigating the Anthropocene: Improving Earth system governance" *Science*, 335(6074), 1306–1307.

Burke, A., Fishel, S., Mitchell, A., Dalby, S. and Levine, D.J. (2016) "Planet politics: A manifesto from the end of IR" *Millennium: Journal of International Studies*, 44(3), 499–523.

Crutzen, P.J. (2002) "Geology of mankind" *Nature*, 415(6867), 23.

Crutzen, P.J. and Stoermer, E.F. (2000) "The 'Anthropocene'" *Global Change Newsletter*, 41, 17–18.

Davies, Jeremy (2016) *The Birth of the Anthropocene* University of California Press, Oakland.

DeFries, R.S., Ellis, E.C., Chapin III, F.S., Matson, P.A., Turner, B.L., Agrawal, A., Crutzen, P.J., Field, C., Gleick, P. and Kareiva, P.M. (2012) "Planetary opportunities: A social contract for global change science to contribute to a sustainable future" *BioScience*, 62(6), 603–606.

Ellis, E.C. (2011) "The planet of no return: Human resilience on an artificial Earth" in Shellenberg, M. and Nordhaus, T. eds., *Love Your Monsters: Postenvironmentalism and the Anthropocene* Breakthrough Institute, Oakland, 37–46.

Frodeman, R., Klein, J.T. and Dos Santos Pacheco, R.C. eds. (2017) *The Oxford Handbook of Interdisciplinarity* Oxford University Press, Oxford.

Hix, S. (1994) "The study of the European Community: The challenge to comparative politics" *West European Politics*, 17(1), 1–30.

Hoffmann, M. (2011) *Climate Governance at the Crossroads: Experimenting with a Global Response after Kyoto* Oxford University Press, Oxford.

Pattberg, P. and Widerberg, O. (2019) "Smart mixes and the challenge of complexity: The example of global climate governance" in van Erp, J., Faure, M., Nollkaemper, A. and Philipsen, N. eds., *Smart Mixes in Relation to Transboundary Harm: Interactions between International, State, and Private Regulation* Cambridge University Press, Cambridge.

Rockström, J., Steffen, W., Noone, K., Persson, Å., Chapin III, F.S., Lambin, E.F., Lenton, T.M., Scheffer, M., Folke, C. and Schellnhuber, H.J. (2009) "A safe operating space for humanity" *Nature*, 461(7263), 472–475.

Steffen, W., Richardson, K., Rockström, J., Cornell, S.E., Fetzer, I., Bennett, E.M., Biggs, R., Carpenter, S.R., de Vries, W. and de Wit, C.A. (2015) "Planetary boundaries: Guiding human development on a changing planet" *Science*, 347(6223), 1259855.

Zeitlin, J. (2015) *Extending Experimentalist Governance?: The European Union and Transnational Regulation* Oxford University Press, Oxford.

Index

For Product Safety Concerns and Information please contact our EU
representative GPSR@taylorandfrancis.com
Taylor & Francis Verlag GmbH, Kaufingerstraße 24, 80331 München, Germany

www.ingramcontent.com/pod-product-compliance
Ingram Content Group UK Ltd.
Pitfield, Milton Keynes, MK11 3LW, UK
UKHW021009180425
457613UK00019B/877